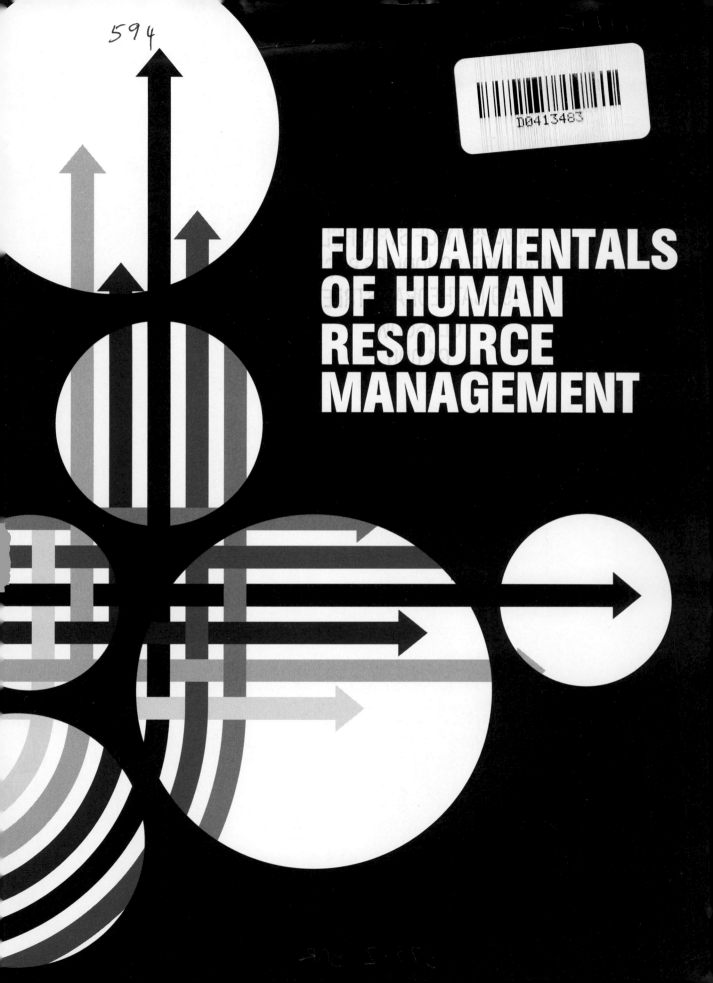

594

FUNDAMENTALS OF HUMAN RESOURCE MANAGEMENT

UNIVERSITY OF STRATHCLYDE
GRADUATE SCHOOL OF BUSINESS
199 CATHEDRAL STREET
GLASGOW
G4 0QU

FUNDAMENTALS OF HUMAN RESOURCE MANAGEMENT
ALAN PRICE

SOUTH-WESTERN
CENGAGE Learning

Australia • Brazil • Japan • Korea • Mexico • Singapore • Spain • United Kingdom • United States

6/1/12

SOUTH-WESTERN
CENGAGE Learning

Fundamentals of Human Resource Management
Alan Price

Publishing Director: Linden Harris
Publisher: Brendan George
Development Editor: Charlotte Green
Content Project Editor: Lucy Arthy
Production Controller: Eyvett Davis
Marketing Manager: Amanda Cheung
Typesetter: S4 Carlisle, India
Cover design: Adam Renvoize
Text design: Design Deluxe

For product information and technology assistance, contact
emea.info@cengage.com.
For permission to use material from this text or product,
and for permission queries,
email **emea.permissions@cengage.com**.

British Library Cataloguing-in-Publication Data
A catalogue record for this book is available from the British Library.

ISBN: 978-1-4080-3212-1

Cengage Learning EMEA
Cheriton House, North Way, Andover, Hampshire, SP10 5BE
United Kingdom

Cengage Learning products are represented in Canada by Nelson Education Ltd.

For your lifelong learning solutions, visit
www.cengage.co.uk

Purchase your next print book, e-book or e-chapter at
www.cengagebrain.com

Printed by RR Donnelley, China
1 2 3 4 5 6 7 8 9 10 – 13 12 11

BRIEF CONTENTS

CONTENTS

10   Reward management   264

11   Flexibility, work–life balance and wellness   287

12   Managing conflict   308

LIST OF FIGURES

LIST OF TABLES

LIST OF CASE STUDIES

xi

ACKNOWLEDGEMENTS

My thanks are due to past colleagues, students and website contributors from many countries who helped me develop and test the contents of this book. I am indebted also to the many people at Cengage Learning, S4 Carlisle, India, Design Deluxe and others for their professionalism in producing the final book.

REVIEWER ACKNOWLEDGEMENTS

Cengage Learning would like to thank the following academics for their valuable suggestions:

Amanda Shantz, Kingston University

Louise Preget, Bournemouth University

Nicolina Kamenou, Heriot-Watt University

Titus Oshagbemi, Queens University, Belfast

Vaughan Ellis, Glasgow Caledonian University

Pam Yeow, University of Kent

Chris Rowley, Cass Business School

The publisher also thanks the various copyright holders for granting permission to reproduce their material throughout the text. Every effort has been made to trace all copyright holders, but if any issues remain outstanding the publisher will be pleased to make the necessary arrangements at the first opportunity. Please contact the publisher directly.

This shortened adaptation of *Human Resource Management*, an extensive text now in its fourth edition, provides a comprehensive and succinct overview of human resource management (HRM), taking the reader through key aspects of an increasingly important topic. The book takes a distinctive approach, locating the subject of human resource management and its various perspectives within a wider international context.

FRAMEWORK FOR THE BOOK

The material in this text has a systematic framework with which we explore the complexities involved in managing people at work. We will see that there is no universal agreement on the meaning of HRM. In fact, there are varying and contradictory models. Yet they embody common elements that distinguish them from previous approaches to managing people – specifically, personnel management.

There are four levels of discussion: environmental, organizational, strategic and operational. At the environmental level we see that the activities of people managers are constrained by a number of factors. For example:

→ Global and national economic activity, affecting organizational growth and funding and subsequently the balance between demand and availability of employees.

→ The actions of government and supranational structures such as the European Union (EU).

→ Legislation on a wide range of employment issues, including hours, diversity, working conditions, minimum pay, redundancy rights, consultation, and so on.

→ Competing demands from stakeholders such as customers, service users, trade unions, shareholders, funding bodies, regulators and senior managers.

At the organizational level, the dimensions of size, structure and culture constrain and sometimes determine the way in which HRM takes place. Organizations range from one-person 'start-ups' to transnationals employing hundreds of thousands of people. As a consequence, HRM can vary from simply managing individuals at a very human level, to the strategic and logistical issues involved in controlling vast numbers. Not surprisingly, HRM in small organizations tends to be commonsensical, with an emphasis on solving day-to-day problems. People management is a natural part of the owner or manager's role, along with finance, production, marketing, customer service and everything else.

By contrast, large organizations require a more sophisticated and structured human resource function. Even where the notion of HRM as an integrated approach has been adopted as a strategy, with operational responsibility delegated to line managers, there is likely to be a major role for a specialist HR function. Such a function may be focused on coordination with operational activities such as resourcing, counselling, employee relations, communications and training/development provided on an in-house or external consultancy basis.

The next level – strategic decision-making – is particularly relevant for this topic since HRM is often viewed as a strategic alternative to traditional personnel management. Employees are a major cost to organizations of any size. Hence decisions about employee requirements are strategic issues with important consequences for the profitability and growth of organizations.

The final (operational) level encompasses the activities of people managers, including recruitment and selection procedures, performance assessment, training and development, and employee relations. Increasingly, these aspects may be outsourced to external providers or delivered through modern web technologies. In this volume we see that they are individually important but also form part of a much wider approach to managing people.

LEARNING FEATURES

The book includes a number of features to help students make the most of this text as a key element in their learning experience:

→ *Learning objectives* – the main learning outcomes that a student should aim to achieve from each chapter.

→ *Key concepts* – highlighted concepts of considerable significance in understanding HRM and related topics.

→ *HRM in reality* – boxed articles relating the topic under discussion to human resource management in the real world. This new edition includes over a hundred new articles, each with a discussion question.

→ *Tables and figures* – providing detailed information and graphical representation of major concepts.

→ *Chapter summaries* – brief outlines of the content and main points in each chapter.

→ *Further reading* – suggested articles and books providing greater depth and alternative perspectives on chapter topics.

→ *Review questions* – to check understanding of the principal issues raised in every chapter.

→ *Case studies for discussion and analysis* – provided at the end of each chapter, designed to stimulate critical analysis, discussion and reflection on the issues raised.

PLAN OF THE BOOK

Chapter 1 addresses the development and scope of HRM as a philosophy of people management, critically examining the claim that it is a coherent and integrated approach to managing people. It also addresses the link between HRM and 'high-performance' or 'high-commitment' management, and the effects of new technology on its practice.

Chapters 2–4 cover the employment market, international human resource management, and human resource strategy, including change programmes and the nature of resourcing decisions. The remaining chapters of the book address the key activity areas, including promoting diversity, recruitment and selection, performance management, reward management, flexibility, work–life balance, and wellness and managing conflict

Each chapter includes a number of boxed articles designed to illustrate particular themes within a real-life context. The flavour of reality is emphasized throughout the book with references to contemporary issues in the media and debate in academic journals. HRM really happens out there – even if it is labelled as 'economics', 'labour' or 'industrial relations'.

RELATED WEBSITES

This text benefits from companion websites:

→ www.cengagelearning.co.uk/price_fundamentals includes additional questions and case studies for students and PowerPoint™ slides and an instructor's manual for lecturers.

→ Sites in HRM Guide Network (http://www.hrmguide.net) – one of the largest and most comprehensive sources of human resource management information available on the internet. HRM Guide is international in its scope with separate sections for a number of countries, including Australia, Canada, New Zealand, the United Kingdom and the United States of America. This is regularly updated with new articles and also provides direct links to human resource journals, societies, associations and business organizations throughout the world.

Alan Price, January 2011

WALK-THROUGH TOUR

CHAPTER 2
HRM and the job market

LEARNING OBJECTIVES

The purpose of this chapter is to:

- Provide an overview of the HR implications of economic growth and stagnation.
- Outline some of the major theories about why people work.
- Develop an understanding of the conditions and salaries for which people work and the expectations they have of employers.
- Determine some of the effects of competitor activities on employee availability.
- Investigate the patterns of work that are replacing 'nine-to-five' jobs.

The employment market 37
Why do people work? 39
Social preferences 43
Individual preferences 45
Participating in the employment market 46
Employee supply and demand 52
Part-time and temporary working 53
Summary 57
Further reading 57
Review questions 57
Case study for discussion and analysis
Rob's career/Jefford Trading 58

Chapter opener Every chapter opens with a list of learning objectives that you should have acquired after studying the chapter, and also an outline of the chapter content.

HRM IN REALITY — DISCREPANCIES IN APPLICATIONS

A 2006 survey checked 2487 job applications for the financial services industry for discrepancies, embellishments and false information. Conducted by Powerchex, a pre-employment screening firm, the research looked at applications from a total of 1029 women and 1458 men over a six-month period. Employment histories, dates, university degrees, professional qualifications and criminal records were verified and checked against information provided by job applicants. With results compiled by the Shell Technology and Enterprise Program, the research was undertaken to discover any trends in discrepancies and the most common embellishments in job applications.

The survey found that 25 per cent of applications had at least one major discrepancy. While the majority of applicants falsifying information did so only once, some submitted forms with up to four major discrepancies. There is no significant difference between men and women in this respect.

The most common discrepancies overall relate to:

- employment titles or duties (12 per cent)
- employment dates
- bankruptcy or county court judgments
- academic qualifications
- reasons for leaving previous employment
- compensation received
- directorships held
- criminal record (less than 1 per cent).

The authors found that 37 per cent of applicants had gaps in their employment history and suggest that giving false information about dates (9.5 per cent of discrepancies) is probably intended to conceal this. The least common discrepancy identified related to criminal records which the authors link to applicants being aware that this can easily be checked against an existing database.

The survey found that the tendency to have discrepancies on applications increased with age, possibly suggesting that older workers feel the need to embellish in order to compete. Discrepancies were lowest in 28 per cent of applications from those aged 51–60, compared with 22 per cent of those aged 21–30. An alternative explanation might be difficulty in remembering the details of a complex employment history. British applicants gave false information in 32 per cent of cases overall (38 per cent of men and 26 per cent of women), compared with 25 per cent of their nonBritish counterparts.

The trend towards jobhopping is reflected in the survey, with 72.5 per cent having held at least two jobs in the last five years. Income had an interesting effect with people earning between £60 001 and £90 000 most likely to give false information (40 per cent) and those earning between £60 001 and £70 000 least likely to do so (9 per cent).

If the authors are correct in the assumption that all discrepancies identified are deliberate – and that is surely questionable – this survey indicates that one in four job applicants to the financial services sector are prepared to falsify information on their job applications in order to gain employment.

Is it reasonable to assume that all discrepancies are likely to be deliberate falsifications?

Source: Reprinted with permission from HRM Guide UK (http://www.hrmguide.co.uk).

leave out crucial items of information, particularly when they are likely to have a negative impact. When and how is this information to be acquired? Interviews are expensive methods for filling in the gaps in a CV or résumé. Moreover, it is unfair to raise hopes, cause inconvenience and possibly expense for interviewees who are disqualified on the basis of information that could be picked up from an application form.

'HRM in reality' boxes HRM concepts are brought to life in every chapter with real recent examples of HRM practice from all around the world.

LEARNING METHODS

HRD managers are presented with an ever-increasing range of learning methods. Traditionally, they have been divided into:

- On-the-job training, including demonstrations of equipment and procedures, instruction manuals, and computer-based training packages.
- Off-the-job training, such as group briefings, projects and formal courses.

Off-the-job training can be in-house, taking place within the organization, or external, for example at a local college or university. Methods of learning can include (Price, 2005a):

- Traditional lectures – good for imparting factual material and relatively cheap for large numbers of trainees.
- Case studies – good for problem-solving and simulated experiential learning.
- Brainstorming – a total contrast to the passivity of the lecture.
- Critical incident technique – can be more focused and directly relevant than a case study.
- Discussion and debate – encourages critical thinking.
- Role plays – another simulated experiential form of learning.
- Exercises and games – useful for developing team cohesion and skills.

Having done this, the criteria for successful training can be established. For example, if delegation skills are a training need, what behaviour needs to be established by the trainee?

9 A pilot training programme This is a prototype used to test the conclusions of the training needs exercise and provide further information for the final employee development programme.

INDUCTION AND ORIENTATION

Starting a new job ('onboarding') has been compared with one's first day at school. The newcomer is bound to be a little nervous, but hopefully enthusiastic; keen to impress, but not wanting to attract too much attention; anxious to learn quickly, but not wanting to be deluged with names, facts and figures; hoping to fit in, but not look too 'new' and inexperienced. The reception from the employer should ideally anticipate these feelings. After all, the organization has spent good money hiring the newcomer and should treat that person as an investment to be nurtured and encouraged. In reality, however, new recruits are likely to receive an induction or orientation which can be anywhere between two extremes:

In at the deep end: expecting the recruit to get on with the job without any real welcome or information.

Overwhelming: providing the newcomer with an avalanche of introductions, site tours, information packs, etc.

In-text boxes Provide practical explanations of key ideas, issues and legislation.

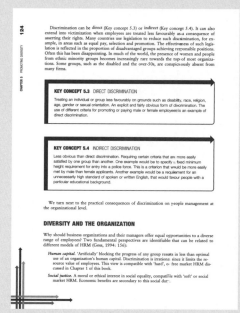

Discrimination can be direct (Key concept 5.3) or indirect (Key concept 5.4). It can also extend into victimization when employees are treated less favourably as a consequence of asserting their rights. Many countries use legislation to reduce such discrimination, for example, in areas such as equal pay, selection and promotion. The effectiveness of such legislation is reflected in the proportion of disadvantaged groups achieving responsible positions. Often this has been disappointing. In much of the world, the presence of women and people from ethnic minority groups becomes increasingly rare towards the top of most organizations. Some groups, such as the disabled and the over-50s, are conspicuously absent from many firms.

KEY CONCEPT 5.3 DIRECT DISCRIMINATION

Treating an individual or group less favourably on grounds such as disability, race, religion, age, gender or sexual orientation. An explicit and fairly obvious form of discrimination. The use of different criteria for promoting or paying male or female employees is an example of direct discrimination.

KEY CONCEPT 5.4 INDIRECT DISCRIMINATION

Less obvious than direct discrimination. Requiring certain criteria that are more easily satisfied by one group than another. One example would be to specify a fixed minimum height requirement for entry into a police force. This is a criterion that would be more easily met by male than female applicants. Another example would be a requirement for an unnecessarily high standard of spoken or written English, that would favour people with a particular educational background.

We turn next to the practical consequences of discrimination on people management at the organizational level.

DIVERSITY AND THE ORGANIZATION

Why should business organizations and their managers offer equal opportunities to a diverse range of employees? Two fundamental perspectives are identifiable that can be related to different models of HRM (Goss, 1994: 156):

Human capital. 'Artificially' blocking the progress of any group results in less than optimal use of an organization's human capital. Discrimination is irrational: since it limits the resource value of employees. This view is compatible with 'hard', or free market HRM discussed in Chapter 1 of this book.

Social justice. A moral or ethical interest in social equality, compatible with 'soft' or social market HRM. Economic benefits are secondary to this social duty.

Key concepts Essential HRM terminology is simply and concisely explained at relevant points in every chapter.

mushroomed at a considerable rate, particularly in the USA. Venkatasubramanian (2009) calculated that the top Fortune 500 CEOs pay had gone up from a ratio of 40–1 (compared to their lowest paid employee) in the 1970s to 334–1 in recent years.

Perkins and Hendry (2005) highlighted the important role of non-executive directors in determining executive pay. They studied the nuances of executive pay decision making, including remuneration committee members' reactions to corporate governance reforms. Such initiatives place non-executive directors in the role of intermediaries, explicitly assigned to resolve the conflict of interest inherent in boardroom remuneration systems, while simultaneously expected to play a team role as board members responsible for the overall strategy and operation of the company.

SUMMARY

Pay is a key element in the management of people. The importance of pay begins with pay administration that deals accurately and swiftly with payroll-related matters. Much of the information used by pay administrators is shared with the human resource function. Pay evaluation systems also impinge on human resource territory. Free market organizations are particularly concerned with performance-related pay as a motivating factor. However, this trend appears to be ideological rather than rational since practical PRP schemes that deliver the results intended are extremely difficult to construct. Current evidence shows that performance pay is likely to demotivate some people more than it motivates others.

FURTHER READING

1 *Armstrong's Handbook of Reward Management Practice: Improving Performance Through Reward*, 3rd edition, Kogan Page (2010) by Michael Armstrong covers the ground thoroughly.

2 *Strategic Reward: Implementing More Effective Reward Management* by Michael Armstrong and Duncan Brown (Kogan Page, 2009) and

3 *Reward Management*, 2nd edition (CIPD, 2011) by Stephen Perkins and Geoffrey White (Kogan Page, 2005) also cover this topic area well.

REVIEW QUESTIONS

1 What is pay for? What effect does the minimum wage have on employer and employee attitudes to rates of pay?

2 What functions should a payroll department fulfil? Is it appropriate to merge the HR function with a payroll department?

3 What are the implications of paying different salaries for the same job?

4 Does job evaluation have a function in a modern pay system?

5 A fair day's work for a fair day's pay'. How can a company's pay system be designed to meet this criterion?

Summary, further reading and review questions Each chapter concludes with a brief review of the chapter content, a list of related reading material, and a set of questions to test your understanding of the chapter.

Case studies for discussion and analysis Case studies situated at the end of each chapter present realistic challenging HRM scenarios inviting you to analyze the situation and discuss potential solutions.

About the website

Fundamentals of Human Resource Management is accompanied by a range of exciting digital support resources, designed to support teaching and enhance the learning experience. Each resource is carefully tailored to the book and the needs of the reader. The website is structured for lecturers and students as follows:

→ A password protected area for instructors with, for example, a testbank, PowerPoint slides and an instructor's manual.

→ An area for students including, for example, multiple choice questions and weblinks.

To discover the dedicated digital support resources accompanying this textbook please go to: www.cengage.co.uk/price_fundamentals

For students

→ Revision multiple choice questions

→ Weblinks

→ RSS feeds from the HRM Guide Network

For lecturers

→ Instructor's manual

→ Case study notes

→ PowerPoint slides

→ ExamView test bank

CHAPTER 1
Introducing human resource management

LEARNING OBJECTIVES

The purpose of this chapter is to:

→ Outline significant developments that led to modern human resource management (HRM).

→ Discuss the main differences between 'traditional' personnel management and HRM.

→ Introduce the key roles played by human resource specialists.

→ Outline the variety of ways in which HRM is defined.

→ Offer a working definition for the aims of this book.

→ Discuss the most influential early models of HRM.

→ Review some of the evidence for the adoption of HRM.

→ Introduce the concept of high commitment/performance work systems.

→ Provide an overview of human resource systems.

→ Evaluate the contribution of HRM and HR technology to business effectiveness.

PEOPLE MANAGEMENT

In this chapter we set out to understand the origins and purpose of **human resource management** (HRM), how it developed and the range of tasks covered by human resource specialists. Arguably, HRM has become the dominant approach to people management throughout much of the world. But it is important to stress that HRM has not 'come out of nowhere'. HRM has absorbed ideas and techniques from a wide range of theories and practical tools. In effect, HRM is a synthesis of themes and concepts drawn from a long history of work, more recent management theories and research in academic disciplines such as psychology and the social sciences.

Organizations are made up of people and there is no management activity that might not be touched on by HRM. In practice, people managers must deal with a continuous stream of organizational and environmental events that are frequently similar but also different enough to require fresh thinking. For example:

→ Organizations expand, contract, merge or close.

→ They innovate or stagnate.

→ They have an emotional dimension, being exciting or unhappy organizations in which to work.

→ Activities are enhanced or constrained by the availability of finance.

→ Stability and change are dependent on the supply and retention of suitable employees.

→ Technology produces new opportunities but also eliminates old procedures and requires new working practices.

→ Staff must be recruited, redeployed, retrained or dismissed.

People management is obviously central to some issues we have listed (for example, recruiting or redeploying employees). The role of human resource managers is less obvious in other areas such as innovation or stagnation but these are affected by having trained, motivated people with suitable skills in place. Superficially, HRM seems irrelevant to activities such as raising finance. However, it has significance even here. Compare two businesses: one has an excellent industrial relations record with no strikes or disputes, while another has many such problems that have been reported in the media. For which company would you find it easier to raise extra finance? Clearly, the correct answer is the first of these.

Human resource management draws on many sources for its theories and practices. Sociologists, psychologists and management writers, especially, have contributed a succession of new and reworked ideas. They offer theoretical insights and practical assistance in areas of people management such as recruitment and selection, performance measurement, team building and organizational design. Many of their concepts have been integrated into broader approaches that have contributed generally to management thinking and ultimately the development of HRM (see Figure 1.1).

THE ORIGINS OF PEOPLE MANAGEMENT

Personnel management has been a recognized function in the USA since NCR opened a personnel office in the 1890s. American personnel managers worked within a **unitarist** tradition, identifying closely with the objectives of their **organization** (Key concept 1.1). It was natural for HRM to emerge comparatively smoothly from this perspective.

FIGURE 1.1

Influences on the development of HRM

Scientific management
Selection of 'best people' for the job
Time and motion
Direction of effort
Minimum staffing
Performance management
Performance-related pay
Anti-union climate

Human relations
People matter
Consultative management
Working conditions
Motivation other than pay
Team working
Informal organizaton
Group phenomena
Peer pressure

Hard **HRM** Soft

Strategic management
Long-term thinking
Missions and objectives
Values
Planned activities
Resource management
Proactive, focused direction

Japanese management
Commitment
Development
Organizational culture
Quality
Just-in-time resourcing
Core-periphery (flexibility)
Continuous improvement

In other countries, the personnel management function arrived more slowly and came via a number of routes. Moreover, its orientation was not entirely managerial. In the UK, for example, its origins can be traced to the 'welfare officers' employed by Quaker-owned companies such as Cadbury. At an early stage it became evident that there was an inherent conflict between their activities and those of line managers. They were not seen to have a philosophy compatible with the world view of senior managers. The welfare officer orientation placed personnel management as a buffer between the business and its employees. In terms of 'organizational politics' this was not a politically viable position for individuals wishing to further their careers, increase their status and earn high salaries.

KEY CONCEPT 1.1 UNITARISM

This concept describes a managerialist stance which assumes that everyone in an organization is a member of a team with a common purpose. It embodies a central concern of HRM – that an organization's people, whether managers or lower-level employees, should share the same objectives and work together harmoniously. From this perspective, conflicting objectives are seen as negative and dysfunctional. By definition it is the opposite of pluralism: the acceptance of several alternative approaches, interests or goals within the same organization or society. Arguably, in the field of HRM, unitarism represents a US tradition, whereas pluralism is more typical of European attitudes towards people management.

Tyson (1989) distinguished between three 'types' of personnel management jobs:

→ *'Clerk of works'.* The majority, involved in the routine of administration, record-keeping, letter-writing, setting up interviews and welfare matters. Reports to personnel or senior line manager.

→ *'Contracts manager'.* Likely to be found in large organizations with formal industrial relations structures. Involved in detailed short-term policy-making and resolving problems. A 'fixer' with some degree of influence on trade unions and senior management.

→ *'Architect'.* Probably highly qualified but not necessarily in 'personnel'. Broad portfolio with a significant strategic role. A business manager first and personnel manager second.

A second tradition – involvement in industrial relations – further compounded the distinction between personnel and other managers. In the acrimonious industrial relations climate prevailing in many developed countries throughout much of the 20th century, personnel/industrial relations managers played an intermediary role between unions and line management. Their function was legitimized by their role – or, at least, their own perception of that role – as 'honest brokers'.

But from the 1980s onwards governments with a neo-liberal or free market orientation, such as Margaret Thatcher's Conservative administration in the UK, reined in union freedom severely. Overall, there was a marked reduction in the importance of collective worker representation in many English-speaking countries. The perceived importance of collective bargaining reduced as managerial power increased. Trade union membership declined along with centralized pay bargaining and other forms of collective negotiation – and with them, the importance of the personnel manager with negotiating experience. The focus switched from the collective to the relationship between employer and individual employee. To support this change, a variety of essentially individualistic personnel techniques were applied to achieve business goals. These included performance measurement, objective setting, and skills development related to personal reward.

As we can see from the list of functions in Table 1.1, personnel had become a well defined but low status area of management by the 1980s. Practitioner Associations in industrialized countries recruited members in increasing numbers, developed qualification structures and attempted to define 'best practice'. Although they drew on psychology and sociology, the knowledge and practices they encouraged were largely pragmatic and common-sensical and did not present a particularly coherent approach to people management. Moreover, in some instances training and industrial relations were considered to be specialist fields outside mainstream personnel management. Traditional personnel managers were accused of having a narrow, functional outlook. For example, Storey (1989: 5) commented that personnel management '… has long been dogged by problems of credibility, marginality, ambiguity and a "trash-can" labelling which has relegated it to a relatively disconnected set of duties – many of them tainted with a low-status "welfare" connotation.'

In practice, the background and training of many personnel managers left them speaking a different language from other managers and unable to comprehend wider business issues such as business strategy, market competition, labour economics, and the roles of other organizational functions – let alone balance sheets (Giles and Williams, 1991). The scene was set for a reintegration of personnel management with wider trends in management thinking.

Like fashions in hairstyle and clothing, management ideas come and go. One year's best-selling management concept is soon overtaken by the next 'big idea'. Significantly, however, a consistent theme has prevailed for more than two decades: the most successful organizations make the most effective use of their people – their human resources.

The emergence of HRM was part of a major shift in the nature and meaning of management towards the end of the 20th century. This happened for a number of reasons. Perhaps

Traditional personnel departments typically encompass functions such as:	
Recruitment	Advertising for new employees and liaising with employment agencies.
Selection	Determining the best candidates from those who apply, arranging interviews, tests, references and so on.
Promotion	Running similar selection procedures to determine progression within the organization.
Pay	A minor or major role in pay negotiation, determination and administration.
Performance assessment	Coordinating staff appraisal and counselling systems to evaluate individual employee performance.
Grading structures	Comparing the relative difficulty and importance of functions as a basis for pay or development.
Training and development	Coordinating or delivering programmes to fit people for the roles required by the organization now and in the future.
Welfare	Providing or liaising with specialists in a staff-care or counselling role for people with personal or domestic problems affecting their work.
Communication	Providing an internal information service, perhaps in the form of a staff newspaper or magazine, handouts, booklets and videos.
Employee relations	Handling disputes, grievances and industrial action, often dealing with unions or staff representatives.
Dismissal	On an individual basis as a result of failure to meet requirements or as part of a redundancy or closure exercise, perhaps involving large numbers of people.
Personnel administration	Record-keeping and monitoring legislative requirements, for example related to equal opportunities.

Using Tyson's classification of personnel work into 'clerk of works', 'contracts manager', and 'architect', what role would each of these three types play in the functions listed in Table 1.1?

most significantly, major developments in the structure and intensity of international competition forced companies to make radical changes in their working practices. From the 1970s onwards, managers in the industrialized countries felt themselves to be on a roller coaster of change, expected to deliver improved business performance by whatever means they could muster. Their own careers and rewards were increasingly tied to those improvements and many were dispatched to the ranks of the unemployed for not acting quickly and imaginatively enough. Caught between the need to manage decisively and fear of failure, managers sought credible new ideas as a potential route for survival.

The development of dynamic new economies in the Asia-Pacific region emphasized the weakness in traditional Western – specifically, American – management methods. To meet competition from East Asia, industries and organizations in older, developed countries were forced to restructure. The Japanese, in particular, provided both a threat and a role model that Eastern and Western companies tried to copy. Frequently, reorganized businesses in Australasia, Europe, North America and South Africa adopted Japanese techniques in an attempt to regain competitiveness. The term '**Japanization**' came into vogue in the mid-1980s to describe attempts in other countries to make practical use of 'Japanese' ideas and practices, reinforced by the impact of Japanese subsidiaries overseas. Initially, the main interest lay in forms of technical innovation and manufacturing methods such as 'continuous improvement' and 'just-in-time'. And their ways of managing people also attracted attention. The message came through that 'essentially, it is the human resource among all the factors of production which really makes the difference' (Storey, 2001: 6).

People management became a central strategic issue rather than a 'necessary inconvenience' (Goss 1994: 4). The early component ideas of HRM theory parallel elements of Japanese people management in that period. Whereas HRM was still a matter of rhetoric for most Western managers, however, the Japanese viewed it as a way of life: an instrumental approach to ever-increasing efficiency focused on employee commitment and skill. Traditionally, Japanese companies placed the interests of their employees first amongst their **stakeholders** (see Key concept 1.2), followed by customers and lastly the shareholders. This is virtually the opposite situation to that found in free market Western countries such as Australia, Canada, the UK or the USA. But the recessions of the last two decades forced a number of Japanese companies to adopt Western ways. For example, there is a general trend across Japanese industries away from a seniority-based reward system towards performance-related pay, a key element of Western HRM practices (Conrad, 2010).

KEY CONCEPT 1.2 STAKEHOLDERS

Employees have rights and interests beyond pay. They are stakeholders along with members of other recognizably separate groups or institutions with a special interest in an organization. These include shareholders, managers, customers, suppliers, lenders and government. Each group has its own priorities and demands and fits into the power structure controlling the organization. Employees have limited importance in free market countries such as the USA, UK, Ireland, Australia or Canada, in comparison with most European and many Asian-Pacific countries. Notionally, shareholders are paramount in English-speaking countries. In reality, top managers normally have effective control and pursue their own interests – often at the expense of their staff.

FROM PERSONNEL TO HUMAN RESOURCE MANAGEMENT

Human resource management-type themes, including 'human capital theory' and 'human asset accounting' can be found in literature dating as far back as the 1970s. But the modern view of HRM first gained prominence in 1981 with its introduction on the prestigious MBA course at Harvard Business School. The Harvard MBA provided a blueprint for many other courses throughout North America and the rest of the world, making its interpretation of HRM particularly influential (Beer, Walton and Spector, 1984; Guest, 1987; Poole, 1990). Simultaneously, other interpretations were being developed in Michigan and New York.

These ideas spread to other countries in the 1980s and 1990s, particularly Australia, New Zealand, parts of Northern Europe – especially the UK, Ireland and Scandinavia – and also South and Southeast Asia and South Africa. Today, the HRM approach is influential in many parts of the world. Typically, in this period HRM was presented in four distinct ways:

First, as a radically new approach to managing people, demarcated sharply from traditional personnel management (Storey, 1989: 4). Personnel management was commonly viewed as having an operational focus, emphasizing technical skills and day-to-day functions such as recruitment and selection, training, salary administration, and employee relations. 'Personnel' was a detached and neutral approach to staff. By contrast, HRM was often portrayed as being proactive – looking at people in economic terms as either assets or costs to be actively managed. HRM was seen to be strategic, tying people management to business objectives. It was an attempt to manage people – not necessarily employees – in the long-term interests of the business.

Second, HRM was seen as an integrated approach which provided a coherent programme, linking all aspects of people management. Whereas personnel managers employed a piecemeal range of sophisticated techniques for assessment or selection, HRM integrated these within a meaningful and organized framework. Each element needed to fit into a pattern that ultimately met business needs. Additionally, HRM was seen to be holistic; in other words, it was concerned with the overall people requirements of an organization. It implied a significant shift towards more conceptual, higher-level concerns such as the structure and culture of the organization and the provision of necessary competences.

Third, HRM represented a consistent view of people management in which employees were treated as valuable assets. An organization's reward systems, performance measures, promotion and learning opportunities were to be used to maximize the utilization of its human resources. In particular, they were focused on the attitudes, beliefs and commitment of employees to achieve behavioural consistency and a culture of commitment.

Finally, HRM was presented as a general management function. Personnel management was often viewed as the work of specialists, whereas HRM was the responsibility of all managers. In some organizations human resource experts provided an internal consultancy service to line managers. There was a particular stress on the role of top management and an overall increase in the status of people management. Traditional personnel managers had little power or prestige.

The renewed emphasis on the importance of human resources drew attention to the practice of people management. Conventionally, this had been divided between line and personnel managers, now frequently called human resource managers. For some, HRM was simply a matter of relabelling 'personnel' to redress the criticisms made about traditional personnel management and sceptics have argued that familiar personnel functions were repackaged and given a more upmarket image – 'old wine in new bottles' (Armstrong, 1987). Indeed, until the early 1990s, 'human resource management' textbooks tended to be slightly revised 'personnel management' texts covering familiar topics in a prescriptive manner.

Writing at that time, Torrington and Hall (1991: 15) concurred that the term was adopted in order to get away from the ineffectual image of previous eras: 'personnel managers seem constantly to suffer from paranoia about their lack of influence and are ready to snatch at anything – like a change in title – that might enhance their status.' It was also fuelled by longstanding criticisms from other managers. This includes a general prejudice that is often expressed within organizations and sometimes finds its way into print. Lucy Kellaway (2001) revisited an article about 'a piece of incomprehensible HR waffle that purported to lay out the future of HR', about which she had made 'a few averagely derogative remarks'. She cited 120 responses she had received of which 115 'referred to the HR profession with scepticism, sarcasm, rudeness or obscenity'. According to Kellaway, no one had a good word to say for HR, 'So demoralized are HR people that they churn out junk and when you attack it they do not even have the spirit to get angry.'

Where does this prejudice come from? Some critics have argued that personnel people should relinquish their ambiguous roles and adopt unashamedly managerialist positions. Others concluded that if human resources were fundamental to business success they were too important to be left to operational personnel managers. One of Lucy Kellaway's e-mailers stated: 'For HR to work it should (a) rename itself personnel and (b) stick to the basics, e.g. payroll, healthcare, training – of other people, not themselves – and pensions.'

But many commentators in the HR and management literature contend that major human resource decisions should be made by top managers and the consequences of those decisions should be carried through by line management. These considerations place HRM on a strategic rather an operational footing and therefore make HRM a concept of greater interest than personnel management to senior executives. However, in an article from the US business magazine *Fast Company* entitled 'Why We Hate HR', Hammonds (2005) repeats some familiar criticisms, stating:

> ...let's face it: After close to 20 years of hopeful rhetoric about becoming 'strategic partners' with a 'seat at the table' where the business decisions that matter are made, most human resources professionals aren't nearly there. They have no seat, and the table is locked inside a conference room to which they have no key. HR people are, for most practical purposes, neither strategic nor leaders.

Whatever the underlying level of hostility, or press disdain, it remains the case that, in larger organizations, there has been a reappraisal of the previously unfashionable and low-status personnel department. 'Personnel' cannot be regarded as peripheral if it controls an organization's people since the rhetoric states that they are its greatest resources. Many businesses have adopted some form of HRM in recognition of this importance. As Fowler (1987) famously stated, 'HRM represents the discovery of personnel management by chief executives'.

Schuler (1990) emphasized that the HR function had an opportunity to shift from being an 'employee advocate' (associated with personnel management) to a 'member of the management team'. Schuler's view was that this required HR professionals to be concerned with the bottom line, profits, organizational effectiveness and business survival. In other words, human resource issues should be addressed as business issues.

In fact, line and general managers have been instrumental in the adoption of HRM, often pushing changes through despite the resistance of personnel specialists (Storey, 2001: 7). Radical changes in business structures and supportive, largely right-wing, governments encouraged a renewed confidence in the power of managers to manage. The balance of power moved away from workers and their representatives with the collapse of traditional heavy industries in Western countries. High levels of unemployment allowed managers to pick and choose new recruits. Existing employees felt pressurized to be more flexible under the threat of losing their jobs. As a result, managers were able to design more competitive organizations with new forms of employment relationships.

Encouraged by the writing of management gurus and, more recently, by the burgeoning legions of consultants (Legge, 2004: 2), managers eagerly adopted new management fads and fashions. Businesses moved away from multi-layered, rigid hierarchies and long-term career paths. Instead we saw an increase in flatter, project-oriented forms of organizations resourced in a flexible way – including short-term, part-time and contract workers. The stage was set for HRM, which was presented as a coherent and integrated philosophy by its originators, covering every aspect of people management (Beer *et al.*, 1984: 1). Yet, the adoption of specific HRM practices is still more dependent on management fashion than research and theory within the HR discipline, whether academic or practitioner (Rynes *et al.*, 2002).

As we observed, human resource specialists have found it difficult to achieve the same esteem and influence as their colleagues in other business functions such as finance and

Function	Roles
1 Planning and organizing for work, people and HRM	Strategic perspective
	Organization design
	Change management
	Corporate 'wellness' management
2 People acquisition and development	Staffing the organization
	Training and development
	Career management
	Performance management
	Industrial relations
3 Administration of policies, programmes and practices	Compensation management
	Information management
	Administrative management
	Financial management

TABLE 1.2

Core roles in human resource management

Source: Plenary group of the Steering Committee for HRM Standards & Qualifications, South Africa, 1999.

Does this list of core HR roles differ in any significant way from the list of personnel functions given in Table 1.1?

marketing, although their status is probably higher in the USA than most other countries. There have been some attempts at a professionalization of HR practice through certification programmes and encouragement of wider-ranging business knowledge within HR qualifications. However, there is some debate about the value of certification. Aguinis, Michaelis and Jones (2005) analyzed 1873 HR job announcements available over a one-week period on four employment websites. Results showed that only nine (0.48 per cent) stated that there was a requirement for a certified HR professional, and only 70 (3.73 per cent) stated that this was a preference. In spite of low overall demand for certified HR professionals, results indicated that demand is slightly higher for jobs posted on a specialist website; certain job titles (e.g. HR director, HR generalist); HR specialty areas (e.g. employee relations, general HR); industries (e.g. manufacturing); and for jobs requiring more years of HR experience.

DEFINING HUMAN RESOURCE MANAGEMENT

Human resource management can seem to be a vague and elusive concept, not least because it has a variety of definitions (see Table 1.3). In fact, pinning down an acceptable definition can seem like trying to hit a moving target in a fog. Keenoy (1999) compares HRM with a hologram:

> As with a hologram, HRM changes its appearance as we move around its image. Each shift of stance reveals another facet, a darker depth, a different contour. As a fluid entity of apparently multiple identities and forms, it is not surprising that every time we look at it, it is slightly different. This is why, conceptually, HRMism appears to be a moving target, and why, empirically, it has no fixed (fixable) forms.

Keenoy's comparison is helpful in explaining why there are so many divergent definitions of HRM. This confusion reflects the different interpretations found in articles and books about human resource management. HRM is an elastic term (Storey, 1989: 8). It covers a range of applications that vary from book to book and organization to organization.

Simple reflection on the three words 'human resource management' does not provide much enlightenment. 'Human' implies it has something to do with people; 'management' places it in the domain of business and organization; but 'resource' is a highly ambiguous concept which many people find difficult to relate to. In fact, much of the academic literature suffers from forgetting the human element in HRM. Most of us would not take kindly to being classified as a 'resource', along with our desks and computers. It seems that there is a fundamental difficulty in considering a person's worth or value to an organization. This arises from that person's humanity. People are different from other resources and cannot be discussed in exactly the same way as equipment or finances. This difference lies at the heart of the antagonism and ambiguity that surrounds HRM in practice.

From an organizational perspective human resources encompass the people in an organization – its employees – and the human potential available to a business. The people in an organization offer different skills, abilities and knowledge that may or may not be appropriate to the needs of the business. Additionally, their commitment and motivation vary. Some people identify with an organization and are motivated to help achieve its objectives. Others regard their employing firm as a vehicle for their personal goals. Some may be overworked while others are underutilized. Invariably, there is a gap or mismatch between the actual performance of employees and the ideal requirements of a business. The thinking behind the models we discuss in this chapter is that human resource management should (somehow) close this gap to achieve greater organizational effectiveness.

HRM IN REALITY HUMAN RESOURCES

Sir, While visiting a patient in Edinburgh's Western General hospital, I was shocked to see a six-foot-long board with large letters proclaiming: HUMAN RESOURCES. This distinguishes people who work in the hospital – doctors, nurses, porters, office workers, painters, managers – from other resources such as computers, laser beams, toilet rolls, refuse bins, beds, etc.

If these human resources are ill, are they labelled 'out of order' or 'broken down' and when being treated, are they being repaired? Are babies listed as 'in process of being manufactured' with an expected date when they will be 'operational'? Are old and dead people 'non-usable human resources' or can they be listed as 'replacement parts'?

When we define humans as resources, we are in danger of forgetting that we are dealing with people!

Source: Cited in Price (1997).

The human potential available to a business includes the recognition and development of unrealized skills and knowledge. Ingenuity and creativity can be tapped to develop innovative services and products. This also extends to people outside an organization – contractors, consultants, freelancers, temporary and part-time workers – who can add expertise, deal with unusual problems and provide the flexibility to give a competitive advantage.

Despite the widespread use of the term 'human resource management' and the proliferation of books, journals, conferences, academic sub-groups, etc., the subject remains 'and always has been from its earliest inception, highly controversial' (Storey, 2001). Storey describes HRM is 'an amalgam of description, prescription and logical deduction' and that it is an 'historically situated phenomenon'. Moreover, for Storey, HRM reflects the beliefs and assumptions of influential 'leading-edge' practitioners. There are grounds also to believe that it arose when confidence had been lost in more traditional approaches to people management because of new levels and types of competition.

Human resource management has often been presented as a proactive approach to managing people in contrast to the stereotypical view of personnel management (Ehnert, 2009: 88). But some commentators see little difference between the two in their effects on the workforce, considering that historical and institutional changes are more significant (Godard, 2010). Proactive management emphasizes long-term thinking, anticipating changes and requirements before they become critical. But, in reality, HRM – like personnel management before it – is a mixture of anticipation and reaction as human resource managers may have to deal with unexpected problems and radical changes in employer policy such as site closures and redundancies because of market changes. To do so, they are expected to react quickly and competently within the bounds of employment law and contractual agreements. This requires that HRM should be both pragmatic and eclectic (Price, 2000): pragmatic because it aims to achieve practical solutions to real work problems; and eclectic because those solutions can be drawn from a variety of theoretical and managerial traditions.

There remain questions about the nature of HRM, the domain it covers, the characteristics of HR practice, the reach of the subject and its antecedents, outcomes and impact. The controversy may have diminished somewhat since or become more focused on specific aspects of the subject (Bach, 2005: 15; Deckop, 2006: 9; Tyson, 2006: 62).

Table 1.3 gives a selection of definitions taken from various books and articles published over the past 30 years. Generally they come from an academic view of HRM.

TABLE 1.3
Definitions of HRM

Definition	Source
Human resource management involves all management decisions and actions that affect the relationship between the organization and employees – its human resources.	Beer *et al.*, 1984, p.1
A method of maximizing economic return from labour resource by integrating HRM into business strategy.	Keenoy, 1990, p.3
A strategic, coherent and comprehensive approach to the management and development of the organization's human resources in which every aspect of that process is wholly integrated within the overall management of the organization. HRM is essentially an ideology.	Armstrong, 1992, p.9
Perhaps it is best to regard HRM as simply a notion of how people can best be managed *in the interests of the organization.*	Armstrong, 1994
A diverse body of thought and practice, loosely unified by a concern to integrate the management of personnel more closely with the core management activity of organizations.	Goss, 1994, p.1
HRM is a discourse and technology of power that aims to resolve the gap inherent in the contract of employment between the capacity to work and its exercise and, thereby, organize individual workers into a collective, productive power or force.	Townley, 1994, p.138
Human resource management is a distinctive approach to employment management which seeks to achieve competitive advantage through the strategic development of a highly committed and capable workforce, using an integrated array of cultural, structural and personnel techniques.	Storey, 2001, p.6
Human resource management is the attraction, selection, retention, development and use of human resources in order to achieve both individual and organizational objectives.	Cascio, 1998, p.2
Human resources can be described as the organizational function accountable for obtaining and maintaining qualified employees. In today's complex environment, fulfilling that mission is a major contributor to an organization's success.	American Management Association, 2000, p.xvii
… The element of managerial work which is concerned with acquiring, developing and dispensing with the efforts, skills and capabilities of an organization's workforce and maintaining organizational relationships within which these human resources can be utilized to enable the organization to continue into the future within the social, political and economic context in which it exists.	Watson, 2003, p.1
Designing management systems to ensure that human talent is used effectively and efficiently to accomplish organizational goals.	Mathis and Jackson, 2007, p.4

Arguably, the definitions may differ from the conceptual equivalent used by practitioners who are actively involved in human resource management. According to Hatcher (2006: 97):

> Definitions of … HRM are in many ways simple intellectual exercises. The extent that any of the many and varied definitions … have been validated by practitioners or the extent they were developed with input from practice remains unclear, yet likely inadequate.

Our working definition of HRM for the purposes of this book is shown in Key concept 1.3. We will see that the variety, scope and intention found in definitions of HRM can be explained, in part, by some of the theories and models of human resource management to be explored in the next section.

KEY CONCEPT 1.3 HUMAN RESOURCE MANAGEMENT

This is a philosophy of people management based on the belief that human resources are uniquely important to sustained business success. An organization gains competitive advantage by using its people effectively, drawing on their expertise and ingenuity to meet clearly defined objectives. Human resource management is aimed at recruiting capable, flexible and committed people, managing and rewarding their performance and developing key competencies.

MAPS AND MODELS OF HRM

There are numerous, widely different interpretations of HRM, some in the shape of formal models. The two most influential are the **Harvard** and **Michigan** models from the 1980s which we will consider later in this chapter. Consistent with the confusion over the definition of HRM, the major models are to some extent contradictory but also have common elements. Partly this is because some of the key concepts have arisen several times in different contexts. Sisson (1990) contends that there are four major features that appear to some degree in all HRM models and theories:

→ Integration of human resource policies with each other and with the organization's business plan. HRM is a key instrument of business strategy, viewing employees as important assets.

→ Responsibility for managing people moves from personnel specialists to senior (line) managers. Specialists provide a consultancy service for line managers.

→ **Employee relations** shift away from **collective bargaining** – dialogue between management and unions. Instead, direct discussion between management and individual employees is encouraged.

→ A stress on commitment to the organization and personal initiative.

KEY CONCEPT 1.4 HARD AND SOFT HRM

Storey (1989) has distinguished between hard and soft forms of HRM, typified by the Michigan and Harvard models respectively. 'Hard' HRM focuses on the resource side of human resources. It emphasizes costs in the form of 'headcounts' and places control firmly in the hands of management. Their role is to manage numbers effectively, keeping the workforce closely matched with requirements in terms of both bodies and behaviour. 'Soft' HRM, on the other hand, stresses the 'human' aspects of HRM. Its concerns are with communication and motivation. People are led rather than managed. They are involved in determining and realizing strategic objectives.

Softer models of HRM typically suggest that HR managers should become:

→ *Enablers* – structuring organizations to allow employees to achieve objectives.

→ *Empowerers* – devolving decision-making to the lowest level.

→ *Facilitators* – encouraging and assisting employees.

From this perspective, managers are no longer supervisors. The organizations move away from rigid hierarchies and power distinctions towards people taking responsibility for their own work. Guest (1987) provides a fusion of various HRM approaches into a theory of HRM which incorporates a number of policy goals:

→ Aim for a high level of commitment from employees, so that workers identify with the organization's goals and contribute actively to its improvement and success.

→ This enables the organization to obtain a high quality output from workers who want to continually improve standards.

→ An expectation of **flexibility** from workers – willingness to depart from fixed job definitions, working practices and conditions.

→ Strategic integration – all these strands link the organization's strategy. They are directed towards agreed objectives and interact with each other in a cohesive way.

These goals require support from top managers and integration of human resource strategy with business policy. The activities we outlined in Table 1.1 are linked and overlaid by HR staff so as to improve communication and increase involvement, commitment and productivity. They are integrated and match the requirements of the organization's strategic plans. We cannot take a decision or make a change in one without having repercussions in at least some of the other areas.

The central aim of the HRM approach is to combine all personnel or human resource activities into an organized and integrated programme to meet the strategic objectives of an enterprise. It moves us away from common sense solutions for day-to-day problems, such as 'get someone to fill that job', towards a conscious attempt to think through the consequences of hiring that 'someone'. Do we want a recruit who is perfect for that particular position right now, or an individual who might require considerable training but shows great adaptability? Do we hire someone for an overworked production department, knowing that the sales department are forecasting a drop in orders later in the year? The essential point of HRM is that the functions should be managed as a whole, and not as stand alone activities.

Legge (1989, 1995, 2001, 2004), for example, has been a steadfast critic of simplistic or evangelistic interpretations of HRM. The rhetoric of HRM claims that personnel and human resource management are distinctively different forms of people management. She demonstrates some flaws in this argument (Legge, 1989: 20; 1995: 36). First, we have seen that 'hard' and 'soft' models of HRM themselves describe very different approaches. The 'soft' model can be identified readily with the welfarist tradition in personnel management in countries such as the UK and Ireland, Australia, New Zealand, and South Africa. Second, most texts do not actually compare like with like:

→ Accounts of HRM are normative – they are theoretical models of how human resource management could or should take place. That is to say, they express an 'ideal' or set of intentions for HRM. They do not tell us how human resource management actually happens in the real world. Moreover, the intentions of soft HRM are often pious and contradictory. We saw earlier that they are derived from much older concepts and techniques. What makes them 'HRM' is that their components are welded together into expressions of a particular, if divergent, philosophy of people management.

→ In contrast, accounts of personnel management are generally descriptive of personnel practice. Models of personnel are grounded in decades of activity whereas HRM is still comparatively new, and empirical evidence of its conduct is only beginning to emerge.

In short, we are comparing the stereotypical theories of a young form of people management (HRM) with the equally stereotyped practices of an old form (personnel management). If we seek out normative models of personnel management, Legge concludes that there is not much difference from normative models of HRM. We can do so by examining textbook accounts of personnel management in the 1980s which used the same terminology of 'integrating with **organizational goals**' and 'vesting control in the line' as newer HRM literature of the 'soft' variety. However, she finds differences in emphasis:

→ Personnel management focuses on the non-managerial workforce. HRM concentrates on managers and the 'core workforce'.

→ HRM is vested in line managers in their role as business managers not people managers. The focus is on managing all resources to maximize profit.

→ HRM models feature the role of senior managers in managing the culture of organizations.

Watson (2003) finds the use of 'hard' and 'soft' distinctions 'utterly unhelpful as an analytical tool', arguing that 'it confuses variations in intellectual or academic emphasis with variations in managerial practice'. More importantly, Watson considers that 'it ignores the political–economic context of managerial practices'. For Watson, the 'hard–soft' distinction is meaningless in a world where managers may choose either approach (or a mixture) on purely business grounds. Watson is equally unhappy with the use of the term 'rhetoric' (as opposed to reality) which he considers should be restricted to 'conceptualize the *linguistic techniques used by social actors to persuade others of the validity of their arguments*' (Watson's emphasis). Tellingly, he argues that:

> To criticize managers for talking rhetorically is like criticizing birds for singing or dogs for barking. It is a manager's job to persuade people to think and work in particular ways.

From an entirely different perspective, Cakar and Bititci (2001) argue that whereas a number of authors, including Legge, have attempted to classify the various models of HRM using terms such as 'descriptive', 'normative' and 'prescriptive' (see Table 1.4), they do not offer precise definitions of these terms. Cakar and Bititci identify two sources

TABLE 1.4
Classifications of HRM models

Storey (1994a)	Legge (1995)	Tyson (1995)
Conceptual	Normative	Normative
Descriptive	Descriptive-functional	Descriptive
Prescriptive	Descriptive-behavioural	Analytical
	Critical evaluative	

of confusion: (a) confusion over the different types of classification, e.g. is there a difference between 'normative' (Legge, 1995) and 'prescriptive' (Storey, 1994a); and (b) a lack of clear definitions for each classification.

Cakar and Bititci (2001) state:

> HRM (people management) is a critical input enhancing the business results. … HRM criteria cover planning, managing and improving the human resources; identifying, developing and sustaining people's knowledge and competencies; involving and empowering people. All these things have an effect on business results, because human resources are key assets. HRM has a significant impact on the performance of the manufacturing business.

Cakar and Bititci locate HRM within business process architecture, a classification of business processes into three groupings: manage processes, operate processes and support processes. They classify HRM as a support process together with finance and IT, arguing that HRM needs to be understood as a business process in order to improve manufacturing performance.

Boxall and Purcell (2003) point to two basic forms of normative HRM models or theories: **best practice** and **best fit**. Best practice approaches have been a feature of the debate since the 1990s, the best known of which are those presented by Jeffrey Pfeffer and David Ulrich. Pfeffer (1998) stresses, in a series of books, that the greatest competitive advantage is to be obtained from people rather than technology. He contends that investment in technology is not enough, because that technology is (or soon will be) available to competitors. And the more complex the technology, the more it requires people skills anyway. Instead we need that variant of HRM described as 'high-performance management' (US) or 'high-commitment management' (elsewhere). Ulrich (1997) argues:

> HR professionals must focus more on the deliverables of their work than on doing their work better. They must articulate their role in terms of value created. They must create mechanisms to deliver HR so that business results quickly follow. They must learn to measure results in terms of business competitiveness rather than employee comfort and lead cultural transformation rather than to consolidate, re-engineer, or downsize when a company needs a turnaround.

Ulrich contends that modern HR professionals should have four roles: strategic partner, agent of change, administrative expert and employee champion. Each role furthers the goals of both the business and its employees. As strategic partner, the HR function must make sure that its practices, processes and policies complement the overall organizational strategy. It must also develop the capacity to execute that strategy in the minimum amount of time.

As we shall see in later sections of this book, organizational change has become a major issue due to speedier communication and global communication. The HR role as change agent, according to Ulrich, is that of a facilitator, involving modelling change to other departments, being a positive advocate of change across the entire organization, resolving employee issues arising from change, and embedding change by implementing efficient and flexible processes.

The HR function spends most of its time as administrative expert, and rightfully so, according to Ulrich. This role covers the infrastructure of people management: recruiting, hiring, compensating, rewarding and disciplining, training, record keeping, and terminating – and all of the other processes that involve people. HR's focus should be on ensuring that these processes are both efficient and optimized. The HR function must track, monitor and continuously improve on these basic processes to give credibility to its own existence.

The final role, 'employee champion', draws on the welfare manager roots of the personnel profession. This requires the HR function to know the concerns of employees and spend time talking to them and listening to their concerns. Moreover, according to Ulrich, the HR function should promote all possible methods of communication, including employee surveys, suggestion programmes, team meetings, and any other means of sharing information and views. A key element of this role is ensuring that employees receive a fair hearing. We will discuss the concept of best practice further in later chapters on strategic HRM and change. We turn now to some of the most influential 'best fit' models of HRM.

THE HARVARD MAP OF HUMAN RESOURCE MANAGEMENT

We noted earlier that the Harvard Business School generated one of the most influential models of HRM. The Harvard interpretation sees employees as resources. However, they are viewed as being fundamentally different from other resources – they cannot be managed in the same way. The stress is on people as *human* resources. The Harvard approach recognizes an element of mutuality in all businesses, a concept with parallels in Japanese people management, as we observed earlier. Employees are significant stakeholders in an organization. They have their own needs and concerns along with other groups such as shareholders and customers.

The Harvard view acknowledges that management has the greatest degree of power. Nevertheless there must be scope for accommodation of the interests of the various stakeholders in the form of trade-offs, particularly between owners, employees and different employee groups. The model also acknowledges the need for mechanisms to reconcile the inevitable tension between employee expectations and management objectives.

Beer *et al.* (1984) argue that when general managers determine the appropriate human resource policies and practices for their organizations, they require some method of assessing the appropriateness or effectiveness of those policies. Beer *et al.* devised the famous Harvard 'map' (sometimes referred to as the Harvard model) of HRM shown in Figure 1.2. This map is based on an analytical approach and provides a broad causal depiction of the 'determinants and consequences of HRM policies'. It shows human resource policies to be influenced by two significant considerations:

→ *Situational factors* in the outside business environment or within the firm such as laws and societal values, labour market conditions, unions, workforce characteristics, business strategies, management philosophy, and task technology. According to Beer *et al.* these factors may constrain the formation of HRM policies but (to varying degrees) they may also be influenced by human resource policies.

→ *Stakeholder interests,* including those of shareholders, management employees, unions, community and government. Beer *et al.* argue that human resource policies should be influenced by all stakeholders. If not, 'the enterprise will fail to meet the needs of these stakeholders in the long run and it will fail as an institution.'

The emphasis is on psychological objectives: the 'human' side of human resource management, including:

→ Motivating people by involving them in decision-making.

→ Developing an organizational culture based on trust and teamwork.

Within the Harvard 'map' four strategic policy areas are addressed: **human resource flows,** reward systems, employee influence and work systems.

1 *Human resource flows:* managing the movement (flow) and performance of people:
   — into the organization, by means of effective recruitment programmes and selection techniques which result in the most suitable people;
   — through the organization, by placing them in the most appropriate jobs, appraising their performance, and promoting the better employees;
   — out of the organization, terminating the employment of those no longer required, deemed unsuitable or achieving retirement age.
   Human resource policies must ensure the right mix and number of staff in the organization. This is achieved by the processes of resourcing and development of employee competences.

2 *Reward systems:* including pay and benefits designed to attract, motivate and keep employees.

3 *Employee influence:* controlling levels of authority, power and decision-making.

4 *Work systems:* defining and designing jobs, so that the arrangement of people, information and technology provide the most productive and efficient results.

FIGURE 1.2

The Harvard interpretation of HRM

Source: Beer *et al.* (1984: p.16) Reproduced by permission of Professor M. Beer. Originally published in 1984 by The Free Press, a division of Simon & Schuster from Managing Human Assets by Beer, M., Spector, B., Lawrence, P.R., Mills, D.Q. and Walton, R.E. Copyright © 2003 M. Beer and B. Spector.

These policies result in the 'four Cs':

Commitment of employees to the organization's mission and values in a way thought to be typical of Japanese workers.

Congruence, linking human resource objectives with the organization's goals.

Competence, developing an appropriate mixture of skills, abilities and knowledge.

Cost-effectiveness, delivering performance in a competitive manner.

The Harvard model is strongly influenced by behavioural research and theory and stands in the tradition of 'human relations'. This is a humanistic and anti-authoritarian viewpoint which holds that employees will only adopt an organization's objectives if they wish to. They will not demonstrate enthusiasm and commitment if they are forced to comply. Accordingly, although strategic decision-making is channelled through top managers there is an emphasis on participation throughout the organization.

A further key point is that HRM is the responsibility of all managers – not just human resource specialists. Delivery of HRM initiatives is pushed down to line managers wherever possible. The Harvard model applies HRM to any manager with staff responsibilities. It should consider issues such as delegation, leadership, participation, team-building and organization from a non-specialist perspective. Taken to its extreme, it can be argued that if managers are sufficiently competent in handling people then personnel or human resource specialists are unnecessary.

Beer *et al.* (1984) argue:

> In the long run, striving to enhance all four Cs will lead to favourable consequences for individual well-being, societal well-being, and organizational effectiveness [i.e., long-term consequences, the last box in Figure 1.2]. By organizational effectiveness we mean the capacity of the organization to be responsive and adaptive to its environment. We are suggesting, then, that human resource management has much broader consequences than simply last quarter's profits or last year's return on equity. Indeed, such short-term measures are relatively unaffected by HRM policies. Thus HRM policy formulation must incorporate this long-term perspective.

Beer *et al.* state that these 'four Cs' do not represent all the criteria that human resource policymakers can use to evaluate the effectiveness of human resource management, but consider them to be 'reasonably comprehensive' although they suggest that readers may add additional factors depending on circumstances.

HRM POLICIES AND THEIR CONSEQUENCES

Beer *et al.* (1984) propose that long-term consequences (both benefits and costs) of human resource policies should be evaluated at three levels:

1 *Individual.* They argue that the well-being of employees must be considered separately and distinctly from that of the organization. Employees can be affected economically, physically or psychologically by HRM policies. But managers have different values and will weight those consequences differently according to those values. Some will focus on the organization at the expense of workers whereas others will regard employees as having legitimate claims to fair treatment.

2   *Organizational.* Human resource policies have to be evaluated in terms of their contribution to business goals and organizational survival. Specifically, HRM policies can increase an organization's:
— efficiency
— adaptability
— service performance
— price performance
— short-term results
— long-term results.

3   *Societal.* HR practices can have wide consequences on society. For example, Beer *et al.* ask: 'What are the societal costs of a strike or a layoff?' They point out that 'alienated and laid-off workers may develop both psychological and physical health problems that make them burdens to community agencies funded by the local, state, or federal government. Today employers pass on many of the costs of their management practices to society'.

Beer *et al.* suggest that managers use their four Cs to analyze the questions raised above:

→   *Commitment:* do HRM policies enhance the **commitment** of employees to their work and their organization – and to what extent? Improved commitment may lead to more loyalty and better performance for the business. It can also benefit the individual through enhanced self-worth, dignity, psychological involvement and identity. And there is a societal spin-off because of these psychological benefits.

→   *Competence:* do HRM policies serve to attract, keep, or develop employees who have valuable skills and knowledge – **competence** – both now and in the future? Again there are benefits at all three levels. If skills and knowledge are there when required, the organization benefits, and its employees experience an increased sense of self-worth and economic well-being.

→   *Cost-effectiveness:* the **cost-effectiveness** of particular HRM policies can be evaluated in terms of wages, benefits, turnover, absenteeism, strikes, etc. The costs can be judged for organizations, individuals, and society as a whole.

→   *Congruence:* the question can be raised about the level of **congruence** in HRM policies between, for example:
— management and employees
— different employee groups
— the organization and the community
— employees and their families, and
— within the individual.

A HARDER APPROACH: PEOPLE AS HUMAN RESOURCES

A different and more clearly 'best fit' view of HRM is associated with the Michigan Business School (Tichy *et al.*, 1982). There are many similarities with the Harvard 'map' but the Michigan model has a harder, less humanistic edge, holding that employees are resources in the same way as any other business resource. People have to be managed in a similar manner to equipment and raw materials. They must be:

→   Obtained as cheaply as possible.

→   Used sparingly.

→   Developed and exploited as much as possible.

Moreover, the same approach should be applied to all people who resource an organization – not just its employees. Human beings are 'matched' to business needs. They are recruited selectively and trained to perform required tasks. Whereas the Harvard approach was inspired by the behavioural sciences, the Michigan view was strongly influenced by strategic management literature. HRM is seen as a strategic process, making the most effective use of an organization's human resources. Hence there must be coherent human resource policies which 'fit' closely with overall business strategies.

In fact, HRM is seen as a secondary product of strategy and planning rather than a primary influence. Within this model, the purpose of human resource strategy is to assist in the achievement of an organization's goals. This requires an alignment of all HR systems with the formal organization. Since the nature of HRM is determined largely by the situation and the environmental context, there is little freedom of operation for human resource managers. At best, human resource managers can only choose from a menu of possible initiatives which fit business strategy. The Michigan School identified the following key areas for the development of appropriate HR policies and systems:

Selection of the most suitable people to meet business needs.

Performance in the pursuit of business objectives.

Appraisal, monitoring performance and providing feedback to the organization and its employees.

Rewards for appropriate performance.

Development of the skills and knowledge required to meet business objectives.

The Michigan model (see Figure 1.3) takes a top-down approach. In contrast with the Harvard viewpoint, control of human resources lies firmly in the hands of senior management. People are selected and trained to meet the performance needs of the organization. However, this is not sufficient. Their attitudes and behaviour must also fit the strategic requirements of the business. The Michigan model advocates that HRM requires that employees show **behavioural consistency** with the ways of thinking and operating necessary to achieve business goals. For example, if strategy focuses on sales, employees will be expected to be extrovert, responsive and attentive to customer needs. On the other hand, an innovative strategy based on research and development will emphasize creativity, technical skill and long-term diligence.

ADOPTING HRM

So far, we have tried to establish a reasonably clear concept of HRM, despite the different emphases between the two major early models. At this point, however, we must inject a necessary element of caution. In the late 20th century human resource management was presented as a radical alternative to personnel management: so much so that it was regarded as a new paradigm (Kuhn, 1962) – a framework of thinking – consisting of exciting, modern ideas which would replace the stale and ineffective prescriptions of personnel management. Enthusiasts saw the transition from 'personnel' to 'human resources' as an inevitable and unstoppable process – a paradigm shift. In fact, the process has proven to be somewhat slow.

The HR function can be organized in a variety of ways. Adams (1991) identifies five main types of HR service, now commonly described as HR delivery models:

1   The traditional personnel department with a range of specialist human resource services.

2   In-house HR agencies which act as cost-centres, charging client departments for activities, e.g. recruitment.

FIGURE 1.3

The Michigan model of HRM

Source: Devanna *et al.* (1984) in Fombrun *et al., Strategic Human Resource Management* © 1984 John Wiley & Sons Inc. Reproduced by permission of John Wiley & Sons Inc.

3   Internal HR consultancies, selling their activities to the organization – possibly competing with outside agencies.

4   Business-within-business HR consultancy, selling services within and outside the company.

5   Outsourcing human resource services to an external provider.

DIFFERENT INTERPRETATIONS OF HRM

As we have seen, HRM is primarily North American in origin but in the USA, far from causing a revolution in people management techniques, acceptance of the new interpretation has not been universal. Kochan and Dyer (2001: 272–3) comment that, despite an explosion of interest in human resource management:

> ... we find that the human resource function within many American corporations remains weak and relatively low in influence, relative to other functions such as finance, marketing and manufacturing ... little progress has been made in developing systematic theory or empirical evidence on the conditions under which human resources are elevated to a position where the firm sees and treats these issues as a source of competitive advantage. Nor is there much research that actually tests the effects of different strategies on the competitive position of the firm.

Why is this so? A number of explanations can be considered. First, there is the issue of perception: many US businesses fail to see the difference between HRM and earlier forms of people management. We observed at the beginning of this chapter that the term 'human resource management' had been used interchangeably with 'personnel management' in the USA. This continues to be the case. For example, many American 'HRM' texts are concerned with the functional activities of personnel specialists – their philosophy is little different from 1970s texts. In part, this is due to the managerialist and anti-union tradition of personnel management in the USA. For US practitioners, HRM was not such a radical departure from previous practice as it seemed to be for welfare-orientated personnel managers and industrial relations specialists in other countries. Legge (2004: 3) has changed her position or, perhaps more fairly, moved with the times, in concluding that the preoccupation with supposed differences between 'personnel management' and HRM is now a moribund, indeed meaningless, debate:

> There is little point in discussing the niceties of the differences between personnel management and HRM when, in the USA, HRM is just another term for personnel management. In any case it was a bit of a straw man debate. Whether HRM was considered to be different from personnel management – in the UK at least – largely depended on the point of comparison. Sharp distinctions and contrasts emerged if the normative aspirations of HRM were compared with the descriptive practices of personnel management, but otherwise faded into several different emphases, all of which, though, pointed to HRM, in theory at least, being an essentially more central, strategic task than personnel management.

Kochan and Dyer (2001: 282) also point to the 'market failures' problem. HRM is generally portrayed as a long-term perspective. Within this context an organization's people are investments for the future. They are not to be hired and fired for short-term purposes. But this concept sits uneasily with the prevailing short-termist ideology of business in the English-speaking world. Long-term investment is expensive and requires the use of money which might otherwise be diverted to dividend payments. This draws unfavourable comment from shareholders. If all businesses in an industry were to take the same human resource initiatives there would be no problem. This is unlikely. Moreover, expensively developed staff can be creamed off by competitors unwilling to invest in training but prepared to pay a premium for competent recruits.

The difficulties associated with long-term, soft HRM are reflected in the history of IBM. As one of the world's major businesses, IBM was used as an example of excellence by Peters and Waterman (1982). It hit its high point in 1984 with profits of over US$6 billion – a sensational 25 per cent return on equity for shareholders. At that time it was the dominant force in world computing with 37 per cent of the total market. IBM was also featured by Beer and his colleagues as an example of a corporation which utilized the Harvard form of HRM. However, recent years have seen a significant shift towards a harder model as IBM encountered serious problems in the 1990s. Despite increases in overall revenues, the company was forced into major restructuring and job losses.

The IBM case emphasizes a number of difficulties associated with the adoption of 'soft' HRM. When business is good and continued growth seems probable, a company can afford to manage its people in a humane and considerate way. However, when the going gets tough and significant change is demanded, profitability becomes the prime consideration. The pressure for action from other stakeholders becomes overwhelming. It appears that, in such circumstances, managers have no alternative to adopting a 'hard' approach. The choice between hard and soft models is governed as much (if not more) by the prevailing market situation as it is by any question of managerial humanitarianism (Watson, 2003).

According to Weiss (1999: 3):

> In the past the HR department attempted to meet the company's needs without actively focusing on the company's direction and the return on investment. Today, however, the conditions under which HR needs to operate have changed. ... Just as the finance department is responsible for overseeing the financial assets of the business, human resources' role is to oversee and be accountable for the investment in human capital (the money it takes to cultivate people and their talents). The company will maximize its return on this investment in human capital when HR maximizes the contribution people make to the company's strategic direction.

Weiss argues for the transformation of the human resource function in terms of its priorities, accountabilities, roles and organizational design. He emphasizes:

Strategic value, ensuring that HR focuses on transforming organizational processes and people management practices in order to achieve competitive advantage.

A *competitive mindset*, awareness that people management processes can be supplied by an outside specialist provider if the HR department is not efficient and proactive.

HRM IN REALITY THE FOURTH BEST JOB IN AMERICA

That's 'human resources manager', in case you're wondering, according to the *Money* magazine and Salary.com list of 50 Best Jobs in America.

The survey of about 250 of the best-paid jobs in 19 industries, mostly requiring higher education, found that software engineers have the best jobs in the USA, with college professors second and (the much better compensated) financial advisors placed third. Online surveys were completed by 26 000 people to rank the best jobs.

The HR profession is rated well on:

→ flexibility

→ overall compensation

→ opportunity for growth

→ level of stress.

Additionally, the survey highlights a trend toward outsourcing operational and administrative tasks, freeing HR to concentrate on a strategic role and adding to the challenge and interest in the profession.

'We're not surprised to see HR rank so highly. We couldn't agree more that HR is a great profession,' said Susan R. Meisinger, SPHR, President and CEO of the Society for Human Resource Management (SHRM). 'The profession is rapidly evolving where HR executives are playing a much larger role in determining the overall direction of their organization. These developments add to the vibrancy of the profession as more organizations look to HR for strategies to align their workforce with the goals of the business.'

'HR is an exciting profession, and with the projected growth and competitive salaries, there will be many opportunities available for bright new HR professionals who want to play a critical role in shaping the success of organizations,' added Meisinger.

Following HR came physician's assistant, market research analyst, computer/information technology analyst, real estate appraiser, pharmacist and psychologist.

To what extent does this survey indicate that HR is a prestigious occupation?

Source: Reprinted with permission from HRM Guide USA (http://www.hrmguide.com).

Process outcomes, achieving a balance between the need for measurable outcomes from HR initiatives and practices and 'excellence in process', i.e. doing it well. In the past human resource departments could have been accused of an obsession with the quality of practices, and showing little concern for the value of their outcomes.

Kochan and Dyer (2001) could find no evidence that American businesses (in general) had taken the value of HRM seriously. They argued that there was little in US management history – or in the behaviour of present-day American managers – 'to suggest that management alone, left to its own devices, will produce the transformation in organizational principles needed to sustain and diffuse the delineated human resource principles'. Accepting that some senior executives may share general values such as those outlined by Weiss, Kochan and Dyer contend that other pressures tend to force them into short-term actions (such as firing people) in order to placate major shareholders. A study by Rynes *et al.* (2002) shows that only one per cent of a sample of HR managers, directors and vice-presidents said they usually read HR research literature and 75 per cent said they never read it at all. Not surprisingly, they made little use of the findings of HR research.

Dipboye (2007) cautions about taking HR research or 'HR science' too seriously. He produces a list of 'outrageous statements' and invites comment:

1   *Rigor in HR research is more façade than reality.* Researchers are using statistical and other mathematical techniques that are becoming too sophisticated for most of their readers to understand. But, Dipboye argues, the sophistication may be more a matter of appearance than reality and the formal models and theories they represent have never been tested empirically.

2   *HRM research is relevant only to academics.* Practitioners, as indicated in the study by Rynes *et al.*, do not read the literature, do not use the findings to improve their techniques, prefer management fads and fashions, and have completely different frames of reference to those of academics.

3   *HR science has not advanced understanding or application.* He argues that research is not going much beyond the trivial and relying too much on existing literature to generate questions rather than to develop theory. He also points to the 'double-edged sword' implications of meta-analysis as an increasingly common technique.

4   *A scientific HR requires monogamy in research questions but promiscuity in methodology.* HR researchers need to widen their methodologies and try to answer 'big questions' rather than narrow fashionable questions.

5   *Recognize that HR is all OB*. Using OB (organizational behaviour) in a loose way he contends that all HR takes place in an organizational context and cannot be abstracted from organizational structures and processes.

6   *Simultaneously embrace the simplicity of science and the complexity of practice.* HR researchers need to recognize the narrowness of analytic approaches and the need to embody paradox and complexity in their theories.

7   *Take the M out of HRM.* Human resource researchers should look beyond the needs of managers to include the interests of all employees.

THE SPREAD OF HRM

When HRM was imported into other countries, it arrived with many of the contradictions inherent in American practice. Further confusion was created as its principles were considered in the light of local people management traditions. As many commentators have been quick to point out, there is a 'central uncertainty' as to exactly what HRM is (Blyton and Turnbull, 1992: 2). The nature of HRM has been the focus of a particularly vigorous debate in the UK. Its meaning and distinctiveness from personnel management have been the topic of numerous articles, texts and conference papers. For example, Guest (1989, 1997) has developed a particularly influential model of HRM with six dimensions of analysis:

→ HRM strategy.

→ HRM practices.

→ HRM outcomes.

→ Behaviour outcomes.

→ Performance outcomes.

→ Financial outcomes.

The model is prescriptive in the sense that it is based on the assumption that HRM is distinctively different from traditional personnel management (rooted in strategic management, etc.). Additionally, it is idealistic, implicitly embodying the belief that fundamental elements of the HRM approach (essentially those of the Harvard map) such as commitment, have a direct relationship with valued business consequences. However, Guest has acknowledged that the concept of commitment is 'messy' and that the relationship between commitment and high performance is difficult to establish. It also employs a 'flow' approach, seeing strategy underpinning practice, leading to a variety of desired outcomes.

Like its American predecessors, this British model is unitarist (tying employee behaviour and commitment into the goals of strategic management) and lukewarm on the value of trade unions. Guest views the employee relationship as one between the individual and the organization.

Paradoxically, attempts to define HRM too precisely seemed to have resulted in confusion and contradiction rather than clarity. Already there are different variations on the terminology such as human capital management and **talent management** and jobs at the 'C' level occur with titles such as chief people officer as well as chief human resource officer. Nevertheless, personnel departments have refused to go away. A casual examination of job advertisements in the press will reveal that applications are sometimes still to be sent to 'personnel managers', 'personnel departments', and even 'staffing officers'. At the same time, advertisements for 'human resource' jobs are common – particularly at a senior level – even if applications are to be sent to the personnel office! Indeed, as we can see in the 'HRM in reality' box, the lead representative body in the UK continues to use the word 'Personnel' in its title, unlike its equivalents in the USA (SHRM – Society for Human Resource Management) and Australia (AHRI – Australian Human Resource Institute).

It is evident, therefore, that defining and accepting HRM comes down to a matter of opinion – or vested interest. Indeed, some interpretations have a strong constituency. It can be seen from Table 1.5 that each of these views has a natural audience able to identify their own interests with a particular interpretation. Hence it is possible to find accounts stressing one of the following:

→ *HRM is really personnel management.* Human resource management is a modernized form of 'personnel', repackaged to enhance the status of personnel managers. It has a hard edge, entitling HR managers to the same respect as finance professionals. HRM is based on integrated and coherent recruitment, assessment and development programmes. It is sophisticated, requiring rigorous training under the auspices of a professional body or university.

HRM IN REALITY

THE MYTHS ABOUT HR CAREERS

A Chartered Institute of Personnel and Development (CIPD) survey published in 2005 found that most HR professionals are happy with their career choice and 81 per cent would make the same choice if they started all over again.

The CIPD report looks at the career experiences of over 1800 HR professionals and challenges many of the negative myths about human resource specialists. According to Jessica Jarvis, CIPD Learning, Training and Development Adviser and author of the report:

'It sometimes seems that it is fashionable for the HR profession to indulge in doom, gloom and self-loathing. But this survey turns some of the myths on their heads. A profession where the vast majority would pick the same career path if they could start over again is a confident one that is happy with itself.'

Main findings:

→ Contrary to the common belief that the most senior people in HR have little background in human resources and are parachuted into their jobs, the average HR director has 20 years' HR experience, has worked in four different organizations, and taken five major career steps to their present jobs.

→ Human resource professionals are (mostly) not serial career changers. They average 15 years' service within the HR profession.

→ HR professionals do not lack experience elsewhere in the world of work. Just 26 per cent of those surveyed began their careers in human resources. Eighty-three per cent of respondents had worked outside HR at some point in their careers – typically, sales/marketing/retail, or possibly general business/management and finance.

→ Survey respondents rated the most important factors in a HR career as personal drive, business/industry awareness and generalist experience.

→ Moving between organizations is seen as important to career progression. On average, respondents had taken four major career steps and worked for an average of three organizations.

Staying in one organization, over-specializing and call centres/shared service centres were highlighted as significant barriers to career progression. Forty per cent of respondents felt outsourcing was having a negative impact on HR careers.

Apart from age, there were few reliable indicators of the chances of reaching senior levels in HR. These were: being a generalist rather than a specialist; having a degree; having worked for a number of different organizations and having had a number of significant career steps. But many other factors – including qualifications, experience and competences – had an influential role in reaching senior ranks. Jessica Jarvis commented:

It seems that this voicing of more positive beliefs about HR from those we surveyed signals a change in attitude within the profession, with people gaining more belief in the function's ability to become a more credible and respected business player. Certainly it seems that the time is now ripe for this to happen. Several factors are coming together to improve the standing of HR in the business community – the rise of business partnering is making HR more integral to the business, and prominent issues such as human capital reporting and corporate social responsibility are carrying HR up the corporate ladder. HR must step up to the challenge and demonstrate how their strategic activities can impact in business terms.

The CIPD report also highlighted some other myths and realities:

→ 'Nobody applies for top jobs any more – it's all done by head hunting'. Not true according to the survey. Job applications were the most likely way to senior HR positions. Only 26 per cent of directors and 17 per cent of senior/group executives were headhunted.

→ 'Consultants are too young to know much about HR'. Not according to the survey, the independent consultant group had an average age of 51. They had also, on average, been in HR for 22 years – longer than the average HR Director.

→ 'People in HR don't understand the business'. A mere 17 per cent of respondents had no experience of working outside the HR function. 'Business awareness/sense' was the second most important factor in getting to the top in HR, and three-quarters agreed that 'Experience in another function (outside HR) furthers HR careers'.

How would you explain the stereotypical views about human resource specialists given the findings in this report?

Source: Reprinted with permission from HRM Guide UK (http://www.hrmguide.co.uk).

→ *HRM is a strategic model.* It employs the techniques of strategic management for the utilization of human resources. It focuses on senior managers' concern with achieving objectives and containing costs. HRM aims for a seamless link between business policy and recruitment, performance assessment, reward management, development and dismissal. HRM is a mechanism for control and the exercise of power by top management. It encourages employee attitudes and behaviour which are consistent with business goals. HRM is just one aspect of a senior manager's strategic repertoire. It requires a wide appreciation of the industry and the organization and fits resource-based theories which are familiar from business strategy literature. This interpretation owes its inspiration largely to the Michigan model.

→ *HRM is people management.* It covers all aspects of managing employees in its widest sense and emphasizes the role of line managers in overseeing their own staff. From this perspective, HRM is a new generic label for all the techniques and tactics available to

TABLE 1.5

Perceptions of HRM

Perspective	Audience	Focus	Interest
HRM as people management	General/line managers	Managing people as a direct, inter-personal activity	Commitment Performance Leadership Team-building
HRM as personnel management	Personnel specialists	Technical skills for assessment, selection, training, etc.	Appraisals Recruitment Selection methods Development
HRM as strategic management	Senior managers	People as assets (and liabilities)	Strategic planning Performance management Development Managing change

manage people. It concentrates on translating organizational objectives into operational achievement by winning employee commitment and gaining high-quality performance. HRM is practical and pragmatic. This interpretation derives from the Harvard model. With some reservations, this is the approach taken in this book.

The value and popularity of HRM may derive from its openness to varied interpretations. It is possible to argue that the term is a useful, 'catch-all phrase, reflecting general intentions but devoid of specific meaning' (Guest, 1989). This allows it to be applied in a variety of circumstances. Individual authors and practitioners interpret HRM according to their own

HRM IN REALITY CHARTERED INSTITUTE OF PERSONNEL AND DEVELOPMENT

'HRM' has never been a favoured title amongst HR practitioners in the UK. In fact the HR community seems to have gone out of its way to avoid using the term. Currently the lead body in the UK calls itself the 'Chartered Institute of Personnel and Development' but this is just the latest in a long list of titles.

It originated as the 'Welfare Workers' Association' in 1913, changed to 'Industrial Welfare Workers' in 1924, changed again to the 'Institute of Labour Management' in 1931 and then the 'Institute of Personnel Management (IPM)' in 1946. The IPM label lasted for almost half a century.

Then in 1994 the 'Institute of Personnel Management' merged with the 'Institute of Training and Development' to become (very imaginatively) the 'Institute of Personnel and Development' (IPD). This was a time when management fashion dictated that basic human resource management should be conducted by line managers and it seemed that the old personnel profession might soon dwindle to a small number of recruitment, development and other specialists. Mike Bett, IPD president, argued that: 'There should be a professional personnel and development specialist on all top management teams: in the boardroom and on the executive committees.' The role of the IPD was to be 'the pre-eminent professional body influencing and improving the quality, thinking and practice of people management and development.' But there was little evidence that the influence and authority of personnel specialists increased during the late 1990s. From 1 July 2000 the Chartered Institute of Personnel and Development replaced the IPD. Geoff Armstrong, Director-General of the CIPD said that: 'To all intents and purposes, the two organizations are the same.' In terms of staff, organization and mission that is. But he identified three benefits from proclaiming the chartership:

→ A recognition of professionalism, a body of knowledge and the practical competence of the membership.

→ It emphasizes the 'must belong' status of the organization for anyone involved in people management and development.

→ A recognition in the charter that this is a body that government and other influential bodies should consult.

Technology, globalization and competition are making renewed demands on the way people are managed. According to Geoff Armstrong: '…. we are the specialists, the experts in the field. As the knowledge economy gathers pace, our colleagues increasingly look to us to deliver the strategies that make the winning difference.'

Time will tell!

Source: Reprinted with permission from HRM Guide UK *(http://www.hrmguide.co.uk).*

background, interests and intended audiences. Applying the principle from *Alice in Wonderland,* 'it is almost as if HRM is whatever you want it to be' (Armstrong, 1989: 60). Indeed, Keenoy and Anthony (1992: 238) consider that we should not look too closely:

> … once we seek to explain HRM, to subject it to any analysis or criticism, it ceases to function as intended. Its purpose is to transform, to inspire, to motivate and, above all, to create a new 'reality' which is freely available to those who choose or are persuaded to believe. To explain it is to destroy it.

In all the debates about the meaning, significance and practice of HRM, nothing *seems* so certain as the link between HRM and performance. But is it? In practice, unpicking the meaning of 'high performance management' from wider notions of management can be difficult. Some scepticism has been shown towards the apparent link between HRM and various interpretations of high performance. However, recent work on the consequences of high performance systems show a positive relationship between high performance work system practices and employee attitudes, specifically on the attitudinal variables of job satisfaction, trust in management, and organizational commitment (Macky and Boxall, 2007). Whereas Combs *et al.* (2006) found positive benefits of high performance work systems in a meta-analytic study, a longitudinal study by a Sheffield team (Birdi *et al.*, 2008) could not find a relationship with productivity. An Irish study (Guthrie *et al.*, 2009) found greater use of high performance work systems to be associated with positive HR and organizational outcomes with lower rates of absenteeism, higher employee retention rates and overall productivity benefits. Boxall and Macky (2009) conclude that the somewhat 'fuzzy' notion of high performance work systems should be grounded in the concept of 'high involvement' rather than 'contentious' selections of 'best practices'.

MEASURING THE IMPACT OF HRM

Human resource departments are often targeted by senior managers wanting to cut budget costs. So it makes sense for HR managers to know how to optimize their practices within tight financial constraints. A study by US **benchmarking** specialists, Best Practices, LLC, explored how businesses focus their limited HR assets into critical areas.

They found that most of the 'benchmark partners' they examined (companies identified as using best practices), outsourced a number of HR tasks in order to release staffing resources for more important functions. The most commonly outsourced functions were benefits and compensations.

Benchmark partners also tracked their HR metrics (measurements) carefully in order to determine return on investment and to evaluate performance. One company used a balanced scorecard, measuring a wide range of financial, quality, operational and strategic metrics to determine the HR department's performance and contribution to business profitability.

KEY CONCEPT 1.5 BENCHMARKING

Direct comparisons of different measures between an organization and 'best practice' competitors in the same business sector. This indicates the gap in performance, costs, morale, etc., between that organization and industry best practice.

Mahoney-Phillips and Adams (2010) comment that many HR initiatives are not taken seriously in the boardroom, largely because of the lack of quantifiable impact measurements. They describe how the HR corporate function in a global financial organization increased the impact of HR initiatives by developing an integrated and benchmarked metrics framework in partnership with divisional HR functions. Tootell *et al.* (2009) note that HR departments continue to be less prepared than other business functions, such as finance, to quantify the impact they have on business performance. In their study of New Zealand organizations they conclude that HR metrics remain elusive as the Holy Grail of HRM. Bourne and Haddon (2010), in a study of strategic change at the UK's Royal Mail, highlighted the value of appropriate metrics in evidence-based change. HR functions needed the analytical skills to combine 'hard' data relating to financial or operational performance measurements with 'soft' data from employee opinion surveys and assessment results.

HRM IN REALITY USING HR METRICS

A report by The Conference Board in 2005 suggested that while few (12 per cent) of the surveyed organizations made significant use of HR measures to meet strategic targets, 84 per cent of 104 HR executives interviewed in the survey say that they would increase their use of people metrics over the next three years.

Stephen Gates, principal researcher at The Conference Board and report author, said:

> When determining how best to demonstrate achievement, human resource managers must choose from the hundreds of metrics that are currently available to track every aspect of an HR department's endeavours to recruit, develop, and retain employees. What's imperative for the health of their businesses, however, is that these HR professionals tie these people measures more closely into their efforts to meet their companies' overall strategic targets.

Lisa Hartley, director HCM Marketing, PeopleSoft, which supported the research said:

> Though widespread adoption has been slow, we all see that our best practice customers are beginning to use people metrics to understand and drive business decisions. We've had great people data for a long time. It's just that it hasn't been presented in a relevant way. That is finally changing. We believe that the use of analytics is nothing less than transformational to making HR relevant to the strategic needs of the business.

Is HR up to the task?

According to the survey, a mere 31 per cent of respondents felt that HR executives in their organizations had a strong understanding of strategic key performance indicators. Even fewer (25 per cent) surveyed considered their HR leaders capable of linking people measures to such indicators or (16 per cent) believed that HR professionals received extensive training to connect people measures to strategy.

Fifty-one per cent of participants in the survey said that HR professionals in their organizations were partially capable of identifying talent critical for implementing strategy but only 22 per cent said that those executives were fully able to identify strategic talent pools.

Effective people metrics

HR professionals have tended to use metrics to study the time and cost of utilizing people, but they are more likely to:

→ provoke discussions with managers that lead to action plans;

→ serve as educational tools that help bring implicit ideas about the value of human capital to the surface; and

→ improve the HR decision-making process when they are used to evaluate the effectiveness and impact of people investments and HR activities.

Correlating popular individual measures with important perceived benefits can lead to a successful linking of certain people measures to specific strategies. The Conference Board report cites the following examples:

→ employee satisfaction and competences/training metrics were found to match a policy of customer responsiveness;

→ leadership and competences/training measures were found to have solid connections to innovation strategies;

→ remuneration and leadership measures can help boost revenue growth.

But most of the organizations surveyed only partially tied their people measures and targets to strategic plans (52 per cent) or annual budgets (46 per cent). Half of the survey participants reported that their people metrics were fully or partially linked to customer data.

Making the case for people measures
Many respondents reported difficulties in implementing HR metrics with only 19 per cent rating their IT systems highly for HR data gathering. There is also an issue of organizational politics since HR metrics have implications on performance ratings, prestige, power, and resource allocation. Many organizations were trying to build support for their HR metrics efforts through collaboration with colleagues from finance

(54 per cent) and strategy (45 per cent) and employing business managers as champions for HR measures (43 per cent).

According to Stephen Gates:

If people metrics highlight a problem that could be interpreted as critical of a business manager's performance, then the manager could be tempted to distort or suppress the negative data. When they point to a problem with HR's functional activities, then HR could also be motivated to hide negative data. In both instances, manipulating people data destroys the diagnostic power of the people metrics effort.

In 78 per cent of surveyed organizations, people measure reports are delivered to senior management. In a few companies, business managers – rather than HR representatives – present information back to business divisions directly, greatly enhancing the credibility of the process with those divisions.

'However, the finding that only 19 per cent of companies distribute briefings on people measurement to all of their business managers indicates that many companies do not view these reports as decision-making tools for managers,' said Gates.

Summarize the main reasons for using HR metrics.

Source: Reprinted with permission from HRM Guide USA (http://www.hrmguide.com).

 SUMMARY

In this chapter we introduced the concept of HRM. One major point of debate has been the difference, if any, between HRM and 'traditional' personnel management. We found that HRM has a variety of definitions but there is general agreement that it has a closer fit with business strategy than previous models, specifically personnel management. The early models of HRM take either a 'soft' or a 'hard' approach, but this may be a simplistic distinction as economic circumstances are more likely to drive the choice than any question of humanitarianism. The status of HRM is also problematic, with a range of views on the value and purpose of the profession. As HR processes become more easily measurable, the need for justification and the means to do so become more obvious. Many consultants have advocated the concept of high performance.

▶ FURTHER READING

There are many introductory texts on human resource management, several with an orientation towards a single country. The following texts are of more general use:

1 *Human Resource Management: A Critical Text* edited by John Storey (3rd edition, Cengage Learning, 2007) provides a wide-ranging and authoritative account of the origins and development of HRM.

2 David Ulrich's *Human Resource Champions* Harvard Business Press (1997), has been a best-seller among practitioners and outlines much of his thinking on the key roles of the HR function.

3 *The Future of Human Resource Management: 64 Thought Leaders Explore the Critical HR Issues of Today and Tomorrow,* edited by Michael R. Losey, Sue Meisinger and Dave Ulrich (2nd edition, John Wiley and Sons, 2006) is a compilation of articles by an international panel of expert contributors who offer their views on the state of HR and what to expect in the future.

4 *How to Measure Human Resource Management* (3rd edition, 2001) by Jac Fitz-Enz and Barbara Davison, published by McGraw-Hill, contains practical information on measuring elements of HR.

▶ REVIEW QUESTIONS

1 What is HRM? Is it really different from personnel management? Summarize the main differences between personnel management and HRM as you see them.

2 Is 'relabelling' personnel as HRM anything more than a makeover or a cosmetic change?

3 How much does the concept of HRM owe to Japanese management practices?

4 Do you consider that the Harvard four Cs model can give us a complete evaluation of HRM in a particular organization?

5 What do you understand by the concept of 'stakeholder'?

6 HRM theorists argue that employees are assets and not just costs. What does this mean in practice?

7 What are the main differences between the Harvard and Michigan models?

8 Compare and contrast the 'hard' and 'soft' forms of HRM. Is this a useful distinction?

9 Does current research show a clear link between HR procedures and high performance?

10 To what extent are HR processes and outcomes measurable?

→ CASE STUDY FOR DISCUSSION AND ANALYSIS

Read the following case study and answer the question that follows.

Characteristics of engaging managers

Research by the Institute for Employment Studies indicates that engaging managers are made, not born – they learn from their own and other people's mistakes and modify their behaviour accordingly. The report is based on interviews with 25 'engaging managers' (identified as having high engagement scores of teams in their last employee survey), 22 'senior managers' (people managing the engaging managers), and focus groups with 25 teams managed by the engaging managers (a total of 154 people) (Robinson and Hayday, 2009). The seven organizations involved were:

→   The Association of Chartered Certified
    Accountants (ACCA)

→   Centrica

→   Corus

→   Her Majesty's Revenue and Customs (HMRC)

→   London Borough of Merton

→   Rolls-Royce

→   Sainsbury's.

The report concludes that great managers are focused on performance, taking the 'good bits' of other managers they have observed and avoiding the 'bad bits' of behaviour. They were effective communicators and showed improvement over time, according to senior managers. They were ready to show honesty and openness when breaking bad news and gave frequent individual feedback to staff. The features of engaging and non-engaging managers included the following:

Characteristics of engaging managers

→   high performers

→   communicators

→   visionary

→   empathizers

→   developers

→   enthusiasts

→   protectors

→   networkers

→   rocks

→   brave

→   jugglers

→   mavericks.

Characteristics of disengaging and poor managers

→   micro managers

→   muddlers

→   blamers

→   egoistical

→   pessimists.

According to Dilys Robinson, Principal Research Fellow at the Institute for Employment Studies:

The excellent and engaging managers we spoke to have very varied jobs, different spans of control and seniority. But one thing they have in common is how very focused they are on performance. They all manage teams that are known to be high-performing within their organizations, which underlines how important engagement is in difficult times.

We asked team members to draw pictures of how they see their managers. Interestingly, several people drew smiling devils, indicating that not all engaging managers toe the company line. The most popular picture of all was of a sun or a smiling face.

The drawings gave us insight into engaging managers' characteristics. The teams value their managers' strategic vision, interest in them as individuals and fostering of positive team culture. Our engaging managers are challenging and approachable, and have good skills in communicating and listening. Their teams also expect them to be honest and development-focused. But engaging behaviours can be learnt and that's good news for aspiring managers.

Other key findings were:

→ Engaging managers, senior managers and teams all had clear views about disengaging behaviours to be avoided.

→ Disengaging behaviours included lack of empathy, poor communication and listening skills, being self-centred, failing to inspire, blaming others, aggression, poor delivery record, lack of approachability, lack of integrity, and micro-managing.

→ Engaging managers were seen to be active internal networkers who did not necessarily feel a need to network externally.

→ Two-way communication was viewed as an essential feature of engaging management.

→ Engaging managers had in-depth knowledge of their organization, how their role fitted into the bigger picture, and were able to communicate this effectively to their teams.

What methods can managers use to gain the trust of their employees?

Source: Reprinted with permission from HRM Guide UK (http://www.hrmguide.co.uk).

CHAPTER 2
HRM and the job market

LEARNING OBJECTIVES

The purpose of this chapter is to:

→ Provide an overview of the HR implications of economic growth and stagnation.

→ Outline some of the major theories about why people work.

→ Develop an understanding of the conditions and salaries for which people work and the expectations they have of employers.

→ Determine some of the effects of competitor activities on employee availability.

→ Investigate the patterns of work that are replacing 'nine-to-five' jobs.

'The modern business has no place to hide. It has no place to go but everywhere' (Lane, Distefano and Maznevski, 1997).

The forces that act on people management are not purely internal to an organization. The most complex of these is the international business environment (see Key concept 2.1). They encompass innumerable active players in the world economy, including international agencies, governments, competitors, unions, speculators and consumers – each pursuing their own goals.

KEY CONCEPT 2.1 THE BUSINESS ENVIRONMENT

'All factors which exist outside the business enterprise, but which interact with it' (Needle, 1994: 26). Government economic, social security, education and training policies affect the supply, cost and quality of available employees. International competition, strategic alliances and supranational organizations such as the European Union are exercising increasing influence on people management.

Changes in the business environment such as the financial crisis of 2007/2008 have major consequences for people managers. These forces may be so powerful that an individual organization loses the discretion to pursue its own strategies (Kochan and Dyer, 2001: 282). In essence this means that factors outside a company's control will affect its requirements for human resources and the way they are managed. For example, unexpected changes in competitor technology or currency exchange rates may compel a business to abandon long-term human resource plans and shed staff in order to survive.

HRM IN REALITY EMPLOYEES VALUE COMPANY STABILITY

Employees of all ages are placing greater emphasis on company stability when making career decisions but four out of ten of those surveyed for specialized staffing firm Robert Half International in 2010 said they are more likely to consider moving to new organizations as a result of the recession.

Kathryn Bolt, president of Canadian operations said:

> Our research reveals that there are several parallels across generations, which may be partly attributed to recent economic challenges. As the job market rebounds, understanding what motivates employees can help companies augment their recruitment and retention efforts.

The conclusions are based on a survey of more than 1400 professionals from Canada and the United States in full-time employment who have, or are studying for, university degrees. This included 502 hiring managers. Respondents came from across the age range: baby boomers (approximately 46–64 years old); Generation X (approximately 32–45 years old) and those from Generation Y (approximately 21–31 years old) meeting the academic criteria for the study.

Other significant findings include:

→ Pay is not keeping up with performance – 37 per cent of respondents felt they were not being fairly compensated for greater workloads associated with the recession.

→ Work is more engaging – 28 per cent agreed they were more involved in their work as a result of the recession.

→ Generational views on post-recession career progression differ – among the youngest employees, the most popular plan was to look for a new job as the economy recovers. Those from Generation X were more inclined to update their skills. Baby boomers most commonly responded that they intend staying with their current employers.

→ Cross-generational teams bring challenges and rewards – while 72 per cent of hiring managers agreed that managing multi-generational teams poses a challenge, more than one-third of employees felt that teams incorporating different levels of experience increase productivity.

→ Retirement plans are being put on hold – 46 per cent of respondents believe they will work beyond the traditional retirement age, more than one-third said the recent recession has had a very significant impact on their retirement plans.

Researchers identified a number of similar responses across the generations surveyed. Working for a stable company and job security were identified as two of the most important aspects of the work environment, valued more than a short commute or working for a socially responsible company. Salary, company stability and benefits were considered the most important factors when evaluating offers of employment. The most valued benefits were extended healthcare coverage, dental coverage, vacation time and Registered Retirement Savings Plan matching. Among those planning to work past the traditional retirement age, the great majority cited the recession as an important factor in their decision, regardless of their current age. The most commonly cited benefit associated with being part of multi-generational teams was the concentration of different experience providing specialist knowledge.

The survey also identified some significant generational differences, especially with regard to post-recession career progression:

→ Thirty-six per cent of respondents from Generation Y planned to look for new job opportunities compared to 30 per cent from Generation X and 24 per cent of the baby boomers.

→ Respondents from Generation X were more inclined to enhance their skills sets (38 per cent) and build tenure with their existing companies (33 per cent) than other generations.

→ More than half of baby boomers surveyed (54 per cent) said they would work past the traditional retirement age compared to 46 per cent of Generation X and 39 per cent of Generation Y.

→ More from Generation X had increased their retirement savings since the recession (34 per cent compared with 27 per cent of baby boomers).

→ Over half of baby boomers (54 per cent) felt the greatest challenge working with multiple generations was 'differing work ethics and approaches to work–life balance' (compared with 45 per cent from Generation X and 35 per cent from Generation Y). Respondents from Generation Y were more likely to identify 'differing communication styles' (29 per cent compared with 16 per cent for both Generation X respondents and baby boomers).

Kathryn Bolt commented:

With the job market stabilizing, many employees, particularly Gen Y professionals, may start to consider other employment opportunities. Developing a sound retention strategy, including the review of top performers' career paths and compensation levels should be a priority for companies looking to maximize emerging growth opportunities.

How would you explain the variation in attitudes towards job security in different age groups?

Source: Reprinted with permission from HRM Guide Canada (http://www.hrmguide.net/canada/).

The **employment or job market** (see Key concept 2.2) is the ultimate source of all new recruits. The dynamics of this market affect human resource managers directly when they deal with employee resourcing or set competitive reward packages. To do so effectively, they need to understand the expectations of prospective employees and have an insight into their decision-making process when applying for, or accepting jobs.

KEY CONCEPT 2.2 THE EMPLOYMENT MARKET

The employment market comprises all those people who are available for work. Neo-classical economics views this potential workforce as forming a labour market. The market is affected by national or regional supply and demand for appropriately skilled employees. It is constrained by demographic factors such as the number of young people leaving schools and universities and by cultural norms such as expectations for mothers to stay at home looking after children.

WHY DO PEOPLE WORK?

The simple answer in most cases is that they have to. Few of us have the private resources needed to maintain a satisfactory lifestyle without an income from employment. This seems obvious but the issue becomes much more complex on examination. For example, many wealthy people (or lottery winners) continue to work even though they do not 'need' to. Moreover, unless they are in a desperate financial state, people pick and choose the type of work they are prepared to do. Professions such as nursing and social work attract large numbers of people despite relatively low rates of pay in many countries. Clearly, there are many other factors, other than money, that have to be taken into account in understanding people's motives in the employment market.

The issue has been made all the more complicated because economists have provided several different and contradictory theories in this area. They can be divided broadly into two main approaches: competitive and institutional.

Competitive market theories

These are derived from the neo-classical economic concepts of rational choice and maximization of utility. The assumption here is that individuals choose jobs that offer them maximum benefits. The utility or value of these benefits – money, vacation time, pension entitlement and so on – varies for different individuals according to their personal preferences. People move from one organization to another if improved benefits are available. At the same time, employing organizations attempt to get the most from their employees for the lowest possible cost. It can be argued that pure competitive theories of the employment market have little to do with HRM since they are not 'concerned with what goes on inside organizations' (Claydon, 2001: 70). It can also be argued that employment markets are never truly competitive because of various 'rigidities' such as union intervention, minimum-wage laws or social protection rights that are not found in other markets.

In reality, it is obvious that the job market does not work in such a simple fashion: people do not move readily between organizations in search of higher wages; most firms do not cut benefits when unemployment levels are high and cheaper workers are available. Such contradictions are partly explained by the omission of HR development issues such as training and career structures in competition theories. More generally, they assume that employment markets are purely external when, in fact, large organizations have internal job markets operating through promotion and transfer of existing employees.

Competition theories assume that job-seekers have perfect knowledge of available jobs and benefits. Job-searching is an expensive and time-consuming business. The unemployed do not have money and those in work do not have time. The result is that few people conduct the extensive searches required to find jobs that meet their preferences perfectly. In practice, most individuals settle for employment which is quickly obtained and which exceeds the 'reserve minimum wage' they have in mind. There is a considerable element of luck involved. Moreover, the job-seeker does not make the choice: in most cases the decision is in the hands of the employer.

Entry barriers to job sectors provide a further constraint on the competitive job market. Many jobs are restricted to people possessing key skills – often specific to a particular firm or industrial sector, or fitting a particular demographic background. In fact, the external job market is made up of many sub-markets with widely different circumstances and constraints.

Competition theories assume that hiring and firing in reaction to changing market conditions is good practice. There are close parallels between this way of thinking and 'hard' HRM. In fact, most firms take active steps to avoid **employee turnover**. This is because turnover is disruptive and costs money. Recruitment advertising and redundancy payments are expensive and training new employees represents a considerable investment in time and effort. Organizations may encourage workers to remain with them by means of HR policies that increase benefits such as annual leave and pensions in line with length of service.

HRM IN REALITY GRADUATES AT HOME

In 2006 Experience, Inc. announced the findings of its Life After College online survey of recent American graduates on the growing 'boomerang kids' trend towards returning to live in the family home, career paths and the overall reality of life after college.

The majority of respondents (58 per cent) returned to live with parents after college, three-quarters did so immediately on graduating and one-third stayed more than 12 months. About half (48 per cent) of those who returned home did so to save money; 37 per cent were unemployed. Returning home was financially advantageous with no contributions paid towards utilities (92 per cent), rent (85 per cent) or groceries (74 per cent). Attitudes to returning to the family home varied: 59 per cent reported feeling 'indifferent or neutral'; 31 per cent 'embarrassed'; and 10 per cent 'proud and happy'.

Job-hopping has become customary for today's graduates; the average tenure at a first full-time job is 1.6 years. Three-quarters had changed jobs in the five years following graduation:

→ up to one year (36 per cent)

→ one to two years (51 per cent)

→ three to five years (77 per cent).

Only 23 per cent had remained with the same employer since graduating. Seventy-five per cent chose to stay within their home state when changing jobs. Respondents cited various reasons for changing jobs, the most common being:

→ salary increase (18 per cent)

→ unhappy with existing employer (17 per cent)

→ to try a new profession, department or company (13 per cent)

→ move home (nine per cent)

→ promotion (three per cent).

Why are graduates keener to change jobs than they are to leave the parental home?

Reprinted with permission from HRM Guide USA (http://www.hrmguide.com).

Institutional theories

An alternative approach places its main focus within the firm rather than the external job market. Institutionalists do not accept the principle of individual maximization of utility, arguing that both individuals and organizations cooperate to some extent and take account of the preferences of others in similar situations. Individual workers are less concerned with maximum benefits than achieving a fair rate compared with their peers. But this comparison may be restricted to employees within the same organization: most people appear indifferent (much of the time, at least) to benefits offered by other employers and large variations occur between firms in the same sector. Employers set wages for a variety of reasons ranging from profitability to tradition – competition with other firms is a relatively minor consideration. As a result, remuneration levels within many firms are relatively rigid. Wage rates are more likely to go up than down and are largely immune to influence from the external job market.

Reflecting on our discussion in Chapter 1, we can conclude that institutional approaches to the job market have a greater affinity with 'soft' HRM. They recognize that group effects underlie notions of fairness and loyalty, fundamental to the notion of employee commitment. They are consistent with the stakeholder concept, recognizing the important roles played by government and trade unions. For example, the 'insider–outsider' model offers an explanation for simultaneously high wages and high levels of unemployment (Lindbeck and Snower, 1988). Insiders have stakeholder status whereas outsiders do not (see Key concept 2.3). Outsider status particularly affects immigrants. Frijters, Shields and Price (2005) found that immigrants to the UK do not compete effectively for employment. Job search methods are less successful; they are as likely to gain employment through informal routes; and the probability of success increases with years since immigration. This may partially explain why immigration has little impact on the job market.

KEY CONCEPT 2.3 INSIDERS AND OUTSIDERS

Employers know that replacing existing workers with others from the outside world has inherent costs. This inhibits recruitment from the external employment market. Also, to some extent, there are costs or risks that inhibit employees from looking for work outside the organization. Consequently, there is rarely a free flow of workers in and out of a business. This disconnection is reflected in the pay and conditions of established employees ('insiders') which may deviate considerably from the 'market rate' in the wider world. Insiders will tend to push for a premium rate of pay, regardless of more competitive rates acceptable to outsiders, because of their perceived power to retain their jobs.

At the organizational level, human resource managers also affect the nature of the market as a result of their recruitment and redundancy strategies. When business is optimistic recruitment numbers increase; if conditions are bad, employees may be shed. Technological change is a further complicating factor, leading to fewer but more highly skilled employees.

Figure 2.1 demonstrates some of the forces that shape the employment market, including the major role played by government, particularly in the shape of legislation.

FIGURE 2.1

Competing influences on job creation within an organization

HRM IN REALITY   JOB SATISFACTION IN THE UK

Results from a survey of over 1000 workers for The Work Foundation conducted in 2006 reveals positive attitudes towards work but also confirms that work remains simply a way of making a living for many people. Commissioned as part of The Work Foundation's campaign for 'good work' the study found most people feel their work has got better since the beginning of their working lives.

The survey found:

→ Sixty per cent said their satisfaction with work had increased, 31 per cent felt it had gone down, and eight per cent said it had stayed the same.

→ Seventy-eight per cent said they found their work 'stimulating and challenging' (55 per cent agreeing strongly with this statement) and 69 per cent said their work was a 'source of personal fulfilment'.

→ Eighty-six per cent did not agree with the statement 'I regard my work as meaningless' with only 9 per cent saying they agreed (the remainder did not express a view).

→ Just over half (51 per cent) said their work was 'a means to an end'. People with lower pay and lower skills tended to be less satisfied with their jobs.

→ Over three-quarters of respondents describe themselves as 'very satisfied' (35 per cent) or 'quite satisfied' (43 per cent) with their current jobs; 10 per cent were neither satisfied nor dissatisfied; six per cent were 'quite dissatisfied'; and five per cent very dissatisfied.

Will Hutton, chief executive of The Work Foundation, said:

Traditionally, work has been seen as purely a grim economic necessity, which there is no getting out of, and little more to be said about. Our survey indicates that that view is no longer a fair reflection of how people feel. Today, work is increasingly thought of as a source of fulfilment, an important aspect of life that matters to people in a very personal way.

Other key findings in the survey included:

→ Women are slightly more likely to be satisfied with their job than men.

→ The over-55s are more likely to be satisfied with their job than younger workers, especially those aged 16–34 years.

→ Managers and professionals are more likely to be satisfied than other occupational groups.

→ People earning over £50 000 per year are more likely to be satisfied than those who earn less.

Will Hutton said:

> Employers and organizations are going to have to think much harder about the jobs they offer. The wage packet still matters, but there are crucially important psychological, social, and personal dividends from work, too – it is about money and meaning. Well over two-thirds of workers regard work as a source of personal fulfilment to them, but only a very few employers ever succeed in making the most of this huge personal appetite for work that more and more people have.

How would you explain the concept of work having 'meaning'?

Source: Reprinted with permission from HRM Guide UK (http://www.hrmguide.co.uk).

SOCIAL PREFERENCES

Participating in employment is not an 'all-or-nothing' decision: individuals also determine the amount of time they are prepared to devote to paid work. The allocation of time is affected by 'expected market earnings', taking travel, clothing and taxation into account. Traditionally, time given to 'market work' is distinguished from that devoted to any other activity – described as 'leisure'. However, it is recognized that time outside paid work is not necessarily devoted to pleasure. Far from lying on a beach, sipping a cool drink, people spend much of their 'leisure' time on some form of work without pay. This could be housework, maintenance, looking after children, cooking or providing a voluntary service.

Deciding to take a job, or not, involves a trade-off between family members. If an additional member works, there should be a reduction or reallocation of that person's unpaid activities. Employment may change lifestyle significantly. In developed countries this can result in the purchase of labour-saving devices such as a dishwasher, changing from fresh to ready-prepared food and hiring a cleaner or child-minder.

The decision to seek employment can be complex and is likely to be taken in conjunction with other members of the household. The household is viewed as the 'decision-making unit' that chooses how to allocate its members' time, evaluating the comparative advantages of working as against not working. Where the possibility of choice exists, the emphasis can be on working for money in order to buy the largest possible house, a brand new car, expensive holidays and consumer goods such as convenience foods. Alternatively, the household can minimize working time and maximize leisure, making do with a more modest home and car, spending effort on home-grown and prepared food.

Doing without paid work in order to maximize free time is an opportunity cost. In other words, if paid work is available, not working has a cost for the household. There may be preferences for particular family members to stay at home – typically mothers – whereas others (fathers) are expected to earn a wage. This pattern has changed radically in most industrialized countries in recent years.

Recognition of household preferences is important to people managers because there are strong cultural differences between one region and another. There are considerable pressures on potential and actual workers to behave in the way perceived as normal for their particular society. However, most organizations pay little attention to the domestic influences on an employee's motivation and performance. Employees are recruited and their performance assessed as if they were entirely free agents with no domestic responsibilities or interests outside work.

When is it worthwhile going to work? The total available resources of the household unit may be weighed up in the equation, including the time available for all its members, other income and total wealth. The financial benefit of work can only be gauged when tax, social security deductions, travelling, child-minding costs and so on have been calculated. This benefit may prove insignificant.

Mathematical models have been developed to predict the hours that people are prepared to work. Empirical studies do not necessarily support this approach – unemployment is an

HRM IN REALITY MOST SENIOR EMPLOYEES NEVER STOP WORKING

A poll of executives and professionals conducted in 2008 by MRINetwork, a major international search and recruitment organization found that the majority rarely stop working. Typically, they worked evenings, weekends and during their commute. Many believed that their employers were responsible for creating the situations that lead to overwork.

Seventy per cent of 500+ people surveyed said the organizations they worked for did not do a good job at fostering a work–life balance. Sixty-five per cent of participants in the poll were frequently still working after normal office hours, a further 19 per cent worked 'sometimes', nine per cent occasionally. Only five per cent said they never did so.

Michael Jalbert, president of MRINetwork, commented:

They often feel they have no choice but to work as much as it takes to meet management's expectations. More enlightened managers, however, are beginning to realize that the X and Y generations are much more committed to forging a balanced life than the retiring baby boomers. This will inevitably lead to a reevaluation of the performance requirements of individual positions within many companies, especially as the younger generation moves into higher management levels.

A number of factors influence the rising number of people whose work day extends far beyond the traditional hours. Obviously technology that makes staying connected almost anywhere in the world

effortless is a significant contributor. And for many people that's led to an almost compulsive need for 24/7 interaction.

He noted that many organizations were understaffed:

Most people simply have more work to do than they can accomplish in eight or even ten-hour days. In some cases, working overtime has masked the need to hire more mid-to-upper-level employees. If the work is getting done satisfactorily, senior management may not be aware of gaps in their workforce.

But many employees love what they do:

The greater their interest and commitment to the work they do, the more they seem to work – even when it's not required of them. To these people, the ability to stay connected to their work via a variety of technological devices is an asset rather than a liability.

Michael Jalbert notes that, especially for telecommuters, there is a blurring of the distinction between being 'at work' and 'off work'. 'As much as employees value flexible work schedules, this arrangement can also encourage working more and playing less.'

Why do executives and professionals tend to work excessive hours?

Source: Reprinted with permission from HRM Guide USA (http://www.hrmguide.com).

experience that can arrive like a tidal wave. There may be no opportunity to make a free decision on whether or not to work. Job choices also reflect individual career plans and preferences.

INDIVIDUAL PREFERENCES

Human behaviour involves deep complexities that bring unpredictability and apparent contrariness into the employment market. Most people's motives and ambitions involve much more than seeking the highest salary. Money is important but to a degree that varies between individuals. People will remain in comparatively low-paid jobs such as nursing because the satisfaction that comes from helping other people can be valued above a high salary. An economic model based purely on income will go some way to explain employment behaviour on the large scale but it will not explain *individual* human behaviour. Other motivations come into play in determining people's approach to work. As we can see from Table 2.1, psychologists have attempted to provide explanations at the individual level.

Factor	Characteristics
Opportunities for control	Limited control over work, or no job at all, leads to higher levels of anxiety, depression, tiredness and psycho-somatic symptoms. Also lower general life-satisfaction and self-esteem.
Opportunities for skill use	People benefit from stretching jobs. Morale, self-esteem, sociability and life satisfaction are reduced when a worker's job is de-skilled or lost. Some people can compensate through hobbies or voluntary work, but many are unable to fill the gap.
Goal and task demands	Jobs set demands on our lives in general. Many unemployed people find it hard to fill their time, often spending a high proportion sleeping, sitting around or watching TV, further contributing to lowered morale.
Variety	Work can increase variety, providing a contrast with home life. It also provides the income to pay for experiences such as cinema, music, sporting activities and holidays.
Environmental clarity	Work helps us understand and predict the world around us. Mental health is better if we are clear about our roles and purpose in life. Conversely, uncertainty is detrimental, especially over a lengthy period.
Availability of money	The unemployed have a lower income level (40–60 per cent on average) than those in work. This can make it difficult to repay credit and keeping up mortgage payments, adding further stress. Expensive activities are curtailed, contributing to feelings of isolation and boredom.

TABLE 2.1
Psychological benefits of work

Source: Adapted from Warr (1987).

TABLE 2.1
(*Continued*)

Factor	Characteristics
Physical security	In Western cultures people are brought up to value personal and private space. To provide feelings of personal security, self-worth and well-being they need a home to call their own. This requires an income.
Opportunity for interpersonal contact	Interaction with other people reduces feelings of loneliness and provides emotional support.
Valued social position	Work provides a self-identity and a feeling of worth.

Ardichvili and Kuchinke (2009: 155) argue that 'work as a process and an institution ... transcends individual frames of reference and links the person to the social, economic and political realms.' The significance of understanding the 'meaning of work' or the 'meaning of working' – some theorists differentiate between the two – is that it underlies one of the most fashionable concerns of HRM or talent management: employee engagement or commitment (Flesher, 2009: 255). It is common to ask the question: 'What do you do?' For many of us, self-identity is provided by a job. Comparing South Korea, Germany and the United States, Kuchinke (2009) contends that the meaning of work varies across the three countries and has changed in different degrees since industrialization. He argues that work is more central to self-identity in the United States than in Germany, where life outside work is equally important.

The psychological benefits obtained from work include the fulfilment of social needs such as companionship, group cohesion and a sense of belonging. Kidder (2006) points to the limitations of an economic model to explain employment behaviour using bike messengers as an example. Bike messengers work in a dirty and dangerous occupation with low pay and no benefits. Nevertheless, many messengers consider their occupation to be their primary source of identity. The creativity and spontaneity of courier work allows messengers to become emotionally attached to their job. It brings the thrill seeking of leisure pursuits into the workplace, which creates an authentic self intimately tied to the occupation, a rare achievement in an increasingly rationalized employment system. Twenge *et al.* (2010) looked at the work values of a nationally representative sample of US high school seniors in 1976 (baby boomers), 1991 (GenerationX or GenX), and 2006 (Generation Me or GenY). They found that leisure values increased steadily over the generations while work centrality declined. Status and earnings were most highly valued by GenX and least by baby boomers. Altruistic work values such as helping and societal worth were the same across the generations. However, social values (for example, friendship) and intrinsic values (such as having an interesting, results-oriented job) were regarded as less important by GenY than by baby boomers.

PARTICIPATING IN THE EMPLOYMENT MARKET

Who is involved in the job market? We have seen that the resourcing of organizations is affected by national or regional availability (supply) and demand for appropriately skilled employees. On the supply side of this balance, people can be divided into three groups, the first two of which are described as **'economically active'** (Key concept 2.4). Rates of economically active participants fluctuate, with a trend towards increasing participation from the 1960s to the early 21st century. For example, the participation rate in Australia increased from 57.4 per cent of over-15-year olds in 1961 to 65.2 per cent in 2008. The bulk of the increase took place among women of whom only 28.9 per cent were economically active in 1961 compared to 58.3 per cent in 2008. In the 15–64 age group of both sexes, the OECD average was 70 per cent in 2007 with rates such as 75 per cent in the USA, 76 per cent in Australia and the UK, 78 per cent in Canada and New Zealand, 80 per cent in Sweden and 81 per cent in Switzerland.

KEY CONCEPT 2.4 ECONOMICALLY ACTIVE

The economically active comprise two groups: (a) *the employed* – those in paid work; and (b) *the unemployed* – those who are looking for paid work but are unable to find it.

Economically inactive people are neither in paid work nor seeking jobs, including people in education, with medical conditions, looking after dependents, and the retired. Proportions of these categories vary from country to country, depending on economic conditions and custom. Accurate figures for each group are not easily calculated. In particular, it is difficult to estimate true unemployment because the unemployed are identified on the basis of registration with state agencies. As an illustration, Table 2.2 shows official figures for a number of OECD countries in 2006 and 2010. Usually the registration of individuals as unemployed is linked to the payment of unemployment relief or other social security benefit. If the benefit system is generous, people are more likely to register. Conversely, if benefits are restricted the registered unemployment figure decreases.

TABLE 2.2

Comparative levels of unemployment (Quarter 1, 2010)

Sources: Labour Force Statistics (MEI), under labour from OECD. Stat Extracts, http://stats .oecd.org, accessed October 2010. Reproduced with permission from OECD.

Country	Unemployment %2010	Unemployment %2006
Australia	5.8	5.2
Belgium	8.6	8.2
Canada	8.7	5.7
Denmark	7.8	4.4
Finland	9.3	8.1
France	9.8	9.4
Germany	8.0	9.1
Ireland	12.9	4.2
Italy	9.1	7.7 (Dec 2005)

TABLE 2.2
(Continued)

Country	Unemployment %2010	Unemployment %2006
Japan	5.1	4.2
Netherlands	5.9	4.2
New Zealand	6.6	3.9 (March)
Norway	3.7	3.9
Poland	10.6	16.9
Portugal	10.6	7.7
Spain	20.1	8.2
Sweden	9.3	5.3
UK	7.9	5.2
USA	10.4	4.8

Developed countries have experienced considerable variations in unemployment levels. This is reflected in changes in public expectations and concern over the level of unemployment. It can be argued that more people would work if jobs were easy to find – but they do not search when work is scarce. This has been called the 'discouraged worker hypothesis' (see Key concept 2.5). Workers calculate the probability of finding a job in relation to the wage they are likely to get and conclude that the effort is not worthwhile. This hypothesis suggests that the number of active job-seekers decreases in times of high unemployment, leaving an unmeasurable hidden unemployment rate behind the official statistics. As with many other Western countries, the 2007–2009 recession seriously affected the UK's economic output – more so than any other recession since the Second World War. However, the unemployment level did not increase to the degree experienced in previous recessions despite being at its lowest level for 30 years. Gregg and Wadsworth (2010) conclude that this difference can be attributed to:

→ High levels of profitability for firms going into the recession.

→ Supportive government monetary and fiscal policies during the period of recession.

→ Reductions in real producer wages.

→ Comparatively stable real consumer wages.

KEY CONCEPT 2.5 DISCOURAGED WORKER HYPOTHESIS

Workers calculate the probability of finding a job in relation to the wage they are likely to get and conclude that the effort is not worthwhile.

HRM IN REALITY — IMMIGRATION AND ITS EFFECTS ON THE JOB MARKET IN THE UK

→ The rate of immigration to the UK rose from 1995 to the recession of 2007–2009 when the stock of immigrants fell back.

→ The level of overseas-born people in the UK's working age population rose from eight per cent in 1995 to 14 per cent or 5.3 million in late 2009.

→ But the UK still has a smaller share of immigrants in the total population (10.2 per cent) than many other developed countries, for example Australia (25 per cent), the United States (13.6 per cent) and even Germany (12.9 per cent).

→ The highest proportion of immigrants to the UK in recent years came from Poland, India, Pakistan, South Africa and the United States.

→ Immigrants are generally younger and better educated than UK-born individuals with most recent immigrants being even more educated.

→ There is a considerable disparity in regional levels of immigrants with an overwhelming concentration in London. For example, about 60 per cent of the working age population in the London Borough of Brent are immigrants while less than three per cent of the working age population of Knowsley are overseas-born.

→ There is a strict 'points' system controlling access to work for non-EU immigrants.

→ Overall, immigration has been positive for the UK as both low- and high-skill gaps in the job market where there are shortages of workers have been filled, with little effect on wage or employment levels.

Why does hostility towards immigration prevail despite the evidence for positive benefits?

Source: Adapted from Wadsworth (2010).

Organizations in free market countries focus on the external employment market, seeking new staff from outside the business. This is compatible with a competitive market approach in which employees are recruited when needed and dispensed with when no longer required. This view also provides a clear rationale for the 'hard' HRM form of employee planning that we will discuss in a later chapter. In the first chapter of this book we observed that the softer Harvard model of HRM emphasizes commitment between organizations and their employees. The latter approach is more consistent with social market and East Asian capitalist models. In Germany and Japan – together with the ideal organizations of 'soft' HRM rhetoric – the traditional focus has been on the internal employment market with:

→ Recruitment taking place almost entirely at the lower levels from the pool of available school-leavers and graduates.

→ Organizations offering a structured career on a lifetime basis.

→ Little movement, or labour turnover, between organizations.

Trends and levels vary significantly between public and private sectors. At the end of the 20th century, public sector tenure levels were over twice those of the private sector. This may be partly explained by the tendency of government workers to be older than their counterparts in private industry. Also, there is a lesser likelihood of public sector employees being laid off or being affected by cyclical factors to the degree experienced by private sector workers – for example those in construction or wholesale and retail trade. However, after the recession of 2007–2009 public sector workers have been targeted in cost-cutting measures in countries such as the UK.

Intriguingly, the archetypal East Asian economy, Singapore, has seen high rates of employee turnover to match its remarkable growth rate due to competition for scarce skills. Similarly, Japanese companies have changed their traditional practices to attract electronics experts with premium technological skills.

Projections of the future size of the employment market are critical to planned economic development. On a local basis, individual companies need to anticipate the availability of suitable recruits to meet business planning needs. These are normally calculated from:

→ **Demographic trends** (Key concept 2.6), including the birth rate at least 16 years previously.

→ Retirement rates: in the last few decades there has been a pronounced trend towards earlier retirement in developed countries, which is likely to be reversed as people live longer and age discrimination is banned.

→ Numbers of people in higher education.

KEY CONCEPT 2.6 DEMOGRAPHIC TRENDS

Long-term changes in the overall population level and age distribution in countries, regions and localities due to variations in birth, death and migration. These changes affect the availability of employable people.

Reductions in demand for manual work have seen many unskilled workers leaving the employment market. Ranzijn *et al.* (2006) studied the impact of mature-aged unemployment on individuals in Adelaide, South Australia and suggest that their quality of life is substantially impaired. Frustration at being unable to contribute to society, support adult children, and use skills can lead to the 'peg-down' phenomenon, described as an intermediate step between becoming unemployed and premature exit from the workforce.

HRM IN REALITY   LIVING LONGER, WORKING LONGER

People in developed countries are living longer and many are working well past traditional retirement age. Some are even returning to work after 'retiring' or opting for 'portfolios' of paid and volunteer positions, according a MetLife Mature Market Institute® study, *Living Longer, Working Longer: The Changing Landscape of the Aging Workforce*, conducted by David DeLong & Associates, Inc. and Zogby International in 2006.

'Today, older workers view retirement as a desirable state, not a particular date,' said Dr David DeLong, author of *Lost Knowledge: Confronting the Threat of an Aging Workforce* and a research fellow at the MIT AgeLab. 'When we conducted the study, we found that mature workers are struggling to balance the conflicting pressures of income security, post-retirement-age employment and, often, age discrimination – perceived or real – as they look for a sense of security and meaning during their "retirement" years.'

This study is unusual in that it examines the actual work experiences of 2719 employees aged 55–70 whereas most other studies offer predictions of aging baby boomers' retirement expectations. The MetLife study shows that the following percentages of respondents are working or looking for work:

→ Seventy-eight per cent of respondents aged 55–59

→ Sixty per cent of 60–65 year-olds, and

→ Thirty-seven per cent of 66–70 year-olds.

Around 15 per cent of employees across all three age groups, have accepted retirement benefits from previous employers, but have chosen to return to work (or are looking for work). These 'working retired', represent:

→ Eleven per cent of 55–59 year-olds

→ Sixteen per cent of 60–65 year-olds

→ Nineteen per cent of 66–70 year-olds.

Motivations to work
There are significant differences between age groups when it comes to the motivation to work. Employees aged 55–59 cited economic incentives as the major motive, with 72 per cent of this group saying that 'need income to live on' was their primary reason for working. Sixty per cent of 60–65-year-olds also cited this as their main motivation, followed by a desire to 'stay active and engaged' (54 per cent) and 'do meaningful work' (43 per cent). However, 72 per cent of 66–70 year-olds cited the desire to 'stay active and engaged' as their primary reason to work, followed by 'the opportunity to do meaningful work' (47 per cent) and 'social interaction with colleagues' (42 per cent).

What does 'retirement' mean?
Respondents in the MetLife study cited the following definitions of retirement:

→ 'freedom from the demands of work' (26 per cent)

→ 'more control over one's personal time' (24 per cent)

→ 'limited financial concerns' (21 per cent)

→ 'the ability to pursue other opportunities.'

'As organizations seek to attract and retain older workers, they must be careful not to lump all "older workers" into the same category – it's important to differentiate the work experiences and motivations of these employees. While some may be working for financial reasons, others place a special premium on feeling engaged and doing work that means something,' says Sandra Timmermann, Ed.D., gerontologist and director of the MetLife Mature Market Institute. 'Recruiting and retaining older workers requires careful consideration of job design, work environment, and creating new and challenging opportunities.'

What motivates the 'working retired'
Twenty per cent of working retireds aged 60–65 said they 'wanted to try something new and different'. However, this option was cited by only 12 per cent of 55–59-year-olds and seven per cent of 66–70 year-olds. Nineteen per cent of 66–70-year-olds cited 'becoming self-employed or starting a business' compared with seven per cent of 60–65-year-olds and eight per cent of 55–59-year-olds.

Twenty-eight per cent of respondents aged 55–59 said they were 'self-employed or business owner'. This increased to 36 per cent of 60–65-year-olds and 42 per cent of 66–70-year-olds.

'Clearly, these findings suggest there are conditions in the job market and in older workers' desire for autonomy and flexibility that make self-employment an attractive option for those in their late sixties,' said Dr DeLong. 'As the oldest Boomers turn 60 in 2006, their desire for autonomy and trying new things could portend a significant wave of departures in the next five years. Employers will need to identify ways to retain the valuable knowledge of these workers.'

Financial reality
Financial necessity underlies the need to work for many older employees. Eighteen per cent of baby boom workers aged 55–59 said that they expected to have no access to retirement benefits (e.g., pension, 401(k), SEP) and are likely to feel compelled to work beyond traditional retirement age. Fourteen per cent of those aged 60–65 and 10 per cent aged 66–70 expected to receive nothing but Social Security when they finally cease working.

'Retirement experts have been predicting for years the serious repercussions that will arise as baby boomers' lack of retirement assets collides with their increased longevity to create widespread economic hardship. The rational solution – to continue working full-time beyond traditional retirement age – is at odds with many Boomers' interests, values and priorities for their retirement,' notes Dr Timmermann.

Some other survey findings
Age discrimination. Older workers frequently cited 'age bias' as a reason for unsuccessful job searches, including:

➜ Thirty-nine per cent of 55–59-year-olds

➜ Forty-two per cent of 60–65-year-olds

➜ Sixty per cent of 66–70-year-olds.

Preference for part-time work. Of those still in employment, 76 per cent of 55–59 year-olds worked more than 35 hours a week, compared with only 39 per cent of 66–70 year-olds.

Portfolio work. Interviews were also conducted for the study, in which some older employees said their lives had taken on a 'portfolio quality' – mixing part-time paid work, volunteer work, and travel, together with more time for hobbies and family. In fact, 25 per cent of survey respondents across all age groups had more than one paid job with about 20 per cent of those working having two jobs, and another four per cent having three jobs.

Why are some older people keen to work while others are not?

Source: Reprinted with permission from HRM Guide USA (http://www.hrmguide.com/).

EMPLOYEE SUPPLY AND DEMAND

Individuals determine how much time they will devote to paid work for a variety of reasons. The proportion of people of working age in work, or seeking jobs, is described as the labour force participation rate. The flow of young people into the workforce is fundamental to the employment market. The underlying demographic pattern is changing throughout the world. Whereas most developing countries have seen an explosion of growth in the youngest age groups, the developed world is experiencing a reduction in birth rate. This follows a baby boom after World War Two which produced a wave of people who will mostly retire in the first quarter of the 21st century. In Western Europe and North America, numbers of people entering the employment market have been falling. This will reduce the overall size of their workforces, shifting the age balance towards older employees. This has been compensated by a massive increase in working women, especially in part-time jobs.

Key demographic trends include the following:

➜ Populations in developed countries are stabilizing or declining. Birth rates are tending to fall below replenishment rates.

➜ Ageing populations in 'first world' countries may be counter-balanced by immigration.

➜ Developing countries experience a period of rapid population growth as infant mortality rates are reduced – well in advance of birth control measures being adopted.

➜ Most developing countries experience population pressure for decades until stability is achieved.

➜ The population balance will change markedly between the developed and developing world. Eventually the developed world will decline in importance, in line with their reduced working population.

Employee demand

Demand for workers is linked to the economic cycle, increasing in boom times and decreasing in recession. Other factors include the adoption of new technology, productivity improvements and changing skill requirements. Superficially, calculating employment supply and demand seems easy. In practice, the combination of variable consumer demand, development of new products and technology, and **economic turbulence** make it extremely problematic. In recent decades, for example, commentators have confidently predicted both permanently high levels of unemployment *and* shortages of labour.

PART-TIME AND TEMPORARY WORKING

Part-time employees contract to work for anything less than normal full-time basic hours. Advantages to employers can include: more intensive work with less time used for breaks; lower absenteeism; enthusiasm and commitment can be higher (less opportunity for boredom); and less unionization among part-time staff.

The main forms of part-time work include:

→ *Classical.* Work that does not require full-time cover, typically restricted to a few hours each day. For example, cleaning offices, or staffing a canteen.

→ *Supplementary.* Where a part-time worker replaces overtime and for example, performs an evening shift, or works short days to cover peak periods.

→ *Substitution.* In which part-timers replace full-timers through job-splitting. It is common for older workers to be retained as part-timers before full retirement.

More recent types of part-time work include key working and job sharing. Key working is typically found in service industries such as retailing. Service work differs from 'traditional' work. Peak activity occurs on days and at times when other workers are at leisure. Peak times may be so short that it is impossible for an employer to use full-time workers effectively. In these circumstances few 'core' full-timers are required. Correspondingly, a large number of 'peripheral' part-timers work at busy periods. Peripheral numbers can be shrunk or expanded as required. This allows greater flexibility than would be possible for a completely full-time workforce.

Job sharing is where two people are responsible for one full-time job, dividing pay and benefits in proportion to the hours worked. Days or weeks may be split or alternate weeks worked. An advantage for some employees, job sharing can also benefit employers. For example:

→ Sharers can overlap hours so that busy periods receive double cover.

→ Jobs are at least partly covered when one person is away through illness or annual leave.

→ Two individuals can bring greater experience and a broader range of views to a job than a single employee.

Job sharing allows skilled people to be retained if they give up full-time employment. However, there are some disadvantages such as:

→ Training, induction and administration overheads for two people.

→ Finding a suitable partner with matching skills and availability if one sharer leaves.

→ Communication on tasks that cannot be dealt with quickly ('hand-over' problems).

→ Responsibility for staff can be problematic; people may find difficulty in working for two supervisors.

→ Fair allocation of work.

Part-time workers come especially from specific groups, including:

1 *Female parents with children.* The largest group, typically working when children are at school.

2 *Retired or semi-retired.* Supplementing pensions, filling time and using their skills. Again, they tend to work during the day.

3 *Moonlighters.* With full-time jobs elsewhere, supplementing income in the evening or at weekends. For instance, driving mini-cabs, delivering free newspapers, or bar work.

4 *Students.* Supplementing grants or servicing loans by delivering papers, pizzas, serving in fast-food outlets. They may also work in vacation periods or undertake seasonal work, for example, in the tourist industry.

Paradoxically, many managers question part-timers' commitment, seeing them as being primarily home-oriented. They are often excluded from interesting and senior positions. Part-time workers tend to get fewer training and promotion opportunities. Some managers have contradictory beliefs about women part-timers. On the one hand they believe them to be reliable, loyal and flexible. At the same time, they consider that they take time off to be with children and give precedence to partners' careers. Webber and Williams (2008) contend that working mothers at both the top and bottom ends of the employment hierarchy are uniquely disadvantaged by their part-time jobs and respond in different ways. However, in general they take responsibility for the 'choices' they have made, thereby absolving their employers of any blame for the exploitation and discrimination against part-time workers.

HRM IN REALITY INVOLUNTARY PART-TIMERS

A report from the School of Social Service Administration at the University of Chicago published in 2010 found that a record number of US employees are involuntarily working part-time as a result of a reduction in their hours or being unable to find a full-time job. This effect of the recession is in addition to unemployment currently affecting nearly 10 per cent of the workforce.

Susan Lambert, associate professor, commented:

> Certainly the current recession is contributing to underemployment, as evidenced by the proportion of American workers classified as 'involuntary part-time'.

Researchers explain that the US Census Bureau applies the term 'involuntary part-time' to those working less than 35 hours a week because they could not find a full-time job or because of 'slack demand'. There were 9.2 million workers in this category in November 2009. Although the largest recorded figure, it reflects trends seen in earlier recessions. The labour market added 1.5 million involuntary part-time workers between 1981 and 1982 (for a total of 6.8 million workers) and 2.3 million between 1992 and 1993 (for a total of 6.7 million workers).

The current study investigated management and employee aspects of scheduling practices in a national retail apparel firm. Researchers explain that the majority of waged and salaried employees are hourly or part-time workers who are particularly vulnerable to imposed changes. They receive limited formal employee benefits, and many are ineligible for public benefits (such as unemployment insurance, cash assistance, or family and medical leave). Their work schedules are typically arranged with little prior notice and are often unpredictable. The researchers call for changes in public policy as well as company practices to address these issues.

Susan Lambert said:

> I think it is important to underscore that employment has become increasingly precarious over the past 30 years, not just during recessionary periods, due to structural changes in the economy, reductions in labour protections and evolving employer practices that pass risk from the market onto workers. The current recession highlights these insecurities, bringing much-needed attention to the plight of disadvantaged workers who are struggling to keep their jobs as well as maintain sufficient hours to make ends meet. The problems faced by hourly, low-level workers are unlikely to go away when the economy fully recovers.

Whatever the economic conditions, employers frequently use 'just-in-time' practices to maintain control over costs and demand. Hourly workers' schedules are used to accommodate fluctuations often with limited notice. This disadvantages workers trying to manage their finances, childcare arrangements and other aspects of family life.

Julia Henly, associate professor, said:

> Unpredictable work schedules can translate into instability in family routines and practices, placing additional burdens on already strapped and busy families, their caregivers and extended family members. We find that hourly retail employees with more predictable work schedules report lower levels of stress, less work-to-family conflict and fewer work interferences with non-work activities such as scheduling doctor's appointments, socializing with friends and eating meals together as a family.

Among other significant findings:

→ Hours vary substantially for both part-time and full-time hourly workers, with full-time employees working more hours but also experiencing the greatest fluctuations in hours from week to week.

→ The more hours employees work and the less their hours fluctuate, the longer they remain at the firm, even after accounting for factors such as age, race and job status.

→ Job turnover is high, particularly for part-time sales associates, younger workers, African Americans and recently hired workers.

→ Management practices contribute to job turnover irrespective of individual worker characteristics. Managers who strategically limit staff numbers with the goal of providing each sales associate with sufficient hours have lower turnover and higher retention rates.

The researchers acknowledge the importance of workplace flexibility in public policy debates as more parents try to reconcile competing demands of work and family life. Common flexibility options include allowing workers to work reduced hours, work at home, or vary the start and end times of the working day. These may make sense for managerial and professional roles but are less applicable to many low-level hourly workers. This issue will be addressed in four government-sponsored regional conferences scheduled for the next twelve months.

The authors comment:

> Fortunately, policy makers, advocacy groups and researchers are becoming increasingly interested in developing and promoting flexibility options for US workers in hourly jobs. As these initiatives proceed, it will be important that they reflect the range of work conditions found in hourly jobs, including low-wage jobs in service industries.

The third author is Anna Haley-Lock, an assistant professor of social work at the University of Wisconsin.

How would you evaluate the consequences on motivation and employee turnover of voluntary and involuntary part-time working?

Source: Reprinted with permission from HRM Guide USA (http://www.hrmguide.com).

Temporary workers

It is frequently assumed that temporary job contracts are increasing but this statement 'needs to be heavily qualified' (Martin and Stancanelli, 2002). An analysis of 1985–2000 data from 13 OECD countries shows that the proportion of temporary employment in total salaried employment has risen (on average) by less than three per cent. France, Italy, the Netherlands and Spain are responsible for much of this less than massive increase. In five other countries, the proportion actually decreased. Countries in this category include the USA. Martin and Stancanelli (2002) suggest, 'one reason for the low recourse to temporary work in the United States may be that US permanent positions are less rigidly protected than in Europe, for instance, so there is less incentive for employers to offer temporary contracts.' On the other side of the Atlantic, Biggs (2006) analyzed data from the employment agency industry plus Labour Force Surveys from 1997–2004 to reveal a reduction of over a quarter of a million temporary workers in the UK over a six-year period. Regional variations were apparent, with increases in Northern Ireland and Wales. This was thought to reflect the impact of new legislation and a stable economy.

The largest temporary staff agency, Manpower Inc. places two million people in a year, over 40 per cent of whom go on to permanent employment. More than 10 per cent of workers in the EU have temporary jobs, with the highest level (30 per cent) in Spain. A UK Labour Force Survey found that 1.6 million British workers were employed on a temporary basis.

Druker and Stanworth (2004) found that employers expected agency workers to show loyalty, commitment and high levels of motivation but the employers gave little in return. Autor and Houseman (2010) did not find any benefits in obtaining consequent long-term employment from temporary work through a scheme in Detroit. Hall (2006) comparing attitudes and preferences of Australian agency workers with permanent employees, found agency workers to be no more satisfied with their level of flexibility than direct workers. Moreover, agency workers were less satisfied with their pay, job security, use and development of skills, autonomy and influence at work. Hall concludes that, in fact, the use of agency workers may be incompatible with human resource strategies based on high performance work practices.

Apart from the familiar 'temps' obtained from specialist agencies, two other groups of temporary workers can be highlighted:

→ *Contingent employees.* In the UK there are 500 000 professional and highly-skilled people working on temporary contracts. For example, 'interim managers'. These are generally freelance executives aged over 40. Most assignments last for 40–80 days, allowing for short-term problems to be handled without long-term commitment to expensive staff. Specialist expertise can be bought in for specific tasks or projects. Contingent managers have been rated highly in functions such as human resources, finance, information technology, marketing, operations and property.

→ *Seasonal employment.* Seasonal workers are hired to cope with fluctuations in demand – to keep down stock volumes, and hence cost. For example, the chocolate industry has especially high periods of demand at times when gifts are commonly given, such as Christmas.

From the employee's point of view, part-time or temporary work may be both convenient and attractive to many people. For most people, however, part-time jobs are no substitute for the loss of full-time jobs but the 20th century concept of the nine-to-five job and a lifetime career may be disintegrating in favour of much more flexible arrangements. Levels of insecurity and stress are rising as people have increasingly uncertain working lives. It has become a truism that most people will experience at least two or three careers in their lifetime. Handy (1989: 46) sees work becoming part of a portfolio of activities. At any one time, individuals may have a number of part-time jobs, together with leisure or study periods.

SUMMARY

Human resource management takes place within a business environment that is increasingly global in its reach. We considered factors which lead to people seeking work and joining that market. We examined key economic and psychological concepts and identified a number of links with fundamental elements of HRM. Participation in the job market was investigated, comparing rates in different countries. Different working patterns were described as a prelude for later discussion of flexibility

FURTHER READING

The range of books on the employment market is vast but tends towards political or economic analysis. The following books are of particular interest:

1 *Global Employment Trends Report*, published by the International Labour Organization each year takes an overview of recent key developments.

2 *Unemployment: Past and Present* edited by Philip Arestis and John McCombie (Palgrave Macmillan, 2008) takes a broad view of unemployment and looks at the lessons of experience and theory.

3 *Employment and the Family: The Reconfiguration of Work and Family Life in Contemporary Societies* by Rosemary Crompton (Cambridge University Press, 2006) takes a gender and comparative perspective on the way employment has changed in recent years.

REVIEW QUESTIONS

1 How is it possible to regard jobs as being in a market? Discuss the usefulness of the competitive market model in describing the ways in which the employment market functions in the real world.

2 Summarize the main differences between competitive market and institutional models of the employment market. How do competitive and institutional models of the job market relate to 'hard' and 'soft' versions of HRM?

3 Describe in your own words what is meant by the 'labour force participation rate'.

4 To what extent do people behave as individuals – as opposed to households – when they seek work? Consider your family, relatives or friends as examples.

5 Is full employment a practical goal for every country?

6 What is the relationship between levels of welfare payment or unemployment benefit and the level of employment?

7 How will demographic trends affect employment in your country in the 21st century?

8 Outline the advantages and disadvantages of part-time jobs for employers and employees.

9 Why has the introduction of new technology not led to a 'leisure revolution'?

CASE STUDY FOR DISCUSSION AND ANALYSIS

Read the following case studies and answer the questions that follow.

Rob's career/Jefford Trading

1 Rob is a student on placement with a thriving media marketing company. As an intern, he enjoys the challenges of dealing with customers and other staff. He prefers work to university where, academically, he is an average performer. Rob enjoys some parts of his course but dreads other aspects – particularly the end of semester assessments. He was pushed into higher education by an ambitious father whose own career was limited by his lack of qualifications. Personally, Rob cannot wait to complete the course and get on with his career.

Rob's placement company has lost a number of key staff to a competitor. Senior managers have looked at the younger staff and highlighted Rob as a potential highflyer. He has the energy and the enthusiasm to cope with the long hours and the considerable travelling required. They have offered Rob a higher level position which is now vacant. The rewards are high and the prospects for the next few years are excellent. However, Rob has been told that he cannot accept this position and return to full-time education to complete his final year.

Rob has to make a choice quickly. What factors should he take into account in making his decision?

2 Jefford Trading is a medium-sized business selling high quality designer furnishings. Originally started 20 years ago from one small shop, Jan and Keith Jefford have built the company into a multi-shop retailer with ventures around the country. In the last three years business has become a struggle: other firms have entered the same market and rental and other costs have risen sharply. The company continues to make a profit but further expansion will be hard work.

There are 57 employees. Apart from the founders there is one other director, Paul Stevens the company secretary (49), who looks after major contracts and personnel. He is competent but not ambitious. There are five middle managers, all graduates under 35 picked by Paul, with responsibilities for buying, logistics, finance, marketing and retailing respectively. The logistics and retail managers are responsible for most of the staff. Junior managers run the shops, all without higher education qualifications but keen. The other head office staff are of mixed ages with little potential for advancement.

The Jeffords have worked long hours developing the company, taking few holidays and little money out of the company. Keith is 48, looks much older and has some health problems. Jan is 43, more determined but worried about her husband. The managers have suggested that they take over the running of the company, allowing the owners to sit back and enjoy life.

The Jeffords' accountants have little faith in the managers: they believe them to be too young and inexperienced. The accountants have advised the sale of the company and investment of the proceeds. The Jeffords accept this is sensible advice but would prefer to keep the company going.

How would you conduct your investigation?

You have been brought in as a consultant to advise them. What would you do?

What are the options?

What do you anticipate your recommendations to be?

How are the Jeffords likely to react?

CHAPTER 3
International HRM

LEARNING OBJECTIVES

The purpose of this chapter is to:

→ Outline positive and negative aspects of the globalization of trade and production that affect human resource management.

→ Critically evaluate the importance of multinational companies in the process of globalization.

→ Highlight human resource issues pertaining to international outsourcing and offshoring.

→ Outline the impact of diverse global cultures on business behaviour.

→ Provide an overview of the role played by governments in creating the context for human resource management.

→ Outline the concept of human capital and its implications for development.

GLOBALIZATION

Why is globalization (Key concept 3.1) important to our understanding of human resource management? Examine the business pages of any national newspaper and you are almost certain to find examples of businesses engaged in cross-border mergers, takeovers or expansion overseas. Moreover, domestic mergers of banks, airline companies and even retailers are often explained as defensive moves by national organizations attempting to build sufficient critical mass to withstand competition from giant multinationals. Businesses simply cannot ignore the global dimension, and neither can human resource managers.

KEY CONCEPT 3.1 GLOBALIZATION

A systematic trend towards integration of production and marketing with brand-named goods and virtually identical 'badge-engineered' products such as cars being made available throughout the world. This process has been fostered by 'transnational' or 'multinational' companies operating in more than one country. Such companies are relatively free to switch resources and production from one country to another.

Physical location is becoming steadily less relevant as new technologies and increasingly complex international supply links are developed. This has a considerable impact on culture, language and working practices throughout the world. The implications for the nature and availability of work and its management are profound. Employees in one country increasingly use the same manufacturing processes as any other and are expected to achieve equivalent standards of productivity. As a result, the costs and skills of human resources have become a matter of competition between countries. The investment that drives such activities criss-crosses between developing and developed countries with investment going from the poorer to the richer countries as much as it does in the opposite direction (Mattoo and Subramanian, 2009).

The International Labour Organization (2000) concluded that globalization intensified in the latter years of the 20th century, especially in terms of trade, investment, financial liberalization and technological change. Despite some fluctuations, growth in world trade has continued into the 21st century. In 2005, for example, the value of world merchandise exports increased by 13 per cent to US$10.1 trillion, while the value of world commercial services exports rose by 11 per cent to US$2.4 trillion (WTO, 2006). But there has been widespread public disquiet due to:

→ Reduction in job security because work (and therefore jobs) can be moved from one country to another.

→ Undercutting of one country's wages by another, leading to erosion of wage rates.

→ Exceeding generally accepted working hours and exposure to health and safety risks in order to cut costs.

In some developing countries globalization has widened inequality. For example, 70 per cent of India's workforce remain in subsistence agriculture. India has more indigenous billionaires than any other country with the exception of the USA, but one in three of its 1.1 billion population are living on less than $1 per day (Thornton and Thornton, 2009). Fofack (2009) shows that despite the deepening integration and interdependency of countries and regions, those that focus on knowledge creation and the production of high-tech and manufactured goods, dependent on leading-edge technology, are those that benefit the most from globalization. Most of sub-Saharan Africa has been relegated to the role of end-users and the income gap with the globalizers has widened even more.

Sen (2002) tries to balance positive and negative views of globalization. He notes that proponents and opponents of globalization tend to perceive it as global westernization. Those who have a positive view of globalization consider it to be a 'marvellous contribution of Western civilization to the world'. But those with the opposite point of view see globalization as an extension of Western imperialism. They see contemporary capitalism as being 'driven and led by greedy and grabby Western countries in Europe and North America' using 'rules of trade and business relations that do not serve the interests of the poorer people in the world'. Preble (2010) contends that a more careful balance of the key issues surrounding globalization, namely jobs, inequality and poverty; national sovereignty and cultural diversity, and the natural environment can make the process sustainable.

The degree of perceived job insecurity is highlighted in the OECD survey shown in Table 3.1.

KEY CONCEPT 3.2 THE INSECURITY THESIS

Heery and Salmon (2000) identify a connection between globalization and the 'insecurity thesis', a belief that: 'Employment in the developed economies has become more insecure or unstable in the sense that both continued employment and the level of remuneration have become less predictable and contingent on factors which lie beyond the employee's control'.

PRODUCTIVITY AND GROWTH

Productivity has a direct relationship with the wealth of any country (see Key concept 3.3). Prior to the global financial crisis of 2007/2008 a study by the Conference Board (Van Ark, 2006) showed that US productivity had outpaced most developed countries in recent decades and that information and communication technologies have been the major drivers of US productivity growth. For example, in 2005, although sharply reduced from the previous year's 3.0 per cent, the USA's productivity growth of 1.8 per cent compared with Japan at 1.9 per cent and markedly outperformed an average of 0.5 per cent in the 15 older members of the EU. Productivity growth in the EU-15 ranged from 1.5 per cent in Ireland to 1.3 per cent in Spain. After the 2007/2008 financial crisis, most Western countries experienced negative growth and consequent reductions in productivity while China, India and other parts of Asia – excluding the moribund economy in Japan – seemed virtually unaffected.

KEY CONCEPT 3.3 PRODUCTIVITY

Productivity may be defined as the amount of output (what is produced) per unit of input used. Labour is one input amongst many. Total productivity is dependent upon a variety of diverse and hard to measure inputs. One simple measure of productivity is the gross domestic product (GDP) per person-hour worked.

TABLE 3.1
Job insecurity across the OECD in 2000

Source: Arnal, E., W. Ok and R. Torres (2001), "Knowledge, Work Organisation and Economic Growth", p.26, OECD Labour Market and Social Policy Occational Papers, No. 50. http://dx.doi.org/10.1787/302147528625 Reproduced with permission of OECD.

Country	Unsure of a job even if they perform well (per cent)
Korea	46
UK	41
Japan	38
United States	37
Australia	37
France	37
Sweden	36
Czech Republic	35
New Zealand	34
Germany	34
Italy	32
Finland	31
Unweighted average	**30**
Greece	29
Spain	27
Canada	27
Hungary	26
Switzerland	26
Belgium	26
Austria	23
Ireland	23
Netherlands	22
Denmark	20
Portugal	21
Norway	17

The British economy has the longest industrial history but UK growth has been consistently slow, rarely exceeding three per cent per annum. There is a tendency for countries that are lower in the GDP league to have higher rates of growth in a 'catching-up' process. China has had remarkable rates of productivity growth in recent years, averaging 8.7 per cent a year since 2000. India has achieved more modest rates, averaging 4.1 per cent in that period, but this reflects around double the increase in employment levels compared with China. However, this is not universal – there has been consistently low growth in Africa, for example. A research report from the Economist Intelligence Unit published in 2006 predicted that more than half the growth in the world's GDP over the period to 2020 will come from China (27 per cent), the US (16 per cent) and India (12 per cent).

The reasons for differing rates of growth have been endlessly debated but the effective exploitation of human resources appears to be a crucial factor and this is reflected in comparisons of relative national competitiveness (see Table 3.2).

Competitiveness indices are calculated by combining hundreds of different measures. These range from GDP per head to estimates of the competence of a country's managers. The World Economic Forum regards government regulation and welfare provision as negative factors for national growth, whereas openness to international trade and investment are viewed favourably. Hence, for example, the UK's comparatively low pension burdens and flexible employment market are seen as strengths. These ratings reflect two important perspectives of the role of human resources in the competitiveness debate. We can regard them as the 'hard' and 'soft' versions of macro HRM.

It has been estimated that some large corporations operating internationally, described as multinationals, are responsible for a greater proportion of international trade than most independent states. At one time, companies such as IBM in the USA, BP in the UK, Volkswagen in Germany and Toyota in Japan were viewed as national champions. They were key players in those countries' economic activities. National champions have become multinational corporations moving functions around the world without loyalty to any nation. Research and development takes place in one country, manufacturing in a second, with sales in different continents. This importance has given them the power to play one country against another and to take actions that would be unacceptable for companies operating within single states. Their ability to switch investment from one country to another has been a significant cause for concern. Multinationals are major determiners of action on the world scene, able to move their operations from country to country in defiance of government attempts to maintain minimum wages or workers' consultation.

Uncontrolled globalization has not gone unquestioned. The possibility of social dumping puts societies and national economies under intense pressure and is generally destabilizing (see Key concept 3.4).

KEY CONCEPT 3.4 SOCIAL DUMPING

The concept of social dumping describes the practice of switching production from countries with relatively high employee costs to those with cheap labour. It is an accusation made against large multinational corporations. Social dumping has led to long-term structural changes including the closure of older, heavy manufacturing industries such as steel and shipbuilding in established industrial countries.

TABLE 3.2
Relative competitiveness

Source: Adapted from International Institute for Management Development, World Economic Forum.

	1995		WEF 2005		WEF 2010
1	USA	1	USA	1	Switzerland
2	Singapore	2	Singapore	2	Sweden
3	Hong Kong	3	Denmark	3	Singapore
4	Japan	4	Iceland	4	USA
5	Switzerland	5	Finland	5	Germany
6	Germany	6	Canada	6	Japan
7	Denmark	7	Taiwan	7	Finland
8	Netherlands	8	Sweden	8	Netherlands
9	New Zealand	9	Switzerland	9	Denmark
10	Norway	10	UK	10	Canada
11	Austria	11	Canada	11	Hong Kong SAR
12	Sweden	12	France	12	UK
13	Canada	13	Austria	13	Taiwan
14	Taiwan	14	Belgium	14	Norway
15	UK	15	Japan	15	France
16	Australia	16	Iceland	16	Australia
17	Luxembourg	17	Israel	17	Qatar
18	Finland	18	Hong Kong	18	Austria
19	France	19	Norway	19	Belgium
20	Chile	20	New Zealand	20	Qatar

Initially, corporations such as Ford adopted a policy of dual-sourcing, in which two or more plants in a regional trading bloc such as Europe or North America had the same function, for example building engines. If there were engineering or industrial relations problems in one plant, the other could supply the required components. Another feature of multinational activity has been the sourcing of components of manufactured products in different countries. Potentially, this had the effect of driving down employee costs. Low skill items were the first affected, but more sophisticated items have followed.

Multinationals have ruthlessly played one country or region against another, accepting the highest subsidies and lowest controls over pollution and workers' welfare. Environmental and employee legislation in their 'home' countries has been cynically avoided by transferring production overseas. Trade unions have been slow and largely ineffective in providing employee protection to match global managers. Admittedly, however, despite the bad press multinationals also produce clearly positive benefits. Multinationals have introduced innovative human resource practices including: mobility packages; cross-cultural and language training; greater sensitivity to national management practices; recruitment and development of local employees; and some exciting international careers.

NATIONAL CULTURES AND BUSINESS BEHAVIOUR

Management practices vary throughout the world. **Culture**, history, language and beliefs underlie much of this variation. More than any other business function, the practice of people management has been closely linked to national culture (see Key concept 3.5).

KEY CONCEPT 3.5 CULTURE

The anthropologist Edward Taylor (1871) defined culture as 'knowledge, belief, art, morals, law, custom and any other capabilities and habits' acquired through membership of society. In a narrower sense the term is used to describe the differences between one society and another. In this context, a culture is an all-pervasive system of beliefs and behaviours transmitted socially. Specifically it consists of the set of values – abstract ideals – and norms or rules held by a society, together with its material expressions (Giddens, 1989: 30).

Comparing one country with another we find components of people management are accorded different degrees of importance and are carried out differently. The activities undertaken by HR managers vary as a consequence. However, there has also been recent consideration of the extent to which globalization, the internationalization of business and consolidation of legal systems dilute the impact of national identity. It is increasingly possible to distinguish practices that are universally applicable from those based on a particular national culture.

ETHNOCENTRISM AND CULTURAL DIFFERENCES

According to Taylor (2006: 12):

> Ethnocentric people tend to form pre-conceived judgements of different cultures based on one experience, or based on limited evidence. Therefore, despite the fact that a person from a different culture may have many unique personal qualities, the ethnocentric person cannot see beyond their own fixed ideas even when those ideas are wrong, so their mind remains closed.

There is a misleading assumption that the social, class and cultural values underlying management ideas are – or should be – 'normal' for every country. Perceptions of normality vary widely and tend to be based on stereotypes (Chakkarath, 2010). The following list (based on the work of Campbell and associates, cited in Triandis, 1990: 35) highlights key conclusions from studies of ethnocentrism. Characteristics of the 'in-group' are that everyone tends to:

→ Define their own culture as 'natural' and 'correct' and other cultures as 'unnatural' and 'incorrect'.

→ Perceive in-group customs as universally valid – 'what is good for us is good for everybody'.

→ Think that in-group norms, rules and values are obviously correct.

→ Consider it natural to help and cooperate with members of one's in-group.

→ Act in ways which favour the in-group.

→ Feel proud of the in-group.

→ Feel hostility towards out-groups.

Scientifically based management methods are regarded as culturally neutral and universal (Chung, 1991). In fact, they are mostly North American and based on that particular culture. English is the major business language, consolidating the spread of largely American business concepts (Brewster and Tyson, 1991). These methodologies were accepted as 'received wisdom' in large areas of the world. However, Eastern countries can be just as ethnocentric. Lee (2006), for example, states that the Chinese are '... a very nationalistic race, they have continued to preserve ethnic practices and traditional customs and characteristics in modern business negotiations.'

Shih, Chiang and Kim (2005) interviewed expatriate employees and human resource managers of five multinational enterprise subsidiaries in the information technology industry. All used standardized performance forms set by headquarters and not tailored to local operating environments. Lack of on-the-job training for expatriates was found to be prevalent. Divergent practices in goal setting, performance appraisal and performance-related pay were largely attributed to the parent company's culture.

Brewster (2002: 14–17) highlights the complexity of integration and differentiation that international HRM encompasses and tensions between global and local practices. He considers that the pat phrase 'think global, act local' used by many consultants is meaningless in practice. Many organizations are divisionalized, one part operating 'globally', another 'locally'.

Walton (1999) distinguishes between a global mindset and an international mindset. Managers in an internationally minded company are 'more one-directional, ethnocentric, outward-looking from the country in which they are based'. Whereas a true global organization will feature highly adaptable managers, and an organizational value structure that allows managers to detach themselves from their original national roots and thereby shed their ethno-centric outlook (Rhinesmith, 1996).

This global-oriented mindset suggests that multinationals should take into account a balance of factors including:

→ Differing national employment legislation, ways of doing business, customs, national investment policies, fiscal incentives, attitudes to foreign investment, and other competitors.

→ Issues related to physical location, including local market potential, geographical and cultural distance from the company's base, transport logistics and communications.

→ Employee costs including wages, training needs, skills availability, social and industrial infrastructure.

→ Fit of new locations with existing customers, management and production.

→ The organizational structure of the firm.

CULTURES AND STANDARDS

Cultures are subjective and we take our own for granted. Each culture has a '**world view**' – a set of values and beliefs. This is meaningful to its members but alien to others. It is normal to 'use our own culture as the standard and judge other cultures by the extent they meet the standard' (Triandis, 1990: 34). As we have seen, this ethnocentrism can be related to the concept of the '**in-group**' – those people we identify with. It can be argued that the export of Western (American) management methods by multinationals and business schools – including HRM – is an example of ethnocentrism on a massive scale.

American business school models commonly have been assumed to represent 'best practice', with universal applicability regardless of local tradition, culture or business history. But there have been occasions when the universality of these methods has been questioned. For example, Brewster (2002: 5) observes that '… in Europe HRM is less dependent, companies have less autonomy and freedom of action, trade unionism is more important, the social partners have more influence, legal regulations are more important, and there is a stronger tradition of employee involvement.'

Trompenaars and Hampden-Turner (1997) point out that international HR (and other) managers have a particularly difficult task. They have to operate in three different cultures at the same time: their culture of origin; the culture within which they are currently working; and the corporate culture of the organization. The training they are offered does not necessarily help. For example, Shen and Darby (2006) examined international training and development policies and practices in ten Chinese multinational enterprises (MNEs). They found that they provided limited training to expatriates and other nationals and lacked any systematic international management development system. They describe the MNEs as having an essentially ethnocentric approach to international training and development, providing different levels of training and development for host-country nationals and others.

Culture is important also when employees in different countries operate as a 'virtual team'. Horwitz, Bravington and Silvis (2006) identified cross-cultural communication improvement, managerial and leadership communication, goal and role clarification, and relationship building as the most important factors leading to effective virtual team performance.

Cultural variety

Cultures should not be confused with countries or so-called 'nation states'. There is a danger in examining cultures as 'wholes': there are not only differences between cultures but also within cultures (Brewster and Tyson, 1991). Hofstede (1994 [1991]: 10) argues that an individual's culture has several levels:

→ National – according to country (or countries for migrants).

→ Regional and/or ethnic and/or religious and/or linguistic.

→ Gender – different assumptions and expectations of females and males.

→ Generation – differences between age groups.

→ Social class – linked to educational opportunities and occupations.

→ Organizational – different organizations have their individual cultures.

We can see that this presents a complex mixture for a selector to attempt to disentangle; for a performance assessor to misunderstand; a management developer to 'correct'. There is massive scope for a clash of cultures – and prejudices. As we shall see in Chapter 5 on the management of diversity, there is a major issue about the real meaning of 'equal opportunities' in this context.

The perception of time

Managing people depends a great deal on our perceptions and expectations of others. We assess, we select, we reward, according to our own criteria. Triandis (1990) identifies a number of dimensions of difference that people managers can be taught to recognize and respect. One example is 'cultural complexity', which particularly affects the perception of time. How do we feel about people who do not turn up to an interview on time, or fail to complete a task within the agreed period? If we live in an industrial culture we will regard them unfavourably.

Another significant time characteristic is that of short or long-term orientation (Hofstede and Bond, 1988). The short-term attitudes of senior American executives have been much criticized. Managers with financial or legal backgrounds have gravitated to the top at the expense of those with technical or scientific expertise. This has led to a prevailing management style emphasizing cash management with fast measurable returns. Mergers and takeovers, disposals and closures fit neatly into this mindset whereas long-term research, product development and people management have been neglected. Senior managers – and governments – elsewhere in the English-speaking world have followed the US lead.

Confucianism

Hofstede and Bond (*ibid.*) attribute the long-term orientation in East Asians to '**Confucian Dynamism**' embodying values from the teaching of Confucius such as perseverance, a need to order relationships by status, a sense of shame and a habit of thrifty saving. Yang (2005) points to the different emphases between various Confucian cultures. In Korea, for example, there is an emphasis on emotion and feelings ('jeong') related to the Western concept of emotional intelligence.

More generally, Tan and Chee (2005) found several factors unique to a Confucian context that facilitated the development of trust: diligence, perseverance, filial piety, thriftiness, respect for authority, a shared value of collective effort, harmonious relationship in the office, humbleness and magnanimous behaviour.

Roles

Triandis (1990) relates cultural complexity to the way we define our working and other roles. In complex societies roles become increasingly specific and compartmentalized. We can behave differently in each role. In less complex societies, roles are diffuse, affecting every aspect of people's lives. Religion, politics and matters of taste are important in diffuse cultures. They are less important in role-specific cultures. Developed countries tend to be role-specific, avoiding role confusion. Theory and best practice in key HRM areas such as selection, performance measurement and development assume an equal opportunities

TABLE 3.3
Ways of thinking

Source: Adapted from
Chung (1991).

	European	Asian
Thinking styles	Causal, clear-cut, single-track thinking – one thing follows another	Network, whole vision, complex, taking in different perspectives
Decision styles	To suit controls Individual, free To suit the majority	Based on trust Group solidarity Reaching consensus
Behaviour	True to principles Based on legal principles Dynamic, facing conflict Open, direct, self-confident, extrovert	To suit a situation To suit a community Harmonious, conservative Restrained, indirect, with self-assurance, introvert

approach in which people are dealt with without favour or prejudice. However, this notion is alien to diffuse-role cultures in which it is natural to favour members of one's own family or community.

Diffuse-role cultures value politeness and courtesy – even towards people who are disliked – something that would be regarded as hypocrisy in specific cultures. Again, human resource texts assume that outright, if tactful, honesty is required in rejecting job applicants, counselling for performance weaknesses and dismissal. This approach can appear arrogant and aggressive to people from diffuse societies.

Psychology and culture

Cultural differences are deeply imbedded. Chung (1991), for example, draws on the psychology of thinking styles to explain differences between business cultures (see Table 3.3). This model provides a cultural explanation of the different forms of people management: contract-based in the West; commitment-based in the East.

CULTURAL TRAINING

Human resource managers have a considerable role to play in preparing staff for work away from their country of origin. Given the range and sensitivity of cultural differences, it is clear that people working in an international context can benefit from tuition in the business customs and social manners of the countries they will work in. Training can encompass language, social behaviour, local business structure and practice. Argyle (1991) details a number of key behavioural features that differ between cultures.

Non-verbal behaviour

Proximity, touch and gaze. Cultures can be classified as contact or non-contact. For example, Arabs and Latin Americans stand much closer to each other than East Asians and Northern Europeans. In Greece, staring is regarded as an expression of interest and politeness, even at a complete stranger in the street. Conversely, a Caribbean employee may avoid eye-to-eye contact with a manager during a conversation, having been taught to regard this as discourteous.

Expressiveness. The Japanese are reluctant to be too expressive for fear of causing offence. Many Northern Europeans are also reticent in showing emotion. By contrast, African-Caribbean people are more likely to be open about expressing opinions, including negative emotions and attitudes.

Gestures. It is dangerous to make use of one's own familiar gestures in another country.

Accompaniments of speech. People often expect listeners to show obvious attention while they are talking. Failure to do so can be interpreted as lack of interest or boredom. This feedback is not expected in all cultures.

Symbolic self-presentation. Appearance, dress, badges and uniforms have significance for individuals in a particular culture but may mean nothing to outsiders.

Rituals. Seating positions at a dining or conference table may be highly significant to one culture and virtually irrelevant to another.

Customs or rules

Bribery. A bribe in one culture is a gift in another. In many cultures it is normal to pay a commission to people involved in a transaction. People such as civil servants, managers and sales representatives expect a percentage of the contract value. Western European and North American tradition regards this as unethical, if not illegal.

Nepotism. Cultures that feature personal obligations to large extended families expect powerful individuals to look after relatives; for example, by giving jobs or contracts. This 'social welfare' system is normally governed by codes of conduct that regulate its abuse.

Gifts. Every culture expects its members to give presents in certain circumstances such as weddings or birthdays. Some cultures extend gift-giving to everyday business meetings.

Buying and selling. The importance of bargaining varies from 'fixed price' cultures where haggling is regarded with distaste, to others where negotiation is expected in any transaction.

Eating and drinking. Every culture has taboos about food and drink, and norms relating to consumption.

Rules about time. Being on time is regarded as polite and a demonstration of business efficiency in Western countries. Conversely, lateness is taken as normal in other cultures.

Language

The use of language has critical implications. For example, in any interpersonal context, people managers must be aware of cultural differences covering areas such as: directness, politeness, acknowledgment of status, use of humour, and forms of address.

Some customs are illustrative of differences in underlying **attitudes** (see Key concept 3.6) and what is regarded as ethical practice (see Key concept 3.7). This has much wider implications for people management. Ethical dilemmas have many cross-cultural dimensions. The position of working children is but one example.

KEY CONCEPT 3.6   ATTITUDES

Attitudes are dispositions held by people, towards or against people, things and ideas. They have individual components based on factors such as personality and understanding, and social elements derived from shared experiences and cultural history. Attitudes are complex systems of belief, evaluation, emotion and behaviour (Eiser, 1994; McKenna, 1994: 251).

KEY CONCEPT 3.7   ETHICS

Standards of personal, professional and corporate behaviour – principles of conduct – that result in the just and fair treatment of others. Some make a distinction between this and moral behaviour that takes into account prevailing social custom and culture in the definition of what is right and wrong.

NATIONAL AND ORGANIZATIONAL CULTURES

Organizations are microcosms of national cultures, reflecting crucial differences. Hofstede (1980: 1994) compared several thousand IBM employees in over 50 countries using attitude questionnaires. He found significant differences between employees in different countries, despite similar jobs and membership of an organization with a strong corporate culture. Using sophisticated factor analysis, Hofstede attributed the variation to four main dimensions: **power distance; collectivism** versus **individualism;** masculinity versus femininity; and uncertainty avoidance (see Table 3.4).

Power distance

How marked are the status differences between people with high and low degrees of power? Questions tested whether:

→ People were afraid of expressing disagreement with their managers.

→ Management style was perceived as paternalistic, autocratic, participative and so on.

→ Employees preferred a particular management style.

Individuals in countries with autocratic management styles preferred their own bosses to have that style. In a culture where respect for authority is a valued quality, participative management can make people feel uncomfortable. Individuals in countries with low power distance scores preferred consultation.

Dimension	High	Medium	Low
Individualism (versus collectivism)	Argentina, Australia, Belgium, Brazil, Canada, France, Ireland, New Zealand, Spain, UK, USA	Austria, Germany, Israel, Italy, Japan, Netherlands, Scandinavia, Switzerland, South Africa	Chile, Greece, Hong Kong, India, Iran, Mexico, Pakistan, Peru, Portugal, Taiwan, Singapore, Turkey
Power distance (inequality between levels in organizations)	Belgium, France, Iran, Hong Kong, Nigeria, Philippines, Singapore, South America, Spain, Taiwan, Thailand	Japan	Australia, Germany, Italy, UK, USA
Uncertainty avoidance (intolerance of ambiguity)	Austria, Argentina, Belgium, France, Germany, Greece, Iran, Israel, Italy, Japan, Spain, Turkey, South Africa, Switzerland		Australia, Canada, Ireland, Netherlands, New Zealand, Scandinavia, UK, USA
Masculinity (competitiveness)	Japan, Austria, Venezuela, Italy, Switzerland	Canada, Jamaica, Greece, India, Hong Kong, Pakistan, South Africa, UK, USA	Chile Netherlands, Scandinavia, Costa Rica
Work centrality	Japan	Belgium, Israel, USA	Germany, Netherlands, UK
Job satisfaction	Canada, UK, Germany, Netherlands, Scandinavia		Greece, Spain, Italy, Portugal, Japan

Collectivism versus individualism

Is a culture focused on individuals or groups? Hofstede describes most societies as 'collectivist' in a non-political sense. In these cultures people obtain their identity from an extended family or a work organization. This is particularly relevant to people management since most of its concepts come from the USA – a strongly individualistic country. Individualistic cultures are characterized by:

→ An emphasis on care for self and immediate family – if necessary, at the expense of others.

→ 'I' consciousness – heightened awareness of the distinction between oneself and other people.

→ Self-orientation – looking for advantage and career progression for the individual.

→ Keen defence of the right to a private life and personal opinions.

→ Emphasis on decisions being made individually.

→ Emotional independence from the work organization.

→ Autonomy and individual financial security.

High power distance and collectivism usually go together. In collective cultures socially respected jobs are valued highly. In contrast, individualistic cultures value personal success, responsibility, and self-respect. Triandis (1995: 33) points to key differences leading to reward and promotion: 'People in individualistic countries have the tendency to emphasize *ability* more than is necessary, and to underemphasize *effort*. In collectivist cultures, the reverse is true.'

Hui (1990: 193) argues that Hofstede's notion of the collective is too vague: people in collective cultures relate to particular in-groups, not to everybody. Collectivist cultures emphasize harmony, and avoidance of shame or loss of face. These are social elements of culture emphasizing obligations to others within the in-group.

Further contradictory evidence was provided by Ramamoorthy *et al.* (2005) who analyzed 180 MBA students from the USA, Ireland and India on their individualism/collectivism (IC) orientations and preferences for HRM practices. Contrary to expectations, the Indian sample tended to be the most individualistic.

Masculinity versus femininity

Hofstede rates the aggressiveness of a culture as masculinity – its level of individual assertiveness and competition. Positive responses to questions relating to high earnings, recognition, advancement and challenging work rated highly on masculinity. Good working relationships, cooperation, living in a desirable area and employment security were scored at the 'feminine' end of the dimension.

Recruitment. Applications in 'masculine' cultures are expected to be couched in positive, achievement-orientated language. Interviews are searching and sometimes aggressive. In contrast, applicants from 'feminine' cultures are expected to be modest about their achievements, giving the opportunity for interviewers to 'discover' undeclared talents.

Meetings. In 'feminine cultures' meetings are held to achieve cooperation, exchange ideas and solve problems. The intention is positive and participative. In masculine cultures meetings are more competitive and are used for displays of power, posturing and political point-making.

Uncertainty avoidance

How do people deal with conflict, particularly aggression and the expression of feelings? **Uncertainty avoidance** measures people's reactions to unusual situations. High uncertainty avoidance favours precise rules and superiors to be obeyed without question. Low uncertainty avoidance leads to flexibility. Arguing with superiors is acceptable.

Dimension mix

The characteristics of national business cultures are further defined by the particular mix of these four dimensions. Hofstede argues that the choice of organization structure is strongly influenced by the prevalent culture. A culture with high power distance and strong uncertainty avoidance prefers a functional 'pyramid of people' hierarchy. Lower power distance but high uncertainty avoidance encourages organizations with a clear structure, rules and procedures. Low power distance and uncertainty avoidance favours a flexible structure focused on human relations. Large power distance and low uncertainty avoidance features a strong paternalistic boss and an organizational model based on the family.

Hofstede's statistics have been questioned but the thesis remains popular. A study by Pheng and Yuquan (2002) compared construction workers in Singapore and two cities in China, demonstrating some interesting variations:

Power distance. Singapore workers showed a higher power distance than their Chinese counterparts. In Singapore, superiors and subordinates were more likely to consider each other as unequal. Chinese employees were likely to regard the hierarchical system as an inequality of roles, established for convenience, which could change in different circumstances. This attitude leads to more decentralized organizations with flatter hierarchies and fewer supervisors.

Uncertainty avoidance. Singapore respondents had a low index value for uncertainty; Chinese respondents had a high index value. According to Pheng and Yuquan: 'In Singapore, people feel less threatened by ambiguous situations. Emotions are shown less in public. Younger people are trustworthy. People are willing to take risks in life. The authorities are there to serve the citizens. Conflicts and competition can be contained on the level of fair play and are used constructively'. In China, on the other hand, 'people tend to establish more formal rules, reject deviant ideas and behaviour, accept the possibility of absolute truths and the attainment of unchallengeable expertise. Younger people are looked upon suspiciously. People are concerned with security in life. Ordinary citizens are incompetent, unlike the authorities. Conflict and competition can unleash aggression and should therefore be avoided.'

Individualism/collectivism. Singapore workers are more individualistic than their counterparts in China, tending to think of themselves as 'I' and also tending to classify people by individual characteristics, rather than by group membership. Employees in China are less inclined to differentiate an individual from the group and put a lower emphasis on self-actualization.

Masculinity/femininity. The masculinity score in the Singapore construction industry is lower than that for respondents in China, meaning that Chinese employees tend to place a greater emphasis on work goals such as earnings and advancement and also on assertiveness. In Singapore, by contrast, respondents showed a greater concern with personal goals, a friendly atmosphere, getting along well with the boss and others, etc.

The accelerating trend towards the internationalization of business is eroding these cultural differences.

THE STATE AND INTERVENTION

National and regional governments have a powerful influence on the practice of HRM because they set the legislative, regulatory and economic contexts in which people work.

Economists typically describe such government initiatives as '**labour market** policies'. Abrahart and Verme (2001) distinguish three broad types adopted around the world: the Japanese, European and American models.

The Japanese model relied (at least until the early 1990s) on full employment as one basic principle of a stable society. The emphasis was on the 'internal labour market' rather than the external job market. Firms were hierarchical, protecting their workers from the consequences of economic fluctuations. Workers were expected to be fully committed to their employers. Government supported business through skills upgrading and training or identifying production alternatives for changing markets. Labour market policies were part of economic and industrial strategies managed by relevant government departments. Abrahart and Verme describe this as an 'enterprise-centred and industry-driven form of labour market management'. The Japanese model was the main frame of reference for many Asian governments until relatively recently.

Abrahart and Verme perceive the European model as one that accepts market laws and the existence of unemployment – but only as a 'necessary temporary condition to facilitate and maximize the allocation of labour'. There is limited government intervention in support of firms. The unemployed are supported by maintaining their income and providing training schemes to help them find jobs. The European model accepts that the market periodically fails to protect the public interest and that governments need to step in to mitigate the short-term economic and social consequences. The American model places considerable limitations on government intervention. Firms can dispense with employees to match economic fluctuations. The role of government is to 'maximize mobility of workers and minimize labour market rigidities such as hiring costs and mismatching of the supply and demand of labour'. Short-term unemployment benefits are provided but the unemployed are expected to very actively seek work. Abrahart and Verme perceive this as an individualistic model. For example, in the area of employee relations:

→ Employment conflicts have been rare in Japan as workers expected to be protected by their enterprises and the government.

→ In the European model the government is seen as a mediator that can protect the interests of both employees and enterprises.

→ In the American model, however, labour disputes are viewed as civil disputes between individuals for lawyers and the courts to settle.

Abrahart and Verme describe the American model as a 'liberal market-driven labour management system'. Before the economic collapse dating from 2008, the USA generated more new jobs than other developed countries through flexible job markets, minimal welfare benefits and comparatively low wages for unskilled work. However, the cost has been considerable social inequality and a high crime rate. In most other developed countries the employment market is subject to a greater level of governmental control.

Underlying beliefs regarding the degree of employment protection, unemployment benefits, and acceptable wages have become tougher throughout developed countries indicating a general swing towards 'the American model'. Parties supposedly at opposite ends of the political spectrum have adopted policies advocating:

→ Restrained and affordable public sector spending (fiscal prudence).

→ Control of inflation.

→ Encouragement of inward investment.

→ Tax rates that compare favourably with those of international competitors.

→ Employment protection that does not cause rigidity or inflexibility in the job market.

→ Maintenance of government legislation restricting the scope of trade union activities.

→ Partnership between public and private sectors to revitalize investment-starved infrastructure.

→ The reform of education to boost the nation's skill base.

In the European Union, the pursuit of a single market has led increasingly to measures allowing free circulation of employees and freedom of residence in any EU country. Other barriers to job mobility are being removed with recognition of different educational qualifications and further social and economic cohesion. There are increasing moves towards standardization of employment regulation and protection measures to further promote a single European job market with the goal of full employment. The result is an apparent hybrid between a US-style, 'free for all' employment market and the former rigid, social protectionism of mainland Western Europe.

The European Union created a new dimension for people management in its member states with initiatives aimed at improving economic conditions in less privileged regions. The differences in income between the EU's richest and poorest regions are dramatic, ranging between 30 per cent and 209 per cent of the average.

Pressure for the EU to adopt a unified, interventionist approach to the unemployment problem resulted in conflict between the majority **social market** (Key concept 3.8) position and those supporting the free market. Countries such as the UK held that the 'market' would take care of the problem if employment laws were relaxed and 'flexibility' encouraged.

KEY CONCEPT 3.8 SOCIAL MARKET

Alfred Müller-Armack, Secretary of State at the Economics Ministry in Bonn, Federal Republic of Germany (1958–1963), defined the social market as an economic system that combines market freedom with social equilibrium. The government plays a regulating role and creates the framework for market processes, going beyond securing competition to ensure social equity.

Further pressure on EU member states comes via three routes (Leibfried and Pearson, 2000):

Direct positive pressures of integration. Actions taken directly by the European Commission to create a social dimension.

Direct negative pressures of integration. Through the market-building process that encourages labour mobility and freedom of provision of services.

Indirect pressures of integration. Stemming from factors such as tax harmonization, common European currency (with implications for setting a unified interest policy), and other economic initiatives.

Less affluent governments have an uphill battle to achieve high growth and reduced unemployment in the face of rapidly increasing populations and low levels of industrialization.

In the Middle East and North Africa, for example, the International Labour Organization estimates the need for at least 5 million new jobs each year from 2000, rising to 6.18 million in 2015. But, according to World Bank estimates, these countries already have among the highest unemployment rates in the world.

LEGISLATIVE FRAMEWORKS

One of the most important environmental constraints on the job market and the activities of people managers comes from the law. Employment law changes continuously and varies extensively in different parts of the world. Much of the legislation relating to business derives from custom or precedent. Within the Anglo-Celtic countries these have been systematized into a common law framework. Many of these countries also have a written constitution which provides a further code. Most European countries employ an entirely code-based system called civil law. In the 21st century, national governments have become law-making machines, creating a complex legal environment for businesses. One of the major complications for human resource managers is that relevant laws differ from country to country, and also between different states within countries with a devolved or federal structure.

Countries with legal systems based on common law, including Australia, Canada, Ireland, New Zealand, the UK and the USA, have used civil rather than criminal law as the main method of counteracting discrimination. Government bodies may assist but, in essence, it is up to individuals to pursue their case. Possible costs are a negative aspect of this approach but there is a benefit in the lower burden of proof required (Lappalainen, 2001). There is also room for compromise and conciliation.

Legislation can take a number of forms:

Positive action. Measures to prevent discrimination and remove inequalities by insisting, for example, on non-discriminatory recruitment procedures, training programmes and pay rates. **Positive action** does not include any preferential treatment for disadvantaged groups.

Affirmative action or positive discrimination. Designed to redress the disadvantage experienced by particular groups including women, members of ethnic minority communities and the disabled. Criticized by some white, middle-class males who argued that laws intended to encourage equality were unfair to them.

Targeting. Quotas for the employment of particular groups.

HUMAN CAPITAL

Personal and national success is increasingly correlated with the possession of skills. Skilled individuals can command a premium salary in periods of high economic activity while a shortage of skilled people can act as a limiting factor on individual organizations and on the economy as a whole. For example, in Canada and the UK small businesses report an inability to expand because of the difficulty in finding people with the right skills. Small firms are also vulnerable because their owners may lack basic marketing and finance skills. It is in the interest of any country to maximize its human resources by investing in the skills of its workforce: its **human capital** (see Key concept 3.9). Human capital is a crucial component of a country's overall competitiveness.

KEY CONCEPT 3.9 HUMAN CAPITAL

Economic growth creates employment but partly depends on skilled human resources – a country's human capital. The concept encompasses investment in the skills of the labour force, including education and vocational training to develop specific skills.

HRM IN REALITY EUROPEAN SKILLS IN DEMAND

According to CEDEFOP (The European Centre for the Development of Vocational Training) most of the projected 8.5 million new jobs created in Europe over the next ten years will be in knowledge- and skill-intensive occupations, including high level management and technical jobs.

Despite the economic crisis, which CEDEFOP estimates has cost the EU some 10 million jobs, slow recovery over the next ten years will bring the total number of jobs close to the 2008 peak of 235 million. Around 80 million job opportunities will become available by 2020, including jobs vacated through retirement or job-changing.

The demand for skilled non-manual workers will grow significantly, but the types of job will be different with marked reductions in conventional office jobs and increases in service work, including security, catering and caring. Many manual jobs will disappear as technology changes the nature of work. The net result is projected as a rise from 29 per cent of jobs requiring high-level skills in 2010 to 39 per cent in 2020. Correspondingly, the percentage of jobs requiring low levels of skill will drop from 20 per cent to 15 per cent.

Balancing high-level skills and suitable job openings

In the long run, there is a need for more people with high-level skills, but the balance between people with available skills and suitable jobs will vary. This is particularly evident at the moment as recruitment of young people has been taking place at a low level because of the recession.

A recent CIPD survey of 700 graduates in employment in the UK conducted by YouGov found that 59 per cent of employees who graduated in the last two years were not working in a field or profession related to their degree subject. Additionally, among graduates not working in a field related to their subject:

→ Fifty-eight per cent said this was because they were unable to find a suitable job.

→ Twenty-eight per cent said that their degree did not equip them with the skills needed for the workplace.

→ Twenty-one per cent said that they chose a new career path after finishing their degree.

→ Twenty-four per cent had since decided to postpone the start of their careers entirely.

The CIPD has queried the British Government's continued expansion of enrolment on university degrees, and the new 75 per cent target for young people to be educated up to degree level, given the results of this study and the contraction of the UK job market.

According to Tom Richmond, Skills Adviser at the CIPD:

> Our survey findings suggest the Government's target of 75 per cent of young people achieving a degree or equivalent level qualification is counter-productive and should be urgently reviewed. As rising youth unemployment threatens to create a 'lost generation' of jobless young people, the rising number of students unable to work in jobs related to the subjects they studied at university threatens to create a 'disillusioned generation' of graduates, unable to find graduate-level employment but still saddled with thousands of pounds worth of debt.

If this is the situation today when our graduation rate is 39%, then the consequences for future graduate job prospects look bleak indeed, if there really is an attempt to nearly double the numbers of graduates in the UK. To compound this, the recent announcement of an extra 20 000 university places in this year's Budget makes the creation of a 'disillusioned generation' even more likely.

Government should focus on understanding the needs of learners and employers, as well as providing young people with better information about the realistic employment prospects and salaries typically available for holders of degrees in different subjects. This will help ensure there is a better link between demand for, and supply of, graduate jobs.

The Government also needs to spend more time and effort developing and promoting the new vocationally-based diplomas for 14–19-year-olds to ensure that more young people have the key skills to enter the workforce at age 16 or 18, rather than encouraging such a high proportion of them to study for degrees. Our survey suggests this over promotion of university or equivalent level study could leave many without the knowledge and skills that will genuinely help them find graduate-level work and apply it in the workplace.

According to CEDEFOP, their research 'suggests that formal overqualification is not a problem per se. But underutilization of skills and competences is certainly a potential problem for individuals, employers and society as a whole.'

Employer training across Europe

According to another of CEDEFOP's recent reports, *Employer-provided vocational training in Europe: Evaluation and interpretation of the third continuing vocational training survey*, training investment by companies had actually dropped by 27 per cent per employee in 2005 compared with 1999. Also, almost two-fifths (39 per cent) of EU enterprises in the EU did not provide any continuing training for their employees, either in 1999 or 2005. CEDEFOP consider that the situation may have worsened during the recent economic crisis.

Some countries are doing better than others with Eastern Europe gaining ground but Western Europe worsening. Slovenia has showed the greatest improvement, rising from a low level of performance to a borderline high performance. France retained its high level of performance, but the other high performers in 1999 (the Netherlands, Sweden and Finland) had worsened significantly by 2005. The Czech Republic had joined the ranks of the high performers by 2005. Belgium and Germany, both medium performers, had slipped a little.

Amongst the low performers, Romania, lowest of all in 1999, had improved in all dimensions, and Spain and Portugal had also improved. But Greece had gone backwards between 1999 and 2005, placing it last in the EU-27.

How critical is it to have employees educated to degree level in modern organizations?

Source: Reprinted with permission from HRM Guide UK (http://www.hrmguide.co.uk/).

Human capital development in the form of education and skills training can be an effective response to constraints imposed on the employment market. Specific skills may be in short supply – even during periods of high unemployment – and technological developments require new competences.

There is considerable variation between education and training levels in different countries. For example, technology and production have long been regarded as high-status activities in Germany. As a consequence, German businesses are much more committed to technical training than their UK equivalents. Ironically, training systems in the two countries are similar, depending on a mixture of academic education and vocational courses – unlike France, Japan and the USA where there is a greater concentration on full-time education. Countries that have shown some of the highest rates of growth, for example Singapore and Malaysia, have invested heavily in the education and technical skills of their population.

Whereas the British apprentice system had been more or less dismantled by the 1980s, it remained intact in Germany. Clarke (2006b) compares attitudes to construction industry labour in the UK and other leading European countries. The UK industry is characterized by casual self-employment, output-based pay, rigid trade divisions, low levels of training and a sharp division between operative and professional/technical skills. Skill shortages beset the industry and the solution focuses not on employment regulation and a comprehensive industry-wide training scheme, but on importing the necessary skilled labour. Other leading European countries rely on higher skill levels, based on knowledge gained through the training process and on a more stable and collectively negotiated structure of training provision and employment.

Reluctance to train apprentices is not confined to the UK. Wolter, Mühlemann and Schweri (2006) looked at why so many Swiss firms choose not to train apprentices when cost-benefit studies of apprenticeship have shown that training costs are offset by the productive work most apprentices contribute during the course of their apprenticeship. Using maximum-likelihood selection models, they estimated the net cost of training for firms without an apprenticeship programme. They showed that switching to a training policy would lead to a significantly higher net cost during the apprenticeship period. This less favourable cost-benefit ratio was determined not so much by cost than by insufficient benefit.

Skill requirements are particularly critical at the managerial level. For example, the arrival of multinational corporations in China has led to an increased demand for professional managers. In the past, Chinese colleges have produced large numbers of technicians but few accountants, lawyers or marketing specialists.

Competition is not restricted to marketing and product development. It also entails competition for staff. Availability of skilled employees in the external job market may constrain growth. Additional expensive advertising may be required, together with the offer of enhanced salaries to attract suitable applicants. Companies that promote training and development risk staff being poached for higher wages by organizations that have not made a similar investment (Kochan and Dyer, 2001: 282).

The reluctance of many employers to engage in training can probably be pinned down to two issues: (a) the short-term, cost-based approach to all management activities (in this case, demand for a quick and obvious benefit from training expenditure); and (b) the difficulty of proving the connection between training and improved efficiency.

Human capital theory also deals with personal investment in self-development, such as enrolling on a degree course. It presupposes that individuals balance the cost of education and training (time, loss of income, fees) against the benefits of a higher income in the future. As such it predicts that the young are more likely to invest in training because their losses

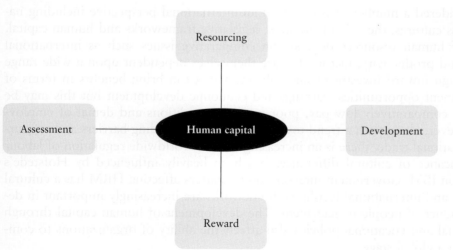

FIGURE 3.1

Human capital and major HR activities

TABLE 3.5
Macro HRM in context

	Levels of analysis			
	Environment	**Organization**	**Strategy**	**Activities**
HRM type	Macro HRM	Organizational HRM	Strategic HRM	Operational HRM
Features	Economy Labour market Culture Political climate	Structure Culture Power Functions	Mission Objectives Policy Planning	Recruitment Development Reward Dismissal
Traditional responsibility	State	Senior management	Senior management	Personnel
Modern responsibility	Supranational National Multinationals	Managers Employees	Senior-middle management	Line managers HR specialists

are relatively less – and the potential gains greater – than for older people. In general, the income of employees with degrees and other higher education qualifications is significantly higher than that of people who ceased education at an earlier stage.

We can see from Figure 3.1 that human capital is a significant unifying concept in HRM. It links four major people management activities – resourcing, assessment, development and reward – with an environmental variable which is a key to both organizational and national success. Each of these areas is further explored in later chapters in this book. Table 3.5 locates macro HRM in the context of a changing world and a background of economic uncertainty.

➤ SUMMARY

This chapter considered a number of issues from an international perspective including national and business cultures, the role of the state, legislative frameworks and human capital. The allocation of human resources depends on comparative issues such as international competitiveness and productivity, factors that are themselves dependent upon a wide range of variables. Foreign inward investment and subcontracting can bring benefits in terms of increased employment opportunities, earnings and economic development but this may be at the expense of comparatively low pay, poor working conditions and denial of employment rights. However, along with a trend towards reduction of trading barriers and encouragement of international trade, there is an increasing call for worldwide regulation of labour issues. The significance of cultural differences has been heavily influenced by Hofstede's pioneering work on IBM. Government intervention in matters affecting HRM has a cultural basis and national and international legislative frameworks are increasingly important in determining the conduct of people management. The development of human capital through national educational and vocational policies also affects the ability of organizations to compete effectively on a global stage.

➤ FURTHER READING

1 *Smart Sourcing: International Best Practice* by Andrew Kakabadse and Nada Kakabadse (St. Martin's Press, 2002) takes a managerial perspective on wider subcontracting issues.

2 *What's This India Business? Offshoring, Outsourcing and the Global Services Revolution* by Paul Davies (Nicholas Brealey, 2004) is a practical guide on offshoring.

3 *Cultures and Organizations: Software for the Mind, Third Edition: Intercultural Cooperation and Its Importance for Survival* by Geert Hofstede (McGraw-Hill Professional, 2010) is a revised and updated account of Hofstede's work.

4 Most books about human capital are focused on the firm, but more generally *Human Capital Management: Achieving Added Value Through People* by Angela Baron and Michael Armstrong (Kogan Page, 2008) cuts through a lot of the mystique.

5 *International Management: Culture and Beyond* by Richard Mead and Tim G. Andrews (Wiley-Blackwell, 4th edition, 2009) covers the ground in its title.

➤ REVIEW QUESTIONS

1 Summarize the main benefits from gaining an understanding of international HRM. What are the arguments against employing the same human resource practices throughout the world?

2 What is 'culture'? Do attempts to classify cultures into groups or types enhance our understanding of international HRM?

3 To what extent do national cultures determine corporate cultures? How many different cultures can you identify in your own country? What are the implications of the differences between these cultures for human resource managers?

4 How can the concept of 'in-groups' help to explain the inadequacies of equal opportunities policies?

5 Is it possible to describe national business cultures without resorting to stereotypes? Does the analysis provided by Argyle go beyond cultural stereotyping?

6 Explain the following terms in your own words: power distance; avoidance; role specificity.

7 How does the notion of time vary around the world?

8 Define the concept of human capital in your own words.

9 What are the most effective measures open to a government for improving a country's human capital? Is it possible to quantify a nation/company's human capital?

10 In what ways do approaches to people management differ between 'social market' and 'free market' countries. Relate these differences to hard and soft models of HRM. Define 'ethics'. What does ethical HRM entail?

CASE STUDIES FOR DISCUSSION AND ANALYSIS

Location choice/Graduate development

1 You have been appointed general manager at a new European subsidiary of a Japanese manufacturer. The subsidiary is controlled by three senior Japanese managers who have been seconded from the parent company for a five-year period. Your first task is to identify and shortlist suitable locations for production and then participate in choosing suppliers and staff.

What elements of employment legislation, government support and industrial relations would encourage you to locate in a particular country?

Describe the likely decision processes and contrast with the way a typical local company would have dealt with the same problem.

2 Leyanne has recently graduated with a degree in business studies, specializing in finance. She has been recruited as a trainee by a large conglomerate involved in airport management and cargo distribution. The company operates in Australia, Singapore, Europe and the Caribbean. Corporate headquarters are in Sydney, Australia but the largest operational units are in Singapore and Germany. The organization prefers to develop its own management and expects a broad range of experience and grasp of different cultural traditions. Leyanne is ambitious and wants to become a senior manager in the company.

Outline a possible career plan for Leyanne, including aspects that the company should take responsibility for and issues for her own self-development.

CHAPTER 4
Strategic HRM

LEARNING OBJECTIVES

The purpose of this chapter is to:

→ Determine the nature and prevalence of strategic HRM.

→ Evaluate the influence and involvement of people managers in high-level decision-making.

→ Identify different approaches to strategic HRM, and outline their strengths and weaknesses.

→ Discuss the HR role in mergers and acquisitions.

→ Provide an overview of employee resourcing strategies.

→ Discuss the purposes and methods of human resource planning.

→ Outline the process of job analysis.

→ Debate resourcing strategy in the context of staff retention and redundancy.

STRATEGY AND HRM

Purcell (2001: 59) concludes that 'the integration with strategy is central to all models of HRM and virtually all authors are agreed that this is *the* distinctive feature of HRM, compared with personnel.' Personnel management, we are told, is essentially reactive whereas HRM, exemplified by HR strategy, is proactive. Typically, it is claimed that **human resource strategies** combine all people management activities into an organized and integrated programme to meet the strategic objectives of an enterprise. For example, HR leaders are seen as being in a unique position 'at the intersection of strategy, communication and talent' (McLaughlin and Mott, 2010). The personnel model focused on short-term, largely operational matters of little interest to strategists. HRM, by contrast, takes a longer perspective and is closer to the heart of the organization. It takes a proactive stance towards the competitiveness and efficiency of the organization, with a particular emphasis on measuring significant workforce elements through HR metrics (Gates and Langevin, 2010).

But human resource strategies are not easy to identify and academics and practitioners find it difficult to understand what HR strategy means in practice. HR practitioners also find it difficult to reconcile some of the requirements of being a strategic business partner with 'personnel manager'-type concerns such as promoting the well-being of employees (Brown *et al.*, 2009).

Rothwell, Prescott and Taylor (1998: 5) compare 'traditional HR' and its more modern (and dynamic) form, 'strategic HR':

1   Traditional HR practitioners do not have enough 'working knowledge of what business is all about or of the strategic goals of the organizations they serve'.

2   They lack leadership ability, especially if they have no line management experience and are viewed as having less interest in helping line managers solve their problems than they have in meeting HR objectives, such as complying with employment legislation.

3   HR practitioners are viewed as reactive. 'They appear unresponsive – and even resistant – to line management needs, interests and business pressures.'

4   They sometimes seem unable to take on 'the lead in establishing a vision for change and garnering the support necessary to lead the change'. The result is that they lose credibility and respect.

5   They are seen as 'fad-chasers' who try to use solutions for problems in other workplaces and 'drop them in place without taking into account the unique business objectives, corporate culture, organization-specific politics, and individual personalities of key decision-makers found in their own organizational settings'.

Such criticisms of 'personnel management' or old-school HR are common and strategic HRM is seen as a possible solution.

HR AND THAT ELUSIVE STRATEGIC ROLE

Recently, Maxxim Consulting interviewed 20 CEOs of FTSE350 companies in the UK and found that only four knew exactly how many people worked in their respective head offices. Also, just four CEOs knew how much their head offices cost to run each year.

It seems that finally senior managers – some of them, at least – are willing to give HR managers a significant role in strategic decisions. But how many human resource managers know how to fulfill that role? Paul Kearns (2003: 4) tells the tale of a workshop exercise for senior human resource managers when participants were given a military scenario. Briefly, they were asked to envisage that they, and a thousand soldiers under their command, had been dropped behind enemy lines – with no information about their opposition. What would they do? The first response he received was 'I'd retreat'. Kearns comments: 'Why does this response from an HR person not surprise me?' It doesn't surprise me either because so many HR managers are used to operating someone else's strategy, rather than participating vigorously in their organizations' strategic decisions.

Noting that 'business partner' and 'strategic thinker' have featured as the most important roles in some recent surveys of human resource management, Jamroq and Overhot (2004) observe that 'there's something elusive and ambiguous about this widely touted goal of becoming a strategic business partner'. They cite a recent conference on the future of HR where a panel of human resource experts came out with the statement that 'I can't define it, but I know it when I see it' when asked to define the term 'strategic business partner.'

Measuring the effectiveness of HRM

Is measurement at the root of the problem? Are HR managers measuring the wrong things? One common approach is to use a 'Balanced Scorecard' which includes a range of HR measures as well as the more traditional financial and other metrics. Gubman (2004) feels that 'Too many HR scorecards focused on operational metrics: Time to hire, cost per hire, percentage of appraisals completed, etc. While important to track, these kinds of measures will not get HR to the strategic partner role. They only reinforce the view of HR as an administrative function. Key HR measures needed to be central to business success.'

More beneficially, according to Gubman, HR managers should focus instead on the same two major issues as their financial colleagues: return and growth. 'HR-things' can only create economic value from three sources:

→ Employee turnover and retention.

→ Productivity – revenue against employee costs.

→ Expenditure on the HR function and related activities.

Providing measures for these three elements does not require any 'rocket science' because they relate to three familiar HR goals:

1 Attracting, developing and retaining staff.

2 Aligning, engaging, measuring and rewarding performance.

3 Controlling or reducing HR costs.

HR-relevant measures for growth are trickier and need to be tailored to the organizations' individual situation. Gubman believes that HR measures can be devised that, like market share, can indicate trends and forecasts for improved revenue in the future. He argues that the following are the most significant growth-related human resource measures at present:

→ Leadership development, to be measured in terms of unique candidates ready to assume executive and other major roles.

→ Engagement – levels of employees' intellectual and emotional commitment to their work.

→ Diversity, particularly the number of women and ethnic minority employees coming through the system or 'talent pipeline'.

Tamkin *et al.* (2008) used a set of criteria described as the '4A model' (Access, Ability, Attitudes, Application) in their study of almost 3000 British organizations and found that the use of 'bundles' of HR practices produced improved performance and profitability. They suggest a number of issues that HR managers should focus on:

→ **Access**. The quality of the recruitment process: putting serious effort into attracting high quality applicants; using policies and practices that 'ensure the ongoing movement of the best people through the organization'.

→ **Ability**. Effective, long-term development plans focused on the needs of employees and the business. These plans should be constantly monitored to ensure their effectiveness. The researchers also highlight the need for a high workforce quality, e.g. possession of degrees.

→ **Attitudes**. Aligning employees to the objectives of the organization – 'vital in terms of capturing discretionary effort'. They emphasize one-to-ones, appraisals and reward strategies related to organizational performance.

→ **Application**. Encouraging autonomy, empowerment and generation of ideas.

Behaving proactively

Weiss (1999) argues that HR managers must demonstrate the ability to provide stimulating ideas and challenge decisions that do not have business value. To do this they need to perform at the same intellectual level as their colleagues in an executive meeting. Most importantly, they need to wear a 'business hat' rather than a 'HR hat' otherwise they will be relegated to the traditional administrative or tactical (second-level) role that has bedevilled the human resource function for decades. Weiss considers that HR managers need to demonstrate the following to show their ability to add value:

→ Broad understanding of the business, thus helping the human resource function to contribute to the overall direction of the company.

→ Knowledge of how all activities need to align, enabling the company to maximize the success of its strategic initiatives.

→ Professionalism in investing in human capital and HR processes, allowing HR to help guide employees and the organization's decision-making.

→ A unique perspective, allowing the HR function to become an 'ideas merchant' so that people and the outcomes of organizational processes can be made into strategic advantages.

Finally, we can consider Gubman's belief:

HR needs to keep moving itself forward, toward the strategic partner role, by becoming better profit-and-loss business leaders. Be the ones to lead companies back into thinking externally, about customers and markets, and how to create unique value for them. What a surprising and powerful role that would be for HR leaders! Start measuring HR impacts on real business results, not HR activities. Instead of measuring time to hire, measure the people aspects of opening up a new market and the returns they generate.

Source: Reprinted with permission from HRM Guide UK (http://www.hrmguide.co.uk).

KEY CONCEPT 4.1 STRATEGY

A strategy is the means by which an organization seeks to meet its objectives. It is a deliberate choice, a decision to take a course of action rather than reacting to circumstances. It focuses on significant, long-term goals rather than day-to-day operating matters.

What does the term 'strategic human resource management' (SHRM) actually mean? (Key concept 4.2) There are many definitions, including:

→ 'A human resource system that is tailored to the demands of the business strategy' (Miles and Snow, 1984).

→ 'The pattern of planned human resource activities intended to enable an organization to achieve its goals' (Wright and McMahan, 1992).

→ 'By *strategic* we mean that HR activities should be systematically designed and intentionally linked to an analysis of the business and its context' (Schuler, Jackson and Storey, 2001: 127).

Such definitions range from a portrayal of SHRM as a 'reactive' management field where human resource management is a tool with which to implement strategy, to a more proactive function in which HR activities can actually create and shape the business strategy and have a decisive role in organizational crisis management (Wang *et al.*, 2009).

KEY CONCEPT 4.2 STRATEGIC HRM

Strategic HRM takes a long-term perspective and is concerned with issues such as corporate culture and individual career development as well as the availability of people with the right skills. It incorporates redundancy and recruitment planning and is increasingly focused on decisions about maintaining the internal capability of an organization's workforce to perform specific functions or to contract out (outsource) an activity to an external provider.

The range of activities and themes encompassed by SHRM is complex and goes beyond the responsibilities of personnel or HR managers into all aspects of managing people. It focuses on 'management decisions and behaviours used, consciously or unconsciously, to control, influence and motivate those who work for the organizations – the human resources' (Purcell, 2001: 64).

STRATEGIC HRM: THEORY AND PRACTICE

Why do management theorists stress the importance of strategy? A number of reasons are apparent:

→ Strategic literature largely emphasizes the internal resources of a business as the source of competitive advantage. This 'resource-based' perspective (Boxall, 1996) views a firm as

a bundle of resources. Such resources must possess four qualities for advantage to be maintained:
— *Value.* They must add value to the organization's activities.
— *Rarity.* They must be rare and (preferably) unique.
— *Inimitability.* Competitors should have difficulty in copying them.
— *Non-substitutability.* They cannot be replaced by technology.

→ Although the resource-based view originally came from economics, commentators such as Boxall have argued that it is particularly applicable in the case of human resources. The resources embodied in an organization's people are found in the form of skills, expertise and experience (Storey, 1995: 4).

Strategy and planning

If strategy is deemed so important by theorists, how much impact has strategic thinking had on practitioners? First, the emphasis given to strategy by HRM theorists has led to significant interest from senior managers. For example, there is a stress on the importance of maximizing the performance and potential of an organization's people. This does not come necessarily from an altruistic and soft-hearted interest in their welfare. More likely, it derives from a hard-headed appreciation of the long-term contribution they can provide to the business. 'Soft' HRM focuses on an organization's people as assets so that time spent on training and development is an investment in human capital. But the organization's strategy for HRM may not see the HR function as a core part of the business, resulting in an outsourcing contract.

On the one hand, business school strategists have tended to minimize human resource considerations because of the ambiguity and uncertainty attached to human behaviour. Humans are the most unpredictable of strategic resources. Michael Porter, the doyen of strategic management, virtually discounted the HR aspects of strategy. On the other hand, personnel departments generally employed practitioners who viewed themselves as pragmatists dealing with practical issues such as recruitment, pay and discipline 'on the ground', remote from the grand theories of strategists.

The second difficulty comes from their historic role of independent arbitrators between staff and management. As conciliators and apologists personnel managers depended on the ability to find compromises and reconcile the two sides rather than developing a clear agenda of their own. As a result, they make uncomfortable stakeholders, unable to fight their corner. Instead they are forced to react to the decisions of more powerful stakeholders. In practice then (Giles and Williams, 1991: 31):

… personnel specialists find strategy difficult. Personnel specialists have not developed the strategic skills needed to contribute to their organization's effectiveness. Current education and training programmes give them little insight into how to link business, technical and human resource management skills in times of great uncertainty. Personnel specialists do not speak the language of top management in marketing and manufacturing and often seem to clam up when confronted with all the noughts on a company balance sheet.

FORMING HR STRATEGIES

Identifying the relationship between HRM and strategy, it seems, is simpler in theory than it is in practice. Frequently, strategic HRM is a matter of rhetoric. Organizations can usefully be grouped into five alternative categories on the basis of their approach towards human resource strategy (Torrington and Hall, 1995: 47):

1 Businesses in which there is no consideration whatsoever of human resource issues in the preparation of organizational strategy. Typical of firms 20 years ago and still found in many small companies.

2 Organizations in which there is a growing understanding of the role of human resources in implementing corporate strategy. The purpose of HR strategy is to match the requirements of organizational strategy, ensuring the closest possible fit in terms of employee numbers, skills and so on.

3 Businesses in which the relationship becomes two-way with some ideas initiated by HR managers. There is an element of debate about the people management consequences of particular strategies before they are implemented.

4 Organizations in which the HRM concept has been accepted and people are seen as the key to competitive advantage. Corporate and human resource strategies are developed simultaneously. They are coherent and comprehensive.

5 Companies where human resources become the driving force in the development of strategy. There is an overriding emphasis on developing their skills and capitalizing on their competences.

In practice, organizations may adopt any of these approaches.

Where organizations are genuinely concerned with their people, HRM normally focuses on certain strategic sub-goals, or second-order strategies in Purcell's (1989) terminology, as shown in Table 4.1. For example:

→ Resourcing an organization with the most suitable people at the right time, in the right place. There are two important elements:

(a) knowledge of and participation in the formulation of 'official' strategy; and

(b) awareness of underlying developments that will produce 'surprises' that lead to about-turns in the official policy, typically with little or no notice.

→ Planning the redeployment or dismissal of staff who are no longer required for specific tasks.

Level	Organizational focus	Environmental constraints
First-order strategies	Long-term objectives Range of activities, markets, locations	Supranational authorities Government Culture and tradition
Second-order strategies	Internal operating procedures, organizational structure	Capital market Product market Consumers
Third-order strategies	Strategic choice in HRM	Job market Workforce Law
Outcomes	Style, structure, conduct of HRM	

TABLE 4.1
Levels of strategy affecting HRM

Source: Adapted from Purcell (1989).

→ Determining the cultural characteristics appropriate to an organization's business objectives.

→ Developing key skills for new products or equipment.

A significant variant of this process emphasizes strategic planning as a process and plays down the role of the chief executive. Its basic premises are that (Mintzberg, 1994: 42):

1 Strategy formation should be controlled and conscious as well as a formalized and elaborated process, decomposed into distinct steps, each delineated by checklists and supported by techniques.

2 Responsibility for the overall process rests with the chief executive in principle; responsibility for its execution rests with the staff planners in practice.

3 Strategies come out of this process fully developed, typically as generic positions, to be explicated so that they can then be implemented through detailed attention to objectives, budgets, programmes and operating plans of various kinds.

Coherent strategies and integrated practices sound fine in theory but how are they to be translated into action? This 'surface neatness' hides an organizational reality that is far from simple (Blyton and Turnbull, 1992: 2). Mintzberg (1994: 26) argues that the strategies that are actually carried through into practice include an unintended element which he terms 'emergent strategies'. This might result from poor strategic thinking, poor implementation or a sound state of realism. It reflects the view that strategic management should not be confined to the top layers in an organization. Emergent strategy rarely comes from the centre but rather from bright ideas and initiatives at a local level, which were not predicted but were found to work and then adopted more widely: '... big strategies can grow from little ideas (initiatives), and in strange places, not to mention at unexpected times, almost anyone in the organization can prove to be a strategist. All he or she needs is a good idea and the freedom and resources required to pursue it' (Mintzberg, 1994: 26).

Further complications arise from the way firms are structured. It is possible to distinguish between corporate strategies (global, company-wide initiatives) that come from head office and business strategies developed by business units or operating subsidiaries (Purcell, 1995: 67). The latter are concerned with product and marketing decisions but also have human resource implications since business units have a closer involvement with employment markets and working procedures. There are no recognized rules on the relation between corporate and business strategies, but it has been argued that strategic HRM should be focused at the business unit level. Nevertheless, business units cannot operate in isolation from the rest of the firm. Overriding issues such as succession planning and media comment on industrial relations demand corporate people strategies.

TRANSLATING STRATEGY INTO ACTION

At this point we turn to the issue of implementing human resource strategies. The classic approach follows the 'matching' process described in the Michigan model of HRM outlined in Chapter 1. The goal is a realization of the organization's strategic human resource requirements in terms of numbers and, more importantly; attitudes, behaviour and commitment. According to Miller (1989), the key lies with 'the concept of "fit": the fit of human resource management with the thrust of the organization'.

Truss (1999: 44), reviewing a number of authors, finds that 'there is no evidence that a tight fit leads to positive outcomes and the concept of fit implies inflexibility and rigidity which could, in themselves, be detrimental to organizational outcomes.' She also notes the underlying assumption of some 'matching models' of hard HRM which contend that every business strategy has one appropriate human resource strategy. This implies a 'simple, linear relationship between strategy and human resource strategy' that does not exist. Such models fail to acknowledge the complex relationship between strategy and HRM and they ignore issues of power politics and culture. Khilji and Wang (2006) argue that much of the apparent confusion about the effectiveness of strategic HRM results from a failure by researchers to distinguish between 'intended' and 'implemented' strategies. They questioned managers and non-managers from inside and outside HR departments to highlight the differences between the HR practices intended by their company's strategies and those that actually were implemented. They found that the two may be substantially different while consistent implementation leads to higher employee satisfaction with HRM, which is positively related to organizational performance.

Armstrong (1992: 53) argues that the significant issue in HR strategy is that of integration with overall business strategy. In practice, this integration is difficult to achieve. Armstrong outlines some crucial difficulties that continue to be important:

Diversity of strategic processes, levels and styles. As we have seen, many organizations do not use neat, traditional approaches to business strategy based on rational planning. It is difficult to discern appropriate HR strategies and the corporate strategies they are supposed to match. Further, in a diversified organization composed of strategic business units (SBUs), each unit may have its own idiosyncratic strategies.

The evolutionary nature of business strategy. It is not possible to provide a rational HR strategy if corporate strategy is evolving quickly and in a piecemeal way.

The absence of written business strategies. This is particularly the case in smaller companies and overwhelmingly in cultural contexts where evolutionary planning is the rule.

The qualitative nature of HR issues. Business plans have tended to be expressed in numerical terms, such as financial data, sales forecasts and competitive position. However, 'soft' or qualitative issues such as culture, motivation and employee relations have become increasingly important – even in free market countries.

Armstrong's solution to these problems is to emphasize the need for human resource practitioners to achieve an understanding of how business strategies are formed. They should adopt a wider point of view and an understanding of key business issues such as:

→ Corporate intentions for growth or retrenchment, including strategic alliances (mergers, acquisitions, joint ventures, discussed earlier), product and market development, disposals.

→ Methods of increasing competitiveness such as improvements in productivity, quality and service, reducing costs.

→ A perceived need for a more positive, performance culture.

→ Other cultural consequences of the organization's mission such as 'commitment, mutuality, communications, involvement, devolution and teamworking'.

Organizations vary considerably in the formality of their strategic planning, ranging from detailed 200-page documents to unwritten 'orientations'. Neat theoretical approaches with successive stages of analysis, choice and implementation are rarely seen in practice. The organizational characteristics of a firm, and the environmental constraints upon it, affect and sometimes transform the process. Another critical factor is that the human resource is but one of the resources of the firm. Strengths and weaknesses in other areas, such as marketing and finance, may obscure the best people management. Individual companies also have their own control and industrial relations traditions.

The greatest difficulties are experienced in large, diversified organizations with a wide range of interests. They are highlighted in recession when the business needs do not fit with 'soft' HR values. HR strategies may focus on redundancies and sacking employees inevitably damages or destroys a caring corporate image. Legge (1995) outlines a strategy described as 'tough love' – being cruel to be kind – in which employees are expected to be both dedicated and disposable.

More positively, human resource strategies can be aimed at improving an organization's competitiveness by increasing its 'knowledge base' or competence. This includes shedding old values and techniques in favour of new ones. It requires a collective change of the organization's shared world view – including perceptions of the company and the market. Proactive SHRM is particularly important in highly competitive conditions where decisions about outsourcing parts of the organization, such as the HR function itself, are key elements of strategic decision-making. As we can see in the 'HRM in reality' box, outsourcing has been claimed to achieve major cost savings but the truth is more complex. Gospel and Sako (2010) consider outsourcing as a form of corporate restructuring, the nature of which depends on the existing organization structure and the paths open to the firm in supplier markets.

In an Australian study, Sheehan (2009) identified training and development, recruitment and selection, and Human Resource Information Systems (HRIS) as the major areas for HR outsourcing. She found that large organizations tended to use consultants to initiate outsourcing. The private sector was more concerned with recruitment and selection and performance-related pay while public sector organizations were most likely to outsource HRIS.

HRM IN REALITY HR OUTSOURCING

Outsourcing basic human resource services can be the key to achieving a more influential and strategic role for the HR function. However, an executive briefing from the Chartered Institute of Personnel and Development (CIPD) also concludes that:

→ the decision to outsource needs to be carefully considered

→ it will not be right for all, and

→ considerable effort needs to be devoted to ensuring a smooth transfer of responsibilities.

Written by Professor William Scott-Jackson, Tim Newham and Melanie Gurney of the Centre for Applied HR Research, Oxford Brookes University, the report – *HR Outsourcing: the key decisions* – draws on the experiences of 17 organizations that are either outsourcing HR services or have considered the possibility and rejected it. The report is intended to offer practical guidance to HR and non-HR professionals responsible for developing and improving the delivery of HR services in their organizations.

Vanessa Robinson, organization and resourcing adviser at the CIPD, said:

> People management plays a crucial role in delivering organizational performance. In today's modern, knowledge economy this is more true than ever before. The decision to outsource HR services is therefore not to be taken lightly.
>
> However, there are many circumstances in which outsourcing HR services can deliver tangible benefits to the organization, for example freeing HR professionals to devote more time to a strategic role in supporting organizational performance.

Advantages and disadvantages of outsourcing
The report identifies a number of 'strategic drivers' for outsourcing HR services:

→ *Reducing costs:* Key determinator in many outsourcing decisions, but should not be considered in isolation from other costs/benefits.

→ *Increasing effectiveness of HR delivery:* Experienced outsourcing providers can often deal with HR processes more effectively. For example, recruitment may be undertaken more quickly, reducing employee turnover costs and speeding up the pace of growth.

→ *Providing greater expertise:* External providers may offer greater levels of specialist knowledge or experience than affordably available in-house.

→ *Moving HR up the value chain:* Outsourcing human resource administration can lead to a shift in HR focus towards policy and decision-making.

→ *To aid organizational growth:* Fast-growing organizations can lack the HR capacity to deliver business objectives, making HR outsourcing an attractive solution.

The report warns against regarding HR outsourcing as a panacea for organizational problems. The potential pitfalls include:

→ According to the report, handing over unnecessarily complex or badly understood systems to an external provider can be like 'picking up spaghetti'. This limits potential benefits from outsourcing. If processes cannot be improved before a move, the organization may have to accept off-the-shelf replacements that are not specifically geared to their needs.

→ The greatest financial benefits of outsourcing often come from using sophisticated software. If effective IT systems already exist in-house, cost savings may not be achieved from an external provider.

→ Good employee management practices remain essential, and the key relationship between staff and their line managers remains in-house, leaving plenty of work on manager/staff relationships that still has to be handled despite the outsourcing relationship.

→ Local knowledge and ownership of human resource processes could be lost.

Vanessa Robinson continued:

The decision to outsource HR services is a complicated one. Cost reasons alone are not sufficient to drive the decision. Decision-makers need to ask whether there is a need to change the way the HR department operates and review existing provision. This review needs to consider cost, administrative efficiency and HR policy strategy and expertise. Where gaps are identified, organizations need to consider whether these are best solved by minor tinkering or major transformation.

It must also not be forgotten that a transition from in-house HR provision to the use of an outsourced provider is a significant change for the organization, and must be managed accordingly. If significant time is not devoted to the process of change, with unequivocal top-level support, there is a danger that staff/line manager relationships and other aspects of people management policy may be neglected.

Overall, is outsourcing the HR function likely to benefit an organization?

Source: *Reprinted with permission from* HRM Guide UK *(http://www.hrmguide.co.uk).*

TRANSFORMATIONAL HR STRATEGIES

Enthusiasts have seen a transformational power in HRM and transformation, or change, is an inevitable consequence of many human resource strategies (Bourne and Haddon, 2010).

Change strategies fall into one of two categories: turnaround change and organizational transformation (Bertsch and Williams, 1994):

1   *Turnaround change.* This is financially driven, often to ensure corporate survival by cutting unprofitable products and services. It involves the redesign of organizational structures (restructuring), disposal of non-core activities and large-scale redundancies. This kind of

change is painful but straightforward since existing hierarchical control systems can administer the process.

2 *Behavioural transformations.* This involves changing behaviour patterns throughout the company. Hierarchical control is inadequate because different power centres are likely to conflict and differences between business units make behavioural consistency a difficult objective to achieve.

Restructuring

Restructuring is the most common form of major organizational change (Key concept 4.3). According to its protagonists, restructuring should not be a defensive cost-cutting process but rather a proactive attempt to achieve innovative products and services by achieving **synergy** (Key concept 4.4).

KEY CONCEPT 4.3 RESTRUCTURING

Breaking up and recombining organizational structures. Advantages include reduced costs, eliminating duplication and greater efficiency. Disadvantages include disorder; interfering with normal activities; destruction of long-term commitment; loss of direction, especially in careers; and overwork from excessive cost-cutting. Recent strategic thinking has also emphasized the importance of relating business objectives to core organizational competencies. In other words, organizations should do what they are good at, leading to a new trend for companies to demerge, splitting into focused activity areas on which separate management teams can concentrate.

KEY CONCEPT 4.4 SYNERGY

Making the new whole worth more than its old parts, sometimes described as '2 + 2 = 5'. Synergies involve economies from integrating activities, horizontally or vertically; but also unrealized potential for new ideas, products or processes by melding expertise from the different sources into centres of excellence.

Restructuring usually involves **reorganization** – a move from one form of organization to another. Restructuring can affect the HR function directly. Pollitt (2005) describes how pharmaceutical giant AstraZeneca changed from site and functionally based human resources teams offering a full range of generalist support, to a 'one team' approach. Use of HR metrics helped to demonstrate the value of HR to the AstraZeneca businesses. The rationale was to create a more efficient and customer-oriented delivery of HR services and to ensure smooth implementation by communicating the new mindset to HR staff, combined with specific skills training to manage customer interactions both at strategic and transformational levels.

Melé (2005) studied the conversion of a medium-sized bureaucratic organization with highly specialized jobs into one in which employees were much more autonomous in managing their own work. Bureaucratic rules were reduced, but not eliminated completely, and management became less authoritarian. Employees could therefore apply greater entrepreneurial spirit, developing their talents in pursuit of company goals.

The difficulty for corporate management comes in the attempt to achieve both synergy and workable new diversified or decentralized structures at one and the same time (Marginson *et al.,* 1993: 7). Public statements through the media and shareholder information normally present such changes as deliberate and thought-through, the implication being that restructuring would be dealt with by means of a project management approach. However, the notion that restructuring is usually decided at the most senior level on the grounds of balance sheet rationality is often illusory (Purcell, 1995: 70). As we observed in earlier discussions on strategy and management, when faced with uncertainty, complex situations and conflict within the organization, managers typically resort to 'political' decision-making. Ficery *et al.* (2007) attribute a failure of synergy to six main causes: defining a synergy too narrowly or broadly; missing a window of opportunity; using incentives incorrectly or insufficiently; not involving the right people in synergy capture; mismatch between systems and culture systems; and (bluntly) using the wrong process. Estimating synergy benefits during the process of agreeing a merger is difficult and there is a tendency towards over-optimism among senior managers often leading to over-payment, which cancels out much of the benefit (Chatterjee, 2007).

Shrinkage

As we observed earlier, focusing on core activities and disposing of others has become particularly fashionable. In some cases, businesses have decided that management control and shareholder value are best served by a demerger. More commonly, shrinkage involves reducing the number of employees or **downsizing** although this has largely been confined to the manufacturing sector. In either case, HR managers are involved with communicating the change, conducting union negotiations and arranging redundancies or redeployment.

A particular concern is the cost-effectiveness of individual employees and departments. The more expensive, the greater the degree of justification required to retain them. For example, the 'de-layering' initiatives of the 1980s and 1990s focused on expensive middle-managers. Kanter (1989: 94) suggests that 'overhead' functions such as divisional headquarters have a duty to justify themselves to the business units they are meant to support. Approval and checking may delay decision-making, hindering the ability to compete. Wherever possible, these should be eliminated completely or transferred to the business units whose activities are involved. Decentralization is a dominant force, leaving small, slimmed-down central functions. Restructuring can be dangerous when companies treat people purely as costs rather than as assets. Kanter points to the inevitable 'discontinuity, disorder and distraction' that interfere with people's normal activities. She concludes that 'top management typically *overestimates* the degree of cooperation it will get and *underestimates* the integration costs'.

Cowboy management in these circumstances can destroy long-term commitment since restructuring removes many of life's certainties. Most of us try to create a state of order and predictability around our jobs. Restructuring can destroy this. No longer can we count on a job for life with any one company, but some sense of direction is essential to preserve motivation and obtain the best performance. Neither can people be expected to cope with overwork caused by excessive cost-cutting. According to American experience, much downsizing is really 'dumb-sizing', since two-thirds of the companies who have slashed workforces in recent years report no increase in efficiency. Often the principal role of human resource specialists is in rescuing the situation after the change has happened. Motivation and commitment must be rebuilt and skills training made available for staff involved in new tasks.

HRM IN REALITY SURVEYING EMPLOYEE OPINIONS

A 2008 survey by Opinion Research Corporation found that many US businesses are missing out on vital feedback and ideas from their own workforces.

Opinion Research Corporation's annual employee research survey shows that 44 per cent of the 1437 respondents do not carry out employee surveys and almost a half (46 per cent) of businesses that conducted surveys did not make any organizational changes as a result of employee feedback.

Employee surveys were most popular in the South (57 per cent of companies questioned) while those in the North Central region (Ohio, Indiana, Illinois, Michigan, Wisconsin, Minnesota, Iowa, Missouri, North Dakota, South Dakota, Nebraska, Kansas) were the least likely (52 per cent) to take any action following employee surveys, compared with 42 per cent in the West.

Terry Reilly, Director of the Employee Engagement practice at Opinion Research Corporation US said:

> Your employees hold the key to your success. An employee survey gives them the opportunity to let their feedback be heard and become part of the ongoing strategy of the organization.

The research shows a strong correlation between positive employee perception and the responsiveness of an organization to employee survey feedback. Eighty-four per cent of workers in businesses that acted on survey feedback felt that the changes positively affected them personally. However, nearly one quarter (23 per cent) of these did not think that the change was communicated well in the workplace.

US results were much better than those from a similar study in the UK where only 32 per cent of respondents thought that change was managed effectively in their organizations – compared to 63 per cent in the US. And only 43 per cent of British respondents said they had the opportunity to contribute their views before changes were made to their jobs. This compared to 62 per cent in the US.

Terry Reilly commented:

> Ineffective management of change within an organization can lead to increased uncertainty in the workforce. Offering employees the opportunity to voice their opinions before change is implemented

can significantly improve employee engagement, and, in turn – the success of the organization.

Top themes in employee surveys

An analysis of employee responses to opinion surveys in 2006 found a number of recurrent themes. HR Solutions, Inc., a Chicago-based management consulting firm specializing in Employee Engagement Surveys, compiled a top 10 list of the issues that concern employees the most:

1 **Higher salaries**. Pay is the number one topic for employee dissatisfaction.

2 **Internal pay equity**. Employees are particularly concerned about 'pay compression' (defined as the differential in pay between new and more tenured employees).

3 **Benefits programmes**. Particularly health/dental, retirement, and paid time off/vacation days. Many employees are unhappy about the cost of health insurance, especially prescription drug programs.

4 **Over-management**. 'Too many chiefs, not enough Indians' is a typical comment.

5 **Pay increase guidelines**. There should be a greater emphasis on merit.

6 **The HR department**. They need to be more responsive to employees' questions and/or concerns.

7 **Favouritism**.

8 **Improved communication and availability**. This applies to both supervisors and upper management.

9 **Over-work**. Workloads are too heavy and/or departments are understaffed.

10 **Facility cleanliness**.

Responses from written feedback can be different to verbal employee feedback sessions, according to Jennifer Rand, Principal Consultant with HR Solutions. 'Most of what the consultants hear during the feedback sessions supports in great detail the themes of the written comments. The comments most prevalent are usually those things that have changed, whether negative or positive, i.e. benefits, since it is human nature to resist change,' she said.

HR Solutions say that organizations should not overlook the write-in comment section of their employee survey as Quick Wins oftentimes originate from it. Quick Wins are easily implemented, actionable improvements to workplace setting or environment involving little resource investment. They can lead to immediate improvements in employee engagement and reassure employees that managers are acting on the survey findings.

How might employee surveys assist in providing a favourable climate for change?

Source: Reprinted with permission from HRM Guide USA (http://www.hrmguide.com/).

Incremental change

In the 1960s and 1970s, change often came under the label of **organizational development** (OD). This is an undramatic – but effective – long-term change process based on incremental improvements, essentially a continuous flow of emergent strategies. With the advent of modern change programmes such as 'business process re-engineering', this low-risk and long-term approach has gone out of fashion to a considerable extent. As we can see from Table 4.2, its underlying principles are similar to Japanese methods of continuous

Theme	Features
1 Top management support	Initiatives will not succeed unless higher management levels are fully committed to the change process and its maintenance.
2 Problem-solving and renewal process	Allows adaptability and viability to be generated in an organization that may be living in the past. This should allow the organization continually to redefine its purpose.
3 Collaborative diagnosis and management of culture	The process of change must involve all levels within the organization in a search for ideas that will lead to improvement. This is a non-hierarchical, shared evaluation of the culture and long-term goals of the organization.
4 Formal work team	Focusing on work groups, group dynamics and team development.
5 Consultant facilitator	Bringing in an external change agent or catalyst, experienced in the mechanics of change, able to spot resistance and unbiased by any prevailing agenda.
6 Action research	A primary feature of classic organization development that is absent in many modern packaged initiatives.

TABLE 4.2
Themes of organization development

Source: Adapted from French and Bell (1990).

improvement and the methodology has considerable parallels with radical change initiatives described later in this chapter.

STRATEGIC ALLIANCES

Redesign or restructuring may take place within one organization, or go beyond its boundaries, perhaps resulting from the combination of one firm with another. There are several relevant variables to consider at the strategic stage:

Strategic intent. Regardless of negotiated positions and public positions of the partner companies, what are their long-term intentions? Are they committed to a joint venture? Does one partner intend to achieve control? Managers will be wary of losing their power.

Consolidation. How much autonomy and organizational independence is to be allowed? Mergers and acquisitions tend towards much greater consolidation than joint ventures and consortia. Employees feel threatened by obvious opportunities for staff reduction.

Cultural integration. Is cultural plurality to be respected? Does the alliance intend a common culture? If so, will it be based on the culture of the dominant partner or a negotiated hybrid? Being forced to change familiar ways is threatening.

KEY CONCEPT 4.5 MERGERS AND ACQUISITIONS

A merger occurs when one organization is combined with and disappears into another organization. Acquisition, on the other hand is a generic term used to describe a transfer of ownership. Here, the two parties in the transaction may continue as entities in some form or other after the acquisition.

Alliances and mergers draw on the capacity and potential of participants but they have a poor history of success. Surveys show that over 50 per cent of mergers and acquisitions fail to achieve strategic objectives – often disastrously. An often-quoted McKinsey and Company study of mergers between 1972 and 1982 (involving 200 of the largest US corporations) found increased value to shareholders in just 23 per cent. The greatest proportion, 33 per cent, was seen in relatively small takeovers of closely related businesses. The explanation seems to have attracted yet another analogy with poultry, although the meaning is quite different: 'You don't put two turkeys together and make an eagle!' (unnamed economist quoted in Peters, 1987). Often the advantages are outweighed by (Porter, 1990; Buono, 1991):

→ Restructuring costs: including redundancy payments, consultancy and legal fees, accommodation transfer.

→ Strategic difficulties: harmonization of goals and objectives.

→ Organizational problems: difficulties in coordinating two different structures; overloading the parent organization's management systems; reorganization taking attention away from day-to-day activities.

➜ Behavioural problems and barriers: managers fight to preserve their territories or take over others; motivation falls when staff feel they have been taken over by remote managers.

Tampakoudis (2010) concludes that apparently irrational takeovers are driven by personal managerial objectives in the face of negative empirical information. Moreover, takeovers take place in surges with the best bargains to be had at the beginning of an economic cycle, while later acquisitions require hefty premiums that cannot be covered by any synergy (Mauboussin, 2010).

From a HR perspective, according to Mackay (1992, p.10):

> Most of the evidence suggests that a failure to acknowledge the human dimension undermines many potentially successful ventures. … There is a feeling that if 'the figures are right' all else will follow smoothly. Wrong! It is precisely 'all else' that can frustrate the best laid plans of marketing men and accountants as cultures fail to gel and key executives engage in destructive battles for dominance.

D'Annunzio-Green and Francis (2005) studied pressures faced by managers in a contract catering firm involved in an organizational change initiative that encouraged them to become self-sufficient and display entrepreneurial behaviours in an environment where they were also expected to comply with new operating procedures aimed at strengthening central control and cutting costs. They highlight the duality between the quantitative need for discipline in managerial procedures, while at the same time paying attention to the qualitative need for investment in human resources.

The nature of the power relationship is particularly significant. Many studies show that acquisitions are notoriously unsuccessful because of the manner of the takeover. Specifically, the benefits of an acquisition or merger can be destroyed by the way in which the merger process is handled. Staff who are working for new owners tend to feel defensive and threatened. It is almost as if they have been colonized. Similar feelings are experienced when internal restructuring results in merged departments or the absorption of one section by another. Frequently, takeovers are handled insensitively. Acquisitions and mergers bring power differences into sharp and highly visible focus. There is a temptation to charge into the acquired firm or department or to take a condescending attitude. Many takeovers have parallels with the sacking of Rome. The new managers are inclined to feel superior and to regard methods which are different from their own as inefficient or second-rate. Arrogance and organizational chauvinism on the 'conqueror's' part lead to defensiveness and concern on the other side. People sense a loss of power to determine their own fate (Kanter, 1989: 65):

> Arrogance can destroy the essence of the company. Strangers in suits wander about the organization, misunderstanding what they see. Observation is accompanied by sniggers and sneering comments, serving to boost the acquiring management team's egos and sense of superiority. Mackay describes this as 'tribal warfare' – one culture trying to assert pre-eminence over the other.

The consequences are serious. This is not simply a matter of upsetting workers, important though that may be in terms of its consequences on morale and cooperation. There is a considerable risk of throwing the baby out with the bathwater by obliterating the victim's processes before their consequences and rationale are fully understood.

Employee fears and anxieties can be minimized but research shows that people who have been 'taken over' continue to be suspicious and uncomfortable in the new organization for some time. Maurer (1996: 11) notes:

> Change is unsettling. It disrupts our world. Some fear they will lose status, control, even their jobs. The larger the change, the stronger the resistance. Successful change requires vision,

persistence, courage, an ability to thrive on ambiguity, and a willingness to engage those who have a stake in the outcome.

Kavanagh and Ashkanasy (2006) examined mergers between three large public sector organizations and found that resulting changes are often imposed on the leaders themselves. Pace of change frequently inhibits successful re-engineering of the culture. A successful merger hinges on individual perceptions about the manner in which the process is handled and the direction of change. Communication and a transparent change process are important, as this will often determine who is regarded as a leader post-merger. Leaders need to be competent and trained in the process of transformation to ensure that individuals within the organization accept changes prompted by a merger.

HRM IN REALITY — MERGERS AND ACQUISITIONS FAILING TO ACHIEVE VALUE

Mergers and acquisitions (M&As) continue apace but many deals fail to create expected value, according to a recent survey by Accenture and the Economist Intelligence Unit. The survey of 420 corporate executives from the United States of America, Germany, the United Kingdom, Sweden, Norway and Finland conducted in March 2006 also found that over half of recent deals in which respondents had been involved were cross-border transactions.

Less than half (45 per cent) of respondents thought that their most recent M&As achieved expected cost-saving synergies, while even fewer (30 per cent) said they had been able to successfully integrate IT systems in their most recent cross-border deal. Also, almost a half (49 per cent) said their deals did not achieve expected revenue synergies.

'Missing synergy goals by even a small percentage can mean losing hundreds of millions of dollars of shareholder value,' said Art Bert, a senior executive in Accenture's strategy practice. 'The most successful deals are approached with a comprehensive integration plan, with core team continuity through most of the transaction life cycle, from target identification, valuation, due diligence, deal execution, pre-close planning, and post-closing integration.'

Fifty-eight per cent of executives involved in a recent deal said their company's latest acquisition was a cross-border transaction. Around one half of respondents to the survey expected businesses in their industries to make cross-border acquisitions over the next five years. The following reasons were given:

→ to guarantee profitability (55 per cent)

→ to hit strategic corporate targets (49 per cent)

→ just to survive (26 per cent).

Almost three-quarters (70 per cent +) of senior executives considered that the identification and execution of cross-border M&As was more difficult than domestic transactions.

According to Art Bert:

There is a growing body of evidence that most large transactions fail to create shareholder value for acquirers. But what makes M&A so alluring is the less common, successfully executed deal that allows an acquirer to create shareholder value far beyond what its peers and competitors can achieve. This is why we see most high-performing companies undertaking a disproportionate number of deals relative to their industry peers.

Almost a third (31 per cent) of respondents attributed 20 per cent or more of their companies' total revenue growth over the previous three years to acquisitions and 83 per cent thought that at least some growth came from deals. Similar responses were given for anticipated revenue over the next three years with 30 per cent expecting M&As to fuel growth of 20 per cent or more and 88 per cent expecting at least some growth from acquisitions.

'M&A remains a vital strategic tool for corporate executives worldwide,' Bert said. 'Yet management teams must not be misled into thinking that deal closing is a prize, in and of itself. Rather, evaluating and integrating an acquired business in a manner that delivers a superior return on investment, demonstrating that a transaction is really the best use of shareholders' money, is what sets a good deal apart from a bad one.'

Respondents identified the following as some of the critical factors for M&A success:

→ Orchestrating and executing the integration process (56 per cent for domestic and 47 per cent for cross-border deals).

→ Conducting due diligence (42 per cent for domestic and 43 per cent for cross-border deals).

→ Achieving an optimal price for a deal (20 per cent for domestic and 19 per cent for cross-border deals).

Most corporate executives thought that their firms were successful at retaining valuable employees from both the target business (72 per cent) and the acquiring company (77 per cent). Similarly, most also agreed or strongly agreed that their transactions did not have a negative impact on customers of the target business (67 per cent) or the acquirer (73 per cent).

What factors make cross-border M&As more difficult than domestic transactions?

Source: Reprinted from HRM Guide USA (http://www.hrmguide.com).

MERGERS AND THE HR FUNCTION

Clemente and Greenspan (1999: 1) point out that:

There are literally hundreds of reasons why the M&A failure rate is so high. But many can be traced to the exclusion of human resource professionals in the pre-deal planning phase and the function's last-minute inclusion after the transaction has closed. It's a classic case of 'too little, too late'.

They present a description of the typical merger or acquisition. The focus is on 'making the numbers work' and the sequence begins with an investment banker or equivalent presenting an apparently suitable candidate company to management. If this makes 'financial sense' the process is launched. In most cases, the deal-making is more or less complete by the time that HR gets involved. HR specialists are left with the difficult role of developing communication strategies; aligning payroll, benefits and compensation systems; and melding different and possibly incompatible processes and cultures. But by this time a number of key personnel may have gone and those remaining may be confused or hostile.

Instead, Clemente and Greenspan argue, HR professionals should be involved in the earliest stage of any acquisition involving people. HR managers have the demanding task of integrating HR practices and performing two other roles simultaneously: a strategic role for company-wide integration and also a support role for business unit transactions (Antila, 2006). This means that human resource specialists must be familiar with the organization's strategic objectives, and its business and marketing plans. Hanson (2001) observes that early coordination between HR specialists in both companies is ideal but due to the 'sensitive nature of many organization transactions, it is possible that the HR team on the receiving side of the transaction will be notified before the team on the sending side, or vice versa.' Antila (*ibid.*) concludes that HR is important in the merger and acquisition process but is not always self-evident.

RESOURCING STRATEGIES

The basis of people management lies in how work gets done and who does it. Therefore, the rationale behind *why* we should decide on one solution rather than another is fundamental to HRM. There are important issues involved at all levels of analysis. At the environmental level, employee resourcing takes place against a background of:

→ Fluctuating economic conditions and global competition.

→ Choice and availability within the local job market.

→ Competition for scarce skills.

At the organizational level, the structure and functions of an enterprise are composed of the tasks that people perform. At the strategic level, **employee resourcing** involves decisions on:

→ Subcontracting or creating vacancies.

→ Allocating tasks.

→ Choice of selection methods.

As an activity, it is a major element of the work of human resource specialists, involving considerable technical expertise. Employee resourcing can involve sophisticated methods intended to realize long-term objectives and balancing considerations such as: (a) satisfying the immediate need to minimize employee costs while maximizing worker contribution to the organization; and (b) fulfilling a longer-term aim of obtaining the optimal mix of skills and commitment in the workforce (Price, 2000). In the context of ageing populations and changes in retirement legislation, there is a need for proactive planning throughout the developed world (McKinnon, 2010).

Employee resourcing is also a subject of vital importance at a personal level because most of us have to apply for a job: probably the first practical aspect of human resource management we encounter. In many cases it is a frustrating and sometimes baffling process of rejection. Readers in employment may well participate on both sides of the issue – as selectors or as applicants. Inevitably, therefore, resourcing deserves serious discussion. Employee resourcing is a fundamental aspect of people management (see Key concept 4.6).

KEY CONCEPT 4.6   EMPLOYEE RESOURCING

Resourcing is the process by which people are identified and allocated to perform necessary work. Resourcing has two strategic imperatives: first, minimizing employee costs and maximizing employee value to the organization; second, obtaining the correct behavioural mix of attitude and commitment in the workforce. Employees are expensive assets. They must be allocated carefully and sparingly. In terms of costs and efficiency, effective resourcing depends on the care taken in deciding which tasks are worthwhile and the levels of skill and ability required to perform them.

During periods of relatively high unemployment in the 1980s and 1990s, and again in the period after the economic crisis of 2008–2009, organizations in many countries felt able to dictate the terms of employment they were prepared to offer new recruits, often moving away from traditional nine-to-five working days. A modern flexible organization may adopt a structure along the lines of Handy's three-leaf 'shamrock' model (Handy, 1989: 70):

→ A professional core made up of managers, technicians, and qualified specialists.

→ Contractors providing non-core activities, who are not direct employees of the organization.

→ The flexible labour force composed of part-timers, temporary staff, consultants and contract staff performing tasks as and when required.

Most large organizations employ human resource or personnel specialists to conduct or, at least, coordinate employee resourcing. Organizations can take one of three actions to fulfil their employee resourcing needs:

1 *Reallocate tasks* between employees, so that existing staff take on more or different work. This may be part of an organizational change programme, such as restructuring or reorganization.

2 *Reallocate people* from the internal employment market, through promotion or transfer between different departments.

3 *Recruit* new staff from the external job market. Countries in the free market tradition have focused most of their resourcing activities on bringing in people from outside the organization. Employers have a choice between:
— *Recruiting anybody and everybody.* This approach predominates for employment at low skill and wage levels. It is especially common in small low-technology companies.
— *Recruiting selectively.* Skilled and motivated workers are selected. This approach predominates in large organizations.

External recruitment has the virtue of bringing in a wider range of experience but limits career opportunities for existing employees. It is predominantly a free market approach to resourcing but even Japanese businesses are now recruiting externally, particularly for scarce technological skills such as software engineering.

Types of resourcing strategy

Resourcing is a dynamic process: the movement of human resources through an organization. Businesses can assign people largely from existing staff or from the external job market. Companies that focus on internal supply are likely to view people as assets, carrying long-term value, rather than as costs. This is in line with practice in social market and Japanese organizations. It also reflects the spirit of the Harvard model of HRM discussed in Chapter 1.

KEY CONCEPT 4.7 GROW OR BUY?

Organizations can focus on internal or external job markets, or draw from both. Firms with an internal focus recruit at junior levels and 'grow' their employees into valuable assets through training, development and experience in the organization. Alternatively, companies can buy talent at a variety of levels from the external employment market. A mixed strategy offers a balance of continuity and commitment from long-term staff together with fresh ideas from imported 'new blood'.

HUMAN RESOURCE PLANNING

For resourcing strategies to be implemented they must be translated into practical action. The strategic process can be organized logically – for example, following the decision sequence shown in Figure 4.1. For these decisions to be taken, information must be obtained, consequences gauged, political soundings taken and preferences assessed.

Resourcing decisions taken at an operational level may lead from departmental expansion or cost-saving, transfer of activities, new product ranges and comparatively small changes in function. In practice, therefore, **human resource planning** has short, medium, and long-term aspects (see Key concept 4.8).

FIGURE 4.1

A resourcing decision sequence

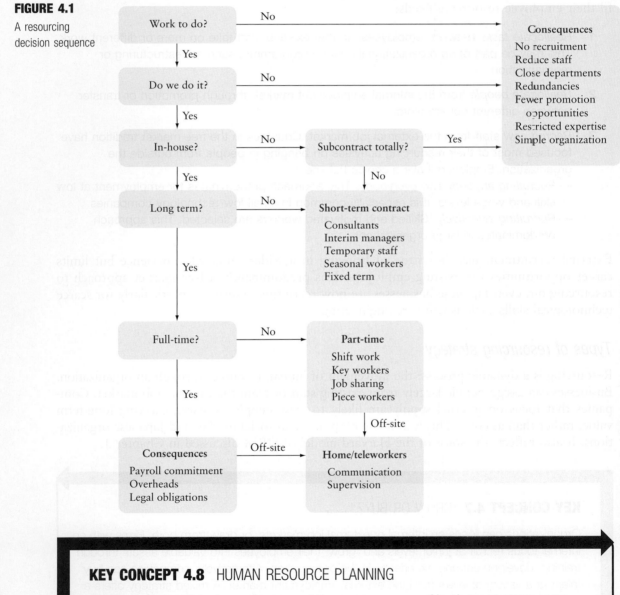

KEY CONCEPT 4.8 HUMAN RESOURCE PLANNING

A process that anticipates and maps out the consequences of business strategy on an organization's human resource requirements. This is reflected in planning of skill and competence needs as well as total headcounts.

Older texts refer to this topic as **'manpower planning'**. Some authors distinguish between manpower planning and HRP as distinct approaches (Hendry, 1995: 190). Primarily a 'numbers game', manpower planning emphasized accurate personnel records and forecasting techniques. It focused on questions such as:

→ How many staff do we have/need?

→ How are they distributed?

→ What is the age profile?

→ How many will leave in each of the next five years?

→ How many will be required in one, five, ten years?

The manpower planning approach regards the human resource manager as a personnel technician. Within this framework, the function of the human resource planner is to provide 'management' with the necessary advice to make decisions on issues such as:

→ Recruitment.

→ Avoiding redundancies.

→ Training – numbers and categories.

→ Management development.

→ Estimates of 'labour' costs.

→ Productivity bargaining.

→ Accommodation requirements.

In this tradition, Graham and Bennett (1992: 175) envisage a long-term human resource plan as a detailed specification, by location, function and job category of the number of employees 'it is practicable to employ at various stages in the future' (see Table 4.3).

Tyson (1995: 80) identifies three distinct approaches to planning:

Formal, long-range planning. Creating a planning framework, usually expressed in financial terms with verbal commentaries. Notably, all the companies studied that used this approach consulted widely with interest groups.

Flexible strategies. Covering most of the organizations studied. Plans changed frequently in response to market changes. Plans were intentionally short-term, often with minimal written detail.

Attributional strategies. 'One step at a time'. Previous actions can be rationalized but, in truth, organizations using this approach are cautious and are not really committed to any specific strategy.

In general it is worth observing (Price, 2000) that:

Modern human resource planners have tended to move away from predicting headcounts towards building 'what if' models or scenarios which allow the implications of different strategies to be debated. However, traditional HR planning techniques have become considerably easier to implement with the spread of Human Resource Information Systems (HRIS) which trap key employee information and generate reports and analyses as a matter of course.

TABLE 4.3
Steps for long-term
human resource
planning

Source: Based on Graham
and Bennett (1992: 174).

Step	Aspects
1 Create a company HRP group	This should include the main functional managers of the company, together with human resource specialists.
2 State the organization's human resource objectives	Within the context of the overall business objectives and considering: → capital equipment plans → reorganization such as centralization or decentralization → changes in products or in output → marketing plans → financial limitations
3 Audit present utilization of human resources	Sometimes described as the 'internal manpower audit', detailing: → number of employees in various categories → an estimate of employee turnover for each grade, analysing the effects of high or low turnover on performance → amount of overtime worked → assessment of performance and potential of current employees → comparison of payment levels with local firms.
4 Assess the external environment	Placing the organization in its business context in terms of: → the recruitment position → population trends → local housing and transport plans → national agreements dealing with conditions of work → government policies in education, retirement, regional subsidies, and so on.
5 Assess potential supply of labour ('external manpower audit')	Including: → local population movements (emigration and immigration) → recruitment and redundancy by other firms → employing new work categories – e.g. part-time workers → productivity improvements, working hours and practices.

People as numbers

Generally, it is accepted that modern workforce or human resource planning should have a wider perspective, in tune with the philosophy of HRM, including 'softer' issues such as competence, commitment and career development. Modern human resource planning continues to use the 'hard' techniques of manpower planning but also includes a new focus on shaping values, beliefs and culture, anticipating strategy, market conditions and demographic change.

Nevertheless, in line with the tradition of formal, observable and 'objective' planning, numerical measurement and forecasting have been favoured over qualitative studies of opinion, attitude and motivation. The growth of information technology and management information systems has made numerical data readily available and possibly further discouraged collection of qualitative information.

Forecasting methods

Human resource planners have a choice of techniques available to them that have become increasingly easier to use as HR technology improves. For example:

Extrapolation. This method assumes that the past is a reliable guide to the future. Various techniques are suitable for short- and medium-term forecasting, such as time series, trend analysis and measures of cyclical requirements.

Projected throughput/production/sales information. As a normal part of the planning process, production, sales and marketing departments and their equivalents in the public services or voluntary organizations will prepare their own forecasts.

Employee analysis. Modern HRIS products offer extensive possibilities for **employee analysis**; modelling the total profile of an organization's human resources. Employees can be classified in a variety of ways, such as function, department or grade. Age and length of service are important predictors of future availability. Skills levels and training or development needs can be compared with annual performance assessments.

Scenario building. Scenarios are not strictly forecasts but speculations on the future.

Employee turnover

In recent years managers have been preoccupied with reducing the size of the workforce, closing plants and encouraging people to leave. In times of economic growth the emphasis changes to retaining the people with required skills. Human resource planning has a role in anticipating wastage. For example, the London Metropolitan Police had experienced difficulty in maintaining the requirement for police constables with the retirement of experienced officers. One way was to extend working life by offering flexible working hours, mentoring roles and pension incentives as alternatives to retirement. However, the consequences of blocking the careers of younger officers had also to be considered (Flynn, 2010). **Turnover** covers the whole input–output process from recruitment to dismissal or retirement and takes the consequences of promotion and transfer into account. Wastage deals only with leavers. Its importance lies in the freedom of employees to leave when they choose and hence its relatively uncontrollable nature for employers.

Early work by Rice, Hull and Trist (1950) identified three main phases of turnover:

1   *Induction crisis.* Individuals who leave shortly after joining an organization: uncommitted employees tend to leave in the first few months.

2 *Differential transit.* During the first year or so, when some employees conclude that the organization is an unsuitable career vehicle or source of income.

3 *Settled connection.* Becoming a long-term 'stayer'.

The degree of wastage can be determined by a variety of turnover indices of varying sophistication. Three examples are:

1 The British Institute of Management (BIM) Index (annual labour turnover)

$$\frac{\text{Leavers in year}}{\text{Average number of staff in post that year}} \times 100 = \% \text{ wastage}$$

2 Cohort analysis – a survival curve is drawn of employees taken on at the same time to determine what happens to a group.

3 Census method – for example, providing a histogram of the length of employee service.

'Soft' planning

HRM implies that planning has to go beyond the 'numbers game' into the softer areas of employee attitudes, behaviour and commitment. These aspects are critical to HR development, performance assessment and the management of change. At this point, we can consider an outline of the **'soft' planning** process:

1 *Where are we now?* Information needs to be gathered through some form of human resource audit. This can be linked to a conventional SWOT analysis of the organization's human capital:
   — *strengths* such as existing skills, individual expertise and unused talents
   — *weaknesses,* including inadequate skills, talents that are missing in the workforce because they are too expensive, inflexible people and 'dead wood'
   — *opportunities,* such as experience that can be developed in existing staff and talent that can be bought from the external job market
   — *threats,* including the risk of talent being lost to competitors.

2 *Where do we want to be?* Essentially, a clear strategic vision and a set of objectives.

3 *What do we need to do?* For example, following the logical sequence in Figure 4.1 decisions must be made on the use of in-house or external staff (see Table 4.4).

4 *Devise an action plan.* Some kind of resource planning is used by as many as 60 per cent of large organizations but it has to be conceded that it is often done poorly. Ideally, it should be linked to corporate strategy but corporate planners tend to ignore the human dimension.

TABLE 4.4
Inhouse or outsourced resourcing.

In-house resources	Outsourcing
Management control	Legal contract
Long-term people (can be developed; build experience; understand organization)	Focus on paying only for work you need
People are hassle	No extra pay/commitment

TABLE 4.4
Continued
Inhouse or
outsourced
resourcing.

111

CHAPTER 4   STRATEGIC HRM

In-house resources	Outsourcing
Contractual arrangements (talent expensive; overheads; large structure; hierarchy; support systems)	Range of options, e.g. consultants (variable expertise; expensive) or contingent workers (usually ex-managers; best for operational work) or homeworkers (lower level/ specialist; low overheads; supervision issues) or subcontracting
People are ambitious (require advancement; can go elsewhere – taking knowledge)	

HRM IN REALITY STRATEGIC WORKFORCE PLANNING

A study from The Conference Board in 2006 reports that the ageing workforce and an emerging retirement wave among 'baby boomers' are driving more businesses toward 'strategic workforce planning'.

Strategic workforce planning is a new approach to traditional human resource planning that involves analyzing and forecasting the talent required by organizations to meet the objectives of their business strategies. It helps:

→ control employee costs

→ assess talent needs

→ make informed business decisions such as whether it's more cost effective to outsource an activity or add full-time employees

→ assess human-capital needs and risks.

In short, according to the study, *Strategic Workforce Planning: Forecasting Human Capital Needs to Execute Business Strategy,* strategic workforce planning is aimed at helping businesses ensure they have the right people in the right place at the right time and at the right price.

'In many companies, traditional workforce planning was an onerous process that HR imposed on management,' said Mary B. Young, senior research associate, The Conference Board and author of the report. 'Too often, the net result was a humongous report, blinding spreadsheets, and a dizzying amount of data that provided very little value to the business.'

Methodology has moved on to meet changing business needs, new tools and technology. The study shows that some businesses have enhanced the simple gap analysis (workforce demand versus supply) used for traditional 'manpower' planning by adopting the logic and analytical tools of other management functions, including finance, strategic planning, risk management and marketing.

Rather than focusing on spreadsheets, the planning process needs to concentrate on the business plan and its implications for the workforce. Consistent, organization-wide data is essential. Other critical areas identified in the study include:

→ making the process and tools simple and efficient

→ developing HR's capabilities and comfort level

→ establishing a common language to describe jobs and required competences

→ integrating workforce planning with business and budget planning

→ driving the plan deep into the organization.

While most companies in the study are finding their way in the process, strategic human resource planning can deliver value already through:

→ generating insights and knowledge to help managers make business decisions

→ providing a deeper and more subtle understanding of workforce dynamics than was previously available

→ enabling more efficient human capital management, for example by evaluating different staffing options for their long-term impacts or creating a stronger internal job market

→ enabling the HR function to achieve a long-held desire to become a player and a valued contributor at a higher level of strategic management.

'Strategic workforce planning enables the organization to slice-and-dice its workforce data to discover critical issues, compare different groups, understand patterns and trends, home in on critical segments of the workforce such as mature workers and top performers, and customize its approach to managing different segments of its workforce,' said Mary Young. 'By enabling leaders to see across lines of business, workforce planning can leverage talent within a company. Ultimately, the same workforce planning database tools will enable employees to shop for new jobs, assess their own developmental needs, and prepare for career moves inside the organization.'

Some of the techniques adopted by companies exampled in the study include:

A workforce analytics approach: mining both current and historical workforce data to identify the key relationships among the variables and between employee and business data. Dow Chemical has used this approach throughout a 10-year evolution of its workforce planning process.

Forecasting and scenario modeling: using data to create forecasts that incorporate multiple what-if scenarios. These enable executives to evaluate strategic options. The study describes how a 'major bank' decides where to locate a new call centre based partly on this approach.

Human capital planning: used by Corning and others to segment jobs on a basis of their 'mission-criticality', making different levels of workforce investment in each segment. This approach focuses on broad three–four-year trends, rather than precise headcounts and short-term plans.

Hewlett-Packard and IBM are cited as being committed to strategic workforce planning, customizing the process to address each company's specific conditions and needs. IBM's HR and finance departments help senior business leaders prepare realistic plans to execute their business strategy and manage drivers of employee costs. At HP, the study states that high-level discussions and a two-way educational process between business leaders and HR emphasizes qualitative over quantitative factors.

'While no organization claims to have achieved it yet, many believe that the ultimate payoff from strategic workforce planning will be a vibrant, internal job market that transcends the boundaries between business units and geographies,' concluded Young. 'The company will be able to mine employee data to locate talent anywhere in the organization, woo passive job candidates, and find the best use for each employee.'

How would you distinguish strategic workforce planning from traditional HR planning?

Source: Reprinted with permission from HRM Guide USA (http://www.hrmguide.com).

RESOURCING INFORMATION

Effective in-house resourcing requires accurate and comprehensive information. Strategies and human resource plans must be translated into actual jobs and people found or developed to perform them. Some basic questions can be asked:

→ What tasks are involved?

→ What skills or competences are required to do the work?

→   Are they to be found within the organization?

→   If not, should extra people be recruited?

Researching the job

Conventionally, the first question is answered by a **job analysis** (Key concept 4.9). It is a more-or-less detailed examination of the sub-tasks within an identified job. Jobs vary between the 'crystallized', such as manufacturing assembly where the job is precisely defined, to managerial and professional jobs in which individuals have considerable freedom to vary their work (McCormick and Ilgen, 1987: 38). The degree of freedom is determined partly by technology or personal expertise and partly by the organization. Job analysis is geared towards tasks that are already being done in some form or can be easily extrapolated from current activities.

KEY CONCEPT 4.9 JOB ANALYSIS

The process of job analysis is that of gathering and analyzing job-related information. This includes details about tasks to be performed as part of a job and the personal qualities required to do them. Job analysis can provide information for a variety of purposes including: determining training needs, development criteria, and appropriate pay and productivity improvements. For resourcing purposes, job analysis can generate job and personnel specifications.

Job analysis techniques vary from the rudimentary to the sophisticated. Long-regarded as a somewhat tedious aspect of the HR function, job analysis has been highlighted as a valuable technique in ensuring compliance with anti-discrimination legislation in the USA. Conversely, the move towards flexible working has deterred many organizations in other countries from closely defining jobs.

The simplest forms of job analysis are conducted by observing or interviewing existing jobholders and supervisors. Alternatively, the same people can produce a self-report according to an agreed format. Information is also available from records, 'experts', training materials, equipment descriptions and manuals. A basic six-step approach could be conducted as follows (Smith and Robertson, 1993: 15):

1   Make use of relevant existing documents such as training manuals.

2   Ask the line manager responsible about the main purposes of the job, the tasks involved and the links with other people.

3   Ask the same questions of jobholders, preferably backed by a detailed activity record over a week or two.

4   Where possible, sit in and observe jobholders at work – preferably on more than one day and at different times.

5   Try to do the job yourself. (This is not possible if specialist machinery or training are required.)

6   Write the job description.

TABLE 4.5
A basic job analysis checklist

Heading	Subject matter
Job identification	Job title, department, grade or level
Relationships	Name or title of immediate boss; number and type(s) of staff jobholder is responsible for; links with other departments
Outputs	What are the end-products or results of the job
Activities	The behaviours or actions of the worker in achieving these outputs
Performance	Required standards, agreed objectives
Individual requirements	Abilities, skills, experience, temperament, training, languages, etc.
Working conditions	The physical and social surroundings of the job such as workspace, working hours, leave entitlement
Equipment	Computers, machine tools, vehicles etc. used as an essential part of the job
Other information	Promotion outlets, training available, transfer opportunities

The job-related information produced by job analysis can be arranged according to a number of headings (see Table 4.5) to ensure that all relevant details are covered. This method is cheap and relatively easy. However, more complex methods may be justified, such as questionnaires, generally purchased 'off-the-shelf' from specialist companies. Questionnaire techniques can provide a wealth of information but are often expensive and time-consuming.

The **critical incidents technique** can also provide a rich, qualitative perspective on a job. Incumbents are asked to describe a number of specific real-life incidents in which they participated. The most effective incidents are those which detail qualities required to do the job well.

Job analysis is not a value-free source of information. Employees are prone to:

Exaggeration. Making jobs seem more demanding or complex than they really are.

Omission. Humdrum tasks are forgotten in favour of less frequent but more interesting activities.

In contrast, information given by supervisors may lead to:

Understatement. Jobs are portrayed as being easier and less complex than they are in reality.

Misunderstanding. Frequently bosses do not know workers' jobs in any detail.

The job description

Whatever the degree of sophistication, the common outcome of job analysis is the job definition or description. In the past, **job descriptions** have been used as quasi-legal documents, with employees declaring their contents to be a definitive list of the tasks they were expected to perform. Uncooperative employees would refuse to do anything that was not on the list and unions and employers would enter into trench warfare over any changes. Today, in a climate of change and flexibility, employers are reluctant to agree to a rigid list of tasks, preferring the employee to be ready to take on any required function. Job descriptions are out of date almost as soon as they are written and cannot be seen as documents to be adhered to rigidly.

Conventionally, job descriptions detail information such as job titles, summaries of main functions and more detailed lists of activities within each job. The 'flexible job description' has a significant role in modern resourcing strategies allowing greater latitude in career development and succession planning (Pennell, 2010).

Researching people

Depending on the method used, job analysis provides a detailed description of the work to be performed but may not indicate the knowledge, skills or abilities needed to do so. The 'right person' model of resourcing advocates a **personnel specification** for this purpose. Personnel specifications translate the requirements of the job into the human attributes necessary to do that job.

Personnel specifications list 'essential' criteria that must be satisfied, and other criteria that rule out certain people from being able to do the job. Competence analyses and sophisticated forms of worker-oriented job analysis generate personnel specifications as part of the package. The step from job to person specification never is entirely objective, requiring inference or intuition. In fact, there is a risk of introducing discriminatory criteria which rule out particular groups. Personnel specifications may be no more than blueprints for 'clones', a matter that will be explored later in this chapter.

Checklists such as Rodger's Seven-Point Plan (Rodger, 1952) have been commonly used for preparing personnel specifications. The desired qualities are categorized under seven headings:

1   Physical qualities, including speech and appearance.

2   Attainments – qualifications, membership of professional associations.

3   General intelligence.

4   Specific aptitudes, such as numerical ability.

5   Interests and hobbies.

6   Personality.

7   Domestic circumstances.

Slavish use of such a plan leads to evident danger. Items one and seven could easily cause discriminatory choices and require rigorous and critical examination. As we shall see in the next chapter, further information is obtained by using selection techniques including formal interviews, psychometric tests, assessment centres and biodata.

STRATEGIES FOR REDUNDANCY

Most of the discussion so far in this chapter has addressed human resource strategies relating to successful, growing companies. Managers are also expected to implement redundancies and closures as a result of strategic decisions. Most job losses are due to age-old causes: business failures, organizational restructuring and cutting back on capacity in response to lower sales or funding levels. Generally, the terms 'redundancy' and 'retrenchment' have lost much of their old stigma.

Planning for redundancies

There are some new features to job-cutting which are indicative of systematic changes in the way that human resource strategists view the process. Despite the emphasis on job security as a prerequisite for an effective human resource strategy, reality in free market economies demands planning for redundancies. These may result from company failure, funding cuts, rationalization or reduction in demand for products and people. There are several terms for the process of losing a job, all with different connotations and nuances: being made redundant, 'letting you go', 'getting the sack' and so on. One euphemism is 'deselection', implying that some form of systematic or thought-out procedure has been used to decide who will lose their jobs.

Hendry (1995: 202) details a number of key issues:

→ To what extent can over-staffing be corrected through natural wastage or redeployment?

→ What agreements constrain the redundancy process. For example, 'last in, first out'?

→ When should a redundancy programme be announced? How much consultation is required?

→ How are redundancy entitlements to be calculated?

→ Is it possible to have an entirely voluntary process? What restrictions should be placed on key staff leaving?

→ Should the organization play an active role in outplacement?

→ When will savings in salary and related items pay for the redundancy costs?

Large companies often employ portfolio management systems that view business units as growth, closure or disposal prospects. A classic, if simple, portfolio planning model is based on the Boston Consulting matrix shown in Figure 4.2. This offers a further typology for resourcing strategy:

Stars. Profitable business units with a dominant market position. Good prospects for employees with promotion opportunities and competitive salaries.

Cash cows. Mature companies with a high market share but low growth rate. Secure but unchallenging for employees – promotions are only possible when staff leave or retire. Comfortable salaries until later stages when hard cost-cutting is required.

Wild cats. New ventures with low market share but high growth rates. A risky environment for employees. If lucky, the group will invest and there will be considerable career opportunities and rapid promotion – provided they work for potential stars. Employees are expected to be flexible and the work can be exciting and fast-moving. If unlucky, they face closure or disposal to another organization.

Dogs. Certain failures. Low growth, low share of market and no strategic potential. The only hope for employees is sale to a more positive owner.

Companies using portfolio planning are likely to take decisions on purely financial criteria without regard to the welfare of employees. HRM in such organizations tends to be tough-minded, favouring employees in profitable business units. Those in less successful areas are likely to be disposed of unceremoniously.

FIGURE 4.2

Boston Consulting Group portfolio planning matrix

Redundancy and retention

Managers in charge of redundancy programmes typically focus on target numbers, with little or no thought about the quality of the staff leaving the business. Retention strategies for key staff are even more important during periods of redundancy. As Thomson and Mabey (1994: 11) point out:

> It is the quality of the staff ... not the quantity, which is the essential factor in downsizing. As we all know from experience, where there are programmes of voluntary redundancy, it is often the most skilled employees who go first because they are more marketable outside.
>
> An obsession with numbers leads to a haemorrhaging of valuable skills: years of work on building a strong competence base can be undone in a matter of weeks.

'Last in, first out', remains a common rule. Lee (2004) investigated the reasons why seniority rules are applied so widely to layoffs and promotion decisions in the USA. Under certain circumstances, he acknowledges, there may be economic benefits from the use of seniority rules but the evidence shows a greater popularity than economic explanations would account for.

HRM IN REALITY TIPS FOR HANDLING LAY-OFFS

Consulting firm Drake Beam Morin (DBM) warned employers against short-sighted workforce decisions and badly handled employee terminations. Lay-offs may be necessary at times, but they can have a negative impact on an organization's productivity levels and affect their ability to retain and attract talented employees in the future.

'From a company's standpoint, the decision to terminate a group of employees is fraught with potential legal, financial and public relations consequences,' said Thomas Silveri, president and chief executive officer of DBM. 'It is critical that managers communicate the news of lay-offs in a professional, legal and humane way in order to treat the departing employees with

sensitivity and to maintain a respectful corporate image.'

DBM conducted a global study revealing that one out of every ten individuals who lost their jobs involuntarily told a colleague first of their job loss. So the manner in which employees are laid off can have a direct impact on the morale, commitment and retention of remaining staff.

Based on extensive experience, DBM recommends a five-step process for managers involved in laying off staff:

1 *Prepare the materials.* Explain the rationale and prepare all severance information in writing (notification letter; salary continuation/severance period; benefits; outplacement, etc.).

2 *Prepare the message.* Write the script you will use during the meeting and the key information you will convey to remaining employees. Keep it short and to the point.

3 *Arrange the next steps.* Schedule meetings with your organization's human resources and outplacement professionals. Review what should be done with the departing employees' personal belongings and specify when the employees should leave the organization.

4 *Prepare yourself emotionally.* Don't assume personal responsibility for the termination. Remember it is a business decision based on business needs. Acknowledge your anxiety, prepare your approach and talk about your feelings with the human resource and outplacement professionals.

5 *Anticipate employee reactions.* There are typically five reactions to termination: anticipation, disbelief, escape, euphoria or violence. By acknowledging these various reactions and learning to recognize them, you will ensure that no matter what the reaction, you will be prepared to handle it in the best way.

DBM recommends that the following 'Dos and Don'ts' should be followed when conducting a termination meeting:

Do

→ invite the employee in to sit down

→ get right to the point

→ explain the actions taken and the reasons for them

→ listen to the employee and wait for a response

→ restate the message if necessary

→ use your prepared notes/guidelines

→ clarify the separation date

→ give an overview of the separation package

→ explain the logistics for leaving the company

→ provide appropriate written materials

→ close the meeting within 15 minutes

→ escort the employee to the next appointment.

Don't

→ say 'Good morning,' 'Good to see you', or 'How are you?'

→ engage in small talk

→ use humour

→ be apologetic

→ defend, justify or argue

→ threaten

→ discuss other employees

→ sympathize

→ try to minimize the situation

→ make promises

→ personalize the anger

→ use platitudes like 'I know how you feel,' or 'You will be just fine,' etc.

'Managers need to learn how to manage this process in a way that preserves the current productivity levels and the company's ability to attract top talent in the future,' said Silveri.

What are the consequences of bad feeling when employees leave an organization?

Source: Reprinted with permission from HRM Guide USA (http://www.hrmguide.net/usa/).

Since the late 1990s, critics have argued that the cutting process has gone too far: as we have noted before, de-layering or downsizing have led to 'dumbsizing'. Organizations have slimmed down to the point where they are denuded of the skills needed to grasp new opportunities and remaining staff are demoralized and overworked. With skilled staff in demand and often difficult to find, there is a greater focus on active retention.

➤ SUMMARY

Human resource strategies tend to focus on numbers and also attitudes, behaviour and commitment in line with harder 'matching' models of HRM but their implementation is problematic. Recent thinking has accommodated the notion that HR strategy is not as simple as some rationalist accounts imply and that strategy itself has the same emotional, irrational and intuitive components as any other form of thinking or decision-making.

Nowadays, change initiatives are common elements of human resource strategies as companies and public sector organizations struggle to achieve their objectives in a competitive environment. Frequently these involve some form of organizational restructuring using a change programme such as business process re-engineering. Some of the most difficult aspects of change management for human resource practitioners come from mergers and acquisitions where their involvement is often late – if not too late to rescue a disastrous situation. Negative attitudes to change are to be expected and are not necessarily unhealthy.

We considered a variety of resourcing strategies. We also discussed some approaches to human resource planning and the use made of information collected during the resourcing process. We reviewed the issue of retention, staff turnover and wastage in terms of measurement, forecasting and action. Some of the limitations of job descriptions and personnel specifications were identified. Finally, we considered redundancies as an aspect of resourcing strategy.

➤ FURTHER READING

1 *Strategic Human Resource Management: Theory and Practice* (2nd edition, Sage, 2005) edited by Graeme Salaman, John Storey and Jon Billsberry is a useful reader.

2 Bernard Burnes's *Managing Change: A Strategic Approach to Organisational Dynamics* (FT/Prentice Hall, 2009) 5th edition places change in a broader context of management theory.

3 John Hayes provides a practical guide for students and managers in *The Theory and Practice of Change Management* (Palgrave Macmillan, 2010).

4 Stephen Taylor's (2008) *People Resourcing,* 4th edition, published by the CIPD, examines the topic of employee resourcing in a practitioner context.

5 *People Resourcing and Talent Planning: HRM in Action* (4th edn, FT/Prentice Hall, 2010) by Stephen Pilbeam and Marjorie Corbridge analyzes contemporary practice.

➤ REVIEW QUESTIONS

1 What is 'strategic human resource management'? Summarize the main goals of strategic human resource management and identify some of the key differences between strategic and operational HRM.

2 When is outsourcing a suitable strategy for the HR function?

3 To what extent is it possible to demonstrate that human resource strategies are vital for business success?

4 What are the ideal conditions for the implementation of a human resource strategy? What deficiencies are commonly found in strategic human resource plans?

5 What do you see as the main barriers to successful implementation of strategic HRM?

6 What is a transformational HR strategy? Define: (a) synergy; (b) restructuring.

7 Why do people resist change? Is it possible for negative attitudes towards change to have positive benefits for an organization?

8 What role should human resource practitioners play ideally in a merger or acquisition? How does this differ from reality?

9 Why do so many mergers and acquisitions fail?

10 Why is employee resourcing a core activity for human resource staff? Summarize the main resourcing strategy options open to modern organizations.

11 Distinguish between 'hard' and 'soft' human resource planning. Which is of greatest value to modern businesses?

12 Are long-term resourcing strategies realistic?

13 What is the relationship between resourcing strategy, HR planning and job analysis? Is human resource planning a worthwhile activity?

14 Why is it important to measure and forecast staff turnover? Is there merit in the claim that resourcing strategies should focus on employee retention rather than recruitment?

15 When and why would you conduct a job analysis? What is the difference between a job description and personnel specification?

16 Are redundancies inevitably a matter of cynical expediency?

➡ CASE STUDY FOR DISCUSSION AND ANALYSIS

West Five Care Trust

The West Five Care Trust controls four hospitals in a suburban area. Two of the hospitals are modern and have extra accommodation space. The other two are old but prestigious specialist units located in expensive areas. The Trust considers that it would make considerable financial sense to close the older hospitals and transfer their functions to the modern sites. Several senior physicians are extremely unhappy about the consequences and have launched a public campaign to save the specialist units. This has angered the general manager who has only just presented the plan as a proposal to the management committee. He considers the physicians to be disloyal as they have taken a confidential business matter to the press. He is also baffled since the new hospitals would offer them far better facilities.

The general manager was recently recruited from industry and has been keen to exercise his right to manage. In his first six months, he successfully outsourced cleaning and catering, brushing aside union opposition. He has also instituted stringent cost-control measures and now vets all budget requests personally, including expenses for attending conferences.

As human resources manager how would you analyze the situation and how could you help?

CHAPTER 5
Promoting diversity

LEARNING OBJECTIVES

The purpose of this chapter is to:

→ Define and distinguish between the concepts of equal opportunity and the management of diversity.

→ Identify the significant barriers to equality and diversity in employing organizations.

→ Outline the nature and extent of discrimination on the basis of sex and gender.

→ Evaluate the causes and extent of racial discrimination in the employment market.

→ Analyze the basis and effects of institutional racism.

→ Assess the effectiveness of legislation in the reduction of disability discrimination.

→ Consider the increasing significance of anti-age discrimination initiatives.

THE MEANING OF DIVERSITY

People are different. They vary in gender, culture, race, social, physical and psychological characteristics. But our attitudes towards these differences can be negative or positive, depending upon individual perspectives and prejudices. Bassett-Jones (2005) argues that diversity is a recognizable source of creativity and innovation that can provide a basis for competitive advantage. Diversity is also a cause of misunderstanding, suspicion and conflict in the workplace that can result in absenteeism, poor quality, low morale and loss of competitiveness. Organizations have to manage the resulting paradox.

There is a tendency for people to form like-minded 'in-groups', to favour members of one's own group and for those in authority to recruit people like themselves. This often goes unquestioned – but is unfair. The consequences include a lack of opportunity for women, ethnic minorities, the disabled, older people and other disadvantaged sections of the community as the best jobs are ring-fenced and barriers are placed to prevent their progress.

As members of organizations, it is difficult to challenge the often subconscious actions and elaborately entrenched justifications for unfairness. Not least, because discrimination and prejudice are expressions of power that includes the ability to prevent, inhibit or punish critical comment. Yet, if people are the key assets of a business it is important to realize the maximum benefit from their human capital. True competitive advantage requires the best from everyone – without restrictions; it demands a prejudice-free and inclusive attitude towards actual and potential employees. It requires diversity (see Key concept 5.1).

KEY CONCEPT 5.1 DIVERSITY

'Diversity is the variation of social and cultural identities among people existing together in a defined employment or marketing system' (Cox, O'Neill and Quinn, 2001: 3).

In reality, this has to be viewed as an ideal since discriminatory and non-inclusive behaviours have a deep psychological basis. Research shows that prejudice is difficult if not impossible to eliminate. For example, if someone is prejudiced against a particular group, meeting someone with positive qualities from that group does not dispel the prejudice.

Nevertheless, equality of opportunity is an objective worth striving for. It can be addressed at all levels: governments have a role to play through legislation to prevent discrimination; organizations need to focus on the management of diversity, making the most of a wide pool of talent; strategists should consider equal opportunity policies, targeting and positive development of under-represented groups; people managers can monitor their activities and increase awareness to minimize discrimination.

SOCIETY AND OPPORTUNITY

Effectively, society determines who is given opportunity and who is not through the process of discrimination. Opportunity is also linked to social factors such as economic conditions and educational attainment: access to and success in education can be responsible for discrimination (Tannock, 2008). Overt prejudice is comparatively easy to observe but the true nature of unfairness lies in the way opportunity has been institutionalized within society. The status quo is constructed to benefit certain types of individual from particular backgrounds or those who are able to adapt most easily to its requirements. Typically this has denied opportunity to women and minority groups.

Most countries have a concentration of particular social groups at the top of their institutions. Others are found further down. As a consequence, skills and abilities are not used to the full – a situation that is detrimental to society as a whole. However, the advantaged are unlikely to admit that their positions come from privilege rather than competence. For them, change is not a priority. This form of '**particularism**' (see Key concept 5.2) is still important, although the influence of convergent forces such as globalization and information technology is becoming increasingly prominent (Horwitz *et al.*, 2002; Good and Taylor, 2008).

KEY CONCEPT 5.2 PARTICULARISM

Discrimination favouring particular groups and individuals over others. It derives from a reliance on personal relationships such as ethnic origin, religion or tribal community. It contrasts with 'universalism' in which personal relationships are ignored and emphasis is on other criteria such as qualifications, expertise and ability to do the job.

Particularism leads to discrimination. This mechanism can be extended to include a number of forms, including discrimination on the grounds of:

Age. Arbitrary age boundaries excluding younger and older workers.

Appearance. Preferring people of a certain height or weight, for example.

Disability. Discriminating against people with special needs.

Gender. Limiting certain types of jobs to either males or females.

Ethnic origin. Preference for particular racial or linguistic communities.

Nationality.

Religion.

Background. Often seen as cliques – networks of people from similar backgrounds reserving the best jobs for themselves. In addition, people with socially undesirable backgrounds, such as ex-offenders, are actively discriminated against.

Nepotism. Common in small companies that rely heavily on family members.

Marti, Bobier and Baron (2000) found that some forms of discrimination are more easily observed and recognized than others. Participants in their studies were more likely to label actions of gender or racial discrimination as prejudice and also tended to rate such examples as more severe than cases of prejudice on the grounds of age or weight. Harper (2000) reports on a study of longitudinal cohort data covering 11 407 individuals born in Britain in 1958. The results showed that physical appearance had a significant effect on earnings and employment patterns for both men and women. Regardless of gender, people assessed as unattractive or short were penalized. At the extremes, taller men tended to receive higher pay than average, while obese women were paid less than those of average weight. The researchers attributed the bulk of the pay differential for appearance to employer discrimination. In a Swiss study, Krings and Olivares (2007) observed prejudice against a disliked group – but only for jobs requiring interpersonal contact, rather than those needing technical ability.

Discrimination can be **direct** (Key concept 5.3) or **indirect** (Key concept 5.4). It can also extend into victimization when employees are treated less favourably as a consequence of asserting their rights. Many countries use legislation to reduce such discrimination, for example, in areas such as equal pay, selection and promotion. The effectiveness of such legislation is reflected in the proportion of disadvantaged groups achieving responsible positions. Often this has been disappointing. In much of the world, the presence of women and people from ethnic minority groups becomes increasingly rare towards the top of most organizations. Some groups, such as the disabled and the over-50s, are conspicuously absent from many firms.

KEY CONCEPT 5.3   DIRECT DISCRIMINATION

Treating an individual or group less favourably on grounds such as disability, race, religion, age, gender or sexual orientation. An explicit and fairly obvious form of discrimination. The use of different criteria for promoting or paying male or female employees is an example of direct discrimination.

KEY CONCEPT 5.4   INDIRECT DISCRIMINATION

Less obvious than direct discrimination. Requiring certain criteria that are more easily satisfied by one group than another. One example would be to specify a fixed minimum height requirement for entry into a police force. This is a criterion that would be more easily met by male than female applicants. Another example would be a requirement for an unnecessarily high standard of spoken or written English, that would favour people with a particular educational background.

We turn next to the practical consequences of discrimination on people management at the organizational level.

DIVERSITY AND THE ORGANIZATION

Why should business organizations and their managers offer equal opportunities to a diverse range of employees? Two fundamental perspectives are identifiable that can be related to different models of HRM (Goss, 1994: 156):

Human capital. 'Artificially' blocking the progress of any group results in less than optimal use of an organization's human capital. Discrimination is irrational since it limits the resource value of employees. This view is compatible with 'hard', or free market HRM discussed in Chapter 1 of this book.

Social justice. A moral or ethical interest in social equality, compatible with 'soft' or social market HRM. Economic benefits are secondary to this social duty.

Goss sees the human capital perspective as fluctuating and opportunistic: a shallow commitment '... capable of being adopted or abandoned, in line with legal or economic expediency'. It is also narrow, restricted to legal requirements and short-term employment market conditions. This contrasts with the more principled social justice viewpoint, that embodies a deeper and wider commitment, extending beyond minimum legal requirements.

According to Ross and Schneider (1992) organizations benefit from a deep, principled commitment to equality of opportunity because it leads to:

→ A diverse workforce that enriches ideas and perspectives within an organization.

→ Imaginative ideas to assist total quality management.

→ Recruitment or promotion of the most talented people.

→ An environment that encourages them to stay.

→ Improved motivation and commitment that raises productivity.

→ Reduced wastage and recruitment costs that increase profitability.

Other commentators contend that, whereas this is valid for the economy as a whole, equal opportunity practices may be a significant expense rather than a benefit for individual firms.

All businesses operate within the national or supranational legislation governing equal opportunities in a specific country. For example, the USA and South Africa have required some employers to take measures of positive discrimination, typically requiring them to fill quotas from under-represented sections of the community. Recruitment criteria such as qualification or skill requirements may be relaxed for members of those groups. This represents an attempt to achieve the **equal share** level of opportunity outlined in Straw's model that also considers **equal chance** and **equal access** (detailed in Table 5.1).

TABLE 5.1
Levels of opportunity

Level	Opportunities	Barriers
1 Equal chance	Everyone has same chance, e.g. right to apply for vacancies; be considered for a position.	Formal or informal barriers, e.g. employers may ignore applications from people living in ethnic minority areas.
2 Equal access	Disadvantaged groups not barred from entry into organizations but may be confined to lower levels of work.	Institutional barriers, e.g. appraisal methods that favour certain groups, or promotion requirements – such as mobility – that effectively bar many married women.
3 Equal share	Access is free. Representation achieved at all levels. Legislation may require quotas for disadvantaged groups, e.g. disabled.	Only those lawful, justifiable and necessary, e.g. specific language speakers to work with ethnic groups.

Alternatively, positive action may be required or undertaken voluntarily by governments or employers. Underrepresented groups are assisted and encouraged to participate in training and development initiatives, support groups and mentoring schemes. This requires that organizations are aware of their disadvantaged employees and the jobs they are doing, so that the problem of **occupational segregation** can be tackled (see Key concept 5.5).

KEY CONCEPT 5.5 OCCUPATIONAL SEGREGATION

Disproportionate representation of particular groups in specific sectors, job types or levels of responsibility. Horizontal segregation places men and women, for example, in different jobs, such as chambermaids (women) and porters (men). Vertical segregation places one group in better-paid positions than another group, so that men are better represented at managerial levels while women are concentrated in lower, administrative jobs.

Turnasella (1999) suggests that the employment process is itself responsible for the persistent pay gap between men and women and between ethnic minorities and non-minorities. Employers usually require a salary history from job applicants and frequently ask questions about salary expectations. Applicants with a record of relatively low pay tend to be offered lower offers of remuneration. Intriguingly, in an experimental study involving 100 participants (50 men and 50 women), Blanton, George and Crocker (2001) found that women compared themselves with other women to gauge satisfaction with a pay rate when it was framed as compensation for past work, but compared themselves with the men when framed as part of an offer for future employment. Drawing on police work as an example, Dick and Nadin (2006) argue that personnel selection alone can make little difference to the unequal position of women given the complex causes of social occupational discrimination and segregation along gendered lines.

Corbridge and Pilbeam (1998) also point out that networking and headhunting are inevitably discriminatory because they involve recruitment from a restricted pool of friends, social acquaintances and school or university peers. People from disadvantaged groups, if they are employed at all, tend to be confined to 'boring jobs with no prospects' in the secondary sector (Molander and Winterton, 1994: 96).

The impact of discrimination on equality of pay is less in a unionized environment (Metcalf, Hansen and Charlwood, 2001). The authors attribute this to two factors:

→ Union members and jobs are more homogeneous than their non-union counterparts.

→ Union wage policies narrow the range of pay rates within and across firms and bring up the lowest wage rates.

STRATEGIES FOR DIVERSITY

Many organizations have adopted **equal opportunities policies** – statements of commitment to fair human resource management. However, such policies are notoriously ineffective and rarely disturb vested interests. Obstacles to creating a diversified workforce are embedded in organizational culture – particularly the sub-culture at the top. Can the human resource function steer employers towards an equality perspective? Woodhams and Lupton (2006) found that the presence of an HR professional in small to medium-sized enterprises is associated with greater take-up of gender-based equality policies but not with greater implementation of associated practices.

According to Molander and Winterton (1994: 102) serious equal opportunity policies require:

→ Allocation of overall responsibility to a specific senior executive.

→ Agreement of the policy with employee representatives.

→ Effective communication of the policy to all employees. An accurate survey of existing employees in terms of gender, ethnic origin, disability, etc. and the nature and status of their jobs.

→ An audit of human resource practices and their implications for equal opportunities.

→ Setting equal opportunity objectives within the human resource strategy.

→ Resources, such as training and development capabilities, to back up these objectives.

This approach can be incorporated within an integrated framework termed the 'management of diversity' (outlined in Key concept 5.6). The pitfalls in the process are evident.

However, the main difficulties arise from cost and lack of commitment, exemplified by '**tokenism**' – the employment or promotion of isolated individuals to represent their gender or colour. 'Paternalism' is a related problem, where discriminatory decisions are taken for the 'benefit' of particular groups.

KEY CONCEPT 5.6 MANAGEMENT OF DIVERSITY

The management of diversity goes beyond equal opportunity. Instead of merely allowing a greater range of people the opportunity to 'fit in', or be an honorary 'large, white male', the concept of diversity embodies the belief that people should be valued for their differences and variety. Diversity is perceived to enrich an organization's human capital. Whereas equal opportunity focuses on various disadvantaged groups, the management of diversity is about individuals. It entails a minimization of cloning in selection and promotion procedures and a model of resourcing aimed at finding flexible employees.

Monitoring of potential discrimination is frequently spasmodic, most commonly undertaken when individuals are recruited, then when they are candidates for promotion, and at exit. Training does not seem to be monitored closely for potential discrimination.

The management of diversity is a natural consequence of human resource strategies that focus on flexible working arrangements. Part-time work and, especially, homeworking are particularly attractive to some women and disabled employees. But men also may benefit from more flexible working arrangements.

HRM IN REALITY   GENDER INEQUALITY IN ACADEMIC RESEARCHERS' COMPENSATION

Research from the Mongan Institute for Health Policy at Massachusetts General Hospital published in *Academic Medicine* found that women researchers in the life sciences still receive lower levels of compensation than their male equivalents, including those at higher academic and professional levels. The study also identified gender differences in career advancement paths.

Lead researcher Dr Catherine DesRoches said:

> The gender gap in pay has been well documented, but what was not understood was whether academic accomplishments could overcome the pay gap. Our study found that, across the board, men are being paid substantially more than equally qualified and accomplished women at academic medical centers.

Researchers explain that previous studies documenting gender inequality in compensation and academic rank did not consider differences in professional activities, such as leadership responsibilities. The current study investigated whether such differences exist, whether productivity (reflected by scientific papers published) continues to vary, and whether salary discrepancies persist after these factors are taken into account.

In 2007 researchers randomly selected more than 3000 life science investigators from the top 50 academic medical centers in receipt of funding from the National Institutes of Health in 2003–2004. Respondents completed anonymous questionnaires including details of professional activities; scientific papers published; hours spent on professional, scientific and clinical activities; and total compensation.

The study found that women with the rank of full professor worked significantly more hours than equivalent men. This difference primarily reflected more time spent on administration and other professional tasks rather than patient care, teaching or research. There was no significant gender difference in hours worked by associate professors. Women at the assistant professor level tended to work fewer hours than men, the most common factor being less time expended on research. After controlling for differences in academic ranking, research productivity and other characteristics, researchers found women earned from US$6000 to US$15000 less per year than their male counterparts.

Catherine DesRoches said:

> These differences may seem modest, but over a 30-year career, an average female faculty member with a PhD would earn almost US$215 000 less that a comparable male. If that deficit were invested in a retirement account earning six per cent per year, the difference would grow to almost US$700000 over a career. For department of medicine faculty, that difference could be almost twice as great.

The researchers did not investigate reasons for differences identified by the survey, but suggest that the greater number of professional responsibilities taken on by female full professors could reflect their organization's attempts to improve diversity at departmental and committee leadership level. Salary discrepancies may reflect on-going discriminatory practices or the specialist areas selected by women.

Principal investigator Eric G. Campbell, associate professor of medicine, concluded:

> Women working in the life sciences should not assume they are being paid as much as equally qualified men, and academic institutions should look hard at their compensation and advancement policies and their cultures. In the end, I suspect major systemic changes will be needed if we ever hope to achieve the ideal of equal pay for equal work in academic medicine.

Why are male and female academics being paid differently?

Source: HRM Guide USA. *(http://www.hrmguide.com).*

Discussion on women in the workplace tends to focus on family, children and marriage. However, Hamilton, Gordon and Whelan-Berry (2006) found that never-married women without children often experience work/life conflict at similar levels to that experienced by other groups of working women. Work/life benefits typically provided by organizations are frequently regarded as less important and used less often by never-married women without children than by other working women.

KEY CONCEPT 5.7 THE GLASS CEILING

The term 'glass ceiling' describes the process by which women are barred from promotion by means of an invisible barrier. This involves a number of factors, including attitudes of people in power and the inflexible processes and requirements geared to the cloning process which ensures that 'men of a certain sort' will generally succeed. In the USA, the term is also used to describe the barrier that prevents progress for other disadvantaged groups – for example, ethnic minorities.

GENDER AND SEXUAL DISCRIMINATION

Women's participation in the employment market has increased rapidly but in most countries their share of senior jobs remains low. The 2009 FTSE Female Index found that women made up 12.2 per cent of directors on the boards of Britain's biggest businesses (Sealy *et al.*, 2009). The report cited a 'discouraging decline' in the number of women executive directors from 16 to 15 and in the number of boards with multiple women directors. A quarter of FTSE boards are exclusively male. Of 14 women appointed who had not previously held FTSE 100 directorships, 13 were not British nationals. The authors contrast the position with that in Norway and Spain. Both countries are actively trying to increase female participation rather than rely on incremental progress. In Norway 30.5 per cent of directors on the top 100 ASA companies are women. In Spain in 2008, 74 per cent of IBEX 35 directors were women.

HRM IN REALITY MORE WOMEN FILL CANADA'S TOP BUSINESS JOBS

More women fill top executive jobs in Canada's largest publicly traded businesses than ever before – but this still amounts to a mere 7.2 per cent, according to a report from executive search firm Rosenzweig & Company.

Rosenzweig & Company analyzed the largest hundred publicly traded companies in Canada, based on revenue. Their annual revenues ranged between $41.3 billion and $1.9 billion. Between them, 544 top executive positions were examined.

Jay Rosenzweig, Managing Partner of Rosenzweig & Company said:

The good news is there are more women rising to top jobs and 15 are newly on the list this year, which may indicate turnover and change is in the air. The bad news is that the number remains inexcusably low and Corporate Canada's 'old boys' network' continues to disregard such a diverse talent pool in the workforce for leadership roles.

Unfortunately, the tough economic times could well serve to slow the pace of change. We'd like to see a big jump year-over-year so that women hold more than 10 per cent of all the top jobs soon, but we may be waiting longer now.

This is the fourth annual *Rosenzweig Report on Women at the Top Levels of Corporate Canada*. It shows that 36 women now hold top officer jobs in Canada's 100 largest publicly traded companies, compared with 31 last year. In terms of percentages, women currently hold 7.2 per cent of the top jobs while men have 92.8 per cent. Last year women held 5.8 per cent, with men holding 94.2 per cent.

All these businesses have to name and publicly disclose compensation for their Chief Executive Officer (CEO), Chief Financial Officer (CFO), and at least the next three highest paid executive officers. Some businesses list more than five top executives. But over two-thirds (69 per cent) of Canada's largest public companies do not have women executives in these categories. Canadian banks take the lead in promoting women to top jobs, including RBC, TD, CIBC and BMO. Overall, six corporations listed more than one woman: ATCO, Canadian Utilities, Linamar Corp., BMO, Canadian Pacific Railway, and Russel Metals.

'We are hopeful the election of Barack Obama to the top job in the free world will boost diversity in North American boardrooms,' said Jay Rosenzweig. 'Clearly, these abysmally low numbers for women – half the population and almost half the workforce – indicate change is needed; and the sooner the better.'

With study after study indicating that increased diversity at leadership levels spreads through organizations and improving financial performance, Jay Rosenzweig concludes: 'This is not simply a social and moral issue, but an issue about maximizing shareholder value.'

Why are the rates of female participation at the top level so low?

Source: Reprinted with permission from HRM Guide Canada (http://www.hrmguide.net/canada/).

The processes of occupational segregation and 'sex-typing' of jobs continue to be prevalent, so that women are concentrated at the base of most organizational hierarchies in jobs that are less prestigious and lower-paid than those favoured by men. As an example, De Graft-Johnson, Manley and Greed (2005) reported on 2003 research indicating that while approximately 37 per cent of architectural students are women, and the percentage is increasing, this is not reflected in the architectural profession. Women represent only 13 per cent of the total and are leaving after qualifying. A multiplicity of factors, such as low pay, poor promotion prospects, discriminatory attitudes and sexist behaviour were found to influence departure.

Fuller, Beck and Unwin (2005) explore the attitudes of young people (aged 14 and 15) and employers to non-traditional occupational choices and recruitment decisions of employers from traditional sectors, such as engineering, construction and childcare. The study finds that organizations with gatekeeping roles between young people and employers are not taking sufficient responsibility for challenging their perceptions and decision-making processes. Occupational stereotypes are deeply entrenched, creating major psychological and social barriers that have to be overcome if a more evenly balanced workforce is to be achieved.

Employer prejudices explain some of the difficulties that women experience. Central to many employers' attitudes is attachment to a family model where the woman stayed at home looking after the children and the man went out to work. This pattern has become uncommon in much of the developed world. Dual-career and one-parent families, equal parenting and the dismantling of life-long career structures have eroded the distinction between male and female roles.

HRM IN REALITY GENDER SEGREGATION

A 2010 study from the Institute for Women's Policy Research in Washington, DC analyzes data from the *Current Population Survey* to assess the state of gender segregation in US employment since the early 1970s.

Researchers found that women are making progress in some lucrative male-dominated professions. For example, the percentage of women lawyers has risen from 4.0 per cent in 1972 to 32.2 per cent in 2009. However, according to one frequently used measure, the *Index of Dissimilarity*, overall progress towards equity has stalled since 1996. Women continue to dominate traditional female professions that are usually less well paid. In 2009, they accounted for over 95 per cent of kindergarten teachers, librarians, dental assistants and registered nurses.

Some sectors have seen a significant deterioration, with the percentage of women computer programmers falling from more than one-third in the late 1980s to less than 21 per cent, and from 13 per cent of civil engineers in 2005 to just over seven per cent in 2009. Researchers found that young women experienced more segregation in 2009 than they did ten years previously, wiping out about 20 per cent of the improvement achieved since 1968.

Heidi Hartmann, president of the Institute for Women's Policy Research said: 'It is very likely that the stalled progress in integrating the labor market is contributing to the failure of the wage gap to close.'

Based on 2009 earnings data, the study examines the relationship between median earnings and the gender composition of occupations. It differentiates between those that are predominantly male or female, and those that are relatively gender balanced, considering low, medium, and high-skilled fields.

The researchers explain that women are now proportionately more likely than men to have some years of post-secondary education. However, the study found that irrespective of whether a job requires college level education, medium or low level skills, those predominantly held by women typically attract lower median earnings than those with either a more even gender balance or predominantly held by men.

The study acknowledges significant exceptions, particularly among medium-skilled occupations. Dental hy-
gienists, the great majority of whom are women, have higher weekly median earnings (US$956) than occupations almost exclusively held by men such as electricians (US$856) or carpenters (US$665). However, over 80 per cent of dental hygienists have at least an associate degree. Only 20 per cent of electricians, and even fewer carpenters, have attained similar levels of education. Researchers point out that women currently require a higher level of formal education to achieve similar earnings.

Ariane Hegewisch, a study director at the Institute for Women's Policy Research explained:

> All workers are likely to do better if they have at least some post-secondary school qualifications. Yet while it is still possible without college to earn a decent wage in some male-dominated occupations, the same is not true in female-dominated occupations. Almost as important as getting a qualification, however, is the field in which you qualify. A speech language pathologist – an occupation that is predominantly female – on average makes US$1153 per week, compared with a pharmacist – an occupation nearly half female – who receives median earnings of US$1841, a difference of close to US$700 for a week of full-time work.

The study found a less significant difference in median earnings for workers in low-skilled occupations. Researchers explain that the Bureau of Labor Statistics identifies nursing and psychiatric aides; maids, housekeepers and cleaners; and personal and home care aides as the largest categories of female-dominated, low-skilled occupations. They are much more likely to result in wages close to the poverty threshold than male-dominated, low-skilled occupations (such as truck drivers, laborers and ground maintenance workers). Median weekly earnings in 2009 were US$553 for this category of male-dominated occupations compared to US$408 for their female equivalents.

Robert Drago, research director for the Institute for Women's Policy Research, commented:

> Policy makers need to pay attention to the stalled progress in gender desegregation. Occupational

segregation carries costs for the economy and employers by exacerbating skill shortages and causing reduced productivity. It also costs working families. Particularly in low-skilled jobs, working in an occupation predominantly held by women instead of one held by men, may be the difference between earning a poverty wage and earning a family supporting wage.

What causes gender segregation?

Source: HRM Guide USA *(http://www.hrmguide.com).*

In other parts of the world, the position of female workers has improved. For example, Hossain and Tisdell (2005) found evidence of growing commercialization of women's work in Bangladesh. Most women are self-employed or employed in low-skill jobs, but participation is increasing in high-skill and entrepreneurial jobs as well as policy-making bodies. Gender wage differentials have been considerably reduced in many industries but women tend to be paid less than men. Remarkable improvements in women's educational attainments are positively correlated with workforce participation.

Gender differences

A further contributor to the problem is our perception of **gender** differences, real or imagined (see Key concept 5.8). There are differences between men and women, other than the physical, but little agreement as to what they are. The common stereotypes are that men tend to favour and aspire towards qualities that are essentially individualistic and competitive, such as intelligence, dynamism, energy and assertiveness. Women, on the other hand, stress qualities of a more cooperative and consensual nature: thoughtfulness, flexibility, perceptiveness and honesty.

KEY CONCEPT 5.8 GENDER

All human societies divide themselves into two social categories called 'female' and 'male'. Each category is defined on the basis of varying cultural assumptions about the attributes, beliefs and behaviours expected from males and females. The gender of any individual depends on a complex combination of genetic, body, psychological and social elements, none of which are free from possible ambiguity or anomaly (Helman, 1990). Traditionally, sexual differences have been used to justify male-dominated societies in which women have been given inferior and secondary roles in their working lives.

They concluded that since male managers are prevalent, females are disadvantaged by being evaluated against male standards of behaviour. Given similar jobs and appraisal ratings, men are more likely to be offered training or promotion. Kramer and Lambert (2001) examined a large, random sample of female and male employees using a survival analysis technique to investigate the time taken from being hired to being promoted to supervisor.

HRM IN REALITY   GENDER STEREOTYPING A KEY BARRIER

A study published in the December 2009 issue of the *Psychology of Women Quarterly* shows that management stereotypes are likely to evolve as more women assume leadership roles in the workforce.

Despite improvements in female participation at management levels, women still fill less than two per cent of CEO leadership positions in the Fortune 500. It is not surprising to find, therefore, that leaders continue to be thought of as men with the management levels in most industries considered to be 'male-typed'. But in a few industries women have moved into management positions. These industries have become more 'gender-neutral' and there are indications that stereotypes of leaders as men may be changing.

The study, *The Evolving Manager Stereotype: The Effects of Industry Gender Typing on Performance Expectations for Leaders and Their Teams* by Susan F. Cabrera, Stephen J. Sauer and Melissa C. Thomas-Hunt of the Universities of Cornell, Clarkson and Virginia respectively, investigates how male and female leaders and their teams are evaluated differently according to the gender-typing of the industry in which they work.

The researchers' findings were that people have higher expectations for the performance of teams when the leader's gender is consistent with the gender typing of the industry in which the team works. However, expectations for performance of leaders' own performance were not impacted by their consistency with industry gender typing. According to Susan F. Cabrera:

> This research demonstrates the power of stereotypes concerning what kinds of people should lead organizations in what kinds of industries. In addition, it suggests that, as more women move into certain sectors of our economy, stereotypes may be evolving in ways that create a more level playing field for women who aspire to leadership positions.

Gender stereotyping

A survey published in 2007 found that gender stereotyping was a key barrier to the advancement of women in corporate leadership, leaving women leaders with limited and conflicting options.

The Double-Bind Dilemma for Women in Leadership: Damned if You Do, Doomed if You Don't was the third in a series of reports examining the effects of gender stereotyping in the workplace by Catalyst, a non-profit organization working to advance opportunities for women and business. The study surveyed men and women business leaders in the US and Europe. Of 1231 participants, 296 were US senior managers and corporate leaders (168 women and 128 men) and 935 were European managers and senior managers (282 women and 653 men). The second part of the study provided qualitative analysis of in-depth, semi-structured interviews with 13 women leaders in a large US corporation.

The report argued that gender stereotyping results in organizations routinely underestimating and underutilizing women's leadership talent. The 2006 Catalyst Census shows that while women make up over 50 per cent of management, professional and related occupations, only 15.6 per cent of Fortune 500 corporate officers and 14.6 per cent of Fortune 500 board directors were women.

Ilene H. Lang, Catalyst president said:

> When companies fail to acknowledge and address the impact of gender stereotypic bias, they lose out on top female talent. Ultimately, it's not women's leadership styles that need to change. Only when organizations take action to address the impact of gender stereotyping will they be able to capitalize on the 'full deck' of talent.

The report highlighted numerous previous studies demonstrating similar leadership styles in men and women. However, earlier research by Catalyst found that women business leaders faced persistent gender stereotyping frequently confronting them with double-bind 'no-win' dilemmas not experienced by men. The current study found that men are still perceived as 'default leaders' while women are considered 'atypical leaders' and as violating accepted norms, irrespective of their leadership style.

The survey identified three common dilemmas currently experienced by women business leaders, supported by comments from participants:

1 **Extreme perceptions**. Women business leaders are perceived as 'never just right'. Those who act in a manner consistent with gender stereotypes are considered too soft, those who go against them are considered too tough.

My observations show senior women to be at either end of the spectrum, drivers that do it themselves (even though they might have given it to someone). This type tends to give little recognition and is a perfectionist. The others are very effective delegators, giving lots of recognition and building loyal teams, but can be perceived as 'not tough enough (US man, age 35–44, level not specified).

2 **High competence threshold/lower rewards**. Women leaders face higher standards than their male counterparts and receive less reward. Often they must work doubly hard to achieve the same level of recognition for the same level of work and 'prove' they can lead.

Men and women are seen differently, and the difference in my experience and observation is that we (women) need to show it more times before they believe it. With a woman, they will want to see the behaviour repeated more frequently before they will say that this is really part of the women (sic) and her capabilities (European woman, high-potential manager).

3 **Competent but disliked**. Women exhibiting traditional leadership skills such as assertiveness tend to be seen as competent but not personable or well-liked. Those who adopt a more stereotypically feminine style are liked but not seen as having valued leadership skills.

…it may just be that people are more sensitive to how women behave in that regard. There does seem to be a little more tolerance for harsh behavior from men rather than women. Women are quicker to get labeled, and with men, it's easier to brush it off… (High-potential woman, US-based manager).

I have experienced in the past that women can be distrusted in leadership roles, especially when they use a dominant style of communication. On the contrary, if they use a collaborative style serving their organization and empowering people, they get more recognition and sincere appreciation from their male equals (Spanish man, age 31–35, middle management).

The report suggested that organizations need to develop strategies to remove the pervasive and damaging impact of gender stereotyping from the work environment to take advantage of the expanding pool of female leadership talent.

Ilene H. Lang explained: 'While women may address double-bind dilemmas with individual strategies this is clearly about organizations shifting their norms and culture to meet marketplace demands.'

The report argues that education about how stereotyping works and holding individuals accountable can decrease the negative impact of gender bias. Actions that organizations can take include:

→ Providing all employees with tools and resources to increase awareness of women leaders' skills and the effects of stereotypic perceptions.

→ Assessing the work environment to identify ways in which women are at risk of stereotypic bias.

→ Creating and implementing innovative work practices that target stereotypic bias, particularly effective when specific areas of risk, such as performance management procedures, are addressed.

The report suggested ways in which organizations can apply this knowledge:

→ Managerial training and diversity education – educating managers and employees about the origin and consequences of bias, inconsistencies between values and actual behavior, and causes and effects of gender inequality in the workplace.

→ Performance and evaluation management – employing objective and unambiguous evaluation criteria.

Where do gender stereotypes come from?

Source: Reprinted with permission from HRM Guide USA (http://www.hrmguide.com).

They found evidence for significant pro-male bias in promotion decisions that could not be attributed to differences in time on the job, education, or parenting responsibilities. Brynin (2006) argues that men have traditionally gained more than women from access to technologies at work that bring prestige, job security, more satisfaction and higher pay. Female jobs associated with technologies tend to involve routine work. Busolt and Kugele (2009) described the low incidence of scientific researchers in Europe and the even lower level of female inventors.

Wilson (2005) examined how women academics in two British universities perceive the assumption that they are receiving different and unequal treatment in appraisal. It has been argued that men and women appear to have learned that women are different and not equal in organizations. Wilson's study found that, while the women did not necessarily perceive themselves as being seen to be different, men saw them as having different and inferior qualities. Women were seen as 'other' when measured against standards and norms set by men.

Hakim (2006) argues that high levels of female employment and family-friendly policies actually reduce gender equality in the workforce and reinforce the glass ceiling. The emphasis placed on equal opportunities by policymakers and feminists assumes that discrimination is the primary source of sex differentials in labour market outcomes – notably the pay gap between men and women. However, some careers and occupations cannot be domesticated and this also poses limits to social engineering. The notion of the glass ceiling is itself challenged by the metaphor of a firewall (Bendl and Schmidt, 2010).

Fortin (2005) concluded that women are more likely to underestimate their own skill levels and, therefore, inhibit their own progress. However, some deal with the situation by playing the game according to male rules. In general, women are more likely to regard themselves as 'enablers' of other people, building up the confidence of their staff and encouraging them to develop and use their skills.

In a study of 176 women managers from a number of industries across Australia, Downey, Papageorgiou and Stough (2006) found that female managers displaying transformational leadership behaviours tended to show higher levels of emotional intelligence and intuition than women managers displaying less transformational leadership behaviours.

Much of the debate about male and female behaviour revolves around sexual stereotyping, which has a significant cultural basis not easily amenable to change. Stereotyping can also influence career aspirations. Harper and Haq (2001) examined British cohort data and found that 16-year-old young men and women showed significant differences in their occupational aspirations, appearing to follow a traditional pattern that influenced their decisions to apply for certain types of job. They found no evidence of hiring bias against women except in manual and craft occupations and that the effect of sex discrimination could be exaggerated if occupational aspirations were not taken into account.

Kraus and Yonay (2000) compared the way in which women and men attained workplace authority in female-dominated, mixed, and male-dominated occupations. They found that women have the greatest chances of being given authority when they work in 'male' occupations, arguing that the competition between men and women is weaker in such occupations so that men have less reason to discriminate against women. They observed that men have similar chances regardless of the type of occupation in which they are employed. By contrast, in a meta-analytic study, Davison and Burke (2000) found that female and male applicants received lower ratings when being considered for an opposite-sex-type job.

HRM IN REALITY   WOMEN PUT OFF COMPUTING CAREERS BY GEEKY ENVIRONMENTS

Recent research led by the University of Washington published in the *Journal of Personality and Social Psychology* in 2010 found that the work environment may be a key factor deterring women from careers in computer science.

Lead author Sapna Cheryan, assistant professor of psychology said:

> When people think of computer science the image that immediately pops into many of their minds is of the computer geek surrounded by such things as computer games, science fiction memorabilia and junk food. That stereotype doesn't appeal to many women who don't like the portrait of masculinity that it evokes.

This helps create what the study refers to as 'ambient belonging' – whether an individual feels comfortable in a particular setting.

Sapna Cheryan explained:

> It is the sense you get right away when you walk into a room. You look at the objects and make an instant appraisal of how you would fit with the objects and the people who are typically found in that environment. You also make a judgment of 'I like it here' or 'I don't belong here.'

Researchers recruited 250 female and male students who were not studying computer science to study why the proportion of women in this speciality is decreasing while the proportion in other sciences such as biology, mathematics and chemistry is increasing.

In the first of a series of experiments, participants spent several moments in a small classroom that either contained objects stereotypically associated with computer science such as Star Trek posters, video game boxes and Coke cans, or non-stereotypical items such as nature posters, art, a dictionary and coffee mugs. The students were told the room was being shared with another class and to ignore the contents.

Participants then completed questionnaires about their attitude toward computer science. Women exposed to the stereotypical setting expressed less interest in computer science than those who saw the non-stereotypical objects. Men did not demonstrate a similar difference.

Other significant findings included:

→ Female participants were given the choice of joining one of two all-female company teams where the only difference was the objects found in the workroom; 82 per cent chose the team with the non-stereotypical setting.

→ Female and male participants were given the choice of similar jobs at one of two companies with equal gender distribution in their workforces. Both groups preferred the non-stereotypical work environment, but women's preferences were significantly stronger. Women also felt less of a sense of ambient belonging in the stereotypical work environment compared to men.

→ Participants were questioned about their attitudes toward a Web design company and were asked to choose between identical job offers from two such companies. Women were more likely to opt for the non-stereotypical company while men had the opposite preference. The more women perceived the stereotypical environment as masculine, the less interested they were in the company concerned.

Sapna Cheryan concluded:

> These studies suggest objects such as science fiction books and Star Trek posters communicate whether or not a person belongs in an environment. Instead of trying to change the women who do not relate to the stereotype, our research suggests that changing the image of computer science so that more women feel they fit in the field will go a long way to recruiting them into computer science.
>
> We want to attract more people to computer science. The stereotype is not as alienating to men as women, but it still affects them as well. A lot of men may also be choosing to not enter the field

because of the stereotype. We need to broaden the image of the field so both women and men feel more welcome. In workplaces and universities we can do this by changing the way offices, hallways and labs look. The media can also play a role by updating the image of computer science. It would be nice for computer scientists in movies and television to be typical people, not only computer geeks.

What inhibits some women from technological careers?

Source: Reprinted with permission from HRM Guide USA (http://www.hrmguide.com).

Sexual harassment

Aspects of male culture can be distinctly unattractive both to women and men. From school to shopfloor, locker room to office, the culture of masculinity expresses itself in 'jokes' revolving around three stereotypes of sexuality (Mills and Murgatroyd, 1991: 78):

→ The ideal, or 'real man' syndrome – toughness, football and so on.

→ Definitions of males as 'not-females'.

→ The normality of heterosexuality.

Ford (2000) found experimental evidence to suggest that when people who are high in hostile sexism are exposed to sexist jokes they become increasingly tolerant of sex discrimination.

In office and managerial environments **sexual harassment** – ranging from unwelcome comments on appearance to physical advances – remains common. Sexual harassment is a difficult topic for managers to deal with, since it involves personal relationships and the individual interpretations of those involved (see Key concept 5.9). The issue has often been trivialized or ignored in a 'conspiracy of silence'.

KEY CONCEPT 5.9 SEXUAL HARASSMENT

Definitions vary considerably but most are agreed that it is sexual attention which is unwanted, repeated, and affects a person's work performance or expectations. However, it is possible for one incident to be sufficiently severe to be regarded as harassment. It differs from sexual banter or flirting since it is one-way; it does not have the involvement and acceptance of both parties. In the USA, the Equal Employment Opportunity Commission has extended the definition of sexual harassment to include a range of actions that lead to a 'hostile work environment'. This definition includes unwelcome touching, joking, teasing, innuendos, slurs, and the display of sexually explicit materials.

Increasingly, employers can face legal action for sexual harassment by one employee against another. Even in situations that do not proceed to formal complaints or tribunals, the consequences for workplace morale can be significant. At the very least, co-workers are likely to be aware of an awkward atmosphere. Victims may suffer anxiety or depression, adversely affecting concentration and productivity. The likelihood of absenteeism is increased and victims frequently leave to escape harassment. There may also be an impact on non-work relationships.

Employers have a moral duty to protect staff from sexual harassment. In general, if employers tolerate sexual harassment they convey the impression that one gender does not deserve respect; they are prepared to sacrifice motivation and commitment; they must accept the consequences for efficiency. Organizations can deal with sexual harassment by (Moynahan, 1993):

→ Surveying the organization to determine the extent of sexual harassment.

→ Writing and circulating a strongly worded policy indicating possible disciplinary action.

→ Providing an effective reporting mechanism, protecting the rights of accusers and the accused.

→ Packaged workshops, which help to define harassment and prevent 'misunderstandings'.

→ Assertiveness training, perhaps particularly appropriate for women working in jobs which have traditionally been regarded as male, which encourages the confidence to provide verbal or even written feedback to unwanted behaviour. The ability to say 'no' firmly and at an early stage is particularly effective.

→ Gender-awareness training to emphasize different perceptions of teasing and 'harmless fun' between men and women.

Some jobs inevitably have greater risk attached from clients and customers, such as social work, nursing and policing. However, in an Australian study of social working, sexual advances were found to be the least prevalent of hostile actions (Koritsas *et al.*, 2010).

Legal definitions of sexual harassment fall into one of two types:

Quid pro quo. A narrow, traditional definition of sexual harassment as a demand by a person in power, for example a supervisor, for sexual favours from a subordinate in return for a job, pay increase, promotion, transfer or other benefit.

Hostile environment. A wider definition, including unwelcome sexual advances that have the effect of creating a hostile, intimidating, abusive or offensive working environment.

Clarke (2006a) examines concerns raised by employers about consensual sexual relationships occurring at work. The study suggests that the link between sexual relationships and sexual harassment is sometimes used as a justification for regulating relationships, particularly hierarchical ones. There also can be a problem of harassment when relationships end. Clarke comments that the willingness of employers, particularly in the USA, to prohibit or regulate relationships might not be motivated by concern for women's equality at work. Recent changes to the law on sexual harassment in the UK might encourage British employers to consider prohibiting or regulating sexual relationships, but there are countervailing legal principles to be considered, such as anti-discrimination law and privacy rights. The study concludes that sex discrimination law should be directed to ensuring that unacceptable behaviour is not tolerated rather than prohibiting consensual relationships.

ETHNIC DIVERSITY AND DISCRIMINATION

Most countries have populations of different ethnic origins, typically highlighted by colour or religious differences. Few countries have true equality between these groups.

Racism is commonly equated with hostility and prejudice. The media tends to associate the issue with abuse and violence perpetrated by neo-fascist groups. In general, however, such organizations lack widespread power and influence. The perception of racism as obvious prejudicial opinions and attitudes obscures more insidious forms of discrimination (Sivanandan, 1991). Racism cannot be reduced to 'human nature and individual fallibility' which leave the state, politics, and 'major structural aspects of contemporary life out of focus' (Husband, 1991: 50).

Howitt and Owusu-Bempah (1990: 397) conclude that 'seeing racism solely as a form of interpersonal antagonism not only sanitizes it, but prevents us from defining ourselves as racist if we do not *feel* racial hatred'. Hence stereotypes appear that are not seen as 'prejudiced': '...Asian women are seen as "passive" or "hysterical" or subject to oppressive practices within the family; there is the stereotype of the strong dominant Afro-Caribbean woman as the head of the household; and the description of the over-aggressive African woman' (Sayal, 1990: 24).

Subeliani and Tsogas (2005) studied the diversity management practices of Rabobank, a major bank in the Netherlands. They found that these were primarily directed at attracting ethnic customers rather than improving the quality of working life and career prospects of ethnic minority employees who remained segregated in lower positions and not allowed openly to express their culture and religion. Indigenous participants in an environmental management programme in Australia were marginalized by the formal governance structure which disguised power imbalances and exploitation (Carter and Hill, 2007). The UK's largest employer, the National Health Service has an extremely diverse workforce but has singularly failed in offering promotion prospects to non-white staff (Kalra *et al.*, 2009).

Foster and Harris (2005) examined the way in which managing diversity was understood and applied in one large, long-established British retailing company. They found that business benefits attributed to diversity management are appealing to employers. However, the concept lacks clarity for line managers both in terms of what it is and how it should be implemented within the framework of anti-discrimination legislation. They suggest that line managers are familiar with the value of demonstrating a common approach in decision-making as the key defence against claims of discriminatory treatment. Consequently they tend to regard a diversity management agenda concerned with recognizing and responding to individual differences as more likely to lead to claims of unequal treatment. They argue that, in addition to the operational context, employers need to take account of the tensions facing line managers, their interpretation of diversity management and perceptions of fair treatment.

Stewart and Perlow (2001) looked at applicant race, job status and interviewers' racial attitudes in relation to unfair selection decisions. They found that interviewers with more negative attitudes toward black people showed greater confidence in their decision to hire a black applicant rather than a white applicant for a low-status job and to give a high-status job to a white candidate rather than a black candidate. Frazer and Wiersma (2001) conducted an experiment with 88 white US undergraduates who were asked to look at paper credentials and then interview a high or low-quality black or white applicant. Black and white applicants were 'hired' in equal proportion. But when the interviewers were asked to recall the experience one week later, they rated the answers from black applicants as being significantly less intelligent than the answers given by white applicants. Frazer and Wiersma explain this by postulating that the undergraduates had negative schemas towards black people which they suppressed in the public situation of making a hiring decision, but these negative stereotypes were revealed when unobtrusive measures were used. A study in Austria and Germany suggests that in the case of Muslims race/ethnicity and religion are compounded (Forstenlechner and Al-Waqfi, 2010).

Murji (2006) examines the use of stereotyped images in a series of advertisements that formed part of the 'personal responsibility' campaign by the Commission for Racial Equality (CRE). The aim was to raise awareness of racial stereotyping and, in one case, to provoke members of the public into complaining about the images presented. The CRE was the main body charged with implementing and monitoring anti-racism in the UK and the use of racial stereotypes has been controversial, though not always in anticipated ways. It has been argued that the CRE's use of stereotypes is based on questionable evidence, on a problematic conception of positive and negative images, and that it fails to consider how the images can be read in diverse ways. Murji argues that the CRE seemed to rely on a quasi-essentialist view of race and racism and consequently appears unable to engage with racism in its diverse manifestations.

Another significant aspect of the problem is not so much **racial discrimination** as racial disadvantage. This arises from the inability of the liberal-minded middle classes to perceive the structural advantages that contribute to their own success. Dominelli (1992: 165) argues:

> It is the subtle presence of racism in our normal activities, coupled with our failure to make the connections between the personal, institutional and cultural levels of racism which make it so hard for white people to recognize its existence in their particular behaviour and combat it effectively.

Mason (2000) evaluates the concept of 'pre-labour market inequality' – essentially, the class and cultural background of individuals – and concludes that it has an undoubted impact on individual well-being and intergenerational mobility. But the manner in which class background has its effects is not clear. A higher class position may create an advantage in skill acquisition. Alternatively, higher social status may increase access to people in positions of power and authority. Research and media comment on issues such as choice of school tend to focus on class while ignoring the racial element (Byrne, 2009). Shiner and Modood (2002) observe that young people from ethnic minority backgrounds in Britain are admitted into university in large numbers but class or culturally based institutional biases result in their concentration in the new university sector. Such universities are grossly underfunded in comparison with more established institutions and are less favoured by 'blue chip' recruiters. In the US, faced with disinterest from hiring organizations, career centre staff were found to be favouring white students in comparison to African-American and Latino students (Damaske, 2009). Also in the US black students tend to be particularly isolated when they do attend an elite university (McClintock, 2010).

HRM IN REALITY BETTER EDUCATION BUT WORSE JOB PROSPECTS FOR MINORITIES

Research by Christian Dustmann and Nikolaos Theodoropoulos from the Centre for Research and Analysis of Migration at University College London, published in *Oxford Economic Papers* in 2010, found that members of Britain's ethnic minority communities, whether born abroad or in the UK, tend to be better educated than their white British-born peers but are less likely to be employed.

The study analyzed data from the British Labour Force Survey from 1979 to 2005. Conducted by the Office for National Statistics, this categorizes ethnic background as white, Indian, Pakistani, black Caribbean, black African, Bangladeshi or Chinese.

Comparing women born in Britain, researchers found that those identifying as Pakistani are 25 per cent less likely to be in employment than their white peers and those as Bangladeshi 47 per cent less likely. In the early 1980s Pakistani and Bangladeshi women born outside Britain had 46 per cent and 60 per cent lower probability of employment respectively than white British-born counterparts.

The study found that British-born members of ethnic minority communities are better educated than their parents' generation born outside the UK and white peers. This improvement is greater for the majority of

British-born ethnic minority groups than for whites. Researchers conclude that this is indicative of the value placed on education but acknowledge differences between communities. The study found that of individuals born in Britain between 1963 and 1975, half of Chinese descent went to university, compared with 15 per cent of black-Caribbeans and 20 per cent of whites.

About 46 per cent of British-born ethnic minorities live in London compared with 10 per cent of their white peers. Consequently the former group tend to earn slightly more, particularly women. However, analysis suggests that if educational attainment and regional distribution were the same in both groups, British-born ethnic minorities would earn less than their white counterparts. This would especially affect men with an estimated discrepancy of nine per cent.

Christian Dustmann commented:

Our research shows that individuals of ethnic-minority descent born in Britain invest considerably into education, and more so than their British-born white peers. However, it is concerning that on average British-born ethnic minorities, and in particular men, would have a wage disadvantage if they had the same education, and lived in the same region, as their white British-born peers.

How would you explain the differences in attainment between the ethnic groups?

Source: Reprinted with permission from HRM Guide UK (http://www.hrmguide.co.uk/).

Ben-Tovim *et al.* (1992) criticize the ideology of 'colour blindness' and note other rationalizations for ignoring racism: that raising the question is divisive; that the problems of the ethnic minorities are the same as those of the white population, or the working-class, the inner cities, and so on. Awad, Cokley and Ravitch (2005) investigated the relationship between colour-blind attitudes, modern racist attitudes, and attitudes toward affirmative action. Detractors of affirmative action maintain that use of race-conscious policies to remedy past discrimination is contra-indicative of a colour-blind society. Supporters maintain that while a colour-blind society may be desirable, acts of past discrimination and current institutional racism make it necessary to use race-conscious policies. The study found that after controlling for race and sex, colour-blind attitudes emerged as the strongest predictor of attitudes toward affirmative action, followed by modern racism.

Braham *et al.* (1992: 106) suggest that widening the definition of discrimination to include indirect or **institutional racism** provides a better understanding of the barriers faced by ethnic minorities (see Key concept 5.10). Institutional racism is virtually unrecognized in commercial organizations but remains a contentious issue in the public sector – for example the London Metropolitan Police (Shiner, 2010). It is important to acknowledge the wide range of practices involved – some much more obvious than others. Rejecting the proposition that all institutions are uniformly racist, Braham *et al.* argue that 'the kind of procedures … that disadvantage black people *also* disadvantage other groups'. The 'cloning' proocess is focused on replicating the people in power rather than discriminating against any particular group.

KEY CONCEPT 5.10 INSTITUTIONAL RACISM

Institutional racism is an indirect and largely invisible process. It is a term encompassing the often unintentional barriers that serve to disadvantage members of ethnic minority groups in all aspects of organizational structure, for example selection and promotion procedures. It can be compared with concepts such as cloning and the glass ceiling.

HRM IN REALITY   DIVERSITY TRAINING DOESN'T WORK

Diversity training programmes have failed to eliminate bias and increase the number of minorities in management, despite the fact that many corporations have spent increasing amounts of money on this area according to a paper published in the *American Sociological Review* in 2006. Alexandra Kalev of the University of California, Berkeley, Frank Dobbin, professor of sociology in Harvard University's Faculty of Arts and Sciences, and Erin Kelly of the University of Minnesota, conclude that such efforts to mitigate managerial bias ultimately fail. In contrast, programmes that establish responsibility for diversity, such as equal opportunity staff positions or diversity task forces, have proved more effective.

Frank Dobbin said:

> For the past 40 years companies have tried to increase diversity, spending millions of dollars a year on any number of programs without actually stopping to determine whether or not their efforts have been worth it. Certainly in the case of diversity training, the answer is no. The only truly effective way to increase the presence of minorities and women in managerial positions is through programs that create organizational responsibility. If no one is specifically charged with the task of increasing diversity, then the buck inevitably gets passed *ad infinitum.* To increase diversity, executives must treat it like any other business goal.

This study is described as the first to examine the efficacy of diversity programmes based on the actual change in minority representation in management positions. The authors examined reports submitted to the Equal Employment Opportunity Commission by private sector establishments and conducted a sample survey on the history of diversity programmes within the companies concerned.

These were categorized into three groups: organizational responsibility programmes such as task forces or staff positions; managerial bias programmes such as diversity training; and programmes that created networking or mentoring opportunities. The data showed that organizational responsibility programmes were the most effective. Diversity task forces yielded the greatest results, increasing the proportion of white women in management positions by 14 per cent, black women by 30 per cent, and black men by 10 per cent.

The study found that diversity training aimed at reducing managerial bias may actually increase it. Programmes in this group were followed by a six per cent decline in the proportion of black women in management. White women benefited modestly with a six per cent increase. Social networking improved representation of white women, but lowered that of black men. Mentoring programmes showed a strong positive effect for black women. Across the board, diversity programmes benefited white women the most, followed by black women, with black men benefiting the least.

Frank Dobbin commented: 'Although the likelihood of minorities holding management positions has increased, the raw percentages of minorities in management remain quite low.'

Why doesn't diversity training work?

Source: Reprinted with permission from HRM Guide USA (http://www.hrmguide.com/).

OTHER FORMS OF DISCRIMINATION

Disabled people are among the most disadvantaged because barriers to work are not only social and psychological but also physical. Quota systems for the employment of disabled people have largely been ineffective because of inadequate supervision by governments. Also, where social legislation for the disabled is weak, companies have found it comparatively easy to argue that they cannot provide suitable access or facilities to meet their needs.

Countries including Canada and the USA have instigated their own legislation. After decades of ineffective quotas, the UK was the first country in the European Union to introduce **Disability Discrimination Acts** in 1995 and 2005 (subsequently subsumed by the **Equality Act** that came into force in 2010). These Acts made it illegal for businesses to discriminate against disabled people as employees or customers. Discrimination on the grounds of age is prevalent but often unrecognized. Some countries such as Canada, Australia, New Zealand and the USA have legislated against **ageism** and a European Union Directive compelled all member states to introduce legislation against ageism by the year 2006. Prior to the introduction of age discrimination legislation, blatant ageism was common in job advertisements.

HRM IN REALITY — EQUALITY REPORT: HOW FAIR IS BRITAIN?

The first triennial report from the Equality and Human Rights Commission (EHRC) published in October 2010 concludes that while Britain has made good progress in addressing inequalities and tolerating diversity, significant barriers to a fairer society remain. 'How fair is Britain?' gives insight into opportunities and outcomes for people in Britain according to age, gender, disability, ethnicity, religion or belief, sexual orientation and transgender status. It considers fundamental areas such as life expectancy, health, education and employment as well as security, support and power.

Trevor Phillips, chair of the EHRC said:

> Britain is a country which is more tolerant than at any time in living memory, more intolerant of discrimination – but which has yet to live up to its own aspirations. In short, we are a more fair-minded people than previous generations – but we are not yet a fair society.

With supplementary research into the area of employment conducted by the Policy Studies Institute, the report confirms that the percentage of women and black people in work has increased by twice the average between the mid-1990s and 2006–2008. The increase for Bangladeshi and Pakistani people is three times the average. Only 25 per cent of British Muslim women are in paid employment. Indian and Chinese people are twice as likely to be employed in the professions as their white British counterparts.

The economic situation is restricting opportunities for those without qualifications. The employment rate for men who also have disabilities has fallen by 50 per cent since the 1970s.

The Commission highlights continuing occupational segregation in the job market. Examples cited include 25 per cent of Pakistani men whose main work is taxi driving and the gender differential in public service employment (over 40 per cent of women compared to 15 per cent of men).

This contributes to a persistent pay gap. The report finds that, on average, a 40-year old man working in the private or voluntary sector earns 27 per cent more than his female equivalent.

The report cites some evidence that black graduates may earn a quarter less than white counterparts. Men with disabilities earn about 11 per cent less than other male employees. Comparing women with disabilities to men without, the gap increases to 31 per cent. Pay gaps and insecure employment contribute to poverty in later life.

In Britain, women workers continue to predominate in some sectors but are significantly under-represented in others. Examples include: personal services (83 per cent); secretarial and administrative jobs (77 per cent); architects, planners and surveyors (14 per cent) and engineering (six per cent).

Lesbian, gay and bisexual employees and those with disabilities are about twice as likely to report discrimination, bullying or harassment in the workplace than other workers.

Trevor Phillips said:

> For some, the gateways to opportunity appear permanently closed, no matter how hard they try, whilst others seem to have been issued with an 'access all areas' pass at birth. Recession,

demographic change and new technology all threaten to deepen the fault lines between insiders and outsiders.

In a report for independent think tank Civitas, Peter Saunders, professor emeritus of sociology at the University of Sussex, challenges some of the conclusions in the report, particularly the notion that unequal outcomes are inevitably unfair. For example, he argues that men and women should be free to choose career paths that best utilize their skills and interests. The low representation of Bangladeshi and Pakistani women in the British workforce reflects a cultural emphasis on traditional gender roles, rather than prejudice on the part of employers.

David Green, director of Civitas commented:

> [The EHRC's] determination to treat every group disparity as the result of discrimination and it's enthusiasm for using 'corrective measures' to alter the facts on the ground is likely to multiply injustices rather than rectify them.

Is it fair to accept inequality on the basis of culture?

Source: Reprinted with permission from HRM Guide UK (http://www.hrmguide.co.uk).

 SUMMARY

Equality of opportunity is both a matter of social justice and sound economic sense. Voluntary approaches to minimize discrimination have been largely ineffective and most developed countries have introduced some form of anti-discrimination legislation. There has been a tendency towards all-embracing laws in recent years, increasingly linked to human rights legislation. Granting opportunity is beneficial to organizational effectiveness as well as personal success. The strategic management of diversity leads to a wider range of ideas and abilities, offering greater scope for innovation and competitive performance in the future.

This chapter focused on four areas of workplace discrimination: gender, race/ethnicity, disability and age. We observed that all societies appear to favour certain groups more than others and that most developed societies have attempted to combat prejudice, favouritism and discrimination by introducing relevant laws. Each of the forms of discrimination that we have covered has complex causes that are not easily countered by legislation.

FURTHER READING

1 *The Dynamics of Managing Diversity: A Critical Approach*, 3rd edition, by Gill Kirton and Anne-Marie Greene (Butterworth-Heinemann, 2010) provides a comprehensive discussion of the subject.

2 *Equality and Discrimination: The New Law* by Brian Doyle, Catherine Casserley, Simon Cheetham, Vivienne Gay and Oliver Hyams (Jordan Publishing, 2010), is a comprehensive, practical analysis of the new anti-discrimination law in the UK.

3 *The Glass Ceiling in the 21st Century: Understanding Barriers to Gender Equality* by Manuela Barreto, Michelle K. Ryan, and Michael T. Schmitt (American Psychological Association, 2009) takes a detailed look at barriers to women's career advancement.

4 *The Spirit Level: Why Equality Is Better For Everyone* by Richard Wilkinson and Kate Pickett (Penguin, 2010) covers a wide range of aspects beyond employment.

REVIEW QUESTIONS

1 Distinguish between equal opportunities and the management of diversity. How is it possible to justify either in a commercial organization?

2 Is positive discrimination an effective method of ensuring equal opportunities? Are there any circumstances in which jobs should be reserved for specific individuals or groups without being unfair?

3 Is it true to say that anti-discrimination legislation has had a major effect on equal opportunities in the workplace?

4 Why are women and members of minority groups placed in unfavourable occupational categories?

5 What is occupational segregation and what part does it play in the process of discrimination?

6 Review the evidence for racial discrimination being a more subtle process than overt prejudice.

7 Why does racial discrimination affect some minority groups more than others?

8 Given the reducing proportion of younger people in most developed countries, what could be done to encourage the employment of older workers?

9 What are the limitations on employment of the disabled? What can be done to improve the situation?

CASE STUDIES FOR DISCUSSION AND ANALYSIS

Frank and Margaret/The Black Workers' Group

1 Most people think Frank is a nice guy. He is a good networker, knows everyone in the company and is always the first to buy a round of drinks at any social event. He is married, has three children and an attractive house in a very expensive area. He is the senior accounts controller in the purchasing contracts department and is thought to run a very efficient department. For several years he had a relationship with Margaret from government sales. This broke up in a somewhat emotional fashion last December when he finally told her that he had no intention of leaving his wife.

Audrey, the government sales coordinator has come to see you regarding some stories that are being told in her department. It seems that Margaret has been telling people that Frank is not entirely honest. She has claimed that he has been taking bribes from contractors, accepting cash, holidays and improvements for his house in return for signing contracts. Margaret has not said this in Audrey's presence because Audrey is a rather straightlaced person who has always made it clear that she disapproved of the relationship. Audrey and Margaret do not get on very well as a result.

You are the general manager responsible for these departments. How would you proceed?

2 The borough of Kenwood is situated on the outskirts of a large city. It is predominantly populated by white, middle-class people and is considered reasonably affluent by comparison with its inner city neighbours. Just under 20 per cent of residents are over pensionable age, of whom seven per cent are over 75 years. The vast majority continue to live in their own homes, an increasing proportion living alone. The ageing population has significant resource implications for the local authority.

The Social Services department is responsible for the home care service that comprises three full-time managers and a team of 40 part-time women workers. In addition to providing practical help and social support to their elderly clients, they are often the first people to be alerted to a deterioration in a person's situation. They are a crucial element in enabling people to stay in their own homes, saving the local authority enormous sums of money. However, their status does not reflect their true importance to the community and the section is regularly scrutinized for potential budget cuts.

The local authority has an equal opportunities policy which 'strives towards elimination of discrimination within the workplace'. The Social Services department had noted that the few black staff recruited were in low-paid or insecure posts and tended not to stay long. To try to prevent the policy remaining no more than a piece of paper, it was decided to set up an equal opportunities monitoring committee. This has met quarterly for the last three years and comprises staff representing all grades within Social Services, plus representatives from the main human resources department and two co-opted councillors. It is seen as undesirable to have such a group entirely made up of white representatives so the few black staff available are under constant pressure to volunteer for membership.

One exception to the tendency of black staff to stay no more than a few months is Mary, a middle-aged black woman who has worked for the local authority for 17 years, always as a home carer. She is a tolerant person who likes the flexibility of the work. She has regularly encountered clients whose questions and comments are inadvertently offensive and insensitive but has said little to her managers. However, having been allocated to a couple whose racism is overt and sustained, Mary made a complaint to her harassed line manager, who sympathized and re-allocated a white worker to the couple concerned. Mary got on with her job without further comment. Over the next few weeks the manager thought about her own response, felt it had been inadequate, and referred the incident to the equal opportunities monitoring committee. The reaction of group members was diverse:

What do you expect? Old people are always unreasonable about everything.

They may well be suffering from dementia; if so, they can't be held responsible.

Living in this area, they're probably not used to black people and don't know how to react.

Would Mary like any further action?

We did all we could in practical terms – we can't withdraw the service from them.

The line manager should have visited and confronted them.

Oh dear, how awful.

Has this sort of thing happened before, do we know?

Black staff are particularly discriminated against and should receive appropriate support.

The final response came from one of two black members. He proposed a Black Workers' Support Group, open to anybody working for the local authority who defined themselves as black. The group would meet every two months within paid working time. The existence and purpose of the group would be made known to other colleagues who would be asked to demonstrate support by enabling participants to attend. Benefits to the local authority might accrue from being seen to be implementing its own equal opportunities policy and potentially retaining staff who would feel less isolated and marginalized.

The majority of group members had considerable reservations about this proposal although most did not say so openly. While most doubts centred on the impact on overstretched departments and the possible adverse reaction of colleagues asked to cover extra duties, one of the councillors was more direct: 'Where exactly will this end? In no time at all we'll be expected to pay for part-time workers' support groups, Irish workers support groups, etc., etc.'

The proposal was referred to the senior managers' meeting for further consideration. There was more support within this forum, but it was felt that the Black Workers' Support Group should be chaired by a senior manager. Black staff pointed out that the group would not operate on such hierarchical terms and, in any event, all managers of the grade proposed were white. Managers'

expectation that they would receive copies of the minutes of each meeting met with a similar response. While uneasy with their lack of control, senior managers felt it would be more controversial to refuse permission. The Black Workers' Support Group went ahead and the local authority began to receive enquiries about the scheme from outside the organization and praise for its initiative. With significant cuts proposed to the home help service in the next financial year, and with school-age children to care for, Mary has felt too busy to attend.

How effective is the equal opportunities policy in Kenwood?

Did Mary's supervisor make the right decision?

What is the value of the Black Workers' Support Group?

CHAPTER 6
Recruitment

LEARNING OBJECTIVES

The purpose of this chapter is to:

→ Discuss the meaning and significance of recruitment in its organizational context.

→ Provide a typology of recruitment strategies.

→ Critically review preliminary information-gathering techniques.

→ Discuss the merits of references and biodata.

RECRUITMENT AS A TEXTBOOK SUBJECT

In Chapter 4 we discussed the 'why' of resourcing, evaluating strategies and plans that guide the process. We considered also the initial information gathering from job analysis and the sometimes unwise strategies employed by selectors. This chapter and the next follow on with an examination of the operational elements of resourcing, commonly termed recruitment and selection.

Recruitment and selection are major issues for human resource specialists. HRM and other management literature puts great emphasis on the process of selecting and orienting new recruits. There is no shortage of material on these topics and, together with performance assessment, they are critical elements of effective people management. Not surprisingly, therefore, these aspects of employee resourcing have attracted a great deal of attention from human resource practitioners and occupational psychologists. As we will see in Chapter 7, the topic range has a well rehearsed familiarity because selection methods are regarded as basic tools for human resource managers. Indeed, the underlying 'best practice' model has achieved the status of holy writ in certain quarters, with any deviation regarded as heresy.

Iles and Salaman (1995: 203) argue: 'The limitation of the psychological and personnel-driven approaches to selection is that they are entirely, if understandably, concerned with improving the efficiency of the processes, and not with understanding their wider provenance and significance.' And again (Iles, 2001: 134): '... despite the need for a fuller understanding of these processes, the bulk of existing social science and HR literature is concerned primarily and solely with assessing the efficiency of these processes, often in rather descriptive, prescriptive and atheoretical ways.'

We cannot discuss how recruitment and selection take place without asking why certain techniques are used in preference to others. Iles (2001) sees much deeper consequences, meaning and significance in the exercise and justification of recruitment and selection processes. Within the HRM paradigm, they are not simply mechanisms for filling vacancies. Recruitment and redundancy can be viewed as key 'push' and 'pull' levers for organizational change. Recruitment and selection allow management to determine and gradually modify the behavioural characteristics and competences of the workforce with a trend towards increasing sophistication in choice of methods in countries as disparate as the UK (Branine, 2008), where management fads are favoured, and Egypt (El-Kot and Leat, 2008), where there is considerable resistance to western notions of selection.

MATCHING PEOPLE AND JOBS

Focusing on in-house resourcing, how can we make the best use of people? In practice, it is rarely possible to match perfectly the requirements of an individual job with the skills and abilities of the people available. Square pegs in round holes are not only bad for the organization: wrongly placed workers are often unhappy and bored, or anxious about being out of their depth. In line with the three basic recruitment strategies outlined in Table 6.1, any mismatch between person and job can be resolved in one of the following ways (Drenth and Algera, 1987):

→ Select the best qualified person for the job ('right person' approach).

→ Change job characteristics to fit the abilities of the people employed ('culture-fit' model).

→ Train people to perform more effectively (flexible person approach).

TABLE 6.1
Recruitment
strategies

Approach	Objective	Organization	HR emphasis
1 *Suitability – right person for the job*	Get the job done	Traditional Hierarchical Fixed job categories	Job analysis HR planning Selection
2 *Malleability – fit the culture*	Fit in with today's organization	Small core Strong culture Variable periphery	Appraisal Job training Development
3 *Flexibility – employee for tomorrow*	Build a competitive organization	Flexible Lean Virtual	Performance Skills training Talent management

An organization may choose any one or a combination of these methods. However, all depend on the ability to identify and measure the characteristics necessary for successful job performance. At first sight this seems simple and obvious but a close examination reveals how complex it can be. People can perform a particular job successfully for varied and sometimes contrasting reasons. For example, a good manager may be personally well-organized and able to clear mountains of paperwork quickly. Another manager may deal with similar tasks equally efficiently through skilful delegation. As such, it is the *totality of effectiveness* of the individual that matters rather than specific skills and abilities. Effectiveness also depends on context. Most jobs require an individual to work within a team where required skills or qualities can be spread between its members. In such a case it may not be necessary for every team member to possess all qualities needed for effective performance.

HRM IN REALITY NEW TRENDS IN HIRING

Organizations are planning to increase hiring as the economy recovers but are making significant changes to their recruitment strategies according to research from *Job Search Television Network* (JSTN), a leading video and social media based recruiting company. Cuts to recruiting staffs and budgets during the recession have resulted in a greater emphasis on lower cost, efficient technological solutions. The report notes increasingly targeted use of social media in the recruitment process.

Roger Stanton, CEO of Job Search Television Network, commented:

> LinkedIn and Facebook with links to video has been hot for a while, but now we're seeing clients 'micro-target' employees using niche blogs and LinkedIn groups. For example, one of our clients successfully uses niche blogs to locate workers with very specific types of financial service backgrounds. They started doing this when a new

blog showed up on JSTN's client metric report. When they posted a video to the blog, it quickly became a 'home run'. Clients are finding sites they weren't aware of because JSTN's video provides highly detailed traffic metrics and they can make changes on the fly.

The study also considered the proportion of viewers who go on to apply for the position advertised.
Roger Stanton explained:

We will usually see an enormous spike in viewership for a position right after a video is placed on websites and social media. With clients hitting average conversion rates of viewers to applicants around 18.8 per cent, the video is far exceeding other sources. In some cases, the conversion rate is as high as 45 per cent! That can mean thousands of people have seen the video for a job, at very little cost to the employer and it provides very powerful employment branding. The candidates who do apply are more likely to be a more qualified fit for the job, since they've seen the video and have responded based on the compelling information they have viewed.

The study found renewed interest in Employment Referral Programs (ERP) in the recruitment process, but again with a different emphasis.
Roger Stanton said:

The idea of ERP programs is coming back in a big way, because it is so much faster and cheaper if you can get a referral from your current employees. The difference this time is that since email readership is going down, particularly among younger employees who prefer social media, companies are using video messaging. The video can be placed on a company's Facebook page, blogs, etc. and is far more likely to get watched and sent to friends via mobile phones. And again,

the traffic results can be closely tracked for ROI [return on investment] purposes.

The study identified mobile phones as the third major trend in hiring for 2010.
Roger Stanton explained:

We knew when payment systems started being developed for cell phones that mobile would replace computers as the center of our digital lives. This is why JSTN was created with the ability to TEXT ID videos to mobile phones. Now with smart phones penetrating the market at exponential rates, we're seeing this really take off. Looking forward, research states that by 2014, over 66 per cent of all mobile data traffic will be video [Cisco Visual Networking Index: Forecast and Methodology, 2009–2014]. One of our clients regularly sends job videos to prospects on cell phones with amazing results. Not only does the receiver actually view the video, they also usually forward it to numerous contacts in their network. The video quickly goes viral.

Roger Stanton concluded:

What these trends point to is that we are truly becoming a video-centric society, with much of that centering on mobile phones. Companies are recognizing that if they want to reach prospective hires, this is where they need to be. And with tight budgets, its not surprising they would turn to these technologies now to reach new candidate pools at low cost while maintaining professional identity. As we come into the fall hiring season, which will ramp up in earnest right after Labor Day, you'll really see these trends as play out in the workplace.

Will the use of social media and mobile videos appeal to all candidates?

Source: Reprinted with permission from HRM Guide USA (http://www.hrmguide.com).

The right person?

Resourcing strategies should maintain the required number and quality of staff within an organization. They should also ensure suitability for its future development. There are two underlying and apparently contradictory approaches in common use (Haire, 1959). The first methodology emphasizes the right (or best) person for the job. The individual is the variable element in the search; the job is fixed. This approach is associated with traditional Western personnel management. People are sought with appropriate abilities and experience to perform the job with minimal training. It implies that individual jobs are relatively long term and unchanging and that people can be 'bought in' at any stage in their careers. Vacancies are filled from the internal or external employment market. When the job is no longer required, the incumbent is disposed of.

This model is conventionally described as 'best practice' in the UK and other free market countries. Accordingly, most texts on recruitment and selection traditionally outline a 'prescriptive approach to recruitment based on a systematic analysis of the requirements of an individual job' (Wright and Storey, 1994: 192). Almost invariably the account focuses on a series of selection techniques with limited discussion of the logic behind the resourcing process. There is rarely a suggestion that any other approach may be worth considering. Wright and Storey also rightly point out that 'best practice' only takes place in the largest organizations. Small and medium-sized enterprises generally recruit in an informal manner and rarely use sophisticated selection methods.

The 'right person' approach attempts to be 'objective'. It requires clear answers to questions such as:

→ Is there a job to fill?

→ If so, what tasks and responsibilities are involved?

→ What qualities, skills or experience are required to perform the tasks?

→ What process will best identify these criteria?

In essence, it is an attempt to find a seven-sided object to fit a seven-sided hole. It is a *discrimination* rather than a selection process: a matching technique that attempts to pin down the 'right' or 'best' applicant. By definition it excludes those people who are believed not to fit – a view of people as objects (Townley, 1994: 94). Townley perceives an underlying belief that 'employees who are carefully and appropriately matched to their jobs are satisfied and productive'. Matching involves generating a taxonomy of qualities and skills (criteria) that are believed to be essential or desirable – including qualifications and experience. In turn a matrix is constructed that ranks candidates in relation to the job criteria and imposes a decision point at which some people are accepted and others rejected. In the simplest case, this process can take place inside a selector's head. In the most complex, it involves elaborate selection techniques, multiple dimensions and rating scales and requires a computer to calculate the resulting matrix. The 'right person' approach functions well when:

→ It is possible to define a job tightly.

→ The job is discrete and separable from other functions.

→ The job is best done by an individual with a specific range of skills.

Frequently, however, these criteria do not apply and jobs are identified for less rational reasons such as:

→ We have *always* had a 'major accounts manager'.

→ Department 'x' *must* handle the task.

→ People *like* it done in a particular way.

The 'right person' model is geared to static, self-satisfied organizations. It meets the needs of the 'job box' model of organizational structure, where people come and go but the job continues indefinitely. It leads to positions being offered to people who match traditional criteria – the kind of people we have always had. It closes the appointments process to people who traditionally have been unsuccessful. In terms of equal opportunities this approach continues to disadvantage people from 'different' backgrounds and alternative outlooks. In essence it is a **cloning** process: resourcing a firm with more of the same people (see Key concept 6.1). It eliminates any opportunity for the organization to be creative or experimental.

KEY CONCEPT 6.1 CLONING

Cloning, or 'elective homogeneity' is the tendency for selectors to pick people like themselves, thereby reducing the breadth of skills and personalities in an organization. Simply matching the set of characteristics possessed by previous successful post holders, it is a safe, conservative way to fill jobs. As a low-risk, but backward-looking approach, it is unlikely to meet the future needs of the organization.

Fit with the organization

The second approach described by Haire focuses on fitting the person to the organization. Jobs are changed and reshaped to make the best use of individuals' skills within the organization. People are permanent but jobs can be varied. If more employees are required, a search is made for individuals who appear to have the personal qualities necessary to 'fit in' with the organization's culture. Personality is more important than technical skills in this context.

Culture fit predominates in the traditional large Japanese company. The emphasis is on matching individuals to organizational culture rather than to organizational structure. Recruitment focuses on young people who can be socialized into the company's way of working. Western managers have taken an interest in this approach in recent decades. It has been justified in terms of attracting creative and innovative employees. However, there is a distinction between creative and plastic minds. In reality, it is a means of hiring more potential clones who have the further 'advantages' of being young, cheap and easy to manage.

Flexibility

A third, more demanding, approach can provide a significant competitive advantage for organizations: recruiting 'flexible employees', prepared for future change and able to contribute rather than conform. Rather than aiming for rigid skills and ability profiles or malleable and gullible personalities, recruit people who are versatile and adaptable. This reflects a long-term strategy, geared towards realizing talent for tomorrow's requirements. It is not simply meeting current needs or filling the organization with compliant clones. The emphasis is on diversity. Organizations should identify a range of individuals required for the future – including 'mavericks to buck the system' and not just 'conformist clones' (Armstrong, 1992: 135). They will require training and development; they will not be docile and managing them may be difficult; but their potential is massively greater than any clone.

Taking this approach, some of the rhetoric of HRM can become reality. Instead of viewing resourcing simply as a matter of recruiting individuals to meet immediate needs, it also widens the long-term pool of skills and abilities. There is a genuine need for integration and coordination between resourcing strategies and other aspects of talent management such as assessment, development and reward. Creative people must be freed from overbearing control. They cannot be managed through compliance: engagement and commitment form the 'glue' that can bind individual talents and innovation to organizational objectives.

All options, including subcontracting, must be considered carefully before hiring new people. This form of flexibility offers long-term benefits but needs people ready for new demands and hence a need for a detailed knowledge of individual jobs, people's capabilities and the range of work to be performed now and in the future.

SELECTORS AND STRATEGIES

The 'right person' approach is entirely concerned with the individual, whereas the 'cultural fit' model is consistent with a focus on teamworking. In practice, the models are easily confused with each other and many selectors apply a mixture of both. Frequently, selectors believe they are using 'best practice' to find the person who meets the specified criteria when, in fact, the person chosen is the one whose face fits. All too often resourcing emphasizes the selection of people who fit existing culture and practice at the expense of future needs.

Why does this occur? Employee resourcing involves risk and uncertainty. Above all, assessors want to avoid the consequences of picking the 'wrong' person. This may be for the valid reason that an unsuitable person will not perform to required standards. However, selectors are also aware of the consequences of an unfortunate choice rebounding directly on themselves (and their reputations). This encourages selectors to take 'safe' decisions minimizing risk of error. The individual clearly identified as a 'good bloke' by the organization and its senior managers becomes an attractive choice.

The in-breeding found at higher levels of management has been described as 'organizational dry rot' (Smith, 1991: 29). Poverty of ideas, stultified thinking and blinkered behaviour can be due to a narrow range of experience. It is imperative, therefore, that resourcing activities should increase the breadth of experience within an organization. To do this the interests of the organization should be divorced from those of any specific stakeholders, including those of its senior managers. However, resourcing costs money directly (e.g. advertising) and indirectly (the time occupied by comparatively well-paid people). As a consequence many organizations avoid the hassle and expense by taking a casual approach to one of the most critical aspects of people management.

HRM IN REALITY WHAT RECRUITERS WANT

A 2010 study from leading North American recruitment firm Rosenzweig & Company highlights how potential employees can best respond to increased use of recruiters as the economy recovers.

Jay Rosenzweig, managing partner said:

> It's been a long while since many people have been in these interviewing situations making it even more important than ever to have a firm grasp of the process well before the interview begins.

The report offers key advice for individuals recruited for a job opportunity:

→ **The headhunter works for the employer, but can also be your friend** – The report points out that recruiters can provide general advice and be used as a sounding board. The recruiter can act as an intermediary between candidates and potential employers, responding to comments or concerns before direct contact takes place.

→ **Retainer v. contingency** – Clarify the basis on which recruiters are being employed. Retainer-based contracts where payment is assured tend to be less focused on quick results and commission, reducing the risk of inappropriate placements.

→ **Sell yourself** – Convey your skills, experience and career plans without overstating your accomplishments. Provide recruiters with sufficient information to promote your candidacy to a potential employer.

→ **Be yourself** – Recruiters and potential employers can detect insincerity. Trying to redefine your background or personality in an attempt to fit a specific role is unlikely to be successful.

→ **Do your homework** – Research your prospective employers including recent financial and operational developments. However, do not present yourself as an expert on the organization.

→ **Try to relax** – Attempting to anticipate questions and preparing answers is likely to be counterproductive. Candidates may be unsuccessful if overeagerness is interpreted as desperation.

→ **Be honest about any other opportunities you are considering** – Both recruiters and potential employers will understand that you may be considering other options but will not appreciate being misled.

→ **Come clean** – Be honest with the recruiter about any past issues that could affect the attitude of a prospective employer. It is better to volunteer potentially negative information than risk it emerging at a later date.

→ **Accept constructive criticism** – If recruiters or potential employers provide constructive criticism, use it as a learning opportunity.

Jay Rosenzweig commented:

Jobseekers have had lean years and very little movement on the jobs front, including at the higher levels. Some people who've survived the recession with their job intact may think they hold all the cards if a company or recruiter calls. But now, more than ever, the best advice is to check your ego at the door and understand the 'buy and sell' process when presented with dream job opportunities. One of the most fundamental rules in this business is to know when to talk and know when to listen.

How important is it for a job applicant to understand the recruiting process?

Source: Reprinted with permission from HRM Guide USA (http://www.hrmguide.com).

Geerlings and van Veen (2006) argue that there is little material in the HR literature on the long–term consequences of selection policies. They simulated job-mobility patterns over time to show how different policies affected different situations. There is a common tendency to take on less capable recruits when there is a shortage of well-qualified people in order to deal with short-term problems. Geerlings and van Veen found that this was counterproductive in the long-term with even a brief deviation from a resourcing strategy inhibiting the achievement of organizational goals for many years thereafter.

MARKETING THE JOB

Following on from our discussion in Chapter 4, if resourcing strategy and planning have identified the need for new or additional work to be performed in-house, it is obviously necessary to make potential applicants aware of any vacancy. Essentially, this is a marketing process conventionally termed 'recruitment' which Lewis (1985: 29) defines as: 'the activity that generates a pool of applicants, who have the desire to be employed by an organization, from which those suitable can be selected.'

Potential candidates may come from an internal trawl of the organization, or from the external job market. The latter are reached through channels such as recruitment advertising, employment agencies, professional associations or word of mouth. Organizations with a strong culture are likely to seek malleable new employees at school leaving or graduate levels. More senior jobs are filled from the internal job market. When companies look for the 'right person', however, detailed personnel specifications may rule out internal candidates.

In each case, the recruitment phase is critical because it determines the range of choice available to the selectors: 'The more effectively this stage is carried out the less important the actual selection of candidates becomes: if a firm can attract 20 high flyers for a job it hardly matters whether they choose amongst these high flyers with a pin, an interview or tests' (Smith, Gregg and Andrews, 1989: 24).

HRM IN REALITY   USING SOCIAL MEDIA TO IMPROVE JOB CHANCES

Until recently, the rules of the game were simple: post your résumé or CV on a host of jobsites and recruiters would come looking for you. But the game has changed and is continuing to evolve, according to recruiters at MRINetwork, one of the world's largest search and recruitment organizations.

Tony McKinnon, president of MRINetwork said:

Social media sites have become increasingly important platforms for finding jobs by facilitating connections and demonstrating the achievements and interests of jobseekers. But capturing the attention of prospective employers and recruiters – who have made the sites a routine part of their searches – has also become more difficult because of the overwhelming amount of information available.

He offers several useful tips to adapt jobseekers' messages so they are more likely to 'go viral':

1 **Keep it simple**. Text should be pruned to a core message and always stick to the point. Don't leave room for misinterpretation. McKinnon advises that any superfluous or flowery language and clever wordplay should be removed. 'Remember, too, that your audience may include many for whom English is a second language.' But, he cautions, brevity should not come at the expense of clarity. People should be able to tell:

→ what your message is

→ why it is important

→ why it affects them personally, and

→ what they should do about it.

2 **Tailor the message to your audience's needs**. The people you want to reach need to see what's in it for them. McKinnon says 'Relate to them by tying your story to what drives them. Make it about them and what they should do about it.' He suggests the use of pronouns such as 'you', 'your', 'our' and 'ours'.

3 **Consider your timing**. Your message could be drowned out if you post at a time when many others do the same. You may get noticed more if you post at an earlier or later time, even if there are fewer people reading their online sources then. Experiment with different timeslots.

4 **Be selective in choosing your channels**. The three most popular channels are Facebook, Twitter and LinkedIn but influential people may be looking at other channels as well such as:

→ Blogs: try blogsearch.google.com, technorati.com, twingly.com, and make friends with key bloggers and try some cross-posting.

→ Groups: with millions of groups a little browsing should locate the most popular ones to join. McKinnon also suggest joining suitable groups on Facebook and LinkedIn where you can post messages and develop a following.

5 **Craft an interesting story**. McKinnon says that, fundamentally, people care about people. 'We all seek connections, so don't just push a bunch of isolated facts. Craft a story and keep spinning it as you send out your messages. Not all your content has to be tied to one single thread, but weaving it into many of your posts will give readers continuity and help keep them coming back for more.'

6 **Push to get the word out**. McKinnon observes that it is hard to predict what might go viral and get noticed. He recommends enlisting the help of friends, colleagues, and other people in your network.

Use every method you can think of, for example: turning your message into a blog post on your own blog, or asking other bloggers to post it or publish a link to it on their blogs. Ask your Twitter followers to re-tweet it. Post it on friends' Facebook walls and ask them to share it with their friends. Post on LinkedIn Groups and send a message to your LinkedIn network to post it as a status update.

McKinnon concludes:

As recruiters, we know how difficult it is for jobseekers to capture the attention of the people who can help them the most. But if you plan your approach, focus your content, pick your medium, and involve your friends, you can significantly increase your chances of getting through the noise.

To what extent is the process of job hunting/ recruitment a game played between applicants and recruiters?

Source: Reprinted with permission from Job Skills Information (http://www.jobskills.info/).

Internal recruitment marketing can take place by word of mouth, staff notices, newsletters, blogs, webcasts, or social networking through media such as Twitter and Facebook. Recruiting may be on a 'one-off' basis or linked to a development programme as discussed in Chapter 9. External recruitment marketing can be done similarly through the Web, other media advertisements, various public and private employment agencies and headhunting. The role of the state varies, with some countries such as Italy requiring official notification to state employment agencies. As with other marketing campaigns the selection of appropriate channels, creativity of vacancy presentation and size of budget will determine success.

INFORMAL RECRUITING

Cultural factors are important in determining the orientation between internal and external job markets. They also influence the nature of recruitment. People may appear to have found their job or career by chance, but this apparent serendipity obscures non-random factors such as personal relationships, social networks and cultural background (McDonald, 2010). In fact, nepotism and cronyism remains the norm in many countries. Arasli and Tumer (2010) point to job stress caused by such practices in the North Cyprus banking sector. Two decades ago Papalexandris (1991) compared multinational corporations operating in Greece and Greek-owned companies. She found that Greek employers preferred to recruit from among relatives, and friends of the owners or existing employees. Advertisements and agencies were used only when this failed to produce suitable candidates. Greek employers paid more attention to recommendations and previous experience than to qualifications such as degrees (Eleftheriou and Robertson, 1999). In contrast, foreign-owned companies followed 'best practice' and focused on younger, inexperienced graduates attracted through agencies and advertisements. Drydakis and Vlassis (2010) studied the consequences of partial attitudes towards applicants in the case of Albanian immigrants to Greece who were 21.4 per cent less likely to be invited for interview than native Greeks.

Formalized introduction schemes along similar lines occur in other countries, serving to perpetuate recruitment from pools of like-minded people. However, they have the benefit of supplying candidates who have a more realistic view of the organization, than people attracted by recruitment advertising. The former have gained their knowledge from the informal network, the latter from PR information. As a result, word-of-mouth applicants are likely to stay longer and be more suitable than recruits obtained by advertising. Word of

TABLE 6.2
Percentage of firms using selected recruitment methods

Recruitment method	2000	2006
Ads in specialist/trade press	86	66
Local newspaper ads	81	79
National newspaper ads	68	45
Jobcentre Plus	68	51
Employment agencies	66	76
Speculative/word of mouth	53+	49
Internet	47	
Company website	–	75
Commercial job board	–	16
Links with education	44	37
Radio/TV	12	7

mouth is discriminatory since it restricts applications to established communities and excludes minority groups who are not part of informal networks (Smith, 1991: 31). Inevitably, people will recommend others from their own in-group even if they have no intention of discriminating.

Informal recruitment is common. More widely, Table 6.2 shows a comparison of UK recruitment methods in 2000 and 2006 (CIPD, 2000, 2006).

At a senior level, **headhunting** has become a common, if not predominant, method of recruitment. Otherwise known as executive search, consultancies are used to locate supposedly 'outstanding' people. The marked absence of women and ethnic minorities in senior positions reveals this to be a further mechanism for cloning.

HRM IN REALITY ANY JOBS GOING FOR ASTRONAUTS?

Superhero, trapeze artist, goddess, astronaut and slave are just some of the jobs people have looked for online, according to an analysis of six million career searches made on Fish4jobs.

'The vast majority of searches done on our site every month are serious ones,' says Fish4jobs publisher Ian Sprackling. However, he continues:

A lot of workers seem to fantasize about a completely new career as a 'superhero' for example, or hope to see a position open as an 'astronaut'. Though we unfortunately can't claim to hold current vacancies for 'billionaires', we do have an enormous range of dream jobs available. For example, the people who thought it would be a laugh to type in 'tree surgeon', 'tarot card reader', 'wine taster' and 'lap dancer' will have been in for a surprise as positions for all four were advertised on the Fish4jobs website over the past month!

The research found that more than 1000 people could not spell common job titles correctly, including 15 different misspellings for 'secretary':

sercretary	sacratary	secreatarie
secrretary	scretary	secutery
secetary	secretie	secitery
sectary	secraterie	secreatire
sacretery	secritarie	secrectree

Apart from 110 people spelling 'secretary' wrongly, 51 people replaced receptionist with anything from 'recepshionist' to 'receiptionist'. Manager became 'meneger', 'managar' and 'manger' for 34 applicants. According to Ian Sprackling:

> Though it's easy to miss out the odd letter here or there when doing a search on a PC, attention to detail is one of the most important things employers look for. Therefore let's hope that the person wanting to become a 'manger' hasn't made the same mistake on his/her CV. However, the people who got it completely wrong and decided they want to become 'recepshionists' or 'secreties' should maybe consider a career change!

Top ten searches for jobs that don't exist comprised:

1 mover and shaker
2 billionaire
3 superhero
4 nun
5 busy bee
6 slave
7 astronaut
8 layabout
9 male porn star
10 trapeze artist.

Top ten unusual searches, where there have been vacancies on Fish4jobs comprised:

1 lap dancer (posted for a club in Blackpool)
2 'car jockey' (an excusive hotel in Scotland wanted 'car jockeys' to park guests' cars)
3 tarot card reader (two vacancies available, one working from a call centre)
4 trainee forensic psychiatrist (postgraduate post in Newcastle)
5 tree surgeon (several vacancies)
6 footwear designer (design company in West Yorkshire)
7 drag racer (company in Basingstoke has sought professional drag car drivers)
8 rectal surgeon (a vacancy was posted for a health professional specializing in 'colorectal surgery')
9 reporter for the local paper (several positions nationwide)
10 'lollipop' lady (over the summer, several councils were seeking school road-crossing attendants).

How would you recruit an astronaut?

Source: Reprinted with permission from HRM Guide UK (http://www.hrmguide.co.uk).

WEB-BASED RECRUITMENT

The Internet has become the dominant recruitment medium in recent years. It has become normal for jobseekers to scan employment sites on the web for opportunities; so much so that many organizations block access to job sites from their workstations to prevent employees from job hunting during working hours.

Most large organizations, and many smaller ones, make extensive use of corporate websites in their recruitment programmes. Typically, general career information is presented in an engaging manner to promote the employer brand and gain interest from prospective applicants. It has become common for the early stages of the selection process to be made accessible online, allowing résumés and CVs to be uploaded, application forms to be completed and preselection tests to be conducted.

HRM IN REALITY RECRUITERS WARY OF SOCIAL MEDIA

Sixty-five per cent of graduate recruiters are wary of using social media and one in seven perceives it as 'dangerous' according to research by recruitment and marketing communications specialists Penna Barkers conducted in 2010. However, nearly half (44 per cent) have some kind of presence on Facebook and one-third have uploaded graduate recruitment videos to YouTube.

Phill Lane, head of planning commented:

We've found that graduate recruiters generally fall into two camps – those that are reticent about using social media to reach out to students, and those that actively embrace these channels. A common concern is that social media allows potential and unsuccessful candidates to post comments that are detrimental to employers' reputations. Such comments are available for all to see, even when they are unfounded or incorrect.

The latest Social Media Audit of 84 graduate recruiters found that 95 per cent acknowledged the importance of keeping up to date with online chatter to assess the impact on organizational image. However 60 per cent felt they did not have sufficient time to do this. More than half (56 per cent) felt unable to monitor their reputation well and more than one-fifth (21 per cent) undertook no monitoring.

The study found that when describing their knowledge and use of social media, nearly a quarter (23 per cent) described themselves as novices and 23 per cent as confident. No respondents considered themselves expert.

Phill Lane said:

Graduate recruiters are often being asked to use social media as part of their day jobs in a way that is very different to their private use of the same channels. They are nearly twice as likely to blog on

behalf of their employer as they are to blog on their own behalf and almost three times more likely to Tweet professionally, so it's no surprise that some of this usage is outside of their comfort zone.

It's also clear that graduate recruiters attach different values to information they view online. We found that they are far more comfortable using traditional recruitment channels to review candidates. Despite the fact that there has been a number of concerns over how much people lie on their CVs, graduate recruiters believe a CV is two and a half times more reliable than information posted on LinkedIn in allowing them to form an opinion of a candidate and eight times as reliable as a Facebook profile.

Other significant findings include:

→ Seven per cent of graduate recruiters are 'evangelical' about the use of social media, 27 per cent 'try not to be too bureaucratic' towards it

→ Ninety per cent think it is important to use social media to manage their reputation

→ Twenty-seven per cent maintain a blog as part of their graduate recruitment strategy

→ Seventy-five per cent are concerned that line managers might be using Facebook to screen candidates

→ Thirty per cent don't know whose responsibility it is to monitor their reputation.

Phill Lane concluded:

What we are trying to do is work with recruiters to develop coherent plans, both for monitoring their reputation online, and also for managing it alongside the rest of their communications channels. By treating social media as part of the channel strategy, offering guidance and training, we are helping employers navigate these challenges and taking away the feeling that getting involved in social media is a risky business.

What are the advantages and disadvantages of online information sources in comparison to more traditional methods?

Source: Reprinted with permission from HRM Guide UK (http://www.hrmguide.co.uk/).

FORMAL RECRUITING

The effectiveness of recruitment is usually measured in terms of expediency – attracting enough minimally qualified applicants. Rarely are the long-term consequences to the organization of cloned and barely adequate employees or the costs of recruitment taken into account. Doubts have also been expressed about the quality of people who are engaged in recruiting. Remarkably, the advertisements placed by recruitment agencies for their own staffing vacancies rarely ask for any knowledge of people management or selection techniques. Almost invariably they emphasize selling skills such as communication, dynamism and youth.

The likelihood of attracting 'suitable' applicants depends on the detail and specificity of the recruitment advertisement or literature. Key factors such as salary, job title, career and travel opportunities obviously influence response rates along with the 'personality' of the organization projected by the advertisement (Nolan and Harold, 2010). Not surprisingly, experienced and inexperienced jobseekers show different reactions to advertisements because the experienced 'read between the lines' (Walker *et al.*, 2008). As examples of marketing, considerable effort and money can be invested in the effectiveness of recruitment advertisements. However, employers do not wish to be swamped with applications from clearly unsuitable people. In some instances, honest job descriptions are designed to put off unwelcome applicants.

HRM IN REALITY JOBSEEKERS WANT TRADITIONAL EMPLOYER CHARACTERISTICS

Interesting work, recognition and reward for good performance and opportunities for promotion attract jobseekers the most, according to an Accenture global recruitment survey conducted in 2006.

The survey also shows that fashionable offerings such as corporate citizenship and diversity programmes are not as attractive to jobseekers as 'traditional' benefits such as robust rewards programmes and personal development opportunities.

A total of 4100 entry-level and experienced jobseekers in 21 countries in the Asia-Pacific region, North and South America, and Europe were surveyed online to identify the career goals they valued most. Accenture carried out the research between November 2005 and March 2006 as part of the company's efforts to make sure that it remains competitive, relevant and attractive to the most talented applicants.

'Challenging and interesting work' was selected as a priority employer characteristic by 60 per cent of all respondents with the potential for accomplishments to be recognized and rewarded coming a close second (58 per cent of respondents).

The others in the top five characteristics of greatest interest to jobseekers were:

→ opportunities for fast career growth (44 per cent);

→ indications that an employer was well-established and likely to prosper in the long term (42 per cent); and

→ indications that an organization has a particular focus on its employees (42 per cent).

Main findings of the survey:

Percentage of jobseekers selecting priority employer characteristic

1   Challenging and interesting work (60 per cent)

2   Recognizes and rewards accomplishments (58 per cent)

3   Provides an opportunity for fast career growth and advancement (44 per cent)

4   Financially strong/will prosper in the long run (42 per cent)

5   People-oriented (42 per cent)

6   Offers flexible work arrangements (41 per cent)

7   Innovative (33 per cent)

8   Approachable (27 per cent)

9   Team-oriented environment (27 per cent)

10   Global company (26 per cent)

11   Offers a variety of work (26 per cent)

12   Smart (21 per cent)

13   Collaborative environment (17 per cent)

14   Committed to the community/corporate citizenship (16 per cent)

15   Diverse workforce (16 per cent)

'Interestingly, we found that what is considered important to potential recruits was remarkably consistent across geographies,' said John Campagnino, Accenture's global director of recruitment. Also notable was the fact that while we know from our own employees that corporate social responsibility and diversity are important employer characteristics – things our employees demand and place high value in – the research also validated what many of us intuitively know: namely, that more tangible benefits such as rewards and recognition are most important from an external recruit's perspective.'

Would you place the employer characteristics in the same order of priority?

Source: Reprinted with permission from HRM Guide (http://www.hrmguide.com/).

TARGETING AND DIVERSITY

In the UK, the recent massive increase in higher education has produced a consequent increase in the number of new graduates. British employers are copying US organizations in **targeting** specific universities, courses and even lecturers. The pecking order favours 'old' universities, reflecting the prejudices of employers. This tendency is as old as the new generation of (ex-poly) universities as we can see from five 'insights' into targeting indicated by a Glasgow consultancy, *Yellowbrick Training and Development* at the time (*Financial Times*, 25 October, 1995; *Guardian*, 26 October, 1995):

→ Competition for the 'best' graduates requires employers to have a clear idea of what they mean by 'best'. Recruitment needs to send a strong, distinctive message to these people.

→ There must be a move away from junior staff indiscriminately attracting as many applicants as possible to a more selective process involving senior management.

→ Target key institutions and specific courses.

→ Recruit whenever the needs of the business dictate, rather than to a fixed 'milkround' calendar.

→ There will be a diminished role for glossy brochures. Instead, vacation and placement jobs will be used to provide 'two-way interviews'.

It is clear that many employers are likely to use this form of targeting to ring-fence jobs so that only specific groups are considered. Essentially, they discriminate against institutions where ethnic minorities and working-class people are more heavily represented.

The choice and variety of new graduates has extended considerably in the UK during recent years as the result of government initiatives to widen access to higher education. A number of institutions have achieved university status, largely catering for students with a lower economic status, ethnic minorities and adult learners. But the people who were intended to gain the most benefit of this expansion in higher education actually 'gain somewhat less than their middle-class peers from achievement of a degree' (Purcell, 2002). And they earn less, on average, than people with similar qualifications who enter the job market with a 'traditional' graduate background.

The UK has moved from an elite to a mass-market system of university education but recruiters have not changed their practices in line with this development. On the contrary, a significant number have introduced or emphasized recruitment practices that act against graduates from non-traditional backgrounds. This is a matter of critical concern to people considering an investment in time and money in order to gain a degree.

Purcell (2002) points to a situation where:

→ Graduates with non-traditional backgrounds complain that they are finding it difficult to access jobs that offer them the fullest range of opportunities and make the most of their skills.

→ Companies appear to find difficulty in understanding the diversity of higher education courses and say that they cannot fill jobs with the right *calibre* of graduates.

Purcell (2002) contends that many of these problems result from the conservative recruitment strategies adopted by many organizations. Additionally, there is evidence to show that such strategies impact more on some groups of 'non-traditional' graduates than others – specifically those in older age groups. They appear to show the highest degree of dissatisfaction with the quality of their subsequent jobs and the value of having a degree. Also, the social background of graduates, regardless of age has a correlation with their levels of pay and job satisfaction after graduation. The lower their economic status before they embarked on higher education, the lower the consequent pay and job satisfaction.

Recruitment can be used to present a more positive, welcoming image to groups which are under-represented but, to be successful, this must be reinforced by similar initiatives further on in selection, induction and development mechanisms. Purcell (2002) identifies a number of key characteristics of 'leading practice employers', a similar concept to that of 'employers of choice' in North America:

→ In line with the concept of employer branding, they understand that recruitment is intimately connected with marketing. This means that they have to actively sell their organizations as equal opportunity employers.

→ They are clear about the skills and competences they need for specific jobs and do not confuse these with (irrelevant) attributes. They target sources of these skills and competences and design their recruitment and selection processes to identify them.

→ Where skills shortages exist they work with regional bodies and higher education institutes to draw attention to vacancies and opportunities, so that under-represented groups are positively encouraged to apply.

→ Expectations of recruits (internal and external) are managed to ensure that they understand the nature of the work, the culture of the organization and the career opportunities available.

→ Work experience and placement opportunities are offered through higher education institutes, to encourage students to gain employment skills and experience and to allow them to make sensible career choices.

→ They provide training and development programmes, plus assessment of progress, making internal progression possible.

→ They recognize the diversity and changing needs of their staff through work–life balance, flexibility and people-friendly working policies.

Ming Chia (2005) looked at the effects of academic performance, extracurricular activities and emotional intelligence (EI) on initial and subsequent interviews and on job offers. The applications of graduates with accounting majors to major public accounting firms were investigated. Ming Chia found that academic performance and extracurricular activities influenced the number of initial interviews offered. The number of subsequent interviews depended on the number of initial job interviews and also the applicant's level of emotional intelligence. Job offers were again affected by the candidate's level of emotional intelligence and the numbers of initial and subsequent job interviews.

HRM IN REALITY JOBSEEKERS WITH NON-ANGLO NAMES FACE DISCRIMINATION

University of British Columbia research published in 2010 has found that jobseekers with typical Anglophone names are more likely to be invited for interview than applicants with Chinese, Indian or Pakistani names.

Thousands of résumés were sent to Canadian employers and the study found that applications using Anglophone names such as Jill Wilson or John Martin attracted invitations for interviews 40 per cent more often than those with names like Sana Khan or Lei Li. This suggests that Canadians and recent immigrants with non-'English' names are facing discrimination from employers. The findings help to explain why skilled immigrants with university degrees and significant work experience still do badly in today's job market.

In a working paper released by Metropolis BC, part of an international immigration and diversity research network, UBC Economics Professor Philip Oreopoulos states: 'The findings suggest that a distinct foreign-sounding name may be a significant disadvantage on the job market – even if you are a second- or third-generation citizen.'

Six thousand mock résumés were prepared for the study. They were intended to represent recent immigrants and Canadians with and without Anglophone names. The résumés were tailored to meet job requirements and sent to 2000 online job postings advertised by employers covering 20 occupational categories in the Greater Toronto Area – the largest and most multicultural city in Canada. Each résumé listed a bachelor's degree and four–six years experience. Names and

Canadian or foreign education and work experience were randomly assigned.

Philip Oreopoulos said: 'If employers are engaging in name-based discrimination, they may be contravening the Human Rights Act,' adding that more research is required to determine whether the behaviour is intentional. 'They may also be missing out on hiring the best person for the job.'

The study also found that apparent work experience in Canada seemed to make a huge difference in employer attitudes. Interview invites were almost doubled when mock résumés with foreign names and education listed just one previous job in Canada.

'This suggests policies that prioritize Canadian experience or help new immigrants find initial domestic work experience might significantly increase their employment chances,' said Philip Oreopoulos, hoping that the study findings will help to improve current immigration and diversity practices.

How can blatant discrimination be identified and countered in the recruitment process?

Source: Reprinted with permission from HRM Guide Canada (http://www.hrmguide.net/canada/).

RESEARCHING CANDIDATES

Recruitment attracts a pool of applicants from whom successful candidates may be chosen. We now move on to the selection stages of the employee resourcing process. If a job analysis has been conducted, the criteria or competences that are deemed necessary have been identified. These may be well-defined and focused on experience and skills, as in the 'right person' approach; or general and related to education, intellect and personality for the 'cultural fit' and 'flexible person' models. Since decision-making is based on these criteria, relevant information must be obtained from applicants. The initial response to a vacancy announcement can take a number of forms but each offers the opportunity for: (a) recruiters to obtain information on applicants; and (b) applicants to gain an understanding of the job and the organization.

The commonest responses requested are by telephone or letter. Telephone responses may be used for an exchange of information or as a means of eliciting an application form and literature describing the job and organization.

APPLICATIONS

Application letters, CVs and résumés

Application or **cover letters** and résumés or CVs (*curriculum vitae*) are typically used initially. There is some variation between cultures. North American résumés are intended to present career objectives and history (usually in reverse chronological order, starting with the present) on one tightly written typed page. CVs in the British tradition are typically more detailed, running into two and sometimes more typed pages. The latter approach is also used by professionals in North America. In France, by contrast, advertisements often request a handwritten application letter, CV and photograph. (Many French companies use graphologists in the selection process.) French CVs are shorter and more factual than the British model and include little or no personal information such as hobbies or sporting interests. Japanese recruiters expect an official family registry record, a physical examination report and letters of recommendation in addition to CV and photographs. The use of photographs arouses disquiet in countries where equal opportunities are a major issue since they imply that selection will be influenced by appearance and colour.

Watkins and Johnston (2000) investigated the effect of physical attractiveness and résumé quality on how job applicants were evaluated during the screening phase of the selection process. A total of 180 participants read a job advertisement and one of two differing quality versions of a *curriculum vitae*. Each CV had a passport-sized head-and-shoulders photograph of either an average or an attractive female attached. A control study was also conducted where a photograph was not attached. Participants were asked to state how likely they were to offer an interview to the applicant, rate the quality of the application and state the likely starting salary to be offered to the applicant. Overall, attractiveness had no impact with high-quality applications but was an advantage when the application was mediocre. For example, average quality résumés were evaluated more positively when a photograph was attached and attractive photographs increased the rating of a mediocre application.

Job clubs and career advisers spend a great deal of time coaching jobseekers on the preparation of polished application letters, résumés and *curriculum vitae*. Paradoxically, however, coaching often results in a bland, standardized application that does not stand out among hundreds of others.

The privacy and data protection issues arising from this practice are complex. The European Union has attempted to control the use of automated selection processes through a directive that forms the basis, for example, of the UK's Data Protection Act 1998 (PPRU, 1999). The code of practice for this Act states in respect of shortlisting:

1 Be consistent in the way personal data are used in the process of shortlisting candidates for a particular position.

2 Inform applicants if an automated shortlisting system will be used as the sole basis for making a decision. Make provisions to consider representations from applicants about this and to take these into account before making the final decision.

3 Ensure that tests based on the interpretation of scientific evidence, such as psychological tests and handwriting analysis, are only used and interpreted by those who have received appropriate training.

HRM IN REALITY — ATTRACTIVE WOMEN CAN BE DISADVANTAGED

Attractive women may experience discrimination when applying for jobs traditionally considered 'masculine' and where appearance is not considered important, according to research led by the University of Colorado Denver Business School published in the *Journal of Social Psychology* in 2010. This includes positions like manager of research and development, director of finance, mechanical engineer and construction supervisor. No such discrimination was experienced by attractive men.

Lead author Stefanie Johnson, assistant professor of management, said:

In these professions being attractive was highly detrimental to women. In every other kind of job, attractive women were preferred.

This wasn't the case with men which shows that there is still a double standard when it comes to gender.

The researchers reviewed numerous studies that conclude physically attractive individuals enjoy considerable advantages such as:

→ higher salaries

→ better performance evaluations

→ higher levels of college admissions

→ better responses from voters when running for public office

→ more favourable trial outcomes.

They cite a Newsweek survey of 202 hiring managers and 964 members of the public which concluded that looks are important in all aspects of the workplace, especially for women employees. Looks ranked third out of nine 'character' attributes above education and sense of humor.

Researchers identified two studies which found that being attractive made applicants for most jobs seem more suitable irrespective of gender. However, women experienced greater benefit when applying for feminine sex-typed jobs compared with less traditional roles.

In one experiment, volunteers were asked to assign photographs of 55 male and 55 female applicants according to their suitability for a variety of jobs. Appearance was considered unimportant for jobs like director of security, hardware salesperson, prison guard and tow truck driver. Attractive women tended to be overlooked in these categories, but were linked with positions like receptionist or secretary.

Researchers caution against allowing stereotypes about physical appearance to influence hiring decisions at the expense of the overall characteristics of the applicant.

Stefanie Johnson commented:

> One could argue that, under certain conditions, physical appearance may be a legitimate basis for hiring. In jobs involving face-to-face client contact, such as sales, more physically attractive applicants could conceivably perform better than those who are less attractive. However it is important that physical attractiveness is weighed equally for men and women to avoid discrimination against women.

Can appearance have any valid bearing on recruitment?

Source: Reprinted with permission from PsyArticles.com (http://www.psyarticles.com).

Application forms/blanks

Both letters and CVs/résumés present a problem in a large recruitment programme: applicants may not provide all the relevant information and what there is will be presented in different ways. Comparison of applicants is easier if data is supplied in a standard form. Therefore, applicants replying to a job advertisement typically receive an **application form** (usually termed an application blank in North America), often asking for information already supplied. Stone-Romero, Stone and Hyatt (2003) found that completing an application blank was regarded as the least invasive of privacy out of 12 selection procedures.

Candidates face a paradox with application forms. Because information is regimented into a particular order and restricted space, jobseekers may present very similar applications. As with application letters, if candidates do not include details that distinguish them from (sometimes hundreds) of others, they stand little chance of being shortlisted. Conversely, if their responses are too unorthodox, the form immediately becomes a test of conventionality.

An applicant's heart sinks when a carefully crafted résumé or CV appears to be ignored and a standard form arrives in the post or email inbox. Hours are wasted completing forms that are not read because applicants are rejected on decision criteria, such as qualifications, not mentioned in the marketing process. However, an organization that does not use application forms has a major problem dealing with hundreds of applications. How are they to be analyzed and compared? How is the choice of a shortlist to be made? Applicants will

HRM IN REALITY DISCREPANCIES IN APPLICATIONS

A 2006 survey checked 2487 job applications for the financial services industry for discrepancies, embellishments and false information. Conducted by Powerchex, a pre-employment screening firm, the research looked at applications from a total of 1029 women and 1458 men over a six-month period. Employment histories, dates, university degrees, professional qualifications and criminal records were verified and checked against information provided by job applicants. With results compiled by the Shell Technology and Enterprise Program, the research was undertaken to discover any trends in discrepancies and the most common embellishments in job applications.

The survey found that 25 per cent of applications had at least one major discrepancy. While the majority of applicants falsifying information did so only once, some submitted forms with up to four major discrepancies. There is no significant difference between men and women in this respect.

The most common discrepancies overall relate to:

→ employment titles or duties (12 per cent)

→ employment dates

→ bankruptcy or county court judgments

→ academic qualifications

→ reasons for leaving previous employment

→ compensation received

→ directorships held

→ criminal record (less than one per cent).

The authors found that 37 per cent of applicants had gaps in their employment history and suggest that giving false information about dates (9.5 per cent of discrepancies) is probably intended to conceal this. The least common discrepancy identified related to criminal records which the authors link to applicants being aware that this can easily be checked against an existing database.

The survey found that the tendency to have discrepancies on applications increased with age, possibly suggesting that older workers feel the need to embellish in order to compete. Discrepancies were found in 28 per cent of applications from those aged 51–60, compared with 22 per cent of those aged 21–30. An alternative explanation might be difficulty in remembering the details of a complex employment history. British applicants gave false information in 32 per cent of cases overall (38 per cent of men and 26 per cent of women), compared with 25 per cent of their non-British counterparts.

The trend towards jobhopping is reflected in the survey, with 72.5 per cent having held at least two jobs in the last five years. Income had an interesting effect with people earning between £80 001 and £90 000 most likely to give false information (40 per cent) and those earning between £60 001 and £70 000 least likely to do so (nine per cent).

If the authors are correct in the assumption that all discrepancies identified are deliberate – and that is surely questionable – this survey indicates that one in four job applicants to the financial services sector are prepared to falsify information on their job applications in order to gain employment.

Is it reasonable to assume that all discrepancies are likely to be deliberate falsifications?

Source: Reprinted with permission from HRM Guide UK (http://www.hrmguide.co.uk).

leave out crucial items of information, particularly when they are likely to have a negative impact. When and how is this information to be acquired? Interviews are expensive methods for filling in the gaps in a CV or résumé. Moreover, it is unfair to raise hopes, cause inconvenience and possibly expense for interviewees who are disqualified on the basis of information that could be picked up from an application form.

Provided that they are not devised as mediaeval instruments of torture, short and pertinent application forms will continue to have a major role in recruitment. Purcell (2002) found that employers were increasingly tailoring application forms to identify specific competences required for individual jobs.

QUALIFICATIONS

We noted that educational qualifications are of major importance in some cultures, for example France and Japan. In other countries their value varies, depending on the level and nature of the vacancy. Purcell (*ibid.*) found that employers tended to use degrees as thresholds for considering applicants in order to guarantee minimum potential and ability. Also, with the massive increase in degree-qualified candidates in the UK, many employers were questioning the need for a degree as a basic qualification for a wide range of jobs. Many had moved, or were in the process of moving away from qualifications as a key element in the selection process. Instead they were looking for evidence of competences, particularly generic competences such as communication and teamworking or personal attributes such as resilience and commitment. In particular, they were increasingly valuing experience.

Purcell (*ibid.*) noted a clear difference between employers seeking to fill professional and technical jobs and those looking for general management or administration candidates. The former emphasized degrees as a qualification, particularly in subjects that featured numeracy, whereas degrees were often thought unnecessary for entry jobs in more generalized fields. Purcell quotes the instance of one high-street bank that sought to obtain A-level (high-school graduate) candidates for a five-year management programme rather than university graduates. They targeted working-class applicants who might consider the programme more attractive than a debt-incurring degree course.

BIODATA

Application forms and model CVs invariably include **biodata**; sections on experience, hobbies and other spare-time activities. Applicants frequently have serious difficulties in providing answers if they have fairly mundane interests. Does a passing interest in stamps and a small collection of DVDs allow us to describe our hobbies as philately and music? Do holiday snapshots justify 'photography'?

KEY CONCEPT 6.2   BIODATA

Roberts (1997: 10) describes biodata as a 'set of questions framed around "coincidences" in the lives of good performers'. People who are good at a particular job are likely to be more similar to each other than to individuals selected at random from the general population. Such similarities extend beyond work-related factors into hobbies, sports and social activities.

Traditionally, little use was made of this type of information. But it can be useful in discriminating (and that word is used advisedly) between applicants who are similar in most other respects. In fact, as we have already mentioned, an increase in coaching, books and professional writers aimed at preparing CVs or résumés and answering conventional forms, has resulted in applications becoming more and more similar. Supposing an employer advertises for trainee customer service assistants. The response is likely to include numerous applications from school-leavers with insufficient qualifications to proceed into higher education. These applicants may seem much the same on paper, but some have greater initiative or people skills than others. Biodata (biographical data) forms have been developed to identify non-academic qualities such as these. Biodata consists of systematic information about hobbies, interests and life history. The underlying rationale is described by Smith, Gregg and Andrews (1989: 54):

> Biodata methods are based on the assumption that *either* our characteristics are formed by the experiences we are subjected to in the course of our lives *or* our abilities cause us to select or become involved in certain types of life event. In either case, it follows that if we can accurately assess the events of a person's life, we can deduce something about their skills and abilities.

Biodata forms request detailed information of this kind, normally in the form of a multiple-choice questionnaire, covering:

→ Age, sex, place of birth, residence.

→ Family background, number of brothers and sisters, parental history.

→ Education, work experience.

→ Marital status, number of children.

→ Physical characteristics (weight, height) and medical history.

→ Hobbies and leisure interests.

→ Reading habits: newspapers, magazines, type and frequency of books read.

Question items are largely factual or 'hard' and could be checked with other sources if necessary. Other items are 'soft' and include opinions, attitudes and feelings. It is also possible to collect the same data in a structured interview. Biodata is an expensive procedure to set up but cheap to administer, especially if the data can be entered on computer by optical scanning.

A typical biodata exercise follows an established sequence (Smith, Gregg and Andrews, 1989):

1 Job analysis identifies criteria for good performance.

2 A 'brainstorming' exercise generates relevant biodata items, such as 'interest in people', 'stability', 'imagination'.

3 Draft questionnaires are given to a large number – ideally over 300 – existing employees.

4 Replies are correlated with job performance. Items which correlate poorly or discriminate against particular groups should be discarded.

5 The revised questionnaire is then given to applicants.

6 Biodata items become out of date quickly. They should be rechecked every two years.

Biodata cannot be used in small organizations or for a 'one-off job. A simplified version could be provided as a decision aid in such circumstances. This would entail interviewers collecting narrative personal histories and scoring the information against a previously determined scale. The main use of biodata is in pre-selection of basic or entry-level jobs such as apprenticeships or posts for trainees. The logic is that if candidates are matched with existing staff, people with similar interests can be found who are likely to be suitable for the job. The greatest value of the technique is its ability to reduce staff turnover.

Biodata is specifically used to select people who are similar to those already employed. Although designed to eliminate unfairness, in a less obvious way it consolidates and makes 'scientific' an embedded practice that is prejudicial to the disadvantaged. Furnham (1992: 231) reviews a number of studies comparing biodata with job performance and finds strong supporting evidence for its usefulness. He instances Russell *et al.* (1990) who examined the life details of 900 naval recruits and measured five biographical features:

→ Life problems and difficulties.

→ Aspects of task performance.

→ Work ethic/self-discipline.

→ Assistance from others.

→ Extraordinary goals or effort.

These were found to relate to other measures such as military performance rating. Furnham notes that factor analyses of biodata information relate to well-attested personality dimensions. Biodata correlate well with later supervisor ratings and can be useful in predicting turnover (Bret *et al.*, 2009).

Roberts (1997) observes that we do not need to know why biodata items are significant in order to use them. In many respects it is similar to the actuarial techniques used by insurance companies to quote for car insurance cover. Clearly, however, there are distinct implications for equal opportunities in a technique which, it could be argued, is designed not to promote diversity and that raises a possibility of breaching anti-discrimination laws unless the biodata items are carefully assessed. There is also the issue of faking to consider (Lautenschlager, 1994; Levashina *et al.*, 2009). The 'correct' (expected) answers to questions on non-cognitive tests such as biodata questionnaires are often easy to guess. In fact present-day biodata questions may be indistinguishable from items on personality tests and may attract the same problems of impression management and dishonesty. The consequent uncertainty about the effect of distorted responses on selection decisions and validity is a matter for concern (Snell, Sydell and Lueke, 1999). However, Anderson *et al.* (2010) found that applicants tended to have positive views towards biodata as a fair method of collecting information.

REFERENCES

Virtually all employers request references as a matter of course, usually without any thought as to their purpose and value. Where a purpose is expressed, they tend to serve one or both of the following functions: (a) a factual check to maximize the probability of a truthful application; and (b) to provide evidence of character or ability.

The latter assumes that the referee is disinterested and capable of making a valid judgement and is frequently misused. Candidates are most unlikely to offer referees who will write unfavourably. A classic study is frequently quoted to demonstrate the dubious value of the reference (Mosel and Goheen, 1958). In the study 1000 applications for the US civil service were examined and it was found that:

→ Fewer than one per cent had poor references for ability or character.

→ Approximately 50 per cent were described as outstanding by the referees.

→ The remaining references were at least satisfactory.

Moreover, when the work performance of successful candidates described by referees as being particularly suitable for the job were compared with those that were not, no difference was found between the two groups.

There is a growing and welcome trend for references to be simple factual checks rather than a source of 'evidence' for the selection process. There is also an issue regarding a referee's liability for the consequences of their comments. This is dependent upon employment law within specific countries.

HRM IN REALITY   REFERENCES CAN BE DECISIVE

Despite the emphasis placed on strong résumés and interview performance, the results of a reference check can be decisive in determining the outcome of a job application, according to a 2010 survey conducted by OfficeTeam, a leading staffing service specializing in the placement of skilled administrative professionals.

The survey was based on telephone interviews with more than 300 Canadian senior managers at companies with 20 or more employees. Respondents reported removing 26 per cent of candidates from consideration after checking their references.

When speaking to reference providers, 29 per cent said they were most interested in information about the applicant's strengths and weaknesses; 27 per cent wanted a description of their past job duties and experience. Other areas of interest included:

→ workplace accomplishments (14 per cent)

→ confirmation of job title and dates of employment (nine per cent)

→ insight into the applicant's preferred work culture (seven per cent).

The report offers advice for jobseekers when selecting reference providers:

→ **Choose wisely**. Identify individuals able to discuss your abilities and experience directly relevant to the position, not just those with the most impressive job titles. Offer a mixture who can address different aspects of your background; for example, a previous co-worker to describe your interpersonal skills, a past direct report to comment on your management style.

→ **Check in beforehand**. Always ask permission in advance. Give all reference providers a copy of your résumés, the job description and the name of the person likely to contact them.

→ **Be prepared**. Provide detailed contact information for your references (including name, title, daytime phone number and email address). Give a brief explanation of the nature of your relationship with each individual. Consider supplying additional references in case the hiring manager is unable to contact one of those on the list.

→ **Think outside the box**. Employers may seek out additional contacts (for example, online or using their own networks) to gain a broader view. Try to remain on good terms with past supervisors and colleagues. Be selective about who is represented in your online network on sites such as LinkedIn.

→ **Give thanks**. Express gratitude to those who agree to give references, even if they are not contacted ultimately. Update them on your progress and offer to reciprocate.

Robert Hosking, OfficeTeam executive director said:

> When hiring, managers narrow the field to a few potential candidates, the reference check often becomes the deciding factor. To distinguish themselves from the competition, jobseekers should assemble a solid list of contacts who can persuasively communicate their qualifications and professional attributes.

Are good references essential?

Source: Reprinted with permission from HRM Guide Canada (http://www.hrmguide.net/canada/).

SUMMARY

Recruitment and selection are core areas of human resource management but are frequently discussed in a prescriptive manner. They are not simply techniques for filling jobs – they are also levers for organizational change, sustaining employee commitment and achieving high performance. In free market countries, the personnel profession has adopted a 'best practice' model which fits the prevailing business ideology. This model prescribes a quest for the 'right (best) person for the job'. The 'best-person' or psychometric model has achieved the status of orthodoxy in free market countries. But different models of resourcing have been developed with a greater concern for personality and attitude than presumed ability. Recruits may be sought who will 'fit in' with the culture of the corporation; who will be content to build a career within the organization; who will absorb the goals of the organization.

FURTHER READING

There are many titles available covering the topic of recruitment, usually in conjunction with selection. Some of the best include:

1 *Competency-Based Recruitment and Selection* by Robert Wood and Tim Payne (John Wiley and Sons, 1998).

2 *Recruitment and Selection* by Gareth Roberts (CIPD, 2005).

3 *A Manager's Guide to Recruitment and Selection* by Margaret Dale (Kogan Page, 2003).

REVIEW QUESTIONS

1 Distinguish between recruitment and selection. What is the purpose of recruitment?

2 Why is employee resourcing more than a matter of filling jobs?

3 What do you see as the main advantages and disadavantages of the 'right-person', 'culture fit' and 'flexibility' models of recruitment?

4 What are the critical characteristics of leading practice employers or employers of choice?

5 Write a covering letter and a résumé or CV that would be suitable for an application to a HR department in a large multinational company.

6 What are the best ways of obtaining basic candidate information? What types of information can be gleaned from application forms?

7 Review the positive and negative aspects of using biodata questionnaires.

8 What roles do the Internet and company websites have in recruitment? How do they compare with other recruitment marketing channels?

9 Evaluate the role of the line manager in resourcing.

10 What are the legal pitfalls in the recruitment process?

CASE STUDIES FOR DISCUSSION AND ANALYSIS

Saveplenty Stores/Recruiting in Paris

1 The general manager of Saveplenty Stores has been interviewing applicants for sales and management jobs for 23 years. She believes that she can identify good and bad candidates by chatting to them for 10 minutes. You have been placed in her department as a graduate trainee and have been given the task of organizing recruitment for a new superstore.

How would you do this and what role should the general manager play?

2 You are a human resource specialist with Online Solutions, a large software company.

The company has agreed to set up a joint venture in Paris with a major French computer manufacturer. The venture will adapt and distribute software in French-speaking countries. Being fluent in French, you have been chosen as HR manager. Most of the other senior staff are long-standing managers from the French company. Your first task is to recruit approximately 60 junior managers and technical staff. The procedures and choices have to involve your French colleagues.

How would you conduct the exercise and what difficulties would you expect?

CHAPTER 7
Employee selection

LEARNING OBJECTIVES

The purpose of this chapter is to:

→ **Evaluate the screening or pre-selection stage of employee resourcing.**

→ **Introduce the concepts of validity and reliability in relation to different selection methods.**

→ **Provide a critical overview of selection methods.**

→ **Investigate the frequency of use of different selection methods.**

RESOURCING DECISIONS

According to *The Dictionary of Daily Wants* (1859):

> In seeking employment, much depends upon the applicant's manner and dress; if he is rude and ungainly, and expresses himself in an awkward manner, an employer will at once conceive a prejudice against him, and curtly decline the proffer of his services. But if, on the other hand, he is pleasing in his manners and dress, he will not only be engaged to fill a vacancy, but will sometimes be taken into the establishment, although no vacancy exists. Applicants for employment should also be scrupulously neat in their attire, and clean in their persons; for an employer naturally argues that a person who is careless of himself will be equally so about about his business.

Selection is a decision-making activity: 'the psychological calculation of suitability' (Townley, 1994: 94). If the recruitment process is open, selection decision-making normally takes place in a series of stages. Recruitment marketing may attract hundreds – sometimes thousands – of responses. The first decision stage is termed pre-selection. Its purpose is to reduce applications to a manageable number with the emphasis on rejection rather than selection. Evidence is gathered from letters, résumés/CVs, application forms, and possibly biodata or screening tests. Preselection increasingly involves telephone screening interviews, ranging from basic checking of information supplied in the application process to a 20-minute question and answer sequence not unlike the formal interview. Regardless of the methods used, the intention is to arrive at a comparatively small number – the shortlist of apparently well-suited applicants.

Pre-selection is open to considerable abuse and plays a major role in the cloning process. Frequently decisions are made on arbitrary grounds, ranging from the absurd – use of the 'wrong' colour of ink, for example – to the discriminatory, excluding particular groups such as women, ethnic minorities and graduates from other than specific schools or universities. Pre-selection offers those so inclined an ideal opportunity to reject unwanted candidates without having to give detailed reasons. Unless the organization has an applicant tracking system, with each application logged, categorized and tracked throughout the selection procedure, pre-selection can be a glaring loophole, allowing hidden and illegal discrimination to take place. It is common for two identical applications to be treated differently if one is sent with an obvious ethnic minority name and the other is evidently from the majority population. Herriot and Fletcher (1990) note the irony that pre-selection and initial interview result in rejection of the largest proportion of candidates and yet these stages are the least valid and reliable.

After pre-selection screening, surviving applicants meet the formal decision-making procedure termed 'selection'. Biased selection processes can result in hiring unsuitable people (false positives); or may lead to a failure to hire applicants who would have been suitable for the job (false negatives). In the 'best person' model, selection is a matching process, where:

→ An applicant's qualities are compared with criteria deemed necessary for the job.

→ When the measurement of the former is extremely difficult.

→ Evidence for the latter is a matter of opinion.

In contrast, 'culture fit' focuses on personality and compatibility with existing staff. In Japan, the traditional approach paid attention to such matters as political views, family background and personal finances – irrelevant to the average Western company (Whitehill,

1991). These two models are frequently confused and decision-making is a matter of identifying the 'ideal' or clone candidate, a process rationalized by talk of 'fitting in'.

An alternative explanation comes from the cognitive process interpretation of selection (Vandenberghe, 1999). For whatever reason, selectors develop a cognitive schema (mental picture) of the 'ideal' candidate for a specific job or more generally as a recruit for their particular organization. The cognitive schema may be a complicated mental network of beliefs and attitudes shared by a group of selectors against which prospective candidates are assessed.

How consistent are selectors when it comes to looking for the qualities they consider important? In a study of selection decisions in Hong Kong, Moy (2006) compared recruiters' judgement on the qualities deemed to be necessary for effective performance and the qualities they actually looked for in their selection processes. She found that conscientiousness was thought to be the most important quality for effective performance whereas the quality that they spent most time assessing during interviews was extroversion.

Sophisticated selection methods are not common in small companies, most of which continue to depend on informal methods for selection decisions – typically references and one or two interviews – although more sophisticated methods such as work samples can be effective (Wyatt *et al.*, 2010). In contrast, large organizations have adopted a range of methods to aid decision-making. Regardless of the resourcing model employed, procedures have become more elaborate. At Mazda in Michigan, USA, for example, the process involved several weeks' assessment and included application forms, aptitude tests, personal interviews, group problem-solving and simulated work exercises. These were designed to weed out 'druggies, rowdies, unionists'. Selection emphasized team-working behavioural traits rather than technical skills and successful candidates had an average age of 31, little or no factory experience and were overwhelmingly (70 per cent) male. Guest (1992) observes that the 'excellence literature', authored by Tom Peters and others, together with accounts of Japanese management methods focused the minds of many Western managers on the importance of recruitment, selection and socialization of employees. This leads to an interest in factors that can be assessed by a range of technical methods such as psychometric tests. In recent years their use has increased in Europe, particularly in the UK, whereas equal opportunities legislation has forced a different approach in the USA.

So, confining our discussion to 'best-person' and 'culture-fit' models for the moment, is selection best conducted subjectively or objectively? Smith and Robertson (1993: 255) compare the two approaches:

→ **Clinical,** or subjective. Just as a doctor diagnoses a medical condition on the basis of perceived sympoms, an 'expert' or experienced person reviews information on candidates. Choice is based on the expert's experience and expertise.

→ **Actuarial.** Comparable to calculating an insurance premium. Various factors are quantified and put into a weighted equation. For example, experience may be given twice the value of educational qualifications. The candidate scoring the highest number of points is selected.

They conclude that the actuarial approach is better than the clinical method, but not to a very major extent. But what happens in practice? Nowicki and Rosse (2002) note that the state of practice in employee selection differs markedly from the state of research. They conducted interviews with 166 line managers and asked them to describe their own successes and failures in hiring. The managers attributed successful hiring largely to luck and intuition, but they also acknowledged the value of more systematic and rigorous approaches to selection. From their comments it seemed that they simply lacked awareness of research on selection such as comparative validities, rather than choosing to ignore this information. There is also evidence for a strong belief among many selectors in the importance of personal experience, intuition and the ability to spot good performers (Highhouse, 2010) – to the point where, in the case of executive selection, decisions may be more often wrong than right (Hollenbeck, 2009).

From a diversity perspective, Peppas (2006) compared Hispanic and non-Hispanic hirers in the USA on the importance they attached to 26 different selection criteria. Peppas found that there were significant differences on 13 of the criteria with Hispanics tending to favour more subjective criteria while non-Hispanics preferred objective criteria.

PSYCHOMETRIC TESTS

Psychological tests have become commonplace. Psychometric means 'measurement of the mind'. Psychometric tests purport to measure psychological characteristics including **personality** (see Key concept 7.1), motivation, career interests, competences and intellectual abilities. Traditionally they take the form of pen and paper multiple-choice questionnaires but modern forms can also be presented on computer screens. Most tests require applicants to work through a large number of items in a given amount of time. Some ask candidates to choose between various alternatives, as in the following example:

'Which of the following best describes you?'

1 I never take time off from work because of illness.

2 Sometimes I take time off work if I am very ill.

3 I believe in taking care of myself. If I am ill, I stay at home.

This kind of item is typical of personality and motivation tests. Other tests use pictures and geometrical shapes. Tests of number ability might offer a series of numbers and ask for the next two:

$$2\ 4\ 8\ 16\ ?\ ?$$

This is a simple illustration – tests normally include items of increasing difficulty. The limited amount of time allowed ensures that few people can complete all items correctly.

KEY CONCEPT 7.1 PERSONALITY

Many lay people and psychologists believe that personality is a definite 'something' with a continuing existence at all stages of an individual's life, manifesting itself in every situation that person encounters. Generally expressed in terms of types or traits, the latter form the basis of most personality tests used for resourcing and the documentation employed for many performance appraisal systems. An alternative approach is to regard personality as an artefact of a particular set of circumstances. In other words, apparent personality depends on the meaning individuals give to a particular situation.

Users argue that they provide valuable evidence that is not revealed by other methods. Additionally, there is a widespread belief that they are somehow objective, contrasting strongly with the subjectivity of interviewing. Candidates often feel that they may justifiably 'sell' themselves in an interview, creating an excessively favourable impression, whereas tests will magically reveal the truth. They give resourcing the semblance of scientific professionalism (Townley, 1989).

Tests are based on the **psychometric model** (Key concept 7.2) which '... assumes that there is an optimal set ... of psychological characteristics for success at any human activity (in this instance, success at a particular job)' (Kline, 1993: 374). However, in our discussion of human resource planning we have seen that identifying such optimal sets is extremely difficult in practice. Specifically, job or personal specifications derived from traditional job analysis are backward-looking: they do not describe requirements for the future, as many tightly prescribed 'jobs' disappear in favour of more fluid, flexible roles. Older notions of psychological 'dimensions' by which jobs and people are matched are being replaced by the more complex multi-dimensional concept of competences.

KEY CONCEPT 7.2 THE PSYCHOMETRIC MODEL

The dominant approach to selection in British and US textbooks. In its traditional form, it grounds the 'best-person' model in psychological theory and testing. It embodies the use of refined techniques to achieve the best 'match' between job characteristics identified by formal job analysis and individual characteristics measured by psychological tests, structured interviews and other assessment methods.

Psychological testing has been used for different purposes in mainland Europe and North America, with the UK taking an intermediate view. The reasons for this are complex and reflect different traditions. The 'softer' European approach has relied on more descriptive, observational methods such as projective techniques and qualitative performance tests that draw on psychoanalytic theory. Conversely, the American approach has been dominated by behaviourist attitudes, emphasizing 'objectivity' and the quantitative use of data. This led to the development of a massive range of 'paper and pencil' tests, suitable for individual or group use. Many European selection theorists have never been convinced of their merits. However, in recent years, growth of a more systematic methodology has meant that the two approaches have converged to a considerable extent. Table 7.1 shows some of the advantages and disadvantages of using tests.

Jenkins (2001) reviewed 17 surveys of psychometric test usage published between the early 1970s and 2000. The wide variation in methodology, sampling sizes and sample frames made it difficult to provide precise estimates of test usage for specific periods. However, a clear growth in use was seen from the 1980s onwards, with evidence of widespread adoption by large organizations in particular. Wolf and Jenkins (2006) used case studies of organizations to identify the factors behind this and checked their consistency with Workplace Employee Relations Survey (WERS) data to see if these were national trends in the UK. The regulatory environment was found to be the most important factor: organizations were using tests as a precaution to protect their selection decisions from any challenge.

TABLE 7.1
Advantages and disadvantages of tests

Source: Adapted from Furnham (1992: 39).

Advantages	Disadvantages
→ Test results are numerical – allowing direct comparison of applicants on the same criteria.	→ Responses can be faked on many tests to give a 'desirable' score. Some include 'lie detectors' to overcome this.
→ Tests provide 'hard' data that can be evaluated for their predictive usefulness in later years – i.e. compare predicted with actual performance.	→ Some people lack sufficient self-insight to give accurate responses.
→ Tests provide explicit and specific results unlike interviews and references that can be vague or 'coded'.	→ Tests are unreliable – temporary factors such as anxiety, headaches, illness can lead to variable results.
→ Tests measure substance rather than image.	→ Tests are invalid – many tests do not measure what they say they measure.
→ A battery of tests can cover a comprehensive range of abilities and personal qualities.	→ Tests are irrelevant – many tests do not measure qualities that are relevant to a specific organization, such as honesty and punctuality.
→ Tests are 'scientific' – empirically based with a grounding in theory. They are reliable, valid and discriminate between good, average and mediocre.	→ Tests require minimum literacy and a grasp of American jargon.
→ Tests provide a conceptual language to users, enhancing understanding of behaviour.	→ Good norms do not exist for most populations – comparison with white, middle-class, male US students has little practical value.
→ Empirical data from tests provide objective evidence to justify decisions.	→ Tests are unfair to anyone who is not a white, middle-class, male American because most have been constructed using them as a reference population.
→ Tests provide insights and explanations for behaviour. They can be used to justify individual rejections.	→ Freedom of information legislation opens 'objective' data to greater scope for challenge than vague, unrecorded interview data.
	→ Firms tend to use the same tests so that practice effects and knowledge of desirable answers can destroy their value.

Jenkins (2001) considers that large organizations are more likely to use tests because they have a greater number of vacancies across which to spread the fixed costs associated with testing, and they are more likely to have specialized human resource specialists who are familiar with and trained for psychometric testing. Wolf and Jenkins (2006) also found the growing formal professionalization of HR departments to be a significant factor.

HRM IN REALITY   MAKING THE MOST OF PSYCHOMETRICS

Change management and training consultancy, cda, believes that too many companies are failing to maximize on the benefits of using psychometrics as an integral part of their recruitment policy. This is restricting return on investment and development of staff potential.

They quote the CIPD Recruitment, Retention and Development Survey 2006 indicating that 60 per cent of organizations are now using psychometrics as part of the recruitment process. Costs are significant, typically averaging up to several thousand pounds including training and licences. Nevertheless, it is said to represent a worthwhile investment. Comprehensive use of psychometrics is thought to result in a 'better-fit' recruit who is more likely to meet an employer's requirements, stay longer, contribute more and generally provide a better return on investment.

However, a significant percentage of firms using psychometrics only do so in the initial recruitment process and are not continuing to apply the approach as part of ongoing development.

Lisa Michelangeli, psychologist at cda said:

> We encounter too many instances of what we call 'Silver Bullet' mentality. While there has been an increased recognition of the value of psychometrics, there can be an assumption that its integration into the recruitment process is a guarantee that it will result in a calibre of recruit who will have a long-term positive impact on the organization.

Some firms are not achieving full-value realization of their investment because they do not use the outputs of the psychometrics to inform development beyond the recruitment stage. For example, if a group of individuals is recruited, the outputs of the personality assessment can inform the development of the team and how they interact with each other. This is an example of the invaluable opportunities that we encounter organizations not always making the most of. Psychometrics are not a one-fix cure-all but have to be an integral part of the ongoing development process.

Consultants with cda report that this situation can be exacerbated by discontinuity between HR and line management. Often the HR function is involved only in the hiring (and firing) process and not in employee development, which can be regarded by line managers as their territory.

Lisa Michelangeli continues:

> Given the sums of money companies are investing, we believe that it is essential for business leaders to ensure that their HR experts are educating and then supporting line management in incorporating the output of psychometrics into the various stages of the employee lifecycle.
>
> For example, when line managers are trained in benefits such as the objective basis for performance management that psychometrics can provide, they embrace the practice wholeheartedly. However, it does need the business leaders to instigate clear policy to ensure that the essential instruction and ongoing support is properly implemented by HR and incorporated by line management. Leaving it to chance is not good enough.

Why do many organizations fail to make use of psychometric results after recruitment and selection?

Source: Reprinted with permission from HRM Guide UK (http://www.hrmguide.co.uk).

CRITICISM OF PSYCHOLOGICAL TESTING

Increasing use of psychological testing has caused disquiet among psychologists for at least 20 years, particularly the proliferation of personality assessments. There are many available on the market promoted by people without adequate training and making extravagant claims about their value and effectiveness. Many employers, including those with human resource specialists, do not have the ability to identify good and bad products. In an attempt to distinguish the trained from the untrained, the British Psychological Society has introduced a Certificate in Occupation Testing Competence. Some of the most important criticisms are:

1   **Justification.** Furnham (1992: 5) criticizes the underlying research which 'justifies' specific personality measures on a number of grounds:
    — The personality characteristics chosen are often arbitrary and uninformed. Often they are historical relics, long-abandoned and condemned by psychologists but still exploited as commercial products.
    — Statistical analyses tend to be simple and naive, leading to more findings of significant differences than there are in reality (type II errors). Usually, simple correlations are used – rather than 'robust and sensitive' multivariate statistics – when all the variables involved are multi-factorial.
    — Most studies are exploratory, with no theoretical basis and are not part of systematic programmes. As a result, they tend to be 'one-off, sometimes with interesting implications but no particular consequence.
    — Organizational and social factors are often ignored – personality may not be the only relevant factor.

2   **Validity.** Blinkhorn and Johnson (1990) criticize personality tests as predictors of job performance when compared with ability and aptitude tests. They argue that their validity coefficients are often no better than chance. However, other specialists consider that personality tests are still valuable if they are used carefully and are not taken to be the main predictors. For example, 'conscientiousness' is linked to job performance and 'extroversion' scores are useful predictors for sales ability. Ironically, projective tests, with the lowest predictive value, have higher 'face' validities – looking as if they do what they are supposed to do – than psychometric tests, especially to younger and less educated people (Sartori, 2010).

The greatest difficulty with personality tests is that candidates can lie. Moreover, they can fake results in different ways and to a varying extent (Zickar, Gibby and Robie, 2004). Individuals may score highly on extroversion because they are extroverts. Alternatively they can present themselves as outgoing because it is clear from the job description that selectors are seeking extroverts. There is also some evidence of a small to medium practice effect when internal candidates take repeated tests for vacancies (Hausknecht, 2010). In a meta-analysis, Li and Bagger (2006) looked at the effects of impression management and self-deception on the criterion validity of personality constructs. They used the balanced inventory of desirable responding (BIDR) and failed to find any evidence that impression management and self-deception created spurious effects on the relationship between personality measures and performance. They also found that removing the influence of these two dimensions from measures of personality did not significantly attenuate the criterion validity of personality variables.

It has also been argued that, since tests are based on personality theory, they cannot be interpreted without knowledge of the theory in which most selectors are untrained. Another contentious issue is the effect of practice. If applicants are exposed to the same test on more than one occasion, they gain from the previous experience, often remembering answers. The doubts about personality tests have become well-known. Lievens, Highhouse and De Corte (2005) asked experienced retail store supervisors to rate job applicant profiles described on two dimensions including General Mental Ability (GMA). Unlike previous research, supervisors were also informed about the method of assessment used. The importance attached to extroversion and GMA decreased when store supervisors knew that scores were derived from a paper-and-pencil test rather than an unstructured interview. Store supervisors with more selection-related experience also attached more importance to GMA.

Wood and Baron (1992: 34) consider the effect of psychological tests in terms of 'adverse impact' on ethnic minority groups: "Adverse impact" occurs when there is a significant disparity in test scores between ethnic groups, resulting in one group being disproportionately preferred over the other. The test is then said to have an adverse impact on the lower-scoring group.' They argue that the greater the degree of adverse impact, the more this has to be justified. Employers must be careful to test strictly for qualities that can be proven to be required for the job. Even when this can be demonstrated it remains important to find the method of measurement with the least adverse impact. A common problem is the effect of language proficiency on test performance. Typically, ethnic minority candidates are undergoing a selection procedure in the dominant community language, such as English, when they are stronger linguistically in another, such as Hindi or Italian. Their performance is masked by their comprehension of the questions and their ability to express their answers in a manner that is meaningful to the testers. Often, tests are time-limited. This is a reasonable gauge of mental speed for native speakers because their use of language is automatic. However, it is detrimental to people answering out of their native languages, since they need to translate at a conscious mental level. In effect the test becomes an assessment of 'proficiency in English' rather than a measure of its true objectives such as 'problem-solving ability' or 'motivation'. The test has become unfair for anyone whose first language is not English.

A classic case involving British Rail (BR) showed that, in an analysis of 4000 tests taken by potential drivers, white people were twice as successful as ethnic minority candidates. Eight guards of Asian origin took BR to an industrial tribunal on the grounds that the tests were discriminatory. The verbal reasoning tests employed were not directly related to the job and were particularly difficult for people who spoke English as a second language. BR admitted that the tests had adverse impact on Asian workers and undertook to seek the advice of the Commission for Racial Equality in developing revised selection techniques.

Similarly, the Council for Legal Education (CLE) introduced a critical reasoning test for around 2300 applicants to the English Bar's training school. The CLE had attempted to provide a test that was as fair as possible, involving two firms of occupational psychologists and Birkbeck College of the University of London. However, the test was trialled on a group of existing students that included very few from ethnic minority groups. According to Makbool Javaid, chair of the Society of Black Lawyers, it was felt that 'some of the questions would be difficult to answer for anyone who was not from a middle-class public school kind of background' (*Times Higher Education,* 18 March, 1994). The results produced a storm of protest and the tests were soon reconsidered. These reservations are widely known among human resource specialists and may explain Storey's (1994) report of a reduction in use of personality tests around that time.

INTERVIEWING

The interview is a social ritual which is expected by all participants, including applicants. It is such a 'normal' feature of filling vacancies that candidates for a job would be extremely surprised not to be interviewed at least once.

Informal interviews

Many employers invite applicants for informal interviews prior to the main selection procedure. These interviews are useful for information exchange, particularly in the case of professionals (Breakwell, 1990: 10). They provide the opportunity to discuss the full nature of the job, the working environment, prospects for further development and promotion. Candidates who decide that the job is not for them can elect to go no further. To avoid interviews degenerating into pointless chats, Breakwell emphasizes that both interviewer and applicant need to have checklists of essential points to cover. Interviewers should:

→ Give a balanced picture of the job, including an honest account of its disadvantages together with a (larger) number of positive aspects. Honesty might seem dangerous but is best in the long run.

→ A description of the organization in the same terms.

→ Introduce the interviewee to other people in the department. This also allows interested parties to vet the applicant.

Blackman (2002a) investigated the common practice of informal telephone interviews. The study was aimed at determining if impoverished personality judgements of job applicants would come from telephone interviews in comparison to face-to-face interviews, given the lack of crucial non-verbal communication. Mock job interviews were used in both face-to-face format and telephone format. A significantly higher correlation was found between personality ratings of face-to-face interviewers and other sources of an applicant's personality ratings. Not surprisingly, face-to-face interviewers also rated applicants significantly higher or more favourably on personality traits that are normally best-revealed by non-verbal communication.

There seems to be some ambiguity as to whether informal interviews should be used as part of the pre-selection process by the employer rather than self-selection by the candidate. The crux of the issue depends on what interviewees have been told. If they have been led to believe that it is a truly informal information session they will not consider the process to be fair if they are subsequently told that they have not been short-listed as a result.

Formal interviews

A selection interview can be defined neatly as 'a conversation with a purpose' but not infrequently the purpose is obscure to the point of invisibility. More often than not 'purposeless chat' would be nearer the mark. It is a form of social interaction in which the interviewer is engaged in active **person perception** of the interviewee (see Key concept 7.3). From the interviewee's perspective 'one is managing a demonstration of knowledge or ability through a social vehicle, and one inevitably needs to attend to the social as well as the cognitive aspect of the interview' (Sternberg, 1994: 181). In other words, the impression created depends as much on social factors as any demonstration of experience or expertise.

KEY CONCEPT 7.3 PERSON PERCEPTION

The perception of other people. Cues such as facial expression, posture, gesture, body movement, tone of voice, etc., are used to evaluate their current mood and overall personalities (McKenna, 1994: 144). Each one of us has an 'implicit personality theory' based on our experience, assumptions about people, beliefs and prejudices. The evidence of our senses is used to collect data about the perceived person and attribute characteristics to them according to our implicit theory. This is a simplification process and leads to a number of well-known errors of judgement, including:

→ *Logical error:* assuming that certain traits are always found together, e.g. if a person is described as 'objective' we tend to perceive them as 'cold'.

→ *Halo effect:* the tendency to perceive people as all 'good' or all 'bad'.

→ *Stereotyping:* seeing all members of a particular group, e.g. Africans, Scots, to have the same characteristics. Stereotyping leads to prejudice.

For many unskilled or semi-skilled jobs, the formal interview tends to be perfunctory and can be over in a few sentences. This is not necessarily a bad thing. For decades, the evidence has been that the more sophisticated and lengthy proceedings entered into by major organizations often have been no better in terms of outcome. According to Sternberg (1994: 182):

> Interviewers tend to prefer interviewees who are relaxed, who put the interviewers at ease, who are socially as well as verbally facile, and who have some degree of interpersonal sparkle.

In fact, the interview has attracted severe criticism for a very long time. W.D. Scott is quoted as having said in 1915 that the selection interview is not a dependable selection method (Lewis, 1985: 150). Since then the interview has been attacked on the grounds of its subjective nature, questionable validity and unreliability. Webster (1964) noted some significant findings:

→ First impressions count. Interviewers make their minds up in the first few minutes, then seek evidence to support their opinion.

→ The candidate's appearance is the most significant factor, followed by information on the application form.

→ Unfavourable evidence is valued more strongly than favourable evidence.

→ The interviewer's opinion 'comes over' to the candidate during the interview and influences the candidate's further performance in an unfavourable or favourable direction.

A study of medical students in Canada (Razack *et al.*, 2009) found that sequential 'mini-interviews' were preferred to traditional unstructured interviews. Candidates felt they were enjoyable and allowed them to be competitive.

Hebl and Skorinko (2005) investigated the significance of acknowledgments made by physically disabled individuals in an interview setting, and looked at timing of an acknowledgment in relation to impressions formed by evaluators. One hundred and thirty-seven participants observed interviews of disabled applicants who acknowledged their disability at

HRM IN REALITY   SNAP JUDGEMENTS ABOUT FACES

Recent research indicates that when we see an unfamiliar face, our brains decide intuitively whether a person is attractive and trustworthy within a tenth of a second – so quickly that reason may play no part in the process.

The study by Princeton University assistant professor of psychology, Alex Todorov, and research student, Janine Willis, published in the July 2006 issue of *Psychological Science* asked about 200 observers to look at 66 different faces flashed onto a screen for one of three time durations: 100 milliseconds, 500 milliseconds or a full second.

The observers recorded whether they found the face to be trustworthy or not, and also how confident they were in their analysis. Similar experiments tested for other traits, such as likeability, competence, and aggressiveness. Judgements made after the shortest exposure time correlated highly with those made without time constraints. With more time to decide, observers' judgements did not change, but their confidence in them increased.

Alex Todorov said:

The link between facial features and character may be tenuous at best, but that doesn't stop our minds from sizing other people up at a glance. We decide very quickly whether a person possesses many of the traits we feel are important, such as likeability and competence, even though we have not exchanged a single word with them. It appears that we are hardwired to draw these inferences in a fast, unreflective way.

Todorov said that it is not yet clear why the brain makes such snap judgements. However, functional magnetic resonance imaging of brain activity suggests that the part of the brain that responds directly to fear may be involved in judgements of trustworthiness.

'The fear response involves the amygdala, a part of the brain that existed in animals for millions of years before the development of the prefrontal cortex, where rational thoughts come from. We imagine trust to be a rather sophisticated response, but our observations indicate that trust might be a case of a high-level judgement being made by a low-level brain structure. Perhaps the signal bypasses the cortex altogether,' Alex Todorov continued.

He cautioned that the findings do not imply that quick first impressions cannot be overcome by the rational mind:

As time passes and you get to know people, you, of course, develop a more rounded conception of them. But because we make these judgements without conscious thought, we should be aware of what is happening when we look at a person's face.

If our brains are 'hard-wired' to make snap judgements on faces, what are the likely consequences for fair selection?

Source: Reprinted with permission from HRM Guide USA
(http://www.hrmguide.com).

the beginning, middle, or end of a job interview or made no acknowledgement at all. Applicants who acknowledged their disability early in the interview were perceived more favourably than those who acknowledged at the end of the interview or not at all.

In a Canadian study, Chapman and Webster (2006) also found that signal and expectancy mechanisms influenced candidate intentions and job choice. These effects appeared to be most important for applicants who had multiple job opportunities and less pre-interview knowledge of an organization. Comparing two impression management techniques used by Belgian candidates Proost *et al.* (2010) found that ingratiation was more effective than self-promotion.

HRM IN REALITY JOB HUNTING ADVICE

Today's competitive market requires considerably more effort than in recent years according to a survey conducted in 2010 by Canadian specialized staffing service The Creative Group.

The survey, based on over 500 telephone interviews with advertising and marketing executives, found that an average of six applicants are interviewed before a vacancy is filled.

The report offers advice to improve the chances of job seekers meeting with potential employers:

1 **Do your prep work.** Applicants with more than basic knowledge of the job and company are better able to comment on their potential contribution. The researchers suggest visiting the organization's website, Facebook page or Twitter feed; searching online and using your personal network for additional information.

2 **Put your best foot forward from the start.** Be polite to reception staff, smile and behave warmly with everyone you meet. Resist the temptation to contact friends while waiting; you'll make a better impression by remaining focused.

3 **Be aware of body language.** Factors such as eye contact, facial expression and posture will affect the impression you make on hiring managers. When practising for an interview, ask friends or family for feedback on any off-putting mannerisms.

4 **Have a good story to tell.** Prepare appropriate examples of how you have helped solve business problems. Outline the challenge faced, your actions and the outcome achieved.

5 **Come with interesting questions.** This isn't the time to inquire about salary or paid vacation. Asking about aspects of the job you might not have anticipated or the process for collaborating on projects confirms your interest while providing information to help determine if the job and company is right for you.

6 **Be yourself.** A hiring manager wants to experience a genuine person who is right for the position. Avoid rehearsed or contrived responses.

7 **Remain positive.** If you are unsuccessful use it as a learning experience. If you have developed good rapport with the interviewer, request feedback on how you might improve. Accepting rejection graciously will leave a positive impression.

Lara Dodo, a vice president for The Creative Group's Canadian operations commented:

> Given the high calibre of talent currently available, employers are being prudent in their hiring and are weighing their options before extending an offer. By taking the time to thoughtfully prepare for the interview, including researching the company and substantiating previous accomplishments, job seekers can impress hiring managers and land the job.

Can you suggest ways in which prejudice based on names may be avoided?

Source: Reprinted with permission from HRM Guide Canada (http://www.hrmguide.net/canada/).

EVALUATING METHODS

How do we judge the value or effectiveness of interviewing – or any other method of selection? Before going further it is useful to consider the four basic requirements (Smith, 1991: 32):

1 *Practicality.* Selection methods must be practical in a given situation – for example, cost, convenience and time available. Attitudes of employers and candidates to the methods are also relevant.

2 *Sensitivity.* The ability of a method to distinguish one candidate from another. Interviews may rank a number of candidates fairly closely, whereas tests may give a wide range of scores.

3 *Reliability.* How consistent are the results? Conventionally, there are three forms of reliability measure:
— Comparison over time. If a method is used on the same group of candidates on different days, are the scores likely to be similar? This is sometimes called test–retest or intra-rater reliability.
— Inter-rater reliability. If two or more assessors are involved, how much agreement is there between them?
— Internal consistency. If several items in a test or procedure are meant to measure the same characteristic, such as sociability, how close are the ratings?

4 *Validity.* Does the method achieve its purpose in distinguishing the most suitable applicants from the others? Three measures of validity are available:
— Face validity. Does the method appear to be measuring what it is supposed to measure? This is important because it is essential that candidates believe that they have been fairly treated. Disappointed applicants frequently complain about apparently irrelevant interview questions or test items. For example, one selection test includes the question: 'Do you like tall women?' Whether or not this has deep psychological significance, its appearance is enough to bring derision on the test.
— Construct validity. To what extent does the method measure a particular construct or human quality such as commitment?
— Predictive validity. How well does the method predict the suitability of a successful candidate?

Reliability and validity are expressed as correlational coefficients where perfection is represented by 1.0 and pure chance is shown by zero. Table 7.2 shows the estimated validities of different selection methods. Establishing the validity of a particular procedure logically requires the employer to take on a large number of applicants, good and bad, and then compare their job performance with that predicted by the selection method. This kind of predictive validity study is impractical in most circumstances. Sometimes termed 'the one that got away' problem, we never know how the people we did not select might have performed.

TABLE 7.2

Comparative validities

Source: Based on Bertua *et al.* (2005), Smith (1991) and Roth *et al.* (2005).

Validity range	Methods	Rating
0.5 to 0.6	Cognitive ability tests	Good to excellent
0.3 to 0.39	Work sample tests Biodata Assessment centres Structured interviews	Acceptable
Less than 0.3	Personality tests Typical interviews References Graphology	Poor
Chance (0)	Astrology	

Research shows that similar results can be obtained by a method termed 'concurrent study' where selection methods are employed on existing employees at the same time as the selection procedure is taking place. Performance of existing employees is then correlated with prediction scores of the selection method. Again, however, this is rarely done, partly because accurate performance measures are difficult to obtain for many jobs.

In a meta-analysis on the validity of over 500 tests of general mental ability and specific cognitive abilities, Bertua, Anderson and Salgado (2005) found that both types of tests are valid predictors of job performance and training success. They calculated that operational validities were in the magnitude of 0.5 to 0.6, in line with previous meta-analyses in the USA.

Fairness is a further requirement: specifically, candidates' perceptions of the equity of the process. Good candidates are more likely to accept an offer if they consider that the procedure has been fair, effective and considerate while rejected applicants will continue to have a positive view of an organization's employer brand if they feel they have been fairly treated. Schleicher *et al.* (2006) looked at a sample of 754 applicants to a US government agency. They found evidence that candidates' perception of their 'opportunity to perform' was an important predictor of their overall feelings about the fairness of the selection process, and was the single most important procedural rule after receiving negative feedback. Intriguingly, in a simulated exercise, Schinkel, van Dierendonck and Anderson (2004) found that rejected candidates who were given performance feedback were more likely to show negative effects on core self-evaluations and affective well-being than those who were simply given rejection messages.

People have different perceptions of fairness. Truxillo *et al.* (2006) related the 'Big Five' personality measures (neuroticism, extroversion, agreeableness, conscientiousness and openness to experience) to candidates' perceptions of post-test fairness, themselves, and the hiring organization. After controlling for gender and test score, they found that personality accounted for significant variance in all three, although the relationship with fairness was weakest. Neuroticism and agreeableness were the personality factors that most consistently predicted candidate perceptions. In a later study (Truxillo *et al.*, 2009) candidates showed more favourable attitudes towards the selection process when they were provided with explanations of various procedures.

Moscoso and Salgado (2004) examined students' reactions to selection methods in Spain and Portugal. They found similar results in both countries with interviews, résumés and work sample tests being rated most highly and contacts, integrity tests and graphology being judged least favourably. Face validity and opportunity to perform were the most important bases for a favourable judgment. In a meta-analysis including samples from 17 countries, Anderson *et al.* (2010) found three clusters of perceived favourability among candidates:

→ *Most preferred* – work samples, interviews.

→ *Favorably evaluated* – résumés, cognitive tests, references, biodata, personality inventories.

→ *Least preferred* – honesty tests, personal contacts, graphology.

In a study of 255 HR professionals involved with selection, assessment and training, Furnham (2008) found that assessment centres, cognitive ability tests and work samples were considered to be the most valid techniques. However, interviews came first in terms of practicality. The professionals had positive views about personality and ability tests but were only familiar with a limited range of tests, particularly those related to personality and motivation. Table 7.3 shows the relative usage of different selection methods in the UK.

TABLE 7.3
Selection methods
used by large
organizations in the
UK, 2006

Source: Based on CIPD
(2006).

Method	%
Interviews	
Structured panel	88
Structured one-to-one	81
Biographical	85
Competency-based	85
Telephone	56
Tests	
Specific skills	82
General ability	75
Literacy/numeracy	72
Personality/aptitude	60
Online selection	25
References (pre-interview)	
Employment	50
Academic	37
Assessment centres	48
Group exercises	48
Other	6

INTERVIEWS REVISITED

Since the late 1980s there has been a revision of opinion concerning the value of interviews (Smith, 1991; Eder and Harris, 1999). Earlier research findings were based on small samples. The use of meta-analytic techniques allows the combination of statistics from a number of small studies to give much larger samples. For example, Weisner and Cronshaw (1988) combined validity coefficients from 150 studies and conclude that interviews can be more valid than suspected. In fact, their validity depends on the type of interview. Traditional, or unstructured interviews comprise the vast majority and are generally no more than cosy chats. Their validity was found to be 0.2 (very poor) whereas structured interviews, especially those based on job analysis, were found to be significantly better with a validity of 0.63.

Structured interviews are conducted to a format, rather than a script, and focus questioning on the job rather than irrelevant incidentals such as holidays and golf. Two standard methods are:

→ Criterion referenced interviews, based on job analysis with a set of questions geared to experience and skill for interviewers to choose from.

→ Situational interviews, based on the 'critical incidents' technique. A reasonable number (typically 20) of real-life work incidents are obtained from jobholders or their supervisors. Possible ways of dealing with these situations are outlined and rated as suitable or unsuitable, frequently on a points system. These situations are presented to candidates as hypothetical problems and responses evaluated against predetermined ratings.

Peeters and Lievens (2006) investigated how structured interview formats, instructions to convey favourable impressions, and applicants' individual differences influenced the use and effectiveness of verbal and non-verbal impression management (IM) tactics. They found that interview format affected the kind of tactics used, which in turn positively influenced interviewer evaluations. Behaviour description interviews triggered self-focused defensive tactics, whereas situational interviews triggered other-focused tactics. Instructions to convey a desirable impression also enhanced the use of specific tactics (self-focused and other-focused verbal IM) and moderated the effects of individual

HRM IN REALITY SUPPORT FOR SITUATIONAL INTERVIEWS

Research from the Richard Ivey School of Business at the University of Western Ontario published in *Applied Psychology: An International Review* found that employers using situational interviews (a structured format in which all candidates are scored on the same job-related questions) introduce less bias and are fairer when recruiting women and visible minorities, irrespective of the strength of any associated employment equity programme.

The researchers explain that these programmes, a legal requirement for some larger Canadian organizations, are intended to increase the recruitment of under-represented groups. However, they are subject to criticism for encouraging reverse discrimination and contributing to low workplace morale.

The current findings suggest that the qualifications of visible minorities recruited under an employment equity programme are less likely to be questioned if situational interviews are used. This affects a significant minority of the Canadian population (currently 10 per cent rising to 20 per cent by 2017, according to Statistics Canada).

Situational interviews present job applicants with potential workplace dilemmas. Candidates' responses to the same predetermined questions are scored as 'outstanding', 'minimally acceptable' or 'unacceptable'. The researchers contrast this with the free-flowing nature of an unstructured interview that may result in the hiring process appearing inconsistent and subjective, especially when used by organizations with employment equity programs.

Lead author Gerard Seijts, associate professor of organizational behaviour said: 'The situational interview encourages organizations to treat job applicants consistently. It allows job candidates to be hired on the basis of merit.'

Are situational interviews likely to be as enjoyable for a candidate as unstructured interviews?

Source: Reprinted with permission from HRM Guide Canada (http://www.hrmguide.net/canada/).

differences on IM use. They suggest that non-verbal behaviour might be less intentionally controllable in selection situations.

Moscoso (2000) reviewed evidence on the criterion and construct validity of the interview. Based on the content of questions included in selection interviews, Moscoso identified two types of structured interview: the conventional structured interview and the behavioural structured interview. Criterion validity studies generally support the view that behavioural structured interviews show the highest validity coefficients. Moscoso found a lower level of investigation into construct validity but concluded from studies available that conventional structured interviews and behavioural structured interviews were clearly measuring different constructs. Also, behavioural structured interviews seemed to produce more frequent negative applicant reactions than conventional structured interviews.

A further study by Salgado and Moscoso (2002) included a series of meta-analyses on the construct validity of conventional interviews and behavioural interviews. Conventional interviews typically include questions aimed at checking credentials, description of experience, and self-evaluative information. Behavioural interviews consist mainly of questions regarding job knowledge, job experience, and behaviour descriptions. They found that conventional interviews assessed general mental ability, job experience, the 'Big Five' personality dimensions and social skills. Behavioural interviews, on the other hand, mainly assessed job knowledge, job experience, situational judgement and social skills. Although there was some overlap, the two main forms of interview seemed to be different.

In a more recent study, Krajewski *et al.* (2006) analyzed data from 157 applicants to managerial positions and found a significant correlation between predictions from past-behaviour structured interviews and subsequent job performance. Situational interview formats did not produce a significant correlation. They also found a closer relationship between past-behaviour structured interviews and relevant cognitive ability measures, assessment centre exercises and personality traits.

Van Iddekinge *et al.* (2006) examined differences in criterion-related validity estimates among ratings from individual interviewers and interview panels in the US army. They found considerable variation in interviewer validity coefficients in relation to multiple performance criteria. Results also indicated the importance of adopting a multivariate perspective when evaluating interviewer validity differences. Similar findings emerged for ratings averaged within interview panels. However, most or all of the variance for some interview-criterion combinations appeared to be due to statistical artefacts.

To be effective, an interview must be more than a friendly chat. The greater the degree of planning beforehand, the greater the likelihood of a higher degree of validity as a selection tool. The function of the interview is to obtain predictive evidence regarding a candidate's likely performance on specific criteria. The questioning style can be linked to the kind of evidence required and may take one of three principal routes:

(Hypothetical) problem-solving questioning in which the candidate is presented with situations to evaluate or solve and which can be expected to test the candidate's abilities in a number of respects, e.g. intellect, grasp of information, problem-solving ability, lateral thinking, practicality, creativity, etc. Situational interviews have been found to increase candidates, perceptions of fair selection (Seijts and Kyei-Poku, 2010).

Behavioural (past) event questioning, which assumes that previous handling of situations and problems predicts an individual's future performance in similar circumstances.

Patterned behavioural event (life) questioning, which attempts to identify an individual's career or life strategy, establishing how rational and sensible changes in that person's life have been and drawing conclusions about stability, seriousness of application and likely motivation. The 'culture fit' approach emphasizes this perspective. For example,

Japanese companies such as Toyota are more interested in personality than technical skill. They look for a personal philosophy that fits the corporate culture. Modern call centres similarly seek a range of competences from customer care through to commitment-related qualities (Callaghan and Thompson, 2002).

Kutcher and Bragger (2004) investigated the potential of structured interviews for mitigating biases. They asked 133 participants to observe videotaped interviews, varying between structured or unstructured interview scripts and average weight or overweight job applicants. The results confirmed a bias against overweight interviewees which was moderated by the use of structured interviews. A further study with a greater level of structure in the interviews appeared to increase the moderating effect.

Blackman (2002b) investigated structured and unstructured employment interviews in relation to the assessment of applicants' job-related personality traits. The hypothesis was that unstructured interviews would lead to more accurate personality assessments since interviewees would feel less constrained by a script and more readily manifest their true selves. Behaviour in mock job interviews (structured and unstructured) was coded by an independent rater. Self-ratings of job-related personality traits on the California Q-set were obtained for each interviewee, together with ratings of their personality from the interviewer and a peer of the interviewee. A correlation analysis supported the original hypothesis, showing that average self–interviewer and peer–interviewer agreement was significantly greater when interviews had used the unstructured method.

Barclay (2001), however, comes out in favour of the behavioural structured interview. A survey of the use of behavioural interviewing in selection for UK organizations showed that both interviewers and applicants were positive about the method. Barclay identifies the following as key benefits:

→ Better quality information-gathering leading to improved selection decisions.

→ More consistency and improved skills of interviewers.

→ Better opportunities for applicants to explain their skills.

But Barclay also recognizes limitations in respect to training, practice and time required and scoring.

Other approaches that have ethical considerations to take into account include stress interviewing and 'sweet and sour'. Stress interviewing, where the candidate is pressurized, sometimes aggressively, is justified on the basis that the job is pressurized and, therefore, it is important to establish how the candidate is likely to perform under stressful circumstances. 'Sweet and sour' interviews are those where interviewers take completely different approaches, one pleasant, one unpleasant in an attempt to gain a wider range of responses from the candidate.

Preparation for interviews

Training for interviewers stresses a number of factors conducive to making a good impression on the candidate. The interviewer should ensure that relevant information (application form, etc.) is read beforehand – it is surprising how many interviewers are found to be reading such material for the first time *during* the interview. The interview should take place in an appropriate environment – a quiet room without interruptions, with comfortable but business-like furniture and so on. The candidate should be put at ease as much as possible.

A major change in recent years has been the improvement in applicants' interview techniques. Redundant staff are commonly given the opportunity of outplacement counselling,

HRM IN REALITY — CANDIDATES WHO PERFORM LAST FINISH FIRST

It isn't surprising when singers who advance to the next round in competitions such as 'American Idol' each week are those who performed at the end of the previous week's episode. Researcher Wändi Bruine De Bruin of Carnegie Mellon University has found that participants appearing towards the end of juried competitions seem to do better than those performing at the beginning – and this finding has implications for recruitment and selection.

Bruine De Bruin's latest paper, published in the journal *Acta Psychologica* (2005), describes her studies on European figure-skating competitions and the Eurovision Song Contest, a pop song competition that has taken place in Europe since 1956 (and which, like American Idol', includes voting by fans watching at home). Bruine De Bruin found that participants appearing near the end of the contests received higher marks from judges than those who performed earlier. This phenomenon, known as the serial position effect, doesn't just affect would-be pop idols; it is possible that the effect may occur in other situations such as job interviews and student exams.

Bruine De Bruin found that the effect was progressive, with scores increasing throughout the competitions, not just when judges evaluated all candidates at the end of each contest, but also when they were asked to rate each individual performance after it had been completed. Bruine De Bruin conducted some of her research at Eindhoven University of Technology in The Netherlands.

'A friend of mine asked to go last in a series of job interviews, after hearing about my research. She got the job. I like to think that she got the job because she has great skills, but order effects may have tipped the balance for her,' Bruine De Bruin said.

Can you suggest any ways to minimize order effects in selection procedures?

Source: Reprinted with permission from HRM Guide USA (http://www.hrmguide.com).

---

which normally includes advice on CV preparation and coaching in interview technique. Managers who are rarely involved in selection, perhaps only conducting interviews once or twice a year, are at a disadvantage against trained applicants. Interview coaching is similar in principle to training politicians for television appearances. Astute trainees can learn how to mask insincerity and to promise the earth with apparent conviction.

Against trained interviewers, the most useful tactic for applicants is to become familiar with the company they are applying to join. This requires research on the company's history, products or services and its reported strategy. Knowledge of the industry or sector in which it operates is also valuable. This information should not be acquired by pestering the recruitment section on the telephone. Given the number of applications to advertised vacancies at present, this is likely to be unwise. Whether or not any direct questions are asked on these subjects, applicants who have researched the territory will be able to form their responses in a way which makes it clear that they have done so.

Interviewing techniques

There are significant variations in the way employers conduct interviews. The most common method is the 'singleton' interview when the candidate's fate is determined by one session with a single interviewer. For obvious reasons, this method is likely to be regarded as unfair by interviewees who are not selected. There is no check or record of bias on the part of the interviewer who may have made a judgement on a complete whim.

A long-standing method which attempts to overcome this problem is the panel or board interview, involving a number of interviewers. The use of interviewers with particular experience of the job being filled has been identified as a strength of the European Union staffing model – although many other aspects of the EU's selection procedure have been castigated (Ban, 2010). Typically in a panel interview, two or three people ask questions in turn. A classic format involves an 'operational' interviewer, usually a line manager from the department offering the job and a personnel interviewer, normally from the HR department. There may be an additional chairperson. Each asks questions appropriate to their areas of expertise, the operational assessor asking task-related questions and the personnel assessor investigating career aspiration and motivation. The board is sometimes much larger: there are instances of seven or nine interviewers.

Superficially, the panel interview is judged to be fairer since all questioning takes place in a public arena and candidates' responses are heard by all parties. It also offers the candidate a more varied range of questions, expanding the evidence available to the assessors. As a consequence, personal bias should have less effect. However, the situation is likely to be more stressful for candidates. There are also opportunities for organizational politics to enter the situation, especially when the procedure is an internal selection.

Dipboye *et al.* (2001) looked at unstructured panel interviews for corrections officers and found a weak aggregate level of validity in the prediction of job performance and training success. Aggregate analyses also showed only a small incremental contribution to the prediction of job performance from panel judgements relative to paper credentials, and found the two sources of information to be only weakly related. But there was a considerable variation in simple and incremental validity at the level of individual panel members and among subgroups of panels. They conclude that aggregate analyses underestimate the validity of the typical unstructured panel interview.

A further variant is the 'sequential' method, with two or more interviews but with the candidate only being expected to face one interviewer at a time. This method carries most of the advantages of singleton and panel interviews with fewer of the disadvantages.

It is possible to use group interviews in certain circumstances. We will see later in this chapter that they are useful within assessment centre programmes as information sessions.

As with many other aspects of selection, interviewing has been formalized and packaged into training programmes available for both selectors and candidates. Untrained assessors are likely to conduct interviews in an unstructured way. Interview training is a useful component of management training. The best training programmes encourage people to become aware of their body language and questioning styles, helping them to develop interview techniques that open up fresh areas of evidence. Many junior managers and job club participants have had the opportunity to see themselves 'in action' on video, taking part in mock interviews. Initially demoralizing (for most), it is an invaluable method of feedback.

Packaged training methods have led to a certain sameness, however, and seasoned job applicants and interviewers now enter into formalized duals where each participant is aware of the underlying dynamics. Typically, interviewers are taught to:

→ Ask open, not closed, questions to elicit the maximum information. Questions beginning with how, what, why, when, reduce the frequency of yes/no answers and force candidates to think about their replies.

→ Provide supportive body language that suggests interest in what the candidate is saying without indicating approval or disapproval.

→ Employ questioning styles such as the use of funnelling. Here the interviewer asks a succession of how, what, why, questions on the same subject in an attempt to achieve a depth of evidence.

→ Consider factual or hypothetical questions, such as 'How would you go about setting up a telephone system for a remote island in the Pacific?' Provided that the interviewee is not a qualified telecommunications engineer, an applicant for a totally unconnected job will have to think hard to provide a full, imaginative but practical answer.

WORK SAMPLES

Interviews suffer from a basic problem: they obtain answers from candidates which, in effect, are unverifiable claims. When asked what they would do in a particular situation it is only natural for candidates to give the answer which they feel the interviewer wants to hear. There is no guarantee that a candidate would actually behave in that way in a real situation. In addition, it is common for candidates to exaggerate their abilities or experience and play down their inadequacies.

The work sample technique attempts to overcome this problem by asking candidates to take on 'mini jobs' in a selection situation. Properly designed work samples capture key elements of a real job. As such, they are realistic rather than hypothetical or abstract and should include features of the context in which the job functions. Work samples have shown some of the highest validity scores compared with other selection methods (Smith, Gregg and Andrews, 1989: 70). Roth, Bobko and Mcfarland (2005) re-examined classic literature supporting work sample tests as among the most valid predictors of job performance and suggest that the level of the validity may be approximately one-third less than previously thought. They also found that work sample tests were associated with an observed correlation of 0.32 with tests of general cognitive ability.

Work samples are comparatively easy to organize and even the smallest of companies could employ the simpler forms such as:

→ A typing test for jobs requiring keyboard skills.

→ Bricklaying.

→ Role playing.

→ Group decisions.

→ Presentations.

→ Reports.

The most sophisticated of work sample procedures include in-basket tests, sometimes called in-tray exercises. Normally used for managerial jobs, candidates are given a typical in-tray containing a selection of material such as letters to be answered, reports to be analyzed, items to be prioritized, etc. They are given instructions on what to do and a time limit. Standard scoring methods are available. Work samples are often used as part of an assessment centre programme. Wyatt *et al.* (2010) found that high and low performers in a medium-sized recruitment company could be distinguished using two work sample tests that had been constructed using the critical incident technique. In fact, there was a high correlation between test results and individual performance.

ASSESSMENT CENTRES

Recent surveys indicate increasing use of **assessment centres**, especially by large companies. They have been heavily researched in recent years, with the emphasis on their reliability and predictive validity. They show up well in comparison with most other forms of selection or assessment such as interviews and psychometric tests (e.g. Krause *et al.*, 2006) Meta-analyses indicate respectable validity coefficients for assessment centres in predicting managerial success (Hermelin *et al.*, 2007). However, as we will discuss shortly, their use is not entirely without difficulties.

 Assessment centres are procedures and not necessarily places. They function on the principle that no individual method of selection is particularly good and no individual assessor is infallible although overall assessment centre ratings correlate well preliminary interviews and cognitive tests (Dayan, 2008). Accordingly, they use multiple methods and several assessors in structured programmes that attempt to minimize the inadequacies of each method and cancel out the prejudices of individual selectors. Inevitably, assessment centres are very expensive methods of selection. However, cheaper methods are focused towards past or present performance. This may be adequate where applicants are being assessed for jobs that are broadly similar to their current or previous work. When this is not the case, and applicants are being considered for more stretching tasks, they fail to provide the evidence as to how candidates are likely to perform. Most management promotions come into this category. Good managers need to demonstrate knowledge, skills and abilities that may not have been required at lower levels. How can we identify these characteristics? Assessment centres are particularly useful in this respect because they are focused on potential. They bring taxing problems and challenges to candidates in a situation that allows systematic observation and measurement of their performance.

 The origins of the assessment centre lie in the violent history of the 20th century and the need for officer selection. Originally devised by the German army in the 1930s, assessment centre techniques were soon taken up in other countries. The British War Office Selection Board subjected candidates to a three- to four-day assessment, geared to evaluate leadership and organizational abilities. This included exercises in which intending officers had to negotiate obstacles such as rivers with a motley collection of squaddies and an assortment of ropes, planks and oil drums. They also included lengthy interviews and long written reports.

 Some modern assessment centres with an 'outward bound' inclination continue to include such exercises, but most consist of group discussions, psychometric tests, interviews and exercises such as 'in-basket' work samples and presentations. The underlying intention is to measure applicants on the competences deemed to be appropriate to the job. Simulations in the assessment centre are designed to bring out the behaviour which demonstrates possession of these competences. The intention is not to estimate current ability but to predict future performance, possibly at higher management levels.

 After World War II the method spread to the public sector and then to industry. The first industrial application was at the American Telephone and Telegraph Company (AT&T). Their experience had a major influence on subsequent use elsewhere, following a number of studies in which employees were compared with initial assessment centre evaluations. These studies showed a significant correlation between the evaluations and subsequent work performance (Smith, Gregg and Andrews, 1989).

 The model form of assessment centre is an expensive process (Byham, 1984). A typical assessment centre involves six participants and lasts from one to three days. As participants go through the simulations they are observed by assessors (usually three) who are specially trained in observing and evaluating behaviour. Assessors observe different participants in each simulation and take notes on special observation forms. Then, after the simulations are completed, assessors spend one or more days sharing their observations and reaching agreement on evaluations of participants. Their final assessment, contained in a summary report for each participant, gives a detailed account of participants' strengths and development needs as well as an evaluation of overall potential for success in the 'target' position. Based on Blanksby and Iles (1990), the following list sets out the seven conditions that classically characterize assessment centres:

1   A number of assessment techniques must be used, of which at least one must be a simulation. Simulations could take the form of work samples, group exercises and in-baskets. Simulations are designed to bring out behaviours that are related to dimensions of performance on the actual job in question.

2   There must be multiple trained assessors.

3   Ratings must be pooled between assessors and assessment techniques in order to provide a judgement on selection, training or development programme.

4   Overall assessment of behaviour has to take place at a different time from the observation of behaviour.

5   Simulation exercises must be pre-developed to elicit a number of desired behaviours. They must be tested in advance to ensure that the results are relevant to the organization and that they are reliable and objective.

6   All dimensions, qualities, attributes or characteristics to be measured by the assessment centre must be determined by some form of job analysis.

7   The assessment techniques used must be designed to provide evidence for the evaluation of these dimensions.

Problems with assessment centres

Whether or not it is costed in financial terms, the impact of assessment centres on management time is considerable. Managers may appreciate the value of high-quality selection procedures, but will be reluctant to devote so much time unless all other parts of the selection process have been thorough. For example, Hilton Hotels International conducted a one-day assessment centre as a final stage in a selection process for general managers. They contracted an outside provider to conduct exhaustive online tests to ensure that candidates who got that far deserved their place (Beal, 2004).

The effectiveness of an assessment centre depends upon its design and the anticipation of problems. Additionally, the traditional process is group-based and is unusable in situations where only one or two candidates are being considered. Common design faults have been well documented (Dulewicz, 1991):

→   The criteria for measurement are too woolly. Often, the competences on which candidates are being assessed are very poorly defined and not expressed in behavioural terms that can be measured.

→   The competences are not mutually exclusive and overlap each other. Candidates are rewarded or penalized twice, depending on their strength in a particular area. Moreover, if candidates become aware of the criteria on which they are being assessed they can skew their behaviour accordingly (König et al., 2007).

→   Criteria are tied to the past, rather than being forward-looking.

→ Exercises are badly designed and do not relate to experiences that are likely to occur within the organization. Alternatively, and perhaps because of this, they do not relate to the assessment criteria.

→ Assessment centres contain a wide range of procedures, from group exercises to psychometric tests. Results from these procedures take a variety of forms. Integrating the results is complex, particularly when combining evidence on single competences from a number of procedures. Poor technical design at this stage will lead to misleading findings.

→ Poor assessor training. Line managers are unlikely to be good assessors unless they have been trained to avoid pitfalls such as 'halos and horns'. Also they require guidance on the range and skew of their assessments. Assessors need to be consistent in how they pitch their ratings, avoiding over-leniency or severity. For example, in a study of the rating of ethnic minority candidates for the Dutch police, de Meijer *et al.* (2007) found that assessors were using more (and irrelevant) cues to judge minority candidates than those from the ethnic majority. Having to assess too many candidates at the same time can also lead to poor rating quality (Melchers *et al.*, 2010).

→ Poor pre-selection and briefing of candidates. The consequence is that some candidates flounder from the beginning of the programme. Others become hostile towards a procedure that appears to them to be unfair or disorganized.

→ Poor programming, leaving both assessors and candidates unsure of what they are supposed to be doing. They may be allotted too little or too much time at different points in the assessment.

→ Inadequate handling of the programme events due to lack of coordination or commitment.

→ Inadequate (or non-existent) follow-up. This may occur in the form of badly handled feedback counselling or inaction on assessors' recommendations.

→ Poor evaluation of candidates' experience and assessors' performance on the programme.

Dulewicz (*ibid.*) considered that there were three broad phases that accounted for most of these difficulties:

1 Programme design.
2 Selection and training of assessors.
3 Effective follow-up action.

He attributed many of the shortcomings to inexperience. Assessment centres are involved and complex. Good design is dependent on the knowledge and skills to design and develop what is a 'highly precise and sophisticated tool'.

Graphology

Graphology, or handwriting analysis, has a long history on the mainland of Europe dating back to the Ancient Greeks and Romans (Thomas and Vaught, 2001). Its modern form originated in Italy in the 17th century and was further refined in France and Germany where it is used widely. The essence of graphology is that analysts claim to be able to describe an individual's personality from a sample of their handwriting. Their theoretical base is that of trait psychology which holds that personality has a number of fixed dimensions that are relatively unchangeable and do not depend on the situation. This is not to say that people do not change, indeed many graphologists believe their strongest asset to be the identification of neurotic or stress-related conditions that may be transient. Some graphologists also claim to be able to detect such characteristics as alcohol problems, homosexuality and dishonesty.

For example, the following excerpt from a press report stated that the British company S.G. Warburg accepted a graphologist's opinion that 'cramped' handwriting indicated drug addiction:

> The recent candidate interviewed for a junior job in Warburg's computer department
> provided an excellent CV, and seemed able and confident in the course of two interviews. His
> handwriting sample, however, was abnormally cramped. The lines were crooked and the letters
> spidery and badly squashed. At best, it seemed the writing of an ill-educated child. But Mrs
> Nezos [graphologist] thought otherwise. For an employer like Warburg, the prospect of hiring
> a drug addict is too frightening to contemplate. The man was turned down for the job.
> (*Independent on Sunday,* 20 October, 1991)

It is commonly believed that handwriting analysis is routine and highly respected in many continental European countries whereas it is generally regarded with disdain in most English-speaking countries. However, there are signs of increasing acceptability in countries such as the USA: In the trade journal *Pest Control,* a contributor lauded the services of a handwriting analyst (Tennenbaum, 2005):

> Heidi mentioned that she could do analysis for potential employees. 'I can tell you everything
> about them, whether they'd be better in sales, for example,' she said. All she would need is a
> page-long essay from each candidate … the content doesn't matter as much as the handwriting
> itself.

The contributor was so impressed, it seems, that he no longer takes on new employees for his US$2 million company without her verbal approval (at less than US$75 a time) or a more expensive typed report. 'With that report in hand, I can decide whether I still want the person based on résumé, references and overall "gut feeling". … Nothing else work[s] this consistently well. It's amazing.'

In a similar pitch at a trade audience in New Zealand (Hogenesch, 2004: 10) another graphologist acknowledged that handwriting analysis has not yet caught on in that country, but that it is 'a science' and 'recognized as an authentic tool': 'Handwriting … is like body language. It is virtually impossible to hide or disguise personality characteristics by altering one's handwriting. In the eyes of a skilled handwriting analyst the true personality is unfailingly revealed.'

The evidence is not so flattering. Cox and Tapsell (1991) compared analyses by graphologists and non-graphologists of 50 handwriting samples provided by managers on a training course. When assessment centre results were compared with the handwriting analyses, they found that the graphologists did slightly worse than the non-graphologists in rating the candidates. Moreover, the two graphologists failed to agree with each other! Thomas and Vaught (2001: 35) surveyed the available literature on graphology and concluded that there was no evidence that handwriting analysis was a valid method of predicting job performance:

> … there is virtually no research that supports the use of graphology as an effective selection
> technique. At its best, it has only moderate reliability. There is little evidence that graphology is
> accurate in predicting personality traits, or that the narrow traits that many analysts infer from
> handwriting samples correlate with job performance. Finally, there is no evidence of a direct
> link between handwriting analysis and various measures of job performance.

Some critics are even more damning, for example Dr Barry Beyerstein, professor of biological psychology at Simon Fraser University in British Columbia (Ellin, 2004: 10). Dr Beyerstein said:

> Graphology is a pseudoscience that claims to be a quick and easy way of saying how someone's wired, but there's no evidence that this is encoded in handwriting.
>
> In these litigious times, you can't ask people about their sexual orientation or previous run-ins with the law or their home life or marital status. But graphologists make statements that no legitimate personnel person could make with such a degree of certainty and you can find a lot of gullible people who'll sign on. You'd think hard-nosed business people would be the last to be taken in, but they lap it up.

Why is graphology apparently so popular in continental Europe and supposed to be increasingly used in the USA and the UK (Ellin, 2004)? Thomas and Vaught (2001) speculate that one reason may be that it has an apparent face validity that people can relate to: it looks like it 'should' work as a method. However, in studies on selection techniques in a number of countries (Anderson and Witvliet, 2008, Anderson *et al.*, 2010), graphology was one of the least favoured by candidates. Finally, Bangerter *et al.* (2009) found that graphology is not as popular in continental Europe as claimed, that few job advertisements asked for handwritten letters and the handwritten letters that were received by employers were rarely analyzed by graphologists. They concluded that the popularity of graphology is a self-perpetuating myth.

 SUMMARY

In free market countries, the personnel profession has adopted a 'best practice' model that fits the prevailing business ideology. This model prescribes a quest for the 'right (best) person for the job'. To achieve this goal, criteria are used to rate prospective applicants by means of selection techniques, including biographical data, interviews, psychometric tests, group exercises, simulated work samples and even handwriting analysis. The most definitive form of selection is likely to take place within the context of assessment centres, involving several assessors and a variety of selection techniques. The 'best-person' or psychometric model has achieved the status of orthodoxy in free market countries. Elsewhere different models of resourcing apply. For example, in Japan there is a greater concern with personality and background than presumed ability. Recruits are sought who will 'fit in' with the culture of the corporation; who will be content to build a career within the organization; who will absorb the goals of the organization.

FURTHER READING

1 *The Professional Recruiter's Handbook: Delivering Excellence in Recruitment Practice* by Jane Newell Brown and Ann Swayne (Kogan Page, 2009) is based on techniques used by successful companies.

2 *The Assessment and Selection Handbook: Tools, Techniques and Exercises for Effective Recruitment and Development* by Ian Taylor (Kogan Page, 2008) is a 'how to' on the assessment centre approach.

Books on interviewing include:

3 *The Interview Book: Your Definitive Guide to the Perfect Interview Technique* by James Innes (Prentice Hall, 2009); and

4 *Effective Interviewing* by Robert Edenborough, (Kogan Page, 2002).

5 Robert Edenborough has also written *Assessment Methods in Recruitment, Selection and Performance: A Manager's Guide to Psychometric Testing, Interviews and Assessment Centres* (Kogan Page, 2005).

REVIEW QUESTIONS

1 Are selection methods objective?

2 When and why would you conduct an informal interview?

3 Discuss the merits and disadvantages of unstructured, structured and behaviourally structured interview methods. Evaluate Peters' approach against our discussion on the various types of interview.

4 Review the advantages and disadvantages of using psychometric tests for small and large organizations. Are psychometric tests fair?

5 What criteria can be used to judge the effectiveness of selection methods?

6 Define 'validity' and 'reliability' in your own words.

7 Why are some selection methods used more often than others?

8 What are the arguments for and against the use of assessment centres for employee selection?

9 Explain why hiring managers do not necessarily use the best decision-making practices in employee selection.

10 Is it possible to guarantee equality of opportunity in a resourcing process?

CASE STUDY FOR DISCUSSION AND ANALYSIS

Everylang

Everylang is a small, fast-growing translation bureau. It needs to keep tight control of its costs in a very competitive market. The owner considers that its success depends on quality, presentation, speed of work and the ability to provide translations to and from any language. Most of the work is from the main European languages and into English. The company employs 12 staff, while the remaining work (over half) is farmed out to freelance translators who are only paid for the work they do. They communicate with the office by a variety of means, including courier, post, fax and email. It is sometimes difficult to get and maintain relationships with top-quality freelancers.

Situation
Everylang has now grown to the point where the owner-manager is too busy with marketing, finance and developing new customers to be able to cope with the

day-to-day operations. You have been invited as an external consultant to advise on selecting an office manager for Everylang. It is apparent that the owner knows a great deal about the translation market but is inexpert in managing people. The owner is keen to promote a member of the existing staff, partly in order to improve motivation but mainly in order to keep costs down. Five have applied and you have been provided with the following job summary on which to base your initial thoughts.

Title:	Office manager.
Pay:	Translator salary + 30 per cent + profit-related bonus and benefits.
Main purpose of job:	Day-to-day running of Everylang office, ensuring that incoming work is dealt with and returned to agreed standard of quality and delivery time.
Functions:	Providing quotations for customers; dealing with enquiries; allocating work to full-time staff or freelancers; recording and progressing all incoming work, delivery on time and to the agreed quality; dealing with complaints; finding and monitoring new freelancers; completing computer records for billing and administration; and dealing with any personal problems among staff.
Personnel specification:	None existing.

Applicants

Helen. Age 42. Five years with Everylang. No formal qualifications. Translates French and Spanish. Ex-secretary. Has been translating for almost 20 years and knows a large number of other translators. Very efficient, quick and accurate. She is keen on long legal translations and has developed a considerable knowledge of business law in French-speaking countries. Pleasant personality but a little short-tempered. She has a good working relationship with other staff members but tends to keep her distance and does not socialize with them. Likes to take a six-week holiday at her parents' home in France every summer. She

has an arrangement with the owner to take this partly as unpaid leave.

John. Age 36. Has been 12 years with Everylang. High school qualifications in French and Italian. Also has a diploma in translating and interpreting in the same languages. A great language enthusiast, he is proud of his standard of work. He translates mostly from French, specializing in letters and product information. Takes a keen interest in the welfare of the other staff. They have a considerable regard for him, respecting his professionalism and his interest in them. Over the last year he has had arguments with the owner over policy and thinks the company is growing too fast. He believes that the ever-increasing pressure of work is leading to inadequate checking of translations. Personally, he is quite efficient but pays too much attention to small details. Has been thinking of going self-employed.

Jill. Age 32. Three years with Everylang. Left school at 16. Took evening classes in French for several years. Cheerful, chatty person who gets on well with customers. Not a particularly good translator but useful for short French translations needed quickly. Can understand Scandinavian languages quite well, particularly Norwegian – she worked in Norway as a managing director's personal secretary for two years. The other staff do not respect her as a translator and often patronize her. She copes well, brushing off their remarks and getting on with her job. She has applied for a number of other jobs recently – without success.

Francesca. Age 26. Graduate in Spanish and Italian. Diploma in Translating. Also speaks Portuguese. Has 18 months' service. Undoubtedly the best translator in the office. She had considered becoming a language teacher but dropped out of the training programme after a year and joined Everylang. She is younger than the other staff and relations are not particularly good. Gets on extremely well with major clients who find her vivacious personality attractive to deal with. She gives customers a feeling of confidence in her abilities. Francesca sees Everylang as a long-term career job, is ambitious and enthusiastic about major expansion. At the moment, she is having major problems with her pre-school age child who suffers from asthma. Sometimes she takes time off with little notice. She has promised the boss that her difficulties will be sorted out soon.

David. Age 55. Three years with company. BA and MA in German Literature. Former export manager, made redundant from a major company. He translated on a freelance basis before joining Everylang. He is the only full-time German translator. A workaholic – he never seems to leave the office and is always ready to work overtime to complete a piece of work. He is regarded as bookish by the other staff. Sometimes David is extremely critical of other people's standard of work.

He considers the qualifications of some of the other translators to be inadequate for the jobs they are doing. In general, he thinks that the owner is unimaginative and has failed to capitalize on non-European languages. He is very unhappy about his salary which is much lower than his pay as export manager. However, he knows that he cannot cope with the uncertainties of being a freelancer.

The company does not have a performance assessment system.

What criteria would you apply in seeking the most suitable applicant?

What methods would you use to obtain further information about these candidates?

What are the likely advantages and disadvantages of promoting any one of these individuals?

CHAPTER 8
Performance management

LEARNING OBJECTIVES

The purpose of this chapter is to:

→ **Determine the criteria that distinguish 'good' from less acceptable performance.**

→ **Evaluate the most common techniques for measuring performance.**

→ **Investigate how performance management can be used to reinforce an organization's human resource strategies.**

→ **Consider whether or not performance management really encourages desirable work behaviour.**

PERFORMANCE ASSESSMENT

In the last chapter we looked at how the performance of potential recruits can be predicted from evidence collected during selection procedures. In this chapter we extend our debate to the evaluation of current employee performance.

Performance assessment has a long history based on comparative judgements of human worth. In the early part of the 19th century, for example, Robert Owen used coloured wooden cubes, hung above workstations, to indicate the performance of individual employees at his New Lanark cotton mills in Scotland. Various merit ratings were represented by different coloured cubes, which were changed to indicate improvement or decline in employee performance (Heilbroner, 1953, cited in Murphy and Cleveland, 1995: 3). As with the employee selection techniques described in Chapter 7, modern performance assessment developed from sophisticated rating systems designed by work psychologists for military use during the two world wars. By the 1950s, such methods had been adopted by most large US business organizations, spreading worldwide thereafter. Initially, performance assessment was used to provide information for promotions, salary increases and discipline. More recently, performance measurement has had wider purposes:

→ To identify and enhance desirable or effective work behaviour.

→ Reinforcing this behaviour by linking rewards to measured performance.

→ Developing desired competences and building human capital within organizations.

Enthusiasts for performance assessment argue that it serves a key integrating role within an organization's human resource processes. First, it provides a checking mechanism for resourcing policies and procedures, evaluating the quality of recruits and hence the underlying decision-making process. Second, it monitors employee commitment and the relevance of their working behaviour to business objectives. Third, it provides a rationale for an organization's pay policies. Taken at face value, these intentions seem entirely compatible with an integrated and strategic approach to human resource management. In reality, however, the definition and measurement of good performance is a controversial matter, involving fundamental issues of motivation, assessment and reward.

All aspects of **performance management** (see Key concept 8.1) arouse controversy, especially appraisals and **performance-related pay**. Critics point to weaknesses in their methodology and basic philosophy. There is also some debate about the use made of performance information, particularly in public services (Moynihan and Pandey, 2010; Al-Raisi *et al.*, 2010). Employees are often dissatisfied with the methods of performance management systems and managers are frequently reluctant to engage in the process because of its confrontational nature. At a deeper level, it can be argued that if true commitment exists, performance management is superfluous. In too many organizations it enforces the compliance of an unhappy workforce. However, Pettijohn *et al.* (2001) demonstrated that a positive attitude towards appraisal – from employees and managers – is possible if managers are provided with information designed to increase the benefits of engaging in the evaluation process and more thought is given to the appropriateness of measurement criteria.

KEY CONCEPT 8.1 PERFORMANCE MANAGEMENT

A holistic approach to assessing and improving the performance of an organization's people in line with business objectives.

Despite its problematic reputation, the use of performance assessment has been reinforced through the increasing prevalence of performance-related pay (PRP). As we will see in Chapter 10 this is based frequently on an oversimplified view of work motivation. Employers, consultants and neo-liberal politicians remain wedded to PRP schemes despite considerable evidence against their effectiveness as motivators. Fletcher (2001) argues that performance assessment has widened both as a concept and as a set of practices, becoming more obviously a part of HRM's strategic integration of human resource activities and business policies. Consequently, research and discussion of the topic has moved beyond measurement issues and criticisms of the accuracy of performance ratings to encompass the social and motivational aspects of assessment. Fletcher divides current concerns into two thematic groups:

→ The content of appraisal: contextual performance, goal orientation and self-awareness.

→ The process of appraisal: appraiser-appraisee interaction, and multi-source feedback that have cross-cultural implications and are open to technological change.

We begin with a discussion of the environmental factors that have led to the widespread use of performance assessment techniques. These include legislation, the demands of technological change, increasing flexibility and diversification, and changes in workforce composition. We proceed to look at the way in which organizations favour certain stereotypes of good performance. The next section evaluates decision-making underlying the adoption of performance assessment strategies. Finally we discuss the activities involved in assessment such as appraisal and counselling.

THE ENVIRONMENTAL CONTEXT

The business environment exercises both a direct and an indirect influence on the conduct of performance assessment. Whereas legislation has specific consequences, particularly in the USA, most environmental factors have a diffuse and often unrealized effect on assessment and pay structures. It is likely that different individuals – and organizations – will respond in varying ways to these factors. Some will be highly sensitive to possible legal implications, practice elsewhere, and the state of the job market; others will be virtually immune to these influences. The main environmental factors identified as having a contextual influence on performance management are examined in the following sub-sections.

Business culture

At a national level, culture affects performance management through socio-political traditions and attitudes that determine whether assessment is acceptable, and to what degree. Cultural norms dictate 'acceptable' standards of performance and the management methods by which they are assured. For example, in a number of Asian societies, the employment relationship is a matter of honour, and obligations are regarded as morally, rather than contractually, binding between the two parties. In a situation where people are automatically expected to do the job as agreed, the role of performance assessment is questionable. Entrekin and Chung (2001) and Hempel (2001) conducted studies of Hong Kong Chinese and Western managers in Hong Kong. Both studies found considerable differences in attitudes towards appraisal and the attribution of good performance between Hong Kong Chinese managers and their counterparts from the UK or the USA. Entrekin and Chung (2001) concluded that Western managers and Chinese managers in Western-owned firms regarded performance assessment more highly than Hong Kong Chinese managers in Hong Kong-owned firms. And, given a choice, supervisory (top-down) appraisal was preferred by Chinese managers over other approaches such as subordinate or peer evaluation. However, Paik, Vance and Stage (2000) examined the characteristics of performance assessment systems in four South-East Asian countries – Indonesia, Malaysia, the Philippines, and Thailand – and found significant differences in managerial practices and behaviours relevant to the design and conduct of performance appraisal. They suggest that the cultural context of performance assessment is complex and that the familiar clustering of cultures is too simplistic to explain the differences that exist. Similarly, in a comparison of public sector performance management in Ontario (Canada) and Ghana, Ohemeng (2010) concludes that a 'one size fits all' approach is ineffective.

Legislation

In free market economies, the employment relationship between workers and employing organizations is seen as a contractual matter. This relationship is expressed in formal or legalistic statements of obligation between the two, such as written employment contracts, job descriptions and performance objectives. Performance measurement has the purpose of ensuring that the employee fulfils the contract. Commitment in Western organizations is rarely a 'hearts and minds' phenomenon and this is exemplified in the policing nature of performance management. It is a modern version of scientific management in which the detail of work is supervised in a sometimes overbearing way. Within English-speaking countries, performance-related pay encapsulates a fusion of the work ethic (Key concept 8.2) and free market ideology: work is virtuous and virtue should be rewarded generously – bearing in mind that there are generational differences in attitudes (Meriac *et al.*, 2010).

KEY CONCEPT 8.2 THE WORK ETHIC

The belief that work is virtuous in itself. Hard work is to be admired and leisure is equated with laziness. Spare time is perceived as evil: 'the devil makes work for idle hands'. In some societies the work ethic became a fundamental religious principle, the Puritans and Calvinists holding it to be such a virtue that Max Weber termed it 'the Protestant work ethic'.

Performance measurement has become a sensitive legal issue in the USA because of possible consequences for equal opportunities (Murphy and Cleveland, 1995: 11). Since the 1970s, assessments have been regarded as tests and are subject to guidelines enforced by the Equal Employment Opportunities Commission. Employers taking personnel decisions on the basis of performance assessment have to be mindful of possible legal action on one of two grounds: (a) the validity or accuracy of assessment ratings as predictors of future performance and promotion potential; or (b) the validity or accuracy of ratings as measures of past behaviour. This legislation is specific to the USA, but all human resource managers have to be mindful of possible breaches of equal opportunities legislation in their own countries.

General economic conditions

Prevailing attitudes towards employees and, in turn, their response to performance assessment are considerably affected by issues such as unemployment. In line with our earlier discussion, growth and shrinkage in the job market is conventionally believed to be followed by changes in the behaviour of workers and employers. At times of high unemployment, workers are thought to be concerned about losing their jobs and hence are more conscientious and tolerant of strict management. When suitable employees are scarce, managers must be cautious – unflattering assessments can trigger an employee's move to another organization. With fluctuating levels of organizational commitment, managers may attempt to increase levels of support for employees who have low levels of commitment (Perryer *et al.*, 2010)

The relationship between the economy and assessment is circular and complex. Performance management is justified by organizational efficiency, and the overall efficiency of organizations in a country is crucial for its economic well-being. Income generated by effective, as opposed to inefficient, performance encourages economic wealth. Performance management has become the chosen Western instrument to drive out ineffective activity. It incorporates both stick and carrot: the first in terms of sanction, criticism or discipline; the second in the form of praise or cash.

Industry sector

Methods of performance management vary considerably between different industrial sectors, partly as a function of the nature of the work involved, tradition and fashion. Sales-dominated industries, such as financial services, tend to have clear individual or team objectives that can be translated readily into performance targets. Performance-related pay is common in this sector and commission-only contracts are not unusual. In other sectors, objectives are more diffuse and difficult to measure so that PRP is not easily justified.

Technological change

The advent of technological advances such as wi-fi and mobile broadband have made work outside conventional offices much easier to perform but, in some respects, more difficult to manage. This raises intriguing issues for performance management. For instance, how does a manager assess the performance of a homeworker when there is little or no personal contact between the two? Technology has the power to provide extensive statistics such as the the time an individual spends logged on to a system, number of key strokes and volume of output; but does this information provide a meaningful measure of job performance? If the employee's task involves elements of creativity, accuracy and thoroughness, how can these be assessed? Being at the work location, and even being busy, is not the same as being effective. Performance management hinges inevitably on results.

Flexibility and diversification

As we have already seen, in the 1980s and early 1990s, the traditional nature of the employment relationship in free market countries changed, moving the balance of power firmly in favour of employers. We noted that job descriptions have disappeared or, at least, have been diluted, so that employees can be asked to do virtually anything required by the organization. Conversely, performance criteria have been more tightly defined, typically expressed in the form of demanding objectives: forever-moving goalposts. Performance assessment has become the crucial means of monitoring this relationship.

Employee relations

Performance management is a means of enhancing managerial control, particularly through individual performance-related pay schemes. In Chapter 10 we will see that the individualization of pay diminishes or neutralizes the role of collective bargaining. The purpose and influence of trade unions is undermined, reducing both their effectiveness and attractiveness as an alternative focus for employee commitment. Brown and Heywood (2005) used data from the Australian Workplace Industrial Relations Survey to estimate the determinants of performance appraisal systems. As we might expect, complementary human resource management practices, such as formal training and incentive pay, are associated with an increased likelihood of performance appraisal, but union density is associated with a reduced likelihood of performance appraisal.

Workforce composition

Largely forgotten in the controversy over PRP, the other main function of performance assessment is the identification of individual strengths and weaknesses. As we will see in Chapter 9, the latter can be targeted for improvement through training and development. Strengths may indicate a potential star performer, worthy of a management career route and promotion. Assessment employed to determine development needs ultimately serves to increase a nation's human capital.

Less positively, demographics and a history of unequal opportunities affect the conduct of assessment, since they largely determine who assesses whom.

THE ORGANIZATION AND EFFECTIVE PERFORMANCE

How do organizations decide which performance criteria should be measured? How do they differentiate between a good, average or indifferent employee? Two central propositions can be used to justify performance assessment (Armstrong and Baron, 1998):

1   People, either as individuals or teams, put the greatest effort into performing well if they know and understand what is expected of them and have had an involvement in specifying those expectations.

2   Employees' ability to meet performance expectations is based on:
   — individual levels of capability
   — the degree of support provided by management
   — the processes, systems and resources made available to them by the organization.

Noblet *et al.* (2005) suggest that wide-ranging changes that have occurred in the public sector over recent years have placed increasing demands on employees. They found that the presence of support at work, the amount of control employees had over their job, perceptions of pay and the perception of a lack of human resources were found to predict employee outcome variables. They emphasize the impact that middle managers and HR managers can have in reducing detrimental effects caused by introduction of new public management. Public sector managers can use design of jobs and development of social support mechanisms, such as employee assistance programmes, to sustain the quality of working life for their employees.

In practice, according to Armstrong and Barron (1998), performance management has the following aims:

→   Assisting in achieving sustainable improvements in an organization's overall performance.

→   Serving as a lever for change in developing a more performance-oriented culture.

→   Increasing employee motivation and commitment.

→   Giving individual employees the means to develop competences, improve job satisfaction and reach their full potential to their own benefit and that of the organization.

→ Improving team spirit and performance.

→ Offering a mechanism for regular dialogue and improved communication between individual employees and their managers.

→ Providing an outlet for employees to express their aspirations and concerns.

What is the reality? DeNisi and Pritchard (2006) argue that almost a century of research on performance appraisal has resulted in very few specific recommendations about designing and implementing appraisal and performance management systems whose goal is performance improvement. They suggest that there has been too great a focus on measurement issues and not enough attention has been paid to the outcome of the performance management exercise.

Organizations take many forms. No matter how an organization is structured, its output is the product of an interaction between different employees, departments, divisions and so on. Frequently, it is difficult to determine whose performance has been critical, or most significant, to the completion of a particular task. Current trends towards networking and team-based projects make individual performance even harder to gauge. Claus Offe once stated that identifying an individual's contribution to meeting an organization's goals is like listening to the sound of one hand clapping. Yet some people are singled out as key performers. On what basis? It is arguable that they may not be outstandingly good performers in an absolute sense but, simply, the people who conform most closely to the organization's norms.

Each organization defines effective performance in its own terms: being a 'good' manager in one organization is not the same as being good in another (Gunz, 1990). Company cultures and management styles vary and effective performance often translates as conformity to the house-style. According to Gunz, organizations differ greatly so that:

1   The contexts in which managers operate vary considerably.

2   This leads to different ideas about effective management so that some companies, for example, emphasize engineering quality, others financial performance or market dominance.

3   In each case people find it comparatively easy to recognize good management but may find it hard to say why. This leads to certain types of people being promoted. As these people are seen to succeed everyone else draws their own conclusions about what it takes to get ahead.

4   This closes the loop, reinforcing the dominant image of effectiveness.

As Gunz concludes:

… promotion patterns in a firm will be resistant to change because of the model's closed loop. The system is remaking itself in its own image, something organizational managers are usually aware of even if they do not always admit it openly.

This is consistent with evidence from a large number of studies reviewed by Campbell *et al.* (1970) who found that judgements of managerial effectiveness or *good*ness are actually measures of personal success. When people are asked to identify a good manager, they do so on the basis of an individual's promotion record, salary, global ranking of success and so on. Often the identification of promotable staff is devolved to individual managers. They tend to favour subordinates who are reliable – that is, they do things in the way the managers would – or who have skills the manager does not possess.

Most of all, as we have noted already in previous discussions of the cloning process, they favour employees who are similar to themselves. Bates (2002) investigated 'liking' and two types of rater–ratee similarity to predict ratings of managerial competencies. The study showed that technical proficiency, rater–ratee liking, demographic and attitudinal similarity about work were all significant predictors of proficiency ratings. Technical proficiency was the strongest predictor of ratings, followed by attitudinal similarity. A combination of liking, attitudinal and demographic similarity seemed to have a significant influence on ratings, over and above technical performance.

Morgan (1986: 144) draws parallels between organizations and political systems in that both vary from autocracy to the democratic decision-making seen in some voluntary organizations. He attributes a major role in determining successful performance to political processes such as conflict, power-play and intrigue. Following this line of logic, it is clear that any performance assessment system is vulnerable to the cloning process. Without thought, performance management can drive out diversity. It is also open to manipulation by employees who can identify the qualities necessary to 'get on' in a particular organization.

Behaviour can be fine-tuned to meet the organization's expectations. The latter can be termed '**impression management**' (see Key concept 8.3).

KEY CONCEPT 8.3 IMPRESSION MANAGEMENT

Image is created as part of one's self-identity. It is a product of individual and social elements, constantly shaped and reshaped to fit the expected behaviours of the current role. In other words, people act. An image can be learned or acquired through training – a deliberate process called impression management.

Impression management

Every organization has its cultural symbols and rites: standards of dress and personal appearance, time-keeping, participating in semi-social activities, etc. We choose to conform or not. We may pretend to be enthusiastic, agree with management opinions, or even take up golf for networking rather than sporting reasons. Such behaviour can be described as 'manipulating the impression others gain about us' (Hinton, 1993: 23). The archetypal example is the selection or promotion interview where most of us make a special effort with appearance and manner to achieve a favourable impression. This is easy to sustain for 20–40 minutes, but not necessarily convincing. Long-term success requires a consistent and believable image sustained over a considerable period.

The most significant quality required for selection to top jobs is the ability to create a good impression (Miller and Hanson, 1991). The key feature of a well-honed image is that it gives the impression that applicants have qualities they do not possess: a false portrayal of abilities, disguising the lack of true competences behind socially valued characteristics.

Control of one's public image depends on self-awareness. Degrees of self-awareness vary. Some people are invariably 'themselves' whereas others are acutely sensitive to the impression they convey and modify their behaviour constantly. For example, salespeople are much more likely to succeed if they can 'fine-tune' the impression made on customers. Snyder (1974) attributed this to 'self-monitoring'. Good salespeople are high self-monitors, responding quickly to customers' reactions. Low self-monitors make little effort to modify their behaviour, even in an employment interview. Day and Schleicher (2006) reviewed empirical and theoretical evidence on the importance of self-monitoring and concluded that high self-monitors are particularly good at 'getting along', for example in meeting others' social expectations, and 'getting ahead', instancing job performance and leadership emergence. Hinton (1993) points to skilled politicians who change their message depending on the audience, and are thereby perceived as being 'in-touch with the people'. They may make contradictory statements to different audiences and portray themselves as liberal or conservative as required.

Some images derive from the role models around us: successful people in the company or media stars. In the UK – particularly in England – the class structure, education system and institutions such as the civil service and the City serve to create and promote specific images. Finding people like ourselves to join our in-group is symptomatic of this condition at a national or institutional level. Too many organizations are dominated by identikit clones with similar images and ideas, whose concept of talent-spotting is finding more of the same. Women in particular are disadvantaged in their stock of relationships (social capital), and impression management may be one approach to compensate for this (Kumra and Vinnicombe, 2010).

Influencers

Miller and Hanson (1991) note that our ability to recognize real ability 'is contaminated by what we have come to call *the smile factor*' – closely related to the halo effect. The one-to-one interview is the most susceptible but at assessment centres 'the fish-bowl setting gives influencers/impressers space to perform'. A classic example is the excellent salesman who fails to perform well after promotion to sales manager. Time and time again the different requirements of the two jobs are ignored. Miller and Hanson studied four groups of widely different US executives and people deemed to have 'high potential' by their organizations. They describe their results as: '… to put it mildly, alarming. These organizations seeking leaders for major responsibilities were apparently confusing demonstrated leadership with some of the behavioural characteristics which some leaders exhibit.'

They found that all the people studied were particularly good at influencing others. They communicated well and were able to get other people to accept their ideas. They were generally sensitive and articulate, able to listen as well as talk. However, few had the motivation and the ability to manage or exercise leadership. They termed the majority 'influencers', people who wanted 'to have an impact on others but who did not want continuing or complete responsibility for the performance of others'. They were natural coaches and facilitators but reluctant to confront staff over missed deadlines or other forms of poor performance.

Admitting that influencers are likely to be bright and analytical, Miller and Hanson consider them to be too aware of the complexities inherent in any situation. They lack the confidence to take one direction as opposed to any other and, therefore, cannot be proactive or take risks. Further, because they are not aware in detail of the activities of their staff, they are unable to monitor changes effectively. Leaders are able to take tough decisions, can handle ambiguity and give direction. Miller and Hanson concluded that 'as many as eight out of ten people promoted into executive positions are influencers rather than leaders: most of the people running these organizations are not leaders; they only look as though they are.' Mount, Ilies and Johnson (2006) explored the hypothesis that personality traits will differentially predict counterproductive work behaviours. They found that direct relationships between traits such as 'agreeableness' and interpersonal behaviour, and 'conscientiousness' and organizational behaviour at work are partly explained by an employee's level of job satisfaction.

There is nothing new in saying that 'real self' and 'outward image' are different constructions and that success is probably more dependent on the latter than the former. However, it is worth stressing that organizations do not benefit from this process. **Images** are distracting and misleading. Promotion on the basis of image does not produce employees capable of doing the job to an internationally competitive standard. Performance assessments tend to value image qualities: apparent self-confidence, the ability to talk charismatically, etc. Indeed, '**charisma**' – the essential characteristic of the successful double-glazing salesman – is much admired and respected in a leader (see Key concept 8.4). According to Bryman (1992: 22):

> In business and management periodicals the term is employed a great deal in the context of discussions of certain prominent figures. In such discussions, the term is often employed to describe someone who is flamboyant, who is a powerful speaker, and who can persuade others of the importance of his or her message. The non-charismatic leader, by contrast, is often depicted as a lacklustre, ineffectual individual.

KEY CONCEPT 8.4 CHARISMA

Weber (1947) regarded charisma as one of three sources of authority (the other two being 'rational-legal' and 'traditional'), portraying it as a magical and hypnotic force based on direct personal contact. In modern life charisma is often fake – a product of carefully orchestrated mass communications.

Charismatics are perceived as having the power to transform organizations; as having a mission; able to inspire awe and obedience. For example, in a study of large French organizations, Bacha (2010) found that employees' perception of energetic, charismatic CEOs was associated with firm performance. They can also be lethal: a poison-pill for the ultimate well-being of any organization. Yet, like particularly dim lemmings, people managers – from personnel officers to boards of directors – will opt for the charismatic in preference to the non-charismatic.

It can be argued that at senior levels managers need to be figureheads and spokespersons for their organizations. For these roles, the required fluency, credibility and general communicating skills are those of a charismatic person. Indeed there may be a case for such a role to be entirely that of figurehead, not requiring any substantive abilities beyond those required for that role. A monarch or president, for example, can serve as a figurehead without executive power, allowing a prime minister to administer and direct. However, the tendency to overvalue charismatic skills has repeatedly led to foolish choices for 'number one' in large and small organizations. A further danger for performance assessment lies in the tendency to use cloning criteria at junior levels that are only relevant for people at the top of the organization.

Image can be construed as a decorative edifice built on the foundation of **substance**. An image which satisfies an audience does not necessarily preclude ability. Curiously, failure does not seem to dent common belief in the value of charisma. Similarly, the success of people with image and substance is commonly attributed to charisma – reinforcing belief in its necessity. Countering this process is difficult. It requires a recognition by senior managers that they may have succeeded by cultivating successful images rather than being the best available. Their organizations need assessment methods that are immune to this process: techniques to identify substance or necessary competences, rather than the obscuring irrelevances of a polished image (Key concept 8.5).

KEY CONCEPT 8.5 SUBSTANCE VERSUS IMAGE

'Substance' can be defined as that body of competences, knowledge and experience required to fulfil a particular function. Image' is the *apparent* totality of such knowledge and abilities as outwardly presented by an individual or group.

Langtry and Langtry (1991) compare two extreme management types which are over-simplified but identifiable within most organizations. 'I' stands for image or 'me', 'O' equals objective or 'others':

→ *I* managers maintain a high profile, speak well at meetings and are particularly effective at interviews. They are good networkers and make a point of getting to know the right people. They develop a good 'veneer', deliberately projecting a positive and confident image. Effective self-publicists, they make sure that everyone knows how hard they work and how successful they are. They are skilled careerists, and with sufficient emphasis and repetition they ensure that myth becomes reality.

→ *O* managers do not indulge in such elaborate charades. Innovative and supportive, they are quietly hard-working, getting on with the job as efficiently as possible. They only come to the attention of senior management when they challenge simplistic ideas which the *I* manager enthusiastically adopts. The tendency is for their work to be ignored in favour of the *I* manager's claims and their criticism to be interpreted as negative. Their fatal mistake is to assume that recognition will follow a job well done. Usually, however, the *I* manager goes streaking past them up the career ladder.

Obviously, this delightful typology divides managers too sharply into two simple categories but it captures the essence of the problem.

Assessment and organizational change

The conduct of performance management is affected also by the success of the organization. Assessors and assessed may vary their standards depending on their perception of the organization's overall performance, career prospects and, consequently, their feelings of security and optimism. The emotional background to assessment can be directly affected by the prevailing culture of the organization. Attempts to develop a strong, cohesive culture encourage closer agreement between raters on the standards they expect.

As we observed in the early chapters of this book, de-layering and downsizing have had the effect of increasing the ratio of staff to managers throughout the Western business world. As a consequence, managers have a greater number of assessments to conduct on people they know less about. Widespread structural changes in large organizations also bring new combinations of people together with little knowledge of each other – but, perhaps, fewer longstanding prejudices.

Intriguingly, managers' routes to power appear to have a direct effect on the way they assess subordinates (Murphy and Cleveland, 1995: 415):

> Attribution theory suggests that raters who have risen through the ranks will have a distorted perception of how well they performed in the job (they will readily recall good performance and will discount poor performance), which may lead to unrealistically high standards.

On the other hand, managers look after their own and assess their own staff generously. It is well known that performance ratings tend to the positive, with more people being judged as good performers than one would expect from a normal population. This is termed 'rater inflation'. It happens generally, but is particularly evident when assessors rate employees they have themselves previously promoted or selected. Rater inflation is common also when the process involves an element of self-assessment. Dunning, Heath and Suls (2004) argue that several psychological processes conspire to produce inaccurate self-assessments. People's self-views hold only a 'tenuous to modest' relationship with actual behaviour and performance.

The correlation between self-ratings of skill and actual performance in many domains is only 'moderate to meagre'. At times, other people's predictions prove more accurate.

Dunning *et al.* suggest that there is a tendency for individuals to overrate themselves:

> People say that they are 'above average' in skill (a conclusion that defies statistical possibility), overestimate the likelihood that they will engage in desirable behaviours and achieve favorable outcomes, furnish overly optimistic estimates of when they will complete future projects, and reach judgments with too much confidence.

In the workplace, flawed self-assessments occur at all levels. Employees tend to overestimate their skill, making it difficult to give meaningful feedback. CEOs can be overconfident in their judgements, particularly when developing new markets or projects. Dunning *et al.* suggest that possible solutions include training in routine correction for bias in self-assessments and requiring people to justify decisions in front of their peers. They conclude that self-assessment of skill, expertise and knowledge is intrinsically difficult, and should be approached with caution.

Most explanations of rater inflation are couched in terms of organizational politics:

Preserving morale. A positive performance assessment – whether or not it is deserved – is an act of praise. It offers an opportunity for a manager to say 'thank you' and 'well done', boosting morale and commitment. It engenders good working relationships between managers and subordinates. It maintains a cosy atmosphere.

Avoiding confrontation. Conversely, a critical assessment is likely to have the opposite effects.

Management image. If managers rate staff poorly there is an implication that they make bad selection decisions and run poor-quality departments. This can have unfortunate consequences on their own performance ratings.

From a psychological perspective, it can be argued that managers develop a bonding, or personal working relationship with their favoured staff that inevitably leads to biased assessments of their performance. The organization's human resource strategies should be focused, in part at least, on overcoming this problem. In the next section we consider the strategic choices that are open to us.

PERFORMANCE STRATEGIES

'Organizations face a critical paradox. No other management tool is more critical to productivity than effective performance appraisals, yet they can actually impair employees' performance' (English, 1991: 56).

As we observed at the beginning of this chapter, performance assessment or appraisal has been in use for a considerable period, particularly for management and sub-management grades in large corporations. The range of jobs covered by performance assessment is steadily increasing but there remain areas of employment where performance measurement does not yet feature and there is a great deal of conflict over its introduction.

From a strategic perspective, the process of assessment is an exercise in management power and control. It is a method by which an enterprise can evaluate its employees and feed back the organization's views to them. Furthermore, evaluation can be linked to 'stick and carrot' measures in the form of critical comment indicating the firm's disapproval, and incentives to reward and encourage 'good' performance in the form of enhanced pay and promotion prospects.

We saw in Chapter 1 of this book that 'behavioural consistency' is a major focus for models of HRM which hold that business competitiveness is improved by enhancing employee attitudes, behaviour and commitment. To do so, it is imperative that the organization has effective methods of communicating its standards or norms of behaviour. Assessors and assessed may have entirely different perceptions of both the reasons for performance appraisal and the criteria for judgement. Proponents argue that performance management should be: 'a process or set of processes for establishing shared understanding about what *is* to be achieved, and of managing and developing people in a way which increases the probability that it *will* be achieved in the short and longer term' (Armstrong, 1992: 163).

Performance management strategies are particularly concerned with workforce motivation or, more accurately, management belief in the factors that lead to employee effort and commitment.

Motivation and performance

A considerable body of literature exists on the relationship between motivation and work performance. Theories range from the simplistic rational 'economic man' concepts underlying scientific management – implying that workers are only interested in money – to complex 'expectancy' theories which explain motivation in terms of a calculus of conflicting needs. Morgan (1986: 149) points to the diverse range of interests that people bring to the workplace:

→ *Task interests:* focused on the job being performed so that, for example, someone in sales is committed to selling, enjoys dealing with customers and takes pride in being able to clinch a sale.

→ *Career interests:* aspirations and visions of one's future – which may or may not include the current job.

These are complemented by extramural interests which incorporate leisure pursuits and domestic relationships. They cannot be divorced from work, since they compete for an individual's time and psychological or physical effort. Performance management strategies must take account of people as whole beings, with work forming just a part of their lives.

Gazioglu and Tansel (2006) analyzed job satisfaction with respect to a variety of personal and job characteristics using data from 28 240 British employees in the 1997 Workplace Employee Relations Survey. Four measures of job satisfaction were considered: influence over job; amount of pay; sense of achievement; and respect from supervisors. They found that those in education and health were less satisfied with their pay but more satisfied with their sense of achievement. Employees who received job training were more satisfied than those who had not. Women are more satisfied than men, and there is a U-shaped relationship between satisfaction and age. Unlike previous studies, they found that married individuals have lower job satisfaction levels than the unmarried.

Achievers and non-achievers

A number of researchers have attempted to identify the important factors leading to successful performance by comparing recognized high achievers with average performers. This method focuses on distinguishing key psychological differences between people in the two groups. However, as Furnham (1990: 30) notes: 'it cannot be assumed that these factors *caused* the success, indeed they may have been a *consequence* of success.' Factors such as confidence and knowledge of a particular area may have been present at an early stage in a person's career or, alternatively, developed as that career became successful. For example, Charles Handy uses the term 'helicopter view' to describe the broad strategic grasp of business expected from senior managers. They are unlikely to have achieved this perspective without wide experience at lower levels.

Reviewing some of the vast selection of books on the rich and famous, Furnham finds consistent themes such as:

→ *Perseverance:* tenacity, single-minded determination and concentration.

→ *Ability:* especially in creating and exploiting opportunities.

→ *Contacts:* knowing the right people.

→ *Self-reliance:* striving for independence.

→ *Thinking big:* but taking modest risks.

→ *Time management:* making the best use of time and planning progress.

The weakness in these studies lies in their essentially retrospective and descriptive nature. They do not set out to test the hypothesis that individuals setting out on a career with a particular set of personality characteristics will be more successful than average. Nevertheless, Furnham *(ibid.:* 31) finds that certain values that he describes as PWE (the Protestant work ethic) recur, providing: 'some evidence for the fact that specific PWE values – namely tenacity, perseverance, autonomy, independence, and hard work – are to be found in financially successful individuals and companies alike.'

HRM IN REALITY   OVERACHIEVING EXECUTIVES

Business executives are showing a dramatic boost in their achievement drives, according to a new study by Hay Group's McClelland Center for Research and Innovation. In fact, they are overachieving to the point of harming not only their own careers, but also the organizations they lead.

The study, 'Leadership Run Amok: The Destructive Potential of Overachievers' by Scott W. Spreier, Mary H. Fontaine and Ruth L. Malloy in the *Harvard Business Review* (June, 2006), shows that executives' achievement motives – defined as 'an innate drive to continually

improve performance or meet or exceed a standard of excellence' – have risen sharply in the last 10 years. This has happened at a time of innovation and rapid business growth, but also in a period of business scandals and public loss of confidence in senior managers.

The authors of the study argue that this is not a coincidence. Overachievement often leads to ineffective and sometimes unethical leadership. They cite Enron's Jeff Skilling as an extreme but classic example of an organizational overachiever driven to continually improve results – without regard to the ways in which they were achieved. They also note that the desire to continually do better and to be the best remains a growing problem in other organizations.

According to Scott Spreier, one of the study's authors: 'Achievement has long been an important ingredient in the recipe for individual, organizational, even national success. And in today's uber-competitive environment, it is fast becoming the performance enhancer of choice as more organizations hire, promote, and reward achievement-driven leaders.'

Spreier observes that, like most stimulants, it's easy to overdose on achievement. 'Be careful what you ask for,' cautions Spreier. 'It can backfire big-time. We've seen highly ethical, well-meaning executives transformed into vicious louts who behave very badly. They focus on the end to the exclusion of the means and become coercive and demanding, destroying morale and motivation. The really hard cases cut corners, lie, even cheat, all in the name of outstanding results.'

The dark side of achievement

The authors say that the key to avoiding this is to become aware of how easily our achievement drive can become aroused, and then learning how to better manage it.

'The most effective executives acknowledge their strong need for achievement and its importance in driving organizational performance,' says co-author Mary Fontaine, who directs the McClelland Center. She argues that they also recognize their own drive can often diminish their impact as leaders. So they adopt styles of leadership that more effectively drive performance through others.

'The best leaders aren't out there blindly setting a blistering pace themselves and demanding the same from others,' Fontaine says. 'Instead they take a step back, create the vision, set the direction and standards, and then coach and engage others. In the process, they create energizing work climates in which people feel they have the flexibility, autonomy and clarity they need to continually perform at the top of their game.'

However, even savvy and self-aware executives find it hard to take such an approach in today's competitive climate. They may realize that channeling their achievement drive through others by collaborating and coaching is the best approach but they can lose control in the heat of battle and resort to coercion and control.

Balance is the key, says Ruth Malloy, also a co-author of the study. 'Good leaders know when to draw from their achievement drive and when to control it so that it doesn't get in the way of their effectiveness.'

What are the likely consequences of having over-achieving managers assessing employee performance?

Source: Reprinted with permission from HRM Guide USA (http://www.hrmguide.com).

Locus of control

Performance management is based on the underlying belief that managers can influence behaviour and, therefore, that rationality is the basis of human action. Unfortunately, the available psychological evidence suggests that this is not the case. Research shows that people vary significantly in their reactions to the persuasion or coercion of others, depending on their perception of the ability they have to control their own lives. At one extreme, some individuals will believe that what happens in their lives is the consequence of their own decisions, abilities and behaviour. These people are judged to have an 'expectancy of internal control'. There is evidence that individuals who have an expectancy of internal control ('internals') are better performers and tend to occupy most of the higher level jobs (Andrisani and Nestel, 1976). Internals take more notice of the feedback provided by performance management but do so according to their own agenda. If good performance produces appropriate rewards, they will deliver more of the same. If it does not, they are likely to devote their internal strengths to finding another job. Such individuals have core self-evaluations, considered to be 'a broad, integrative trait indicated by self-esteem, locus of control, generalized self-efficacy, and (low) neuroticism (high emotional stability)' (Judge, 2009).

At the other extreme are individuals who attribute events to fate, to God, luck, or to more powerful people. They consider life to be outside their personal remit and are permanent victims of chance or the wishes of others. They are said to have an 'expectancy of external control' (Furnham, 1990: 42). People with an expectancy of external control ('externals') will be more compliant at the surface level, following instructions from supervisors and fitting social expectations. 'Following orders' they will fit neatly into bureaucratic structures but will demonstrate little initiative. Externals see little connection between their own performance and eventual success. When criticized for below-average work they will attribute their failure to causes outside themselves and the disapproval of the appraiser to personal dislike.

Are you in charge of life, or is life in charge of you? Most people have times when the former is true, and other times when the progress of life is firmly out of their hands. Some are permanently in one camp or the other. It is clear that being in charge of one's own life, career and circumstances leads to feelings of well-being and confidence and equates with successful and happy times. This is true 'empowerment'. However, it is doubtful whether performance management is entirely compatible with this state. In the next section we elaborate on how organizations can place performance assessment within a wider framework of human resource management.

PERFORMANCE MANAGEMENT SYSTEMS

Among the 10-Cs checklist criteria for HRM discussed in Chapter 1 and elsewhere we placed consistency, coordination and control. These strategic aspects of performance assessment are exemplified in the integration of appraisal and performance-related pay processes within performance management systems and for those systems to be computerized, even in developing countries, for example in Ugandan universities (Kagaari *et al.*, 2010). Armstrong (1992: 162) sees the functions of such systems as:

→ Reinforcement of the organization's values and norms.

→ Integration of individual objectives with those of the organization.

→ Allowing individuals to express their views on the job.

→ Providing the means for managers and staff to share their expectations of performance.

Management by objectives

The origins of strategic performance management can be traced to the concept of management by objectives (Raia, 1974). This is a technique to establish individual performance objectives that are tangible, measurable and verifiable. Individual objectives are derived or cascaded from organizational goals. Top managers agree their own specific objectives compatible with the organization's goals but restricted to their own areas of responsibility. Subordinates do the same at each lower level, forming an interlocked and coherent hierarchy of performance targets. Hence management by objectives lies within the strategic way of thinking that forms a key element in HRM (see Table 8.1). Management by objectives (MBO) encompasses four main stages as detailed in the following sub-sections.

Essential elements	Key stages
Goal-setting	**1** Establish long-range strategic objectives
	2 Formulate specific overall organizational goals
	3 Agree departmental objectives
	4 Set individual performance targets
Action planning	**5** Draw up action plans
Self-control	**6** Implement and take corrective action
Periodic reviews	**7** Review performance against objectives
	8 Appraise overall performance, reinforce appropriate behaviour and strengthen motivation through: — management development — reward — career and HR planning

TABLE 8.1
The management by objectives process

Source: Adapted from Raia (1974).

Goal-setting This is the heart of the MBO process. Goals are specific and desired results are to be achieved within an agreed period of time. They must represent real progress. They should be:

→ *Challenging:* stretching the individual beyond comfortable performance.

→ *Attainable:* realistic within cost and resource constraints.

→ *Measurable:* specific, quantifiable and verifiable. Objectives are best set in numerical terms such as 'increased sales by x thousand', 'reduced staff by y per cent'.

→ *Relevant:* directly related to the person's job and consistent with overall organizational objectives.

Alternatively, goals are sometimes set against the acronym SMART, linked to: Specific or Stretching; Measurable; Agreed or Achievable; Realistic; Time-bounded.

Action planning Goals or performance targets are the 'ends' of the MBO process, action plans are the 'means'. They require individual employees to ask themselves what, who, when, where, and how an objective can be achieved.

Self-control MBO is a self-driven process with each person participating in setting their own goals and action plans. This results in greater commitment to their own objectives and an improved understanding of the process. They are expected to control their own behaviour in order to achieve performance targets. In return it is essential that they are given sufficient information and feedback to gauge their progress.

Periodic reviews It is not sufficient to review progress at the end of the MBO process. Individuals must be provided with an opportunity to check their performance at regular intervals so that obstacles can be identified. Reviews should take a positive, coaching approach rather than a critical approach.

MBO pre-dates human resource management and derives from a period when strategic thinking and the integration of organizational objectives were being emphasized by management writers. Since then, the development of HRM has preserved the focus on strategy and integration. This has been reinforced by the fashion for performance-related pay, fostered by the prevalent belief that reward should be firmly tied to results. Whereas MBO concentrated on individual management of one's own performance, the spread of PRP is underpinned by the use of assessment systems to manage the individual. MBO has gone out of fashion to a considerable extent although its basic techniques have been absorbed into newer approaches. It has been criticized for the paperwork involved, the administrative burden it creates and the realization that goals set for individuals are actually dependent on a team, a department or even a substantial part of the organization (Armstrong and Baron, 1998).

Prescriptions for performance management systems

Bevan and Thompson (1992) describe a model performance management system:

→ The organization has a shared vision of its objectives or a mission statement that is communicated to its employees.

→ There are individual performance management targets, related to unit and wider organizational objectives.

→ There is a regular formal review of progress towards achieving the targets.

→ There is a review process that identifies training, development and reward outcomes.

→ The whole process is itself evaluated – feeding back through changes and improvements.

Rather similar to the MBO approach, the central features of such a system are an objective-setting process and a formal appraisal system. Typically, the performance management system is owned and implemented by line managers. The role of human resource specialists is to aid and advise line managers on the development of the system. In a slightly different approach, English (1991) argues for a 'rational' system of performance management which should have the following characteristics:

→ A clear statement of what is to be achieved by the organization.

→ Individual and group responsibilities support the organization's goals.

→ All performance is measured and assessed in terms of those responsibilities and goals.

→ All rewards are based on employee performance.

→ Organizational structure, processes, resources and authority systems are designed to optimize the performance of all employees.

→ There is an ongoing effort to create and guide appropriate organizational goals and to seek newer, more appropriate goals.

Many organizations consider that they have a performance management system along these lines. Often they do not because one or more of the following conditions are missing:

→ Agreement among all critical parties on what is to be performed.

→ An effective way to measure desired performance.

→ A reward system tied directly to performance.

→ An environment conducive to successful performance.

→ A communication programme to gain understanding, acceptance and commitment to the system.

→ A performance-based organizational culture.

THE ASSESSMENT PROCESS

In this section we consider performance assessment as an activity. Traditionally, performance assessment uses a rating system known as **appraisal** (Key concept 8.6). In most companies it is a matter of something being done to the employee rather than a process in which the employee plays a valued and important part. Assessments are generally an annual exercise, although some organizations may undertake them more frequently, perhaps every six months, especially with new entrants or recent promotees. For lower-grade employees, some companies are content with an assessment every two years.

KEY CONCEPT 8.6 APPRAISALS

Performance assessment is one of the many people management techniques that 'classify and order individuals hierarchically' (Townley, 1994: 33). Appraisals rate individuals on quasi-objective criteria or standards deemed to be relevant to performance. Traditional appraisals rated individuals on a list of qualities – primarily work-related attitudes and personality traits. Modern assessment is often focused on competences.

Appraisal and conformity

Appraisals tend to be formalized. In many organizations they take the shape of pre-printed forms or web input screens and instructions prepared for the appraising manager or supervisor. Dates of completion and return are fixed and the whole process monitored and administered by the personnel or HR department. Theoretically, appraisals can be completed in a number of ways:

→ *Self-assessment.* Individuals assess themselves against rating criteria, or targeted objectives.

→ *Peer assessment.* Fellow team members, departmental colleagues, or selected individuals with whom an employee has working interaction, provide assessments.

→ *Line management.* The employee's immediate supervisor(s) provide the assessment. Alternatively, other line managers may be involved.

→ *Upward appraisal.* Managers are appraised by their staff.

→ *360-degree or multi-rater feedback.* Raters may include anyone with a direct knowledge of an individual's performance, including colleagues, direct reports, managers and internal customers.

The traditional performance appraisal was completed by the immediate supervisor or line manager with, usually, further comments or countersignature provided by the supervisor's own manager. This has been described as the 'father and grandfather' system – appropriate terms, given the essentially paternalistic nature of the process.

Appraisal normally requires rating on a series of categories. Management and lower-level appraisals are commonly conducted in different ways. Management assessments tend to feature results-oriented criteria, typically against objectives agreed at the beginning of the year. Non-managerial appraisals are more likely to be 'trait-ratings' – no matter what the questions may ask overtly, they are actually rating the employee on behavioural or personality criteria. In essence, they are no more than crude personality questionnaires. This remains the case if the criteria are couched in terms of job-related qualities.

HRM IN REALITY — PERFORMANCE MANAGEMENT SYSTEMS FAIL TO MOTIVATE

'Most organizations have lost sight of the fact that performance management systems should aim to enhance performance by motivating staff.' This is the conclusion of recent research by The Work Foundation in six case study organizations. The report suggests that 'HR professionals are too concerned with "tweaking" PM forms and software rather than focusing on what should result from the process – improved performance.'

The report, 'What Makes for Effective Performance Management', by Kathy Armstrong and Adrian Ward, published in 2006, identifies 'profound confusion' about what PM is for. It is treated as a reward mechanism, a learning and development experience, or an exercise in control. Motivation appears to be less of a priority. The report argues that while the task of managing performance was universally held to be a 'good thing' by the organizations concerned, they were unable to identify any concrete organizational benefits to justify this opinion.

Marianne Huggett, a consultant with The Work Foundation, said:

An awful lot of organizations appear to be perpetually tweaking the process of performance management while ignoring the bigger picture of what it is supposed to be about in the first place – improving an organization's performance. In too many organizations, performance management is a matter of elegant bureaucracy – a tiresome form-filling exercise staff and managers could cheerfully live without. Meanwhile, there is a reluctance to

ask hard questions about what really comes out of it. In some cases, organizations might be well advised not to worry so much about the forms and bureaucracy, and simply try and encourage ongoing dialogue and quality conversations between line managers and employees instead.

Armstrong and Ward say that 'process can take up the most time and resources, but add only a small amount of value. This can be particularly dangerous where there is little or no attention paid to improving management's skills in managing performance – where the system itself is hoped to solve all the performance management issues, rather than the managers.'

The report cautions against crude use of measurement in PM. The case study organizations use various techniques including 360-degree feedback to 'vast amounts' of quantitative data. Often, this data is synthesized into a single rating that is intended to represent an individual's net contribution and determine their remuneration. This frequently describes an individual's performance as 'satisfactory' or 'average' – which the authors suggest is 'not an overly motivating message'. Furthermore, some managers use performance-related pay mechanisms to compensate staff they regard as being poorly paid.

'The real danger of becoming embroiled in the technical debates about rating, ranking and quotas is that it can drain the capacity of performance management to be a powerful vehicle for feedback, motivation and, yes, performance improvement' the authors say.

The report identifies seven critical issues of process and people management capability that organizations should debate when setting the parameters of performance management:

Process: the means by which individual performance is directed, assessed and rewarded.

People management capability: the skills, attitudes, behaviours and knowledge that line managers need in order to raise performance.

Armstrong and Ward argue that successful PM depends on the interplay of all of these factors.

Why is a rating of 'satisfactory' unlikely to motivate an employee?

Source: Reprinted with permission from HRM Guide UK (http://www.hrmguide.co.uk/).

According to Philp (1990):

The disadvantages of this approach are numerous. For instance, the terms themselves are extremely ambiguous and it is unlikely that any group of managers would share exactly the same interpretation of any of them. Any appraisal using such words would be extremely subjective and, as a result, totally unfair. Also, because assessment in these terms deals with the individual rather than with the results they produce for the organization, it is very difficult to communicate with the individual involved. The person being appraised is likely to see any critical assessment of this type as a personal attack. The factors deal with the emotive areas closely concerned with personality, and the majority of people will tend to react defensively.

Nurse (2005) studied workers' perceptions of performance appraisal to determine whether they experienced fair outcomes, and whether it was seen to contribute towards career advancement. Non-union respondents expressed fewer unfavourable perceptions about the interaction than did their trade union counterparts. Workers who believed that performers were not treated fairly as a result of performance appraisal similarly agreed that their expectations regarding development and advancement were not being met. The study found moderate relationships between perceptions about treatment of performers and their expectations about career advancement, as expressed through opportunities for training and development, pay for performance and promotions. Brown *et al.* (2010) point to the need for organizations to evaluate the cost of improving the quality of appraisals against the potential consequences on job satisfaction, commitment and intention to quit.

Appraisals are generally disliked by employees and employers alike. Human resource practitioners are often made responsible for the paper distribution and then for policing the process, coercing unwilling participants into completing the paperwork and holding one-to-one confrontations with appraisees.

Despite the fact that most assessors are completely unqualified to make judgements on anyone's personality, even in the most general of terms, the traditional appraisal form asks for a numerical rating on a scale of 1–4 or 1–7 (from excellent to appalling). More detail is asked for as supplementary verbal comments, which could range from one word such as 'good' to a paragraph or more of detailed criticism or praise. Moreover, there is usually an overall rating that may be tied to promotability and a section to indicate areas for development or training. Finally, there are normally sections for comments by the person being appraised, possibly in the form of notes of a counselling interview and comments by the appraising manager's own supervisor.

HRM IN REALITY PERFORMANCE REVIEWS STILL VALUABLE

A 2010 survey of human resource managers found that performance reviews are still considered a valuable element in staff assessment. Conducted on behalf of *OfficeTeam*, a leading Canadian staffing service specializing in temporary placement of office and administrative support personnel, the survey was based on telephone interviews with more than 150 managers in organizations with at least 20 employees.

Over three-quarters of respondents (78 per cent) felt that formal evaluations are effective in improving job performance. Half said they conduct appraisals once a year; one in five (20 per cent) hold them at least quarterly.

Asked to rate their organization's performance appraisal process in improving employee performance, over one-quarter of respondents (27 per cent) felt it was very effective and 51 per cent that it was somewhat effective. The responses of a further 15 per cent were less positive.

Respondents were asked about the frequency of formal performance appraisals. The majority conducted them annually (50 per cent) with 22 per cent conducted 'as necessary', 15 per cent twice a year, five per cent quarterly and nine per cent 'never'.

The report suggests five ways in which employees can achieve the best outcome from performance appraisals:

→ **Sort out the details**. Preparation is important. Ask your supervisor for a copy of the assessment form and clarify any additional expectations (such as bringing information about specific projects to the meeting or completing a self-evaluation).

→ **Showcase your accomplishments**. Highlight any praise or awards received since your last formal review. Keep an ongoing list of achievements to remind you and your supervisor of how the company has benefited from your work.

→ **Make it a two-way conversation**. Your manager will identify areas where you are excelling and where improvement is needed. In turn, ask questions about the assessment and request support or guidance.

→ **Share your ideas**. Discuss what you hope to achieve in the future and ensure these goals are compatible with your long-term professional objectives.

→ **Follow through**. Regularly review agreed goals and keep your supervisor informed about your progress.

Robert Hosking, executive director, commented:

Despite their bad rap, performance reviews benefit both managers and employees, provided adequate preparation goes into them. It's understood that supervisors must take the time to provide constructive feedback to team members, but workers also should play an active role in the process. This is their chance to highlight key accomplishments and discuss career aspirations.

What do you consider to be the ideal period between assessments?

Source: Reprinted with permission from HRM Guide Canada *(http://www.hrmguide.net/canada/).*

The document is usually signed by all the contributors and forms part of the company's HR records. It can be used for promotion boards, training and management development programmes. What happens if an employee disagrees with the assessment? Despite its critical consequences for promotion prospects and, perhaps, remuneration, only one half of all organizations allow any form of appeal.

Upward feedback

The emphasis of performance management has been on top-down assessments open to a degree of power play by managers and senior executives. Over the last decade or so there has been a trend towards constructive, developmental approaches and moving away from a fixation with ratings. It has also become increasingly acceptable to take views of individual performance from a wide range of perspectives. Upward feedback is a process whereby managers receive comments and criticisms from their subordinates. This may be facilitated by an intermediary to organize the process and maintain a positive and non-acrimonious climate.

Upward feedback is not an appraisal as such and is not linked to standardized competences. Instead (Forbes, 1996):

→ It is intended to deliver candid, accurate feedback from a team to its manager.

→ The basis lies in the team's perception of the actions of its manager.

→ Upward feedback is not a system of judgement 'but only asks him or her for more, less, or the same of a broad series of behaviours'.

→ Leadership, management, task and people factors are given equal weight.

→ The facilitator gives confidential feedback, initially to the manager, then between the team and its manager.

→ Team members and the manager – and that person's manager – can compare their views on what is required, bringing areas of misunderstanding or disagreement out into the open.

Because upward feedback is not formal appraisal, managers do not need to fear being judged. Conventionally, upward feedback begins with the most senior executive and cascades downwards, with each level in turn receiving feedback.

Based on Forbes (*ibid.*), the benefits of upward feedback can be summarized as follows:

1 Individual/team action plans can improve cooperation between team and manager.

2 Supervisors are encouraged to vary their management style and emphasis.

3 Ideas, problems and suggestions can be collected across a range of individuals or teams. In turn these can be used to set up new cross-functional teams or aid in the management of change.

4 Training requirements can be pinpointed and linked to specific outcomes for the team.

5 It facilitates empowerment and self-management.

6 A benchmark is gradually developed taking the form of an organizational map and data on how employees, managers and senior executives view requirements in 20 defined behavioural areas in up to 100 practices. An annual comparison can be made from this.

7 It opens up a more communicative culture where different forms of performance assessment can be introduced.

Dierendonck *et al.* (2007) concluded that managers tended to have low awareness of the effect of their behaviour on subordinates and that upward feedback did not lead to much long-term improvement in this respect. Upward feedback also has its disadvantages. Managers may receive negative comments from assertive and ambitious employees intent on undermining their confidence and authority. No one likes to be rated as a poor performer and some managers may be less firm or directive, even when appropriate, in order to avoid criticism. Similarly, managers may be less critical or demanding of their subordinates in order to reduce the probability of unfavourable feedback.

Waldman and Atwater (2001), in a study of upward feedback in a large telecommunications firm, found that managers who receive poor formal appraisal scores from their bosses are more likely to value the usefulness of upward feedback. Managers who receive lower subordinate ratings are more likely to ask for additional feedback. In general, subordinates are more likely than managers to believe that upward feedback scores should be incorporated into formal performance assessments. Waldman and Atwater also found that subordinate ratings were correlated with formal appraisal scores. Kilburn and Cates (2010) observed that leaders who emphasized relationships with followers were more likely to receive voluntary upward feedback.

360-degree or multi-rater assessments

Multi-rater assessments have been used by large US corporations for some time and have gradually become more common in other countries. The evolution of business organizations into flatter, team-based structures has led to multiple reporting lines and wider spans of command for managers, so that assessments by single line managers are not as appropriate as they were in the past (Kettley, 1996). A multi-source rating system such as 360-degree performance profiling typically involves information collected from the people working with the person being appraised, managers, staff reporting to that individual and internal (or, exceptionally) external customers. The process follows a sequence such as the following:

1   A skill model or competence framework is devised that lists essential job skills and behaviours.

2   A performance management survey is defined on the basis of the skill model.

3   Individual employees are each asked to recommend eight to 12 raters for their personal reviews. Immediate supervisors choose six to ten of these to complete performance surveys, rating the employee on each skill area, typically on a scale of 1–10. Raters need to have direct knowledge of the employee's performance but supervisors need to ensure that they are not all friends of the appraisee.

4   The reports are collected together and a summary is given to the appraisee, highlighting both strengths and development needs.

This method of performance assessment has its advantages and disadvantages over more traditional methods. It is clear that the number of people involved, and the amount of form-filling required, can lead to a considerable expenditure of time and effort, even when online forms, data-scanning and report-producing software are used. The anonymity of the process may also allow malicious and undefended negative ratings to be given.

Morgan, Cannan and Cullinane (2005) examined the introduction of 360-degree feedback in the civil service as it underwent modernization. They found that at an organizational level it failed to develop the self-awareness anticipated. It was not aligned with other development plans or the organization's core competences. At an individual level some participants believed that they achieved little from the process overall. The authors suggest this may be related to an expectation that the HRM system would be more proactive in planning development action on their behalf.

LIMITATIONS OF PERFORMANCE MANAGEMENT

Performance appraisal has become one of the most widely used management tools despite widespread criticism of its effectiveness. To add to the controversy, Strebler, Robinson and Bevan (2001) from the UK's Institute of Employment Studies (IES) argue from research on over 1000 British managers that many performance appraisal systems have a limited impact on overall business performance and fail both employees and organizations.

Many organizations try to use performance appraisal and review as a 'strategic lever', not just for the performance of individuals, but also the performance of the whole business. However, according to Strebler and her colleagues:

> This assumes that managers have the ability and motivation to make performance review work, by translating strategic goals into operational practice. Ideally, they should use the appraisal to help the employee see how their contribution adds value to the business as a whole. Too often, however, they are rushed discussions where performance ratings are handed out, where petty lapses in performances are picked upon, or where performance-related pay is awarded.

Additionally, Strebler *et al. (ibid.)* contend that performance review is rapidly becoming an 'over-burdened management tool'. Along with its appraisal and objective-setting aspects, line managers are expected to pinpoint staff training requirements, provide career counselling, identify future star performers and do something about poor performers. These are all important elements of people management but the attempt to do so much at the same time often leads to poor results from appraisal schemes.

Performance review systems are frequently rooted in the hierarchical organizations of the past, and often still drive pay or promotion decisions. Organizations are flatter today and there may be limited opportunities for upward progression. Rewards can also take forms other than pay increases. So, according to Strebler *et al. (ibid.),* new systems are needed that meet the requirements of individual organizations: textbook models might not be suitable for particular strategies or structures.

They advise a transformation of the performance review 'from a beast of burden into a thoroughbred', starting with business strategy, then being clear about the roles, skills and behaviours required for delivering that strategy. There are some simple rules:

→ Clear aims and measurable criteria for success.

→ Involving employees in design and implementation of the system.

→ Keeping it simple to understand and operate.

→ Making its effective use one of managers' core performance goals.

→ Ensuring that employees are always able to see the link between their performance goals and those of the organization.

→ Using it to keep roles clear and focus on performance improvement.

→ Backing up the system with adequate training and development.

→ Making any direct link with reward crystal clear, and providing proper safeguards to guarantee equity.

→ Reviewing the system regularly and openly to make sure it's working.

Strebler *et al. (ibid.)* conclude that human resources functions that can deliver this will be making a real and visible strategic contribution to their organizations.

COUNSELLING INTERVIEWS

Having tested the manager's talents as untrained psychologist, the next part of the process expects the manager to be a qualified counsellor! This **counselling interview** takes the form of a face-to-face dialogue between (normally) the appraising manager and the appraisee, although it is sometimes done by the countersigning manager. The whole process is designed to focus the power of the organization on a direct and individual basis. However, it is also clear that the scope for conflict and its avoidance are considerable.

Many, perhaps most, managers are reluctant to engage in the appraisal process. It is difficult to criticize someone's performance honestly, knowing that the appraisee will read the comments. Potentially, the whole exercise is confrontational and many counselling interviews have turned sour because of carelessly worded appraisals. Most people find criticism difficult to accept and registering a point with an employee without causing offence requires diplomatic skills.

The process is dependent on the personality and management style of the appraising manager. Some managers will be blunt and, perhaps, brutal in their approach. As a consequence, they may not produce any improvement in behaviour but, rather, sullen resentment and a reduction in quality of performance. Others will regard the whole exercise as something to be avoided. As we noted earlier, the result will be rater-inflation: an assessment that is over-generous or, at best, neutral in order to avoid conflict. The process also depends to a great extent on the quality of the appraising manager. If that individual is not particularly capable, the evaluation of the subordinate may well be inaccurate or misleading and may blight the person's career.

HRM IN REALITY — CEO PERFORMANCE AND EDUCATION

CEOs with top college degrees do no better at improving their organization's long-term performance than average and are as liable to be blamed for poor results, according to 2010 research led by the Whittemore School of Business and Economics at the University of New Hampshire.

Lead researcher Brian Bolton, assistant professor of finance said:

> These findings suggest that both boards and researchers should use caution in placing too much emphasis on an individual's education when trying to assess their ability to lead the company and maximize shareholder value.

The study reviewed data covering nearly 15 000 years of CEO experience and more than 2600 turnovers between 1992 and 2007. Researchers analyzed the role educational attainment played in decisions to remove a current CEO, selection of a replacement, and organizational performance. Six main measures were used: whether or not the individual had attended a top 20 undergraduate school; had an MBA, law or master's degree; and whether or not the higher degree was from a top 20 programme.

The study found that poor performance is the most significant factor in a decision to replace a CEO, regardless of education. However, researchers found a significant positive correlation between the education levels of new CEOs and those they replace. For example, a board will seek to replace a poorly performing CEO with an MBA degree with someone similarly qualified.

Researchers found that hiring new CEOs with MBA degrees tends to produce short-term improvements in operating performance that may not be maintained. They conclude that CEO education does not necessarily equate with talent and ability.

Brian Bolton commented:

Even though CEO education does not lead to superior performance by firms, firms may rely on CEO education in hiring decisions because they have few other identifiable and measurable criteria to use. All else being equal, they rely on what they believe to be the observable pedigrees of the executive. Of course, all else is rarely equal, especially when dealing with something as nebulous and potentially unobservable as managerial talent. Interpersonal skills, leadership ability and strategic vision are among the traits that CEOs should possess; these can be difficult to identify and even more difficult to measure. As a result, boards rely on those characteristics which they may be able to observe: work experience, track record, and education.

Why is it that good leaders do not necessarily need a good education?

Source: Reprinted with permission from HRM Guide USA (http://www.hrmguide.com).

It can be argued that there is an increasing tendency to focus on marginal performers in the light of harsh economic conditions. Companies consider that they are unable to carry inefficient employees and the assessment procedure offers a source of data that will support dismissals. In theory, performance appraisal provides documentary evidence of inefficiency that would be hard to refute. In practice, rater-inflation often undermines the process, providing generous appraisals for questionable performances.

OBJECTIVITY AND SUBJECTIVITY IN ASSESSMENT

As we have seen, some of the key issues of performance management revolve around questions of fairness, judgement and interpretation of both results and behaviour. Serious attempts have been made to address these areas. Performance assessment focuses on one or more of the following criteria:

Results. In line with MBO and similar objectives-based systems, employees are rated on their achievements, expressed as well-defined, personal or organizational targets. For example, a salesperson may be given the objective of US$x thousand worth of sales in the year. How this is achieved is not the subject of assessment. As we have already observed, objectives are easier to define for some jobs than others. This approach can be complicated by the use of a 'moving target'.

Processes. In this case the emphasis is not on measurable results but on *how* the outcomes are achieved. It can be argued that compliance with quality procedures or, alternatively, provision of a particular level of service are examples of process assessments. However, if these are measurable in some way, they can be translated into results – for example, proportion of defective items or number of complaints.

Behaviour. Weaker and less objective assessments – but probably the most common – focus on employee behaviour which is only tangentially connected with either achieved results or work processes. A favourite approach for managers incapable of seeing the 'wood from the trees', they allow ample opportunity to dwell on personal prejudices over appearance, dress and manner. Such assessments provide a direct feeder mechanism into culture-bound and organizationally unhealthy practices designed to increase conformity and eliminate diversity.

A number of large organizations have countered this tendency by using behaviourally anchored scales.

> *Behaviourally anchored scales (BARS).* These are relatively expensive techniques to maintain, requiring 'experts' to develop rating scales anchored to real-life behaviour through critical incidents. However, they force appraisers to make comparatively objective judgements, placing individual behaviour in the context of the organization as a whole, rather than on inadequate personality categorizations. They are less usable in situations where new technology or procedural changes require frequent updating of scales.

> *Behavioural observation scales (BOS).* These are constructed in a similar way to BARS but assessors are required to list the frequency of occurrence of particular behaviours within a particular period, rather than make comparative judgements of better or worse performance.

Different behaviour-oriented rating formats may enhance or inhibit the value of performance appraisal as a development tool. Tziner, Joanis and Murphy (2000) compared the effects of rating scale formats on a number of indices of the usefulness of performance appraisal for employee development. Using simple graphic scales, behaviourally anchored rating scales or behaviour observation scales, ratings were made of the job performance of 96 police officers. The BOS ratings produced both the highest ratee satisfaction with the performance appraisal process and the most favourable perceptions of performance goals. Additionally, experts judged the performance improvement goals for officers appraised with BOS to be the most observable and specific.

Competence ratings

In recent years the trend in performance management has been towards assessing people on 'dimensions' of suitable attributes or 'competences'. These may be derived from job analyses and describe a limited number of core skills or behaviours necessary to do a certain job. In fact, such competences aggregate to form a key strategic element of business competitiveness – the overall competences of the firm. There is some ambiguity about the meaning of the term at the level of the individual – it is sometimes used as an equivalent for a psychological trait (perseverance) and, at other times, as a complex hybrid of learning and skill (ability to use computers).

Armstrong and Baron (1998) suggest that competences should address the following points:

1 What are the 'elements' of the job – its main tasks or key areas?

2 What is an acceptable standard of performance for each element?

3 Which skills and what knowledge does a jobholder need to have in order to be fully capable in each of these job elements – and at what level?

4 How will employees or their managers know that they have achieved the required levels of competence?

▶ SUMMARY

HRM is associated with sophisticated and intensive performance assessment, typically involving performance-related pay. The assessment of performance can be beneficial to personal development. We considered performance management as an integrated system.

Theoretical descriptions of such systems emphasize their value to the link between individual employee performance and the achievement of strategic goals. However, there are philosophical issues of what precisely represents 'good' performance, and further technical problems of measurement. We completed the chapter with a critique of appraisal methods and a discussion of recent attempts to objectify their use.

➡ FURTHER READING

1 *Armstrong's Handbook of Performance Management: An Evidence-Based Guide to Delivering High Performance*, 4th edition, by Michael Armstrong (Kogan Page, 2009) is a wide-ranging text that conveys the full flavour of the subject.

2 *Managing Performance* by Michael Armstrong and Angela Baron (CIPD, 2004) is another example.

3 *The Manager's Guide to Performance Management* by Robert Bacal (McGraw-Hill Education, 2003) is particularly reader-friendly.

4 Clive Fletcher's *Appraisal and Feedback: Making Performance Review Work* (CIPD, 2007) is written by a major researcher in the field of assessment.

5 *Abolishing Performance Appraisals: Why They Backfire and What to Do Instead* by Tom Coens and Mary Jenkins (Berrett-Koehler Publishers, 2002) takes an original but positive approach to the process of assessment.

➡ REVIEW QUESTIONS

1 Why is performance assessment important? What factors determine individual success in an organization?

2 Summarize the external factors that can affect the process of performance assessment within an organization. Do they help or hinder that process?

3 Do organizations prefer conformists? What are the implications of the personal relationship between manager and employee on performance assessment?

4 Should males and females be assessed differently?

5 Discuss the view that performance appraisals are unnecessary.

6 Explain the following terms: (a) behavioural consistency; and (b) competences.

7 Compare and contrast Bevan and Thompson's textbook model of performance management with English's rational model.

8 Evaluate a significant business (or political) leader. How much of that person's success is due to charisma or impression management?

9 Discuss the ways in which externals and internals react to performance assessment. Would an objective-setting method such as MBO produce the same effects on performance for a person with an internal locus of control as it would for someone with an external locus of control?

10 Is management by objectives discredited as a performance management technique?

11 How would you conduct a 360-degree performance assessment? Compare and contrast the processes of upward feedback and 360-degree profiling.

12 Define 'rater-inflation'. What are its causes and implications? Is it possible for appraisals to be objective?

➡ CASE STUDIES FOR DISCUSSION AND ANALYSIS

The consumer relations department/ International Holidays

1 As general manager, the consumer relations department has been the source of considerable difficulties for you this year. The manager, Jean Davis, her assistant Lyndon Greaves, and the six staff are involved in a constant battle with the sales department. They say that the number of complaints has gone up substantially. Jean says that customers seem far more ready to find fault with deliveries than ever before. She blames the salesforce for errors in order-taking. She has become aggressive in the way she deals with sales and has accused you of ignoring the problem. Lyndon is more reasonable but says that his people are grossly overworked. They have developed a backlog in clearing customers' emails and phone calls and sick leave has increased.

Conversely, the sales department is working better than ever before. They have a new PRP system in place, based on targets for orders taken by each person. The field sales force have embraced PRP enthusiastically with orders 20 per cent up on last year. Most have received generous bonuses. The board are very pleased with this and have asked you to extend PRP to other departments, including consumer relations. However, Jean and Lyndon are very negative about the idea, demanding to know how they are likely to be assessed when they are behind on their targets.

What is your analysis of the situation and how would you deal with it?

2 International Holidays is a travel agency group. The company has 43 shop units, each employing between four and eight front-office staff. Each unit has a manager. The company has been suffering from low trading levels in recent years. The situation has not been helped by the trend towards Internet booking which has reduced the number of people coming to the company's retail units and threatens the viability of several locations. The managing director has asked you to set up a performance management system to improve the motivation of the staff.

How would you do this? What difficulties would you expect in ensuring that the system achieves its objectives?

CHAPTER 9
Human resource development

LEARNING OBJECTIVES

The purpose of this chapter is to:

→ Outline the concept of human resource development.

→ Debate the need for distinctive management and gender-focused HRD programmes.

→ Introduce the concept of mentoring.

→ Distinguish between learning in organizations and the 'learning organization'.

→ Discuss the relationship between empowerment, self-development and learning.

→ Debate the role of the trainer in the context of proactive learning methods.

→ Evaluate the use of new learning technologies.

HRD STRATEGIES

People with appropriate skills, abilities and experience can be bought from outside the organization through recruitment, consultancy and subcontracting, or grown by training and developing existing employees. This chapter focuses on the second approach. The strategic choice between buying and growing is made on the basis of cost-effectiveness, urgency of requirement and the need to motivate staff. Political, cultural and historical elements also influence the decision. Organizations with an internal job market orientation, for example most large German and Japanese companies, have made a practice of growing their own talent whereas the externally-oriented businesses typical of anglophone countries have tended to buy in skilled people.

KEY CONCEPT 9.1 HUMAN RESOURCE DEVELOPMENT

Human resource development (HRD) is a strategic approach to investing in human capital. It draws on other human resource processes, including resourcing and performance assessment, to identify actual and potential talent. HRD provides a framework for self-development, training programmes and career progression to meet an organization's future skill requirements.

Learning in the workplace also enhances employee engagement and motivation. For example, Rowden and Conine (2005) found a statistically significant relationship between workplace learning and job satisfaction in small US banks. They highlight the importance of informal and incidental learning and emphasize the need for managers to make learning opportunities available to enhance overall job satisfaction. In an Italian study, Panari *et al.* (2010) also showed that workplace learning opportunities have a role in promoting job satisfaction, reducing stress and improving work–life balance while Alonderiene (2010) found a correlation between informal learning and job satisfaction among SME managers in Lithuania.

Systematic **human resource development** (see Key concept 9.1) maximizes the human capital of an organization, devoting time, money and thought to improving the pool of essential competences among its staff. It has a general impact on business performance by enhancing product knowledge and service expertise, motivating staff, drawing on their talents and demonstrating that they are valued by the organization. It is also claimed to empower staff, allowing individuals to take a measure of control over their own careers and develop life patterns that offer increased opportunity and satisfaction. However, Gibb (2002: 138) takes the following view:

> The idea of HRD promises a great deal, and is seductive; but whether there is evidence of organizational examples of this being delivered is questionable. Indeed the 'rhetoric' involved is arguably being used to cover changes which are far removed from the espoused aims; instead of better valuing the human resource, such re-inventions can mask the greater exploitation of people.

According to Sambrook (2001) HRD has its roots in the early organization development interventions of the 1940s, but the term was first used by Nadler in 1972. Nadler (cited in Nadler and Nadler, 1989: 4) described HRD as 'organized learning experiences provided by employers, within a specified period of time, to bring about the possibility of performance improvement and/or personal growth.'

What is the relationship between HRD and training? The two terms are sometimes used to mean the same. However, there is a longstanding tendency to regard training as something done to lower-level workers, whereas development is a process experienced by managers – hence 'management development'. This seems to be incompatible with the central rhetorical principle of HRM that all employees are assets whose competences need to be developed. It is appropriate, therefore, to regard training as an integral aspect of HRD.

Sambrook (2001) argues that HRD can be thought of as a construct, like 'love' or 'quality'. It is intangible in itself since it cannot be found, touched or seen, but it may be investigated through features associated with the concept that might distinguish it from training and development. She argues that training and development was focused on operational issues and took a short-term or reactive approach in which specialists 'did training', delivered it to passive trainees and usually conducted it in classrooms. Sambrook describes this as the 'tell' approach as opposed to 'sell' or 'competent' HRD. Competent HRD focuses on competences and takes a wider approach, encompassing self-development, employee development, management development and organization development. Probably delivered by facilitators, there is two-way communication and some consultation together with far more diverse training methods. There is an attempt to link HRD to other HR processes and take a wider organizational perspective. Finally, Sambrook identifies strategic HRD or 'gel'. Here the HRD function and the organization are strategically and totally interlinked and there is an emphasis on learning. Individuals are encouraged to take responsibility, to share learning and to be participative and collaborative. Others prefer the label of 'learning and development' while in recent years it has been swept up in the topic of 'talent management'.

Discussion of training and development in the media and management literature tends to become idealistic and evangelical. In reality, many employers take an extremely hard-nosed attitude towards the topic, particularly, as we have seen, in countries such as the UK with a notoriously short-termist view of business. Employer reluctance to embark on training young recruits can be attributed to various factors (Stevens and Walsh, 1991: 37).

Poaching

Some employers train while others do not. The non-trainers are likely to poach trained workers from those who train. Whereas Australian and UK firms are afraid of 'free-riders', their German counterparts see themselves as having a responsibility to contribute to the common good. Along with the activities and support of government this attitude maintains a high level of training in Germany. Elsewhere – in France, Japan and the USA, for instance – the poaching problem is less evident since the training of young people takes place largely within the formal education system. Most of the burden and costs are placed upon the trainees.

Cost

Young trainees anticipate higher wages in comparison to recruits for semi-skilled jobs. The reduction in numbers of young people coming onto the employment market has increased competition and wages for higher calibre trainees. Also, people are paid when training but do not produce anything and occupy trainers who are not managing or supervising during this period.

Individual disinterest

Human capital theory predicts that the young are more likely to choose training than the old because their indirect costs are lower than those of older workers. It also predicts that there should be a direct relationship between additional training and increased income. But the perception of young workers may be that there is no direct link: the skill differential may be small or non-existent. They also see that promotions are not based on qualifications.

Weak links between training and performance

Training does not have strategic importance for many companies, partly as we have noted, because of the difficulty of proving the connection between training and improved performance.

DEVELOPMENT PROGRAMMES

The fundamental principle of human resource development is that it goes further than piecemeal training and should be part of a planned and systematic process in which:

→ Competences or capabilities are identified by a performance management system.

→ These are matched with needs specified by the human resource strategy.

→ Gaps are addressed by the development programme.

Within a HRD programme, training is geared towards planned development rather than being an isolated activity unconnected to the organization's objectives. McDowall and Saunders (2010) observed that UK managers favoured the combination of training and development and tended to regard formal training more highly than other forms of learning because its value was easier to assess. In fact, HRD programmes can use a combination of organized patterns of experience as well as formal training. Dechawatanapaisal and Siengthai (2006) studied factors that shape learning behaviour in the workplace and found that psychological discomfort blocks people from acquiring and learning new knowledge during periods of change. However, effective HR practices can help to moderate individuals' inconsistent attitudes, avoid dissonance and facilitate their learning work behaviour. Development programmes that fail to treat employees as individuals may be counterproductive. McDermott, Mangan and O'Connor (2006) examined the perceived progress of graduate recruits and assessed their expectations and corresponding satisfaction levels. Surprisingly, they found that graduates recruited by organizations offering a graduate development programme were less satisfied than their counterparts in organizations with no such programme.

MANAGEMENT DEVELOPMENT

The main focus of HRD for many organizations lies in management development. In principle, anyone can become a manager and many do so without any formal training or development. However, graduates typically aim for formally designated management trainee positions that promise a structured development programme and steady progression through the management ranks.

The trend has been away from long induction ('onboarding') or orientation periods and work shadowing towards immediate 'real' jobs in which trainees perform useful activities, often with management responsibilities. Traditionally, trainees remain in particular functions for fixed periods of time – perhaps six months, a year, or longer. Of late, competence-driven development programmes have required trainees to achieve a certain standard before moving on.

Storey (2001) justifiably observes that 'the panoply of HRM technology is seen in its fullest form in the management of managers'. General management capabilities are developed in various ways. Companies such as Mars, Proctor & Gamble and Unilever have highly structured programmes. Others are more individually based or informal. Training may also involve academic study. At this point it is useful to consider the role of management education.

Many development programmes involve formal business education, including diplomas, business degrees and, above all, the Masters in Business Administration (MBA). MBA programmes have emphasized rational decision-making and a top-down strategic approach to business. In the 1980s, MBA graduates could guarantee substantial salary increases and the likelihood of 'fast-track' careers. More recently, their prospects have become less assured. Nevertheless, academic courses can stretch the boundaries of managers' experience, exposing them to a wide range of concepts, theories and ideas they would never come across otherwise. They also provide students with the means to understand and communicate with people in different business specialisms. Formal education and experiential learning can be used to build a combination of skills, knowledge and abilities – the management competences necessary for effective managerial performance.

There are two main perspectives on competences necessary for management:

1   *One best way.* The generic approach assumes that there is a range of competences or portable techniques that can be learned and used in a variety of organizational settings.

2   *It depends.* The **contingency** view holds that running an organization efficiently requires competences or methods unique to that enterprise. This approach emphasizes commonsense, experience, rule-of-thumb techniques and wisdom. It acknowledges the complexity of the business environment. It also recognizes that what has worked once in a particular situation is likely to work again.

Taking the former approach, in the 1970s the American Management Associations initiated a major study of management competences, whereby 2000 successful managers were studied over a five-year period with the intention of identifying generic (common) competences from actual job performance. The research identified 30 statistically significant competences of which 18 were generic and could be regarded as essential for all successful managers (Boyatzis, 1982). The remainder were related to organizational requirements or individual management styles. The generic competences could be placed in four groups: intellectual, entrepreneurial, socio-emotional and interpersonal (the largest group). Nolan *et al.* (2010) looked at the graduate competences required for entry to hotel management in Ireland and found that interpersonal and product knowledge skills were most important.

The low level of women in management has produced a case for special consideration to be given to the development needs of female managers. For example, the provision of career breaks, refresher training, job-sharing and extended childcare facilities can make a considerable difference in career progress. Specific HRD programmes can be set for women focusing on greater self-awareness, appreciation of career opportunities and encouragement to manage their own careers. This kind of programme boosts confidence and is equally valuable to young trainees and mature returners. However, there are few senior women managers to act as role models. Development programmes involving seminars or attendance on women-only courses allow many female managers to compare notes, discuss issues in common and make sense of advancement in what is primarily a male world. Sharing experiences openly and honestly appears to be easier for women than men.

COACHING AND MENTORING

Mentor relationships have been found to be highly effective (Key concept 9.2). A 2004 CIPD study showed that coaching is increasingly popular as a means of promoting learning and development. Whereas a mere 16 per cent of respondents thought that training courses were the most effective way for people to learn in the workplace, 96 per cent valued coaching as an effective way to promote learning in organizations. Coaching was also viewed as an important way of reducing 'leakage' from training courses and therefore improved their effectiveness. However, coaching is not viewed entirely through rose-tinted glasses. HR professionals are concerned about lack of accreditation and regulation of external providers with only a third of respondents believing that there was sufficient regulation and accreditation of the coaching industry. More than three-quarters of organizations use coaching but a mere six per cent have written strategies for coaching all of their employees. The study shows that most coaches are line managers but just 14 per cent of organizations provide compulsory coaching skills for those who manage staff.

KEY CONCEPT 9.2 MENTORING

Mentors are established managers who can provide support, help and advice to more junior members of staff. A mentor should not be a direct line manager, but should have an understanding of the employee's job. Ideally, mentor and junior should have the same gender and ethnic background, so that advice is based on similar life experiences.

Main findings of the survey:

→ More than three-quarters of surveyed organizations used coaching as a training method.

→ Ninety per cent of respondents considered that coaching was a key mechanism for transferring training skills into the workplace.

→ Virtually all respondents (99 per cent) thought that coaching delivered tangible benefits.

→ More than 90 per cent of respondents believed that coaching applied appropriately could positively influence the bottom line.

→ Line managers were most likely to deliver coaching, but fewer than 20 per cent of organizations had 'all' or 'a majority' of their line managers trained to carry it out.

Thomson and Mabey (1994: 60) consider that successful mentors should be 7–10 years (or, perhaps, more) older than the individuals they are mentoring. The age gap should allow the mentor to reflect on their own careers and work experience and be able to give considered responses. Key points (*ibid.*: 61) are:

→ Meeting with a mentor, typically on a monthly basis, encourages an individual to collect his or her thoughts and structure the learning experience by talking those thoughts through with the mentor.

→ Mentors can help to clarify an individual's thinking by questioning and challenging.

→ In order to do so, mentors must have the ability to listen well and to probe into shallow thinking.

→ The primary role of a mentor is not to advise – although this can occur – but to provide feedback and information on recent developments in the organization.

Mentors can help build the individual's self-confidence in what may initially seem an unfriendly and perplexing environment. Coetzer (2006) investigated the role of managers as formal and informal learning facilitators in the workplace environment. Key factors included providing access to a range of workplace activities; promoting communication; facilitating access to direct guidance from workplace models; and designating other learning facilitators. Management practices could also have unintended positive effects on informal workplace learning. Observing that some individuals appeared to find it easier to receive mentoring than others, Blickle *et al.* (2010) identified a number of predicted perceived barriers to receiving mentoring, including socioeconomic origin, positive affectivity, organizational development culture and previous mentoring experience.

Coaches take a more active role than mentors, appearing in a number of forms, including:

Career coaching. According to Chung, Coleman and Gfroerer (2003: 141) career coaches act as 'personal consultants for any work-related concerns such as balancing home and work, learning interviewing skills, developing better managerial skills, executive personal and career development, and even managerial training to help managers become career coaches to their employees.'

Executive coaching. Coaches are matched with senior executives, providing 'much of the support that more junior employees expect from their managers. Executive coaches may talk through work problems, facilitating decisions, or advise on the executive's own motivation and developing his or her managerial skills' (Price 2005a: 281).

HRM IN REALITY PROFESSIONAL SUPPORT FOR COACHES AND MENTORS

Fifteen per cent of UK organizations have no measures in place to assess the impact of coaching or mentoring programmes and 68 per cent do not use this approach to address corporate objectives, according to a 2010 study by recruitment specialists, Hays Senior Finance, in association with executive and business leadership trainers, LeaderShape. Most initiatives are directed at individuals, with 72 per cent used for talent development or to address personal issues.

Chris McCarthy, director at Hays Senior Finance, said:

In far too many cases companies are leaving it to individuals to set the framework for their own coaching or mentoring — with little or no reference to business needs. They then fail to check the standards of their programmes and show little concern for the outcomes. Support can be extremely effective when a professional starts a new role, but it is essential it is carried out in the right manner by people who understand the specific needs of these individuals.

Responding organizations agreed that if a senior recruit leaves within three months there is both a financial cost and an adverse effect on staff morale. The vast majority (96 per cent) felt that such appointments would benefit from confidential support in the early stages. More than half of respondents said they planned to expand their business coaching provision in the next year with 85 per cent expecting their spending on this area to be maintained at current levels or to increase.

The survey identified a lack of ongoing professional development for providers of mentoring or coaching: Nearly three-quarters of organizations (73 per cent) use in-house resources, but no training or support is given to:

→ Sixteen per cent of coaches

→ Twenty-eight per cent of mentors, and

→ Twenty-nine per cent of team or group facilitators.

To help address this issue, LeaderShape has developed a postgraduate qualification accredited by the University of Chester to enable employees to develop and maintain best practice in the workplace.

Chris Gulliver from LeaderShape commented:

This is a very expensive missed opportunity for UK plc in fast-moving times. Increasing amounts of money are being spent on coaching as a universal panacea but many companies have no comprehensive overview or sense of purpose.

There is a clear lack of framework and training given to those who are delivering many of these programmes with the obvious outcome that they simply don't understand how to use coaching effectively and spend money wisely. In what other area of business would money be laid out with so little thought to evaluating its impact?

Chris Gulliver added:

'Coaching is not regularly applied where it can often be most effective – within the leadership teams. And it is clear that many services are being given to staff, often in difficult situations, by people who are themselves untrained and unsupported. We believe it is essential to upskill internal providers by training them in a range of coach mentoring and facilitation options. It is equally important to track observed outcomes against business objectives. Otherwise businesses could waste time and money and miss the opportunity to boost success.'

Source: Reprinted with permission from HRM Guide UK (http://www.hrmguide.co.uk).

HRD AND THE ORGANIZATION

Priorities have changed in recent years as the focus has moved from piecemeal training activities to more systematic human resource development with organizations re-orienting themselves away from training individual employees towards becoming 'learning organizations' with the emphasis on continuous learning through a range of delivery methods.

Employees learn continuously but this may take place on an *ad hoc* basis, focused on their own short-term needs rather than long-term development to increase their skills and value to the organization. The declared aim of HRD is to direct learning and development towards objectives that are compatible with business strategy. Competitive advantage can come from the development of an organization's human capital: a **learning** experience for employees and the organization as a whole (see Key concept 9.3). For some time, this learning experience was encapsulated within a particular model of training: a comparatively straightforward, organized function which depended heavily on planning.

KEY CONCEPT 9.3 LEARNING

A relatively permanent change of behaviour as a result of past experience. Learning is taken to mean more than acquiring knowledge. It encompasses the way in which outmoded values and techniques are shed in favour of new ones. At an organizational level this requires a collective process of change in its shared worldview, including perceptions of the company and its market.

The systematic training model, or textbook approach, tended to be somewhat prescriptive, laying down stages and techniques to be followed. Depending on a series of logical steps it normally involved (Sloman, 1994):

→ A training policy.

→ A method for identifying training needs.

→ Formulation of training objectives.

→ Development of a training plan.

→ Implementation of a planned training programme.

→ Validation, evaluation and review of training.

The systematic training model assumed an organizational environment based on slow change, hierarchical lines of authority and clear requirements. It was a logical series of steps centred on the use of an objective training-needs analysis. Normally, this would take the shape of an empirical exercise to identify current needs but bringing in the organization's objectives for consideration. It provided a framework within which the trainer could ensure a thorough and 'professional' job. However, it required a methodical and time-consuming series of activities that do not fit so well with modern organizations.

Today's organizations are constantly changing and have much looser systems of control than the companies of the 1960s. The systematic training model does not incorporate a link with development and other human resource initiatives and, consequently, offers an inadequate framework for modern HRD. For example, structural changes may require the movement of people from activities that are shrinking, or even outsourced, to those which are growing. The skills required are those appropriate to the new work area. It is wasteful in both human and budgetary terms to have to dismiss people in one function while simultaneously hiring new people in another.

Learning in organizations can be approached from either a business or educational perspective. Tight (2000) argues that this is an area in which a variety of 'academic tribes' are operating with only limited contacts with each other, including:

→ Adult/continuing/lifelong education.

→ Organizational behaviour/occupational psychology.

→ Management development/learning/studies.

Each of these 'tribes' has a valuable contribution to make to our understanding. There is a conceptual gap between academic literature on the learning organization and that of organizational learning. Huysman (2000) argues that the two streams of theory and research have operated highly independently of each other. The learning organization stream tends to be mainly prescriptive, linking learning to improvement, while the organizational learning stream analyses learning processes without real interest in the outcome.

Whether or not an organization is growing, there is a need to develop skilled people for the future to replace those who are promoted or leave the company. Consistent with human resource strategy, succession planning links development to career structures and promotion policies. It must also take individual career plans and intentions into account. Typically, such a programme is linked to the human resource plans of the company, reflecting its anticipated needs in the relatively long term. Good employers take this seriously.

HRM IN REALITY

THE NEW LEARNING EXECUTIVE – STUDY PROFILES CHIEF LEARNING OFFICERS

A study by the American Society for Training & Development (ASTD) and the University of Pennsylvania has produced a picture of a new breed of learning executive – the chief learning officer (CLO) – that has emerged in the past decade. The challenge of running learning like a business and also making learning a critical contributor to organizational success requires a complex skill set. CLOs must run efficient learning functions that are both strategically aligned with and responsive to the needs of their organizations.

'Profiling a New Breed of Learning Executive', an article in the February 2006 issue of *Training + Development (T+D)* magazine published by ASTD, gives results of the survey of 92 CLOs and identifies the job demands and competences that are critical for success in this position.

Main findings:

→ *Time.* CLOs spend most of their time on strategy development and communicating with corporate executives.

→ *Biggest challenges.* Communicating and measuring the value of learning and resource constraints.

→ *Greatest accomplishments.* Expanding the scope and reach of the learning function and gaining the respect of executives and business unit leaders with whom they partner to improve productivity and performance.

Brenda Sugrue, one of the authors of the study and senior director of research for ASTD says:

> The competences to which these senior learning executives attribute their success emphasize general business skills (leadership, strategic planning and relationship management) rather than specific and deep knowledge of the field of workplace learning and performance.

Additionally, these CLOs recognize the importance of a deeper understanding of the science, technology and measurement of learning and performance.

According to co-author Doug Lynch, vice dean of the Graduate School of Education at the University of Pennsylvania:

> The study results confirm that there are many paths to becoming a CLO and the role requires a combination of business savvy and knowledge of key areas of the learning field. Many CLOs are strong in one but not both of those areas, so the Graduate School of Education and the Wharton School of the University of Pennsylvania is preparing to launch a new curriculum that will prepare professionals specifically for this role.

Daniel Blair, director of ASTD's Learning Executives Network (LXN), added: 'The University of Pennsylvania's initiative to create a targeted curriculum and credential for senior learning executives will help current and aspiring CLOs better prepare to be business partners within their organizations.'

How does the chief learning officer's role differ from that of a traditional senior trainer?

Source: Reprinted with permission from HRM Guide USA (http://www.hrmguide.com).

FROM TRAINING TO DEVELOPMENT

With its incorporation into HRD, training has become a complex topic with a significant shift in both emphasis and importance from the systematic training model. Trainers experience a conflict between, on the one hand, the demand for higher levels of learning to meet the skill needs of new strategic initiatives, and an increasingly decentralized approach to the delivery of learning on the other. There have been changes in responsibility in line with the growth of HRM, new forms of organization and outsourcing. Training may be the province of line managers using specialist trainers as an internal or external consultancy resource or, alternatively, responsibility may lie with a centralized learning delivery mechanism that may come from an external supplier.

New approaches require effective communication between strategic decision-makers, line managers, specialist trainers and learning providers. Together, such changes have made the traditional model of training management obsolete. Almost two decades ago, Sloman (1994) posed some questions that vexed training managers:

→ It is accepted that training should be closely linked with business strategy. But what does this mean in practice? How should this be done?

→ How should training relate to corporate culture?

→ How important a breakthrough are competences?

→ Should the training manager be operating as an internal consultant? If so, what does this mean in practice?

→ Should the company be attempting to become a learning organization, and if so, how?

The strategic link with competitiveness means that HRD has become more important, but there have been pressures on HRD budgets. Critical eyes have looked at development specialists in search of firm evidence of their ability to deliver, in comparison to external providers and new methods of delivering learning. Typically, they are seen more as facilitators and designers of learning programmes than as instructors. Gilley and Gilley (2002: 5) argue that HRD may be sabotaged by trainers who seem more interested in the process of organizing workshops, seminars, meetings and conferences than the organizational purpose of those events. Today's trainers are more involved with strategic decision-makers but often have an unclear career path ahead of them. In many cases they have become managers of externally sourced learning materials, providing advice and acting as internal consultants. The idea of regarding a HRD function as an internal consultancy has attracted considerable support. For example, Mitki *et al.* (2007) describe the use of an internal learning exercise in the construction of a corporate identity for a bank. The notion has an obvious appeal for organizations that divide functions into 'buyers' and 'sellers' and provide an internal accounting system which allocates development costs to budget holders. Separate learning centres can be accurately costed and their value established. The role of 'chief learning officer' has also emerged at a strategic level.

There are some debatable aspects to this approach. If an organization employs external providers for learning delivery, it can do so on the basis of single transactions. Should these prove to be unsatisfactory, the purchaser has the option of changing to a different supplier. In other than the largest organizations, the buyer of an internal consultancy's services does not have this freedom. Additionally, the emphasis on 'independence' sits uncomfortably alongside current management thought which places responsibility for all human resource activities with line managers. Some businesses have rationalized these conflicts by regarding themselves as 'learning organizations'.

THE LEARNING ORGANIZATION

The learning organization 'captured the imagination of trainers and others' in the 1990s (McKenna, 1994: 210). As we can see from Key concept 9.4, it is a view that organizations have to go beyond sporadic training into a permanent state of learning in order to survive in today's business environment. Adapted from Pedler, Boydell and Burgoyne (1989), key characteristics for a learning organization are as follows:

1   The formation of organizational policy and strategy, along with its implementation, evaluation and improvement, is consciously structured as a learning process.

2   There is wide participation and identification in the debate over policy and strategy. Differences are recognized, disagreements aired and conflicts tolerated and worked with in order to reach decisions.

3   Management systems for accounting, budgeting and reporting are organized to assist learning from the consequences of decisions.

4   Information systems should 'informate' as well as automate. They should allow staff to question operating assumptions and seek information for individual and collective learning about the organization's goals, norms and processes.

5   Information on expectations, and feedback on satisfaction, should be exchanged by individuals and work units at all levels to assist learning.

6   Employees with external links – such as sales representatives and delivery agents – act as environmental scanners, feeding information back to other staff.

7   There is a deliberate attempt to share information and learn jointly with significant others outside the organization such as key customers and suppliers.

8   The organization's culture and management style encourage experimentation, and learning and development from successes and failures.

9   Everyone has access to resources and facilities for self-development.

KEY CONCEPT 9.4 LEARNING ORGANIZATION

Not simply an organization which carries out extensive training but rather an organization 'which facilitates the learning of all its members and continuously transforms itself (Pedler, Boydell and Burgoyne, 1989). A learning organization is one that lives and breathes knowledge acquisition and skill development – the ultimate extension of 'learning on the job'.

The concept of the learning organization remains fairly abstract and, as a senior consultant engagingly described it, 'quite fluffy' (Prothero, 1997, quoted in Walton, 1999). The seminal ideas of the concept come from two main sources: the ideas of Pedler *et al.* (1989) on the 'learning company' and Senge's 'five disciplines'. According to Senge (1990, cited in Price, 2000) learning organizations are organizations in which:

→   The capacity of people to create results they truly desire is continually expanding.

→   New and open-minded ways of thinking are fostered.

→   People are given freedom to develop their collective aspirations individuals continually learn how to learn together.

This set of goals may seem somewhat ambitious but Senge contends that they can be achieved through the gradual convergence of five 'component technologies', the essential disciplines of which are (Price, 2000):

Systems thinking. People in an organization are part of a system. Systems thinking is a discipline which integrates the other disciplines in a business. It allows the 'whole' (organization) to be greater than the 'parts' (people, departments, teams, equipment and so on).

Personal mastery. This discipline allows people to clarify and focus their personal visions, focus energy, develop patience and see the world as it really is. Employees who possess a high level of personal mastery can consistently generate results that are important to them through their commitment to lifelong learning.

Mental models. These are internalized frameworks that support our views of the world, beliefs in why and how events happen, and our understanding of how things, people and events are related. Senge advocates bringing these to the surface, discussing them with others in a 'learningful' way and unlearning ways of thinking that are not productive.

Building shared vision. Developing 'shared pictures of the future' together so that people are genuinely committed and engaged rather than compliant.

Team learning. Senge sees teams as a vital element of a learning organization. Hence there is a great significance in the ability of teams to learn.

It is evident that many of the virtuous aspects of 'learning organizations', such as extensive job rotation, mirror practices commonly found in large Japanese corporations. The concept has been much trumpeted but one can justifiably ask if such idealistic objectives can be met in a harsh, competitive business environment. Critics argue that the concept may be unrealistic and, sometimes, counter-productive. Elkjaer (2001) describes a Danish learning organization that did not last very long and suggests that its short life had been due to the emphasis placed on changing individual employees while the organization itself – its management structures and work practices – had remained fairly constant. This emphasis on individual learning may have arisen because of the general and abstract terms in which learning is discussed in prescriptive accounts of learning organizations.

Organizational learning and its offshoot the 'learning organization' have been criticized as a rhetorical device designed to offer senior managers new mechanisms of control over employees. Huzzard (2001) agrees that the learning organization can be criticized on this basis but considers that it should not be dismissed without an adequate alternative. Parding and Abrahamsson (2010) also find problems in reconciling managerial and professional attitudes within a learning organization. Ellinger *et al.* (2002) investigated the relationship between firms' financial performance and the learning organization concept. They found a positive correlation between seven action imperatives for a learning organization and four objective measures of financial performance. More recently the concept has been linked with knowledge management, emphasizing the complex inter-relationships of knowledge sharing, organizational culture and structure necessary for the concept to work (Li *et al.*, 2009; Massingham and Diment, 2009). Similarly, in a Korean study Song and Kim (2009) found positive interactions between the learning organizational and workforce commitment.

EMPOWERMENT AND HRD

The notion of empowerment has a particular relevance in the context of human resource development. There is nothing new in the notion that decision-making should be delegated as low down the organization as possible, and that individuals should take responsibility over their own work, but it has significant implications for the career structures and work behaviour of employees. Empowerment is often presented as something provided for the benefit of employees. In fact, its use is often driven by financial considerations deriving from:

Downsizing. Slimmer companies typically have fewer management layers. The consequence is that the remaining managers are not available for day-to-day decisions – they *must* be taken by lower-level employees.

Speed of response. In an increasingly competitive market, customers expect fast, authoritative decisions on price availability. There is no time for staff to refer to 'the manager'.

In this environment there is a need for confident, speedy decision-making based on a high degree of product expertise. Moreover, in return for empowerment, employees must accept that career opportunities have diminished. As much of the traditional career ladder has disappeared, vertical promotion is only available to a few star performers. HRD in this case is focused on building resilient people, able to gain rewards from existing jobs. Their future lies in 'horizontal promotion', regular moves between different jobs on a similar level.

Specifically, development programmes require an emphasis on decision-making and customer-handling skills, together with in-depth product and service knowledge. In the absence of managerial backup it is necessary that empowered staff have a wide understanding of the organization's functions and goals. They must be able to function well in unclear circumstances, without detailed prescriptive rules and be flexible and proactive enough to make events happen. Ironically, however, Moye and Henkin (2006) found that employees who feel empowered in their work environment tend to have higher levels of trust in their managers.

SELF-DEVELOPMENT

Development is the responsibility of the individual as well as the organization. Career success requires self-control, self-knowledge, systematic career evaluation and frequent role change. Selecting a career path depends on factors such as:

→ *Self-awareness:* being able to accurately assess one's own skills, abilities and interests.

→ *Ambition:* self-esteem, confidence and motivation.

→ *Opportunity:* education, experience and social contacts.

People develop their lives and become distinctive persons through an interaction of three processes: genetic inheritance, life events and self-creation (Glover, 1988). They are so intertwined that we may be unable to attribute a particular event to any one of them. Genetic inheritance determines much of our physical and mental capabilities. Hence the opportunity to succeed in education or business is constrained, to some extent, by inherited factors outside our control. Even health and the duration of our lives are subject in part to genetic determination.

Our lives also depend heavily on accident or chance since the process of living is predominantly an unsystematic series of incidents. We choose to apply for specific jobs, or particular universities, because they meet our needs at a specific point in time. These decisions produce unanticipated side-effects. For example, later we might find ourselves living in a specific location and engaged in projects we would never have contemplated if we had not taken the job or gone to that university.

However, there are major components of life that are controlled by our own actions, leaving scope for intention and direction. The more we plan and take action, the greater the control we have over our lives. To a degree, we shape our own selves by imagining the kind of person we want to be: perhaps being more successful, being respected, or being seen as kind or helpful. When we take actions that contribute to the achievement of these goals we are involved in a process of self-creation. Few of us have a systematic life plan, but rather a loosely organized collection of sometimes minor aims. Viitala (2005) found that many Finnish managers surveyed had no specific development intentions for themselves. In organizations where management development was well-organized and connected to strategic management, managers were more consciously aware of development needs at a personal as well as at a general level. The study revealed that the managers' development intentions differed from those predicted in studies on management competences. Technical and business skills were emphasized at the expense of social and intrapersonal skills.

Most people have restricted opportunities, so that self-creation is a matter of taking account of reality and adjusting to what is possible and some commentators question the concept of self-development (Hallier, 2009). However, from a positive perspective, the following independent development checklist (based on Margerison, 1991: 63) may be useful:

→ What is the best way to spend my time?

→ Who else could do my work?

HRM IN REALITY LEARNING SURVEY

A quarter of British office workers blame their 'David Brent'-style bosses for holding back their development, according to recent research conducted for the online learning specialist, SkillSoft. Sixty-three per cent of the 3000 employees surveyed feel they could be doing better in their career. But many workers say they get no support when it comes to training and career development and bosses fail to recognize and nurture their potential.

The survey also found that public service employees get the most encouragement from their managers with 66 per cent saying their employers are happy for them to develop their skills compared with 56 per cent of people working for private companies. Public sector workers also get more opportunities for on-the-job

training – 40 per cent say they get formal training and mentoring. This compares with 31 per cent in private firms who receive the same level of support.

According to Kevin Young, managing director of SkillSoft: 'It's evident from this study that a large number of people are not being given the opportunity to live up to their potential at work; particularly in the private sector. Just consider the productivity gains that could be achieved if UK businesses stepped up their commitment to developing their employees' skills.'

Sixty-four per cent of those surveyed said their employer allowed them no time in the working day for their professional development. Eighty-nine per cent of employees said they would prefer to be in control of their own learning.

Kevin Young commented: 'This is in line with some research we did last year amongst employees already using e-learning, the majority of whom were taking control of their own professional development by accessing online learning in the office before or after work, or at home in the evenings and at weekends. The effect on their jobs was evident; nearly everyone interviewed could give practical examples of how they had applied their new knowledge at work.' Other key findings:

→ Fifty-three per cent already willingly spend their own free time on professional development. But many more employees said they would spend their spare time studying if bosses allowed them time to learn in the office as well.

→ Forty-three per cent of employees felt that they needed to spend only two–four hours a week on training to achieve their full potential.

→ Asked about the kind of training they needed, 45 per cent said they would like more training in communications and customer relations skills and 50 per cent wanted more management and leadership skills training.

→ Sixty-seven and a half per cent said they deserved higher pay.

→ Most employees enjoy their work – 43 per cent saying that they got some pleasure from their work and 40 per cent go as far as to say they enjoy their jobs 'a lot'. A mere 10 per cent said they don't enjoy their job at all.

Is it possible for self-development to occur without management support?

Source: Reprinted with permission from HRM Guide UK (http://www.hrmguide.co.uk).

→ What am I improving and why?

→ What do I feel strongly about?

→ What are my special strengths and weaknesses?

→ What am I doing to increase my effectiveness?

→ What are the likely benefits and risks of achieving my objectives?

→ What have I learned in the last month?

→ What motivates me most?

→ How many of my objectives do I achieve on time?

→ What is my action plan for: one month, one year, five years?

HRD AS AN ACTIVITY

There is a considerable variation in the way in which HRD is organized and conducted. The difference is greatest between large and small businesses. HRD in small organizations is likely to be unsystematic while large companies may offer sophisticated, highly structured and expensive development programmes. Customer demands are driving training for service and product quality but this is generally focused on 'core' staff with career structures rather than part-time and temporary employees. However, the latter tend to be highly visible to customers, particularly in retailing. In addition we need to distinguish the learning needs of the individual and those of the organization. While individual employees frequently look for wide-ranging courses that will help them in promotion and develop transferable skills which are seen as valuable by other employers, line managers are likely to be more interested in training which improves performance on their present jobs, leading to improved output quality and productivity. In other words, employees seek learning which will make them more marketable whereas organizations prefer training that makes employees more productive.

A training needs model

Nowack (1991) proposes a nine-step model for a training needs exercise.

1 Prepare a job profile Jobs for which training is required need to be identified clearly. The job profile is based on 12–15 dimensions, or job requirements, within which groups of behaviours can be classified. The number of dimensions depends on factors such as what the job involves, its complexity and required skills for effective performance.

Information is obtained from subject matter experts: people who have detailed knowledge of the job(s) being considered. This includes workers currently performing that work, their supervisors and others involved with the input or output to and from those jobs. Information comes from individual interviews, focus groups and survey techniques. Focus groups, for example, discuss the skills deemed important to each job and list them in dimensional categories within broad areas of:

→ Necessary technical knowledge and experience.

→ Communication skills.

→ Decision-making or problem-solving.

→ Administrative skills.

→ Management skills.

Each group indicates how important they feel each dimension is to a particular job – from 'very' to 'not' important. They are also asked to estimate the likely frequency of occurrence of each dimension in terms of 'several times a day/week/month/year'. The lists are compared and integrated to form a definitive job profile.

2 Prepare a learning or training needs questionnaire This is a critical part of the process. Targeted towards particular jobs or job levels in the organization, it is addressed to the people performing the jobs and their immediate supervisors. It includes questions aimed at obtaining three categories of information:

→ *Attitudinal:* describing employees' feelings about their work, their perception of organizational procedures and policies, pay, career, management and environment.

→ *Dimensional:* summarizing views on the job dimensions in terms of their importance and employees' proficiency (expressed on a 1–5 scale).

→ *Demographic:* relevant questions on employees' time within the organization.

3 Administer the questionnaire A decision must be taken on the size of sample required to complete the questionnaire. This will depend on the resources available and the number of people involved in target jobs. In a relatively small organization the questionnaire can be directed to all relevant employees; in larger organizations where hundreds of people may be performing similar tasks, a sample will be more appropriate. The target audience should offer alternative perspectives of specific jobs, for example by asking workers and their immediate supervisors to evaluate the workers' jobs.

The questionnaire should be accompanied by a covering letter describing: the purpose of the exercise; details on how and when to return the questionnaire; and its voluntary, anonymous and confidential nature. Standard methods can be adopted to increase the percentage of questionnaires returned, such as offering incentives (prize draw, restaurant vouchers, etc.).

4 Analyze responses Returned questionnaires are statistically analyzed, preferably by means of a computerized package. A simple mathematical method can indicate the most crucial training needs: each respondent's measure of importance (I) is multiplied by the equivalent rating for proficiency (P) for every dimension. The resulting ($I \times P$) scores can be utilized in a variety of ways. For example, mean scores can be compared across dimensions for a specific group or between groups. Alternatively, supervisors' ratings can be compared with employees' judgements of themselves. It is useful also to compare different departments and to check for differences between new and experienced employees.

5 Interpret the results Nowack suggests that three follow-up questions should be addressed:

→ Is there some commonality between the highest-ranked training needs?

→ What is the explanation for any differences between supervisor and employee assessments?

→ Is there a reason for differences between groups of employees, e.g. senior and junior workers?

Different levels of employee will inevitably have different perceptions of the importance of particular development needs. Workers on the shopfloor may be particularly concerned with day-to-day matters such as dealing with complaining customers effectively, or working a particular machine. Managers may be more interested in longer-term, strategic requirements, such as filling in stock returns accurately and understanding the fine differences between product categories in order to identify trends. These differences have to be evaluated logically.

6 Follow-up focus groups Interpretation of questionnaire results will identify a need for further clarification. This is best provided by small focus groups which can consist of workers, managers or a mix. They can review $I \times P$ scores and offer further explanation. Groups should provide a final executive summary that will be useful for managers and trainees.

7 Feedback A feedback of results to managers and respondents is an essential part of the exercise. Planning and presentation of results is crucial for further progress and as a record of the process for future use.

8 Development objectives The goal is to produce an objective for each dimension identified from the questionnaire and follow-up exercises. They should be tied to an explicit statement of the competences required for effective performance of the jobs in question. Each training need must be categorized as:

→ Imparting knowledge.

→ Changing attitudes.

→ Modifying behaviour.

LEARNING METHODS

HRD managers are presented with an ever-increasing range of learning methods. Traditionally, they have been divided into:

→ *On-the-job training,* including demonstrations of equipment and procedures, instruction manuals, and computer-based training packages.

→ *Off-the-job training,* such as group briefings, projects and formal courses.

Off-the-job training can be in-house, taking place within the organization, or external, for example at a local college or university. Methods of learning can include (Price, 2005a):

→ Traditional lectures – good for imparting factual material and relatively cheap for large numbers of trainees.

→ Case studies – good for problem-solving and simulated experiential learning.

→ Brainstorming – a total contrast to the passivity of the lecture.

→ Critical incident technique – can be more focused and directly relevant than a case study.

→ Discussion and debate – encourages critical thinking.

→ Role plays – another simulated experiential form of learning.

→ Exercises and games – useful for developing team cohesion and skills.

Having done this, the criteria for successful training can be established. For example, if delegation skills are a training need, what behaviour needs to be established by the trainee?

9 A pilot training programme This is a prototype used to test the conclusions of the training needs exercise and provide further information for the final employee development programme.

INDUCTION AND ORIENTATION

Starting a new job ('onboarding') has been compared with one's first day at school. The newcomer is bound to be a little nervous, but hopefully enthusiastic; keen to impress, but not wanting to attract too much attention; anxious to learn quickly, but not wanting to be deluged with names, facts and figures; hoping to fit in, but not look too 'new' and inexperienced. The reception from the employer should ideally anticipate these feelings. After all, the organization has spent good money hiring the newcomer and should treat that person as an investment to be nurtured and encouraged. In reality, however, new recruits are likely to receive an induction or orientation which can be anywhere between two extremes:

In at the deep end: expecting the recruit to get on with the job without any real welcome or information.

Overwhelming: providing the newcomer with an avalanche of introductions, site tours, information packs, etc.

Most large organizations inflict at least some of the following on new hires:

→ Handing out the employee handbook – the HR department may be proud of it but it is not going to be an easy read.

→ Introducing the new recruit to everybody in the business – embarrassing at best, and likely to be off-putting to a new hire who wants to slide into the job quietly. Besides, no one will remember what they have been told or the names of the people to whom they have been introduced.

→ Dishing out even more facts and figures on day one.

→ Doing so in the form of a lecture or presentation – with slides.

→ Doing it again on day two.

→ Not giving the employee their own 'home' – workspace, desk, phone, computer.

→ Having the immediate supervisor away on holiday, in a continuous series of meetings, or just too busy to be involved.

These activities run the risk of boring and confusing, rather than helping, the new employee. Obviously, there is information that new recruits need and administration (payroll details, social security, etc.) that has to be done. Also, there is a degree of ritual – a 'rite of passage' – expected by the new hire, colleagues and the organization. But the process needs to be thought through, especially in relation to timing, quantity and intensity.

The simple truth is that most people responsible for orienting new employees do not put themselves in the new hire's shoes, i.e. do not take account of just what it is like to start a new job – or think of **induction** as an adult learning process that has to be designed to take account of the ways in which people learn. Unfortunately, joiners are commonly 'thrown in at the deep end'. Finding themselves in a strange environment and told to get on with it, they are easily forgotten. Raw recruits are left feeling anxious and vulnerable, forced to make sense of new surroundings and learn correct procedures the hard way. Many managers regard this approach with favour: after all, this was how they learned to cope and get to grips with the business. It is regarded as a test of competence, of machismo, of ability to survive in a demanding environment. This can be a valuable 'growth' experience but there is a considerable risk of individuals becoming disillusioned, leaving or developing bad habits.

There is a well known 'induction crisis' in which a proportion of new recruits leave within the first few weeks. Effective recruitment and selection takes time and costs money. Careless handling of new recruits can render this easily into waste. It is a questionable way of dealing with a significant investment. In the same way as young seedlings and transplanted cuttings are the most vulnerable plants a gardener has to look after, newcomers and promotees are the employees at greatest risk of disillusion and failure. They will worry about their ability to fit in, their competence to do the job, and the impression they are creating in the eyes of their bosses and colleagues.

Induction: getting it right

1   Treat each new employee as an individual, i.e. induction must be tailored to orient individual recruits according to their needs. A school-leaver or fresh graduate will require a different approach to a seasoned professional or experienced worker who can 'hit the ground running'. Don't insult the latter – and waste valuable working time – by putting them through the official HR department induction programme! It is not advisable to have an orientation procedure that is applied to everyone regardless of experience.

2   The immediate line manager should be closely involved, even if arrangements are made by the HR department.

3   It is often useful to allocate a 'buddy' or sponsor on the same working level as the new hire. This allows informal learning to take place about unwritten rules of behaviour, location of important services, and all kinds of 'how-to's that are obvious to an experienced employee, but not to a newcomer. Pick a positive person for this role.

4   Pace the induction process. It is not necessary to do everything on the first morning. The newcomer will still be learning in six months' time.

5   Give the new recruit a real job to do as soon as possible. There is nothing more demoralizing than feeling oneself to be a 'spare part' or a nuisance in a busy department.

Simulation is a key element in several of these methods. For example, Cowey (2005) describes how simulations can be used to overcome the perception of finance training as being dry, difficult and irrelevant. Adobor and Daneshfar (2006) investigated factors that promote the effective use of simulations in management education. They found that the nature of the simulation and team dynamics affected learning and performance. Positive effects were associated with: the extent to which users perceived the simulation as

HRM IN REALITY E-LEARNING IS GAINING GROUND

A report from Ambient Insight, *The US Market for Self-paced E-Learning Products and Services: 2009-2014 Forecast and Analysis* shows that demand for online training is growing by 7.4 per cent and predicts that revenues will reach $23.8 billion by 2014.

According to Chief Research Officer, Sam S. Adkins:

In the past two years, the rate of growth for online learning products has slowed. Yet, despite the recession, and in many cases, because of it, the demand is positive in all the online learning buyer segments. There are distinct revenue opportunities in each of the buyer segments.

E-learning and online training expenditures are estimated for eight buyer segments:

→   consumer

→   corporations

→   federal government

→   state and local government

→   PreK-12 academic

→   higher education

→   non-profits and associations; and

→   healthcare.

The report predicts that corporations will be the top buyers of online training throughout the forecast period, followed by higher education and PreK-12 e-learning buyers.

Ambient CEO Tyson Greer commented:

We see the highest growth rate in the healthcare segment, followed by PreK-12 and higher education. The healthcare industry has been recession resilient and online training suppliers competing in that segment have been relatively immune from recessionary pressures. The rate of growth in the academic segments is due in part to the success and proliferation of the for-profit online schools.

Ambient Insight forecasts spending on six types of Self-paced E-Learning products for each buyer segment:

→ IT-related packaged courseware

→ non-IT courseware

→ custom online learning content services

→ LMS hosting services

→ course authoring tools, and

→ installed LMS platforms.

They predict that non-IT self-paced courseware will generate the highest revenues throughout the forecast period.

Adkins added:

The good news is that there are still large untapped revenues for suppliers. For example, the small and medium business (SMB) buyers were slow to adopt online training until the recent recession. There is now a relatively healthy demand for Self-paced eLearning products and services in the SMB segments.

Why is the market for e-learning growing quickly?

Source: Reprinted with permission from HRM Guide USA (http://www.hrmguide.com).

reflective of real life situations; the ease of use of the simulation; and task conflict, measured by the degree of exchange of ideas. Emotional conflict in the team had a negative association with learning.

KEY CONCEPT 9.5 E-LEARNING

Pantazis (2002) defines e-learning as '… instructional content or learning experiences delivered or enabled by electronic technology.'

E-LEARNING

E-learning has followed the pattern of the Internet – a journey from unrealistic 'hype' to a more modest but increasingly important reality offering personalized web-based learning (Yalcinalp and Gulbahar, 2010)

In the late 1990s and early 2000s e-learning was discussed in dramatic terms as a revolution in learning technology that would become a massive industry in a few years. But uptake was slow and largely confined to organizations with a strong focus on information technology although there are signs of faster growth. Today, e-learning is increasingly seen as one among many possible elements of open learning and workplace training programmes (Price, 2005b). For example, audio and web-conferencing provider Arkadin created learning academies for global talent management that combined e-learning with mentoring and face-to-face training (Mulin and Reen, 2010). In general, however, attitudes towards e-learning vary across organizational cultures (Conboy *et al.*, 2010).

E-learning is computer-based learning, often using Web 2.0 Internet technology such as Wikis, to deliver interactive learning materials to any location. Some of the main reasons for using e-learning include (Driscoll, 2002: 8):

Reducing travel and related costs. Trainees do not need to travel away from the workplace.

Enabling learning any time and any place. Training can be accessed from work, home or anywhere in between.

Providing just-in-time learning.

Leveraging existing infrastructure. Existing equipment, networks and facilities can be used.

Enabling delivery independent of a platform. Accessible from any computer system.

Providing tools for tracking and record-keeping. Can be integrated with human resource information systems.

Making updates easy.

Waight and Stewart (2005) studied factors influencing companies' efforts to value the adult learner in e-learning. They describe an interdependence between:

1   Championing factors – leadership, learning culture, technology infrastructure, finance.

2   Antecedents – needs assessment, learning analysis, work setting analysis, work analysis, content analysis, task analysis.

3   Moderators – return on investment, learning theory application, technology and creativity.

They argue that engagement, learning and transfer can be achieved via e-learning if desirable championing factors, antecedents, and moderators are adhered to.

Servage (2005) suggests that the vagueness of e-learning terminology reflects uncritical approaches to e-learning. Servage's review finds North American practitioner literature dominated by concerns about cost and technology in strategizing and implementation to the near exclusion of workers' learning and affective needs. Servage contends that organizational decision-makers should seek the input and perspective of multiple stakeholders to ensure that e-learning strategies are appropriate not only in terms of financial and technological feasibility but also in the interests of lasting positive effects on employees and organizational culture. In a higher education context, Kirkwood (2009) finds that outcomes of e-learning can be disappointing as context variables such as learner expectations and teachers' beliefs in the system are significant. Again in higher education, Maltby and Mackie (2009) identify four types of e-learner: model, traditionalist, geek and disengaged.

Action learning

Many years before the concept of e-learning was thought of, Revans (1972) argued that classroom-based management education is not adequate. He devised a systematic, experiential or 'action learning' programme based on job exchanges that placed managers in unfamiliar situations and asked them to take on challenging tasks. These tasks should have the following characteristics:

1   Based on real work projects.

2   Projects must be owned and defined by senior managers and be important to the future of the organization.

3   The process is an investment requiring a real return on cost.

4   Managers must work in groups, learning from each other and crossing boundaries between functions and departments.

5   Projects must go beyond analysis – they should require real action and change.

6   Content (programmed knowledge) and process (questions/methods) of change should be studied.

7   There must be public commitment from participants to action/report.

Revans' ideas are consistent with the principles of the learning organization discussed earlier in this chapter. The emphasis lies with learning rather than training and with meeting the changing needs of an organization in a competitive world. His approach is also mirrored in many current programmes aimed at developing leaders. Action learning can be integrated with e-learning. Waddill (2006) investigated the impact of the action learning process on the effectiveness of management level web-based instruction (WBI) or e-learning. Converting a leader-led course proved challenging to facilitate, but the action learning online method was found to be effective.

LEADERSHIP DEVELOPMENT

'I would argue that more leaders have been made by accident, circumstance, sheer grit, or will than have been made by all the leadership courses put together' (Bennis, 1990).

The skills of leadership have attracted management theorists and trainers alike. Whereas good leaders are comparatively easy to recognize when they are in positions of authority, developing people to achieve the necessary qualities is not so easy. Just as the nature of leadership is not fully understood, the appropriate methods of training and leadership are a matter of controversy. At the same time leadership training is a lucrative area for training consultants, and management gurus have been ready to produce packaged methods.

It is arguable that many supposed 'leadership' courses are actually teaching management skills rather than those of leadership. A typical leadership course concentrates on:

→   Identifying the nature of leadership and the form which the individual trainee wishes to adopt. This incorporates a range of options from being able to give orders (to 'boss') to a more inspirational form.

→   Self-awareness – the identification of those leadership skills which individuals feel themselves to be lacking.

→   A general boost in self-confidence.

The focus in each case depends on factors such as:

→   Participants' level of seniority. It would be counter-productive to encourage a junior manager to adopt the manner and style appropriate to a managing director.

→   The organizational culture in which trainees have to operate. Authoritarian forms of leadership would be disastrous in a participative business.

→   Trainees' personalities. People vary in their degrees of assertiveness and sensitivity and need to develop a leadership style that fits naturally with their personality characteristics.

> It is easier to develop abilities that already exist in an embryonic form than to attempt to change an individual's whole character. The latter is likely to be impossible.

Part of the programme would involve a team exercise requiring the solution of a hypothetical problem.

Many courses have taken on 'outward bound' elements. These use sport or other outdoor physical activities that require skill as a vehicle for experiential learning. Such programmes claim to develop management skills such as leadership, teamwork, communication, problem solving, managing change and coping with stress. However, much of this learning does not translate naturally to the office. There have also been lasting physical and psychological effects of a negative kind – particularly with older, unfit participants.

Blended learning

Recently, it has been argued that effective learning needs a combination of methods, an approach described as 'blended learning', integrating best practice in face-to-face and online learning to compensate for the impersonal and isolated nature of e-learning (Sleator, 2010). For example, Collis *et al.* (2005) describe 'putting learning to work', a form of blended learning used at Shell International EP that focuses on learning while in the workplace through work-based activities within technology-supported courses. This has been evolving since 2000.

Graham (2005) looked at IT training of existing employees and argues that it should form an ongoing part of an organization's operations, rather than be reliant on external specialist recruitment and panic reactions to immediate skill shortages. Graham states that a combination of a training needs analysis, psychological, skill-based tests to identify an employee's current ability and willingness to embrace the training, and blended learning, have advantages over other training methods. Ausburn (2004) investigated course design elements most valued by adult learners in blended learning environments that combine face-to-face contact with web-based learning. Most valued were course designs containing options, personalization, self-direction, variety and a learning community. Participants benefit when learning relates to real life situations and participants are actively involved with each other, particularly online (Fontanin, 2010), and received adequate tutor support (Sulcic, 2010).

EVALUATING AND COSTING TRAINING

According to Rosania (2000):

> The fact is that trainers do not inherently lack power; what they lack is the ability to use their power in a way that consistently demonstrates the value of their service to their stakeholders. Trainers do not need fancy titles or affiliation with certain departments to demonstrate their value. What trainers need to change is their thinking about how they can contribute to the success of their organizations.

Of course, one basic issue affecting the credibility of trainers is the need to demonstrate the value of training to the organization. In a review of evaluation methods, Rowden (2001) states: 'The "beancounters" in the organization are likely to know exactly how much training "costs" but they may have little idea of its value. HR must be able to supply that information if it is to truly become a strategic part of the organization.' In general, it seems that the perceived usefulness of the training is a key issue for participants and the sponsoring organization (Giangreco *et al.*, 2009).

What methods are used in practice? The most obvious are 'happy-sheets' or question-naires handed out to participants on completion of a training course. These are forms that ask trainees to rate the presentation and usefulness of the course and invite comments. The inherent flaws of this approach are well known (Lewis, 1991):

→ They are usually completed in the euphoric period at the end of the course when trainees are relieved to have survived, when they are looking forward to going home, and pressure and stress have lifted. At this point in time the world has taken on a comfortable, rosy glow.

→ A personal relationship has been developed with the trainers, so criticism is toned down to avoid upsetting them.

→ Most of all, the evaluation concentrates on the wrong issues. Often there is cursory attention to the value of the training experience to the trainees, their future job performance and hence the organization. Instead, forms are likely to concentrate on the overall enjoyability of the course and the quality of the environment in which it took place. According to McKenna (1994: 212): 'It is known for trainees to be thoroughly satisfied with a programme merely because the instructor or trainer did a good job entertaining them.' Happy-sheets are excellent for comments on the comfort of hotel accommodation, speed and service in the restaurant and the stuffiness of seminar rooms. Usually they tell us little about the cost-effectiveness of the programme.

The evaluation of training has attracted considerable attention. A number of models exist of which Hamblin's (1974) is, perhaps, one of the best known. Hamblin stratified training into five levels, which could be evaluated independently:

Level 1. The reactions of trainees during training to the trainer, other trainees and external factors.

Level 2. Learning achieved during training, assuming basic aptitude and receptiveness on the part of the trainee.

Level 3. Job behaviour in the work environment at the end of the training period.

Level 4. The overall effects on the organization.

Level 5. Ultimate values: factors such as business survival, profit, welfare of interested parties and social/political welfare.

Kirkpatrick (1994) split evaluation into four levels:

Reaction: is the 'customer' satisfied? If the trainee does not like the programme he or she is unlikely to be motivated to learn.

Learning: Brown and Seidner (1998) state that this 'can be described as the extent to which participants change attitudes, improve knowledge, and/or increase skill as a result of attending the programme'.

Behaviour change: how is actual behaviour changed by training?

Results: the return on investment (ROI) or effect of the training on the organization's bottom-line.

Rowden (2001) examines the last two levels in detail. He proposes the following as the most significant for measuring behaviour change: a 360-degree appraisal feedback process and a performance-learning-satisfaction evaluation system. In practice, evaluation is seen as a weak link in the learning process. 'It is the step most likely to be neglected or underdone' (Gibb, 2002: 107). Kirkpatrick's model continues to offer promising theoretical and evidence-based value (Steensma and Groeneveld, 2010).

However, the fact that such models exist has not led many organizations to use them! Hendry (1995: 366) echoes some astute criticisms of evaluation:

> The whole notion of evaluation is based on training as a discrete event – namely the training course – and justifying the substantial visible costs associated with off-the-job courses and full-time training staff. Take these away, as Hamblin (1974) and Crittan (1993) have observed, and the rationale and pressure for evaluation largely collapses. Evaluation of training events was always a fallacy as long as it ignored the equally important process of practice back on the job which ensures that training transfers.

In practice, Hendry (1995: 364) argues that the most progressive firms use a mixture of:

'Hard' evaluation criteria. Short-term improvements in measurable performance, such as individual productivity and quality adherence.

'Soft' criteria. Indirect benefits from intermediate human resource goals, including reduction in staff turnover, promotability and flexibility.

Tamkin, Yarnall and Kerrin (2002) and Gibb (2002) concur that although evaluation has grown in priority in recent years, most evaluation activity is unsophisticated. According to Gibb (*ibid.*: 120):

> So while L&D evaluation is at least now done more widely than ever before it is stuck at the most basic level possible, with the prevalence and preference in L&D for using the basic recipes of levels of evaluation … In the end the formulas and techniques for evaluation of L&D have to balance the demands of scientific rigour with those of professional practice, and the theoretical goals of 'truth seeking' with the practical goals of 'pragmatic management'.

 SUMMARY

Competitiveness demands a diverse workforce and up-to-date skills. The free market belief in 'buying-in' skill has proven inadequate, even in times of high unemployment. HRD can be a proactive aspect of talent management, focusing on developing employees as investments for the organization and planning for skill availability in advance of need. In the context of learning organizations HRD programmes involve more than training and require mechanisms for accurate assessment, counselling and inbuilt personal challenge using a variety of learning methods in an active, self-directed manner.

 FURTHER READING

1 Swart, Mann, Brown and Price, *Human Resource Development: Strategy and Tactics* (Butterworth-Heinemann, 2005) is a wide-ranging discussion of HRD and its methods.

2 Stephen Gibb's Human *Resource Development: Processes, Practices and Perspectives*, 2nd edition (Palgrave/ Macmillan, 2007) provides a good practical overview.

3 *Employee Training and Development,* 5th edition, by Raymond A. Noe (McGraw-Hill Higher Education, 2010) has become something of a classic.

4 *Excellence in Coaching: The Industry Guide,* 2nd edn, edited by Jonathan Passmore (Kogan Page, 2010) is a comprehensive text on the subject as is:

5 *Coaching and Mentoring* by Robert Garvey, Paul Stokes and David Megginson (Sage Publications, 2008).

➡ REVIEW QUESTIONS

1 What are the limitations of the following concepts in describing learning in the workplace: training, education, human resource development, 'knowledge, skills and abilities'?

2 Consider an organization of your choice: (a) Does this organization offer systematic development? (b) Does it aim to develop employee skills as a long-term strategy?

3 How is human resource development distinguished from training?

4 What additional pressures or incentives could be placed on businesses to take vocational education and training seriously?

5 What are the arguments for and against separate development programmes for women and men?

6 Define the term 'mentoring' and explain its benefits.

7 Why has there been such a strong focus on management development?

8 How would you distinguish between learning organizations and learning in organizations? Evaluate the view that 'learning organizations are just hype'.

9 What are the most significant links between performance management and learning and development?

10 There has been a trend towards proactive learning and away from passive training. Should the 'training needs analysis' be modified to become more of a 'learning needs analysis'? If so, how?

11 How has the concept of career development changed in recent years? What are the implications of the reduction in management layers in many large organizations on individual career aspirations?

12 Can anyone be a good trainer? Do we still need training specialists if people can learn for themselves?

13 Outline the essential differences between action learning and formal training.

14 What are the most important features of induction and orientation?

15 Is it possible to prove that training is a worthwhile business investment?

16 What are 'e-learning' and 'blended learning'?

CASE STUDY FOR DISCUSSION AND ANALYSIS

Lisa

Lisa was a recent recruit. The HR manager was very pleased to have taken her on as her assessment centre results were outstanding. She was a graduate in chemical engineering, apparently keen to apply her university training within the organization, a medium-sized manufacturer of aluminium products.

Previous female graduate recruits had received a brief induction period involving visits to all departments, and then been placed in marketing or personnel jobs. None had risen beyond the junior management grades: higher posts seemed to be reserved for men promoted from production and finance. The board had decided that the company's attitude towards women was old-fashioned and was preventing them from making the best use of their human resources. Lisa was the opportunity to do something positive about the problem. With the support of the MD, the personnel manager set out to offer Lisa a development programme that would give her the opportunity to achieve a senior management post within a reasonable period.

Situation

Tina Johnson was a determined and thorough human resource manager. In her late 40s and without much in the way of academic qualifications herself, she was aware that many bright young recruits were going to university before taking their first job. She was also in touch with the greater expectations of young people qualified to this level. She found that they were unhappy with the idea of several years at a junior level before being offered a seriously demanding job.

Lisa did not seem to be any different to the other graduates taken on by the company. Outside the male-dominated production and service areas, there were many female graduates at the lower management levels. Lisa had been with the company for three months and had completed the 'grand tour' which was the company's induction programme.

Tina decided to conduct a development interview with Lisa. She began by asking her how she felt about the company so far.

'It isn't quite what I expected,' said Lisa. She seemed ill-at-ease and nervous.

'Oh, in what way?' asked Tina in a friendly but quizzical tone.

'Well, I suppose I was expecting to use my university training from the beginning … rather than being shown around places like Marketing and Distribution,' Lisa answered in a very apologetic way.

Tina decided to persist: 'Yes, but we think it's important for you to have a proper induction programme so that you get a basic understanding of the way the company operates. We invest a lot of time and money in our new recruits … three months is a long time to spend just on induction, you know.'

Lisa continued to look doubtful, and clearly wasn't convinced: 'I just don't think I learned very much, that's all.'

'Why was that?' said Tina, sensing that she had a problem she had not anticipated.

Lisa took some time composing her answer. It was clear that she was fumbling for words that would allow her to express her opinion without upsetting the HR manager. 'I really wanted to show people that I know a lot about chemical engineering but nobody seems interested. Besides, several people told me that I would probably end up in marketing anyway. Most women do, don't they? Or HR, and I'm definitely not interested in that!' She emphasized 'HR' with a grimace.

After the development interview Lisa wrote a letter to Tina Johnson couched in hostile terms, accusing the company of misleading her and having no idea of how to use graduates. She had been offered a scholarship to study for a PhD at an American university and had accepted it. She would be leaving the company in a month's time.

How would you have designed Lisa's development programme?

What resistance would you have reasonably expected and how would you have overcome it?

CHAPTER 10
Reward management

PAY AND COMPENSATION

Pay is an important feature of human resource management – after all, it is the main reason why people work. It is a sensitive and controversial area that has been extensively debated at both practical and theoretical levels. In the USA the term 'compensation' is used to encompass everything received by an employed individual in return for work. For example, Milcovich, Newman and Milcovich (2001: 6) state: 'Employees may see compensation as a *return in exchange* between their employer and themselves, as an *entitlement* for being an employee of the company, or as a *reward* for a job well done' (original emphases).

The reward or compensation that people receive for their contribution to an organization includes monetary and non-monetary components. Remuneration does not simply compensate employees for their efforts – it also has an impact on the recruitment and retention of talented people.

The term '**reward management**' covers both the strategy and the practice of pay systems. Traditionally, human resource or personnel sections have been concerned with levels and schemes of payment whereas the process of paying employees – the payroll function – has been the responsibility of finance departments. There is a trend towards integrating the two, driven by computerized packages offering a range of facilities.

There are two basic types of pay schemes, although many organizations have systems that include elements of both:

Fixed levels of pay. Wages or salaries that do not vary from one period to the next except by defined pay increases, generally on an annual basis. There may be scales of payments determined by age, responsibility or seniority. Most 'white-collar' jobs were paid in this way until recently.

Reward linked to performance. The link may be daily, weekly, monthly or annualized. Payment for any one period varies from that for any other period, depending on quantity or quality of work. Sales functions are commonly paid on the basis of turnover; manual and production workers may be paid according to work completed or items produced. Catering staff typically rely on direct payment from satisfied customers in the form of service charges or tips (gratuities).

Both methods work smoothly, provided that scales are easy to understand and the methods of measuring completed work are overt, accurate and fair. However, there has been considerable dissatisfaction with the management of pay on both sides of the employment relationship. In recent years, attempts have been made to remedy the situation through new systems and a greater reliance on performance-related pay.

KEY CONCEPT 10.1 REWARD MANAGEMENT

Reward or compensation management is an aspect of HRM that focuses pay and other benefits on the achievement of objectives. Typically, it incorporates other changes in pay administration and policy, including: decentralization of responsibility for setting pay levels; uniform appraisal schemes; flexible working practices; and performance-related pay.

Within HRM literature there is some ambiguity as to whether reward should play a supporting role, a view implicit in the Harvard model of HRM, or, conversely, that it should *drive* organizational performance – an opinion which finds greater favour among exponents of 'hard' HRM (Kessler, 1995: 10). Milcovich *et al.* (2001: 5) take a broad perspective, arguing that:

> In addition to treating pay as an expense, a manager also uses it to influence employee behaviours and improve organization performance. The way people are paid affects the quality of their work; their attitude towards customers; their willingness to be flexible or learn new skills or suggest innovations; and even their interest in unions or legal action against their employer. This potential to influence employees' behaviours, and subsequently the productivity and effectiveness of the organization, is another reason it is important to be clear about the meaning of compensation.

Wolf (1999: 41) contends that compensation programmes have been structured to meet three primary design criteria. They must be:

1   *Internally equitable* and pay people in proportion to the relative value of the job.

2   *Externally competitive* and pay people in proportion to the market price of the job.

3   *Personally motivating* to employees.

Wolf adds a fourth objective, which is often kept from line managers: ease of administration for staff. Wolf comments on these objectives:

> Unfortunately, the first two are almost always at cross purposes with each other, forcing an organization to sacrifice one to achieve the other, and achievement of the third means a high degree of individualization, which complicates the fourth, administration.

Many countries have **minimum wage** rates in place which set the base rate for pay across the job market.

HR AND PAYROLL ADMINISTRATION

Traditionally, payroll sections and the human resource sections that interface with them have suffered from too much administration. Every transaction triggered 'a paper-intensive, repetitive, and inconsistent process' (Hitzeman, 1997). Today, businesses want their pay functions to do more than just administration. They demand efficient payroll processes together with expertise and service. According to Hitzeman such changes in delivery and expectations are forcing pay-related departments to sharpen their focus on key issues.

Hitzeman argues that the pay function is becoming increasingly complex because:

→   Legal aspects have become more involved.

→   Staff expect higher standards of service.

→   Pay staffing levels have been kept steady or even reduced.

To provide the desired level of service to staff and other 'customers', pay departments need to reorganize both tasks and resources around two central themes: transactions and consulting.

HRM IN REALITY — TOP TEN EXCUSES FOR NOT PAYING MINIMUM WAGE

HM Revenue & Customs published the top ten excuses used by employers to avoid paying the national minimum wage in 2006. These excuses were to its 16 minimum wage enforcement teams around the UK. The enforcement teams identified nearly £3.3 million in underpaid salaries across the UK between August 2005 and July 2006.

The top ten unusual or outlandish excuses for not paying the minimum wage were:

1 He doesn't deserve it – he's a total waste of space

2 But she only wanted £3 an hour

3 I didn't think the workers were worth NMW

4 I didn't think it applied to small employers

5 He's disabled

6 They can't cope on their own and it's more than they would get in their own country

7 She's on benefits – if you add those to her pay, it totals the NMW

8 He's over 65, so the national minimum wage doesn't apply

9 The workers can't speak English

10 I only took him on as a favour.

Do these excuses have any justification?

Source: Reprinted with permission from HRM Guide UK (http://www.hrmguide.co.uk).

Payroll sections typically deal with issues which go beyond simple pay calculations. They can include:

→ Health benefit schemes.

→ Pension contributions.

→ Savings.

→ Company share option purchases.

→ Sickness and other forms of paid time off.

→ Expenses.

As a result, payroll staff are involved with the following transactions:

→ Dealing with routine queries.

→ Filling in forms.

→ Issuing forms for staff to complete.

→ Explaining company policies and procedures.

Traditionally, payroll departments handled a great deal of repetitive work and generated mountains of paper. At the same time they tended to be inconsistent in the responses they provided – similar queries often receiving different answers, depending on the staff member involved. Basically, traditional pay sections were too clerical in focus. A solution has been to split information away from administrative functions into specialist areas. This allows consolidation and standardization of transaction handling, leading to a degree of efficiency not possible in a traditional, unspecialized department. In large organizations, such a function can become a centre of excellence, taking advantage of professional techniques and up-to-date information technology. This offers the possibility of: more efficient processes and better customer service; consistent handling of queries and situations; better information; and a recognized 'one-stop shop' for pay-related queries.

As another step in this process, organizations may choose to outsource some of the more routine 'number-crunching' functions to specialist companies. Pension administration is a long-standing example. The most obvious justification for outsourcing is to cut costs by:

→ Benefiting from the economies of scale open to a specialist provider.

→ Reducing the number of internal pay administrators.

→ Minimizing capital investment in equipment.

→ Reducing overhead costs such as accommodation, heating and lighting.

HRM IN REALITY — RECESSION IMPACTS ON JOBS, INCOMES AND EMPLOYEE ENGAGEMENT

Most European businesses are finding it difficult to attract and motivate the skilled individuals needed to recover from the economic crisis, according to research from global professional services company Towers Watson. Cost-cutting has also had a negative impact on existing employees and organizations are looking afresh at how they attract, motivate and engage their workforces.

In fact, the Towers Watson Global Talent Management and Rewards Survey, prepared in conjunction with WorldatWork, the international association of HR professionals, shows that businesses worldwide are finding that attracting critical-skill employees is a major issue. Sixty-five per cent of organizations surveyed around the globe reported problems attracting critical-skill employees. In Europe, 58 per cent of respondents were experiencing these problems to a great or moderate extent and 61 per cent also said they had similar difficulties attracting top performers.

Globally, the economic crisis had forced businesses to cut costs. In Europe the top three actions were:

→ hiring freezes (75 per cent)

→ salary freezes (63 per cent)

→ layoffs/redundancies (57 per cent).

Respondents acknowledged that these cost-cutting measures have been tough on employees.

→ Sixty-one per cent of European respondents said that employees' workload had increased as a result

→ Forty-seven per cent felt they had adversely impacted on employees' ability to manage workplace stress

→ Forty-four per cent said the measures had a negative effect on employees' healthy work–life balance

→ Fifty-one per cent believed that there had been an adverse impact on overall employee engagement.

Carole Hathaway, senior consultant at Towers Watson, said:

> Employers need to address the adverse issues amongst employees caused by cost-cutting. It is critical that companies re-motivate and re-engage their employees as there is a clear link between increased employee engagement and improved business performance. Business leaders therefore need to show their employees how they intend to build trust and demonstrate interest in their employees' well-being – whilst also doing so in as cost-effective ways as possible.

Many companies are re-evaluating reward and talent management programmes because of the impact of cost-cutting on employee:

→ 58 per cent of businesses surveyed are ensuring readiness of skilled people for critical roles

→ 56 per cent are creating more movement, rotation and development opportunities for skilled people

→ 53 per cent are investing more in building internal pipelines of talent.

Carole Hathaway added:

> The business climate has clearly affected companies' ability to attract and re-motivate top-performing employees. At least in part because these key people simply are in no rush to seek employment elsewhere given the uncertainty over economic recovery and the future of their current pay and benefits package. But these are the very people most likely to leave should a better offer come along. Many employers have also underestimated the impact of pensions, job security and flexible working arrangements on employees' decisions whether or not to leave their organization.

What should organizations do to optimize their reward management strategies in times of economic crisis?

Source: Reprinted with permission from HRM Guide (http://www.hrmguide.net).

PAY EVALUATION

What criteria should be used to determine levels of pay? Dickinson (2006) found evidence for widespread social norms about the most appropriate bases for pay differentials with 'responsibility', 'qualifications' and 'performance' being the most commonly cited by employees. However, large organizations have traditionally resorted to job evaluation to provide the justification for different levels of pay. According to the International Labour Organization, 'job evaluation is directed towards rating the job, not the person'. Job evaluation is particularly concerned with:

→ Tasks involved in fulfilling a job.

→ Duties that have to be completed.

→ Responsibilities attached.

It is not concerned with elements of job analysis required for the recruitment process such as qualifications, experience, proficiency, or the key considerations of performance management – job behaviour, proficiency and attendance.

The outcome of a traditional job evaluation process is a set of job classifications, perhaps expressed as a formal hierarchy of jobs. The next stage, job pricing, results in a pay scale. Therefore, job pricing determines the remuneration or compensation for each job.

Traditional job evaluation involves the comparison of jobs in a formal, systematic way to identify their relative value to an organization. It has an underlying premise: that some jobs are worth more than others. Job evaluation has its roots in the scientific management movement (Taylorism) of the early 20th century. The methodology has had a particularly strong influence in the USA, where it has focused on position-based job evaluation systems. These systems define the scope and value of jobs by using comparatively narrow job classification grades.

The end of the 20th century saw some radical changes in the nature of work. Increasingly, the concept of flexibility displaced the notion that work should be composed of a rigid set of pre-defined tasks. The job description seems increasingly inappropriate for the way work is organized today since the content of many jobs varies from one day to the next. This makes job rating and pay evaluation more difficult. Traditional job evaluation is focused on unchanging job descriptions and requirements, encouraging staff to take a rigid attitude to their work. If performance assessment and pay are linked to the completion of specific tasks, the need for change and a flexible approach to customers is ignored. Modern organizations have turned to competency profiles instead. Over the last few decades, pay evaluation systems have swung from having an individual focus to being job-based and, more recently, back again to a stress on the individual.

Market-driven criteria

New skills and occupations are characterized by a greater demand for the right people than the job market can supply. The natural response is to increase pay and benefits on offer to these people. However, this has consequences for other staff in the organization and also for any job evaluation system. Scarcity of skills distorts evaluation systems and raises concerns about fairness. Short-term solutions produce further problems in the future when appropriately skilled staff become plentiful. This situation is common in information technology where, at first, only a few individuals are able to use new applications. Within a matter of months large numbers of trained people become available. A year or two later the applications may be replaced by new products and the once-valued skills are redundant.

Broadbanding and skill-based pay

Broadbanding has been implemented in a number of different ways, but the basic principle is the same: large numbers of individually rated jobs or job types are clustered into a few, much wider job classifications or 'bands'. Although broadbanding was trumpeted as a panacea in the 1990s, Wolf (1999: 45) criticizes the exaggerated claims for its effectiveness, stating that these are made on questionable data. It is clear from a number of surveys that managers are not implementing broadbanding thoroughly – for example, bands often are not broad at all. Many organizations are not measuring the cost or effectiveness of broadbanding in comparison with more traditional methods, and improvements in career management (cited as one of the main benefits by proponents) are not being achieved.

Wolf (*ibid.*: 48) is equally dismissive of skill or competence-based pay systems:

> Whether one relies on old-fashioned job evaluation and traditional job-pay structures or moves to competences and broad bands, employers still pay for what you know and what you do. No matter how you get there, these are the key compensable elements! Attempts to dress this up in modern garb abound, but the underlying premise remains as an eternal verity.

Kessler (2001: 221) also concludes that competence (and team) based pay are superficially attractive, but they are difficult to put into practice as competences are difficult to identify and measure, as are the standards for judging team performance. Kessler considers that:

> It is difficult to avoid the conclusion that while use of pay to encourage the development of employee competences and a team-based work environment are readily identifiable as business priorities, driving the formulation of new pay strategies, there is precious little evidence to suggest that such priorities are being translated into practice.

Can we be confident that pay evaluations are always objective? Mobius and Rosenblat (2006) conducted an experimental study where participants acting as 'employers' determined wages of other participants ('workers') performing a maze-solving task. The skill required had nothing to do with physical attractiveness but physically attractive 'workers' seemed to get a sizeable premium. Three possible explanations were suggested:

→ Physically attractive workers are more confident and higher confidence increases wages.

→ For a given level of confidence, physically attractive workers are wrongly considered more able by employers.

→ Controlling for worker confidence, physically attractive workers have oral skills (such as communication and social skills) that raise their wages when they interact with employers.

MOTIVATION, PAY AND BENEFITS

How important is pay as a motivator? Rynes, Gerhart and Minette (2004: 382) observe that 'practitioner journals present claims about pay importance that are inconsistent with research about the actual motivational effects of pay. In general, there appears to be a consistent (but incorrect) message to practitioners that pay is not a very effective motivator – a

HRM IN REALITY POOR LEADERSHIP IN MOTIVATING POORER-PERFORMING STAFF

A 2008 European study by consultants Watson Wyatt has found that employers need to be more effective at helping managers to motivate poorer-performing staff.

Carole Hathaway, a senior consultant at Watson Wyatt commented:

Managers find it easy to manage top-performing employees but are not so adept when it comes to improving poorer performers. Some of the greatest opportunities for improved organizational performance lie in helping managers raise the bar for moderate and poorer performers but it appears from our study that few employers are doing a good job of this.

Watson Wyatt's 2007/2008 Global Strategic Rewards study encompassed 5500 employees and 175 businesses across Europe. The study found that, compared to their poorer-performing colleagues, top performers were 66 per cent more likely to say that their immediate bosses did a good job of communicating organizational and performance management issues.

Watson Wyatt also found that just a third of poor performers could say that their immediate supervisors were good at:

→ communicating expectations for organizational financial performance

→ establishing goals for their individual performance that were linked to business objectives, or

→ providing direct feedback on their individual performance.

Worse, fewer than 30 per cent felt that their immediate manager did a good job of linking organizational performance to rewards or linking individual performance to rewards.

Carole Hathaway said:

It could be that managers need more support in understanding how to communicate with all their staff, not just the more motivated stronger performers. Employees perform better if they have a clear understanding of their organization's goals and what they can personally do to contribute towards these.

So setting good objectives and getting performance management communication right, especially for the weaker members of a team, is of vital importance.

Poor leadership affecting business performance

A survey for RTL in 2007 indicated that UK bosses' lack of leadership skills in setting objectives, motivating employees and dealing with poor performers has an adverse effect on business performance. Commissioned by Ros Taylor Ltd, a leading firm of Chartered Psychologists, the study drew on responses from 1500 people from organizations of varying sizes throughout the UK about leadership in the workplace.

Key findings include:

→ Seventy-seven per cent of respondents said their boss was not interested in them

→ Ninety per cent said their boss did nothing about poor performers

→ Seventy-nine per cent claimed their boss did not set clear objectives

→ Eighty-nine per cent said their boss lacked innovation and was unreceptive to new ideas.

Ros Taylor, managing director of RTL commented:

That's only 15 per cent of people we asked who thought their boss was any good and eight per cent who thought they were inspirational. I wish I could say I was shocked – but the truth is it's slightly better than I expected. The fact is that while businesses are quite rightly paying attention to their cost base – squeezing every last ounce of value out of the food chain – they are not so cleverly overlooking a very real business and financial asset.

Leadership

Let's forget the old clichés about 'soft skills' – bad leadership costs shareholders and stakeholders real money. While companies are spending millions on automation and the new IT architectures they could be spending thousands and saving millions by sharpening up their leadership assets.

Think about it. Many line managers, heads of department and directors are on a minimum £100K+ pa. These people represent something of the order of a £200K+ investment for the company. As a psychologist I am intrigued that companies who bend over backwards to 'think smart' ignore this area. It's the 'one thing' they could do that would deliver tangible results – and yet the vast majority just don't do it. They probably think that, in the old cliché 'leaders are born, not made' and yet in our business we disprove that on an almost daily basis. They can't leave the innovation and blue sky thinking that comes from truly inspirational leadership to chance – or for that matter to a quirk of genetics – it's odd to think that multinational companies who factor the canteen subsidy into the cost of a sausage roll don't have a 'leadership development plan'.

Why is there a mismatch of perceptions between managers and staff?

Source: Reprinted with permission from HRM Guide UK (http://www.hrmguide.co.uk).

message that, if believed, could cause practitioners to seriously underestimate the motivational potential of a well-designed compensation system.' They argue that most surveys of motivating factors are misleading because employees tend to give 'socially desirable' responses that place pay well down in the list of motivators. They consider that pay is the most important motivator and cite meta-analytic evidence.

Despite its importance, motivation goes beyond pay. Herpen, Praag and Cools (2005) demonstrated a positive relationship between the perceived characteristics of the complete compensation system and extrinsic motivation. Intrinsic motivation, on the other hand, was not affected by the design of monetary compensation, but by promotion opportunities.

They also found that the compensation system significantly affected work satisfaction and turnover intent. Balsam *et al.* (2007) found evidence that stock options reduced employee turnover in the periods when the options could not be exercised.

According to Rosenbloom (2001: 2):

Employee benefits constitute a major part of almost any individual's financial and economic security. Such benefits have gone from being considered 'fringe' to the point where they may constitute about 40 per cent of an employee's compensation, and the plans under which they are provided are a major concern of employers.

See Key concept 10.2.

KEY CONCEPT 10.2 EMPLOYEE BENEFITS

Any form of reward other than regular wages paid to employees.

HRM IN REALITY INCENTIVE SCHEMES DILUTED BY TOO MANY PERFORMANCE MEASURES

A global study by Watson Wyatt in 2007 concluded that the effectiveness of sales incentive plans can be diluted by too many performance measures and shows significant differences between sectors. For example, the banking sector frequently used multiple measures while the hi-tech sector uses far fewer.

At branch management level, the banking sector uses seven dominant measures:

→ revenue volume

→ number of new accounts

→ number of units sold

→ sales growth

→ profit margin

→ expense control, and

→ customer satisfaction.

Conversely, a role at a similar level in hi-tech companies typically uses a mere three criteria: revenue volume; management by objectives; and profit margin.

Chantal Free, European head of sales effectiveness and compensation consulting at Watson Wyatt commented:

We believe hi-tech companies are ahead of the curve by moving away from using lots of measures. We are likely to see other sectors following suit in having fewer measures. Companies are finding that having too many measures dilutes their effectiveness and the laudable intentions behind them risk getting lost. Two is ideal for any sales role, and three is the maximum.

Watson Wyatt's survey of over 200 companies in 22 countries, found revenue volume to be the main measure criterion for most industries and job roles. The study also found that team measures were increasingly used because of account management and cross-selling initiatives.

Why would having too many criteria dilute the effectiveness of incentives?

Source: Adapted from HRM Guide UK (http://www.hrmguide.co.uk).

The US Chambers of Commerce survey of employee benefits (cited in Rosenbloom, 2001: 3) includes the following:

1   Employer's share of legally required payments.

2   Employer's share of retirement and savings plan payments.

3   Employer's share of life insurance and death benefit payments.

4   Employer's share of medical and medically related benefit payments.

5   Payment for time not worked (e.g. paid rest periods, paid sick leave, paid vacations, holidays, parental leave, etc.).

6   Miscellaneous benefit payments (including employee discounts, severance pay, educational expenditure and childcare).

Paid time off is still the most common benefit for employees in US private organizations. All US employers in a survey conducted by WorldatWork in 2010 offer paid time off work and three-quarters of respondents find it necessary to offer paid time off programmes in order to compete in the labour market and have 'traditional' and non-traditional ways of doing so. The report, *Paid Time Off Programs and Practices*, was based on 1036 respondents from the HR, compensation and benefits departments of mostly large US corporations. Lenny Sanicola, benefits practice leader for WorldatWork said:

> With the focus of the Administration and Congress on expanding access to work/life benefits such as paid leave programs, our research report shows that employers recognize the competitive advantage of offering paid time off and believe in continuing these programmes, even through the recession.
>
> Time is the new currency, and employers remain committed to providing paid time off as a key employee benefit and reward.

The report defines three types of programme:

→ **Traditional**. Preferred by large organizations and used by 54 per cent of companies. These programs give employees separate allotments for vacation, personal and sick days. A typical programme offers 21 days (12 paid vacation plus nine sick days) on average for one to two years of service.

→ **PTO bank-type**. This model has increased in popularity from 28 per cent in 2002 to 40 per cent in 2010. Employees are given a pooled number of days off to be used as needed, although fixed holidays, jury duty and bereavement are treated separately. PTO bank programs average a total of 19 days.

→ **Unlimited leave**. Allowing employees to take as many days as needed. This model is offered by mere one per cent of organizations.

On average, employers offer nine paid statutory holidays each year.

Morris, Bakan and Wood (2006) highlight some of the contradictions and limitations of flexible reward systems in a study of employees in a large retail organization in the UK. They found that participation lengthens the reward cycle; employees are encouraged to remain with the firm to maximize their shareholdings. However, workers may have different agendas according to individual choices made regarding the scale of participation in such schemes. Junior employees are less likely to choose to actively buy into profit sharing and share ownership schemes. Workers in lower job bands achieve less reward from participation but the effects of any undermining of collective solidarities are likely to be particularly pronounced in this group.

HRM IN REALITY   EXECUTIVE PERKS

A report from Compdata Surveys shows that cell phones are the most popular executive perks. The *Executive Compensation 2008/2009* survey of 5300 organizations found that 60.2 per cent offered cell phones to executives as a perk with 43.8 per cent of employers providing laptops or home PCs in 2008. Fewer than a third of organizations in the survey provided car allowances or company cars.

The report analyzes both national and regional data collected from 5300 organizations across the United States with almost 25000 incumbents. 45 executive and senior management positions were analyzed by base pay and total cash compensation.

The frequency of most executive perks depends on the revenue size of employing organizations, but cell phones were offered by over half of the companies surveyed, regardless of size. Company cars were also offered by 20 to 30 per cent of surveyed organizations across the board. But businesses with revenues over $20 million were the most likely to provide executives with laptops or home PCs.

Perks mentioned in the survey included:

→ cell phones (60.2%)

→ car allowance (31.3%)

→ company car (26.4%)

→ supplemental life insurance (26.2%)

→ voluntary deferred compensation programs (18.8%)

→ annual physical exam (17.6%)

→ supplemental disability programme (16.9%)

→ club membership(s) (15.7%)

→ supplemental executive retirement plans (10.3%)

→ supplemental medical insurance (6.2%)

→ legal counseling (5.6%)

→ post-retirement insurance (4.6%)

→ supplemental vacations (4.5%)

→ airline VIP lounge membership (3.1%)

→ dependent tuition reimbursement (3.3%).

The number of organizations offering each kind of executive perk has remained consistent over the past four years.

What perks would motivate you?

Source: Reprinted with permission from HRM Guide USA (http://www.hrmguide.com).

Rumpel and Medcof (2006) review research on Total Rewards, an approach to reward management adopted by technology-intensive firms such as IBM, Microsoft, AstraZeneca and Johnson & Johnson. Total Rewards takes a holistic approach, going beyond the traditional emphasis on pay and benefits. It considers all the rewards available in the workplace, including opportunities for learning and development, and quality work environment. These factors were found to be a high priority for technical workers and offer an opportunity to tap an organization's unrealized potential. It is argued that effectively managed rewards will ease the critical attraction, retention and motivation challenges faced by high-technology firms.

PAY AND PERFORMANCE

Many commentators severely criticized the apparently chaotic and disorganized nature of pay management between the 1950s and 1980s. Subsequently there has been an attempt to remedy this situation. The fashion has been towards the development of performance-related pay schemes that are related to assessments of performance through individual employee appraisal. Wolf (1999: 48) sums up a common view:

> Pay for performance is the holy grail of modern compensation administration – widely sought but hard to actually achieve. Pay for performance is the flag, motherhood and apple pie, but it is easier said than done. One primary problem is defining performance properly, so that the organization pays for results and not for effort. Once over that hurdle, there remains the large impediment of finding enough money to make the reward for top performance meaningful.

Pay is a sensitive issue. Most employers have been cautious with the introduction of PRP. Often it is applied to senior managers first, then extended to other employees. Usually, it has been an 'add-on' to normal pay. Rarely does it replace the existing pay scheme completely. More commonly, PRP has:

→ Formed part or (rarely) all of the general pay increase.

→ Been used to extend pay above scale maxima for employees with high levels of performance.

→ Replaced increases previously paid on the basis of age, or length of service.

Such caution is due to the complexity and sensitivity of performance-related pay in the context of employee relations. People take pay scales seriously. Negotiating and justifying radical changes to a pay structure can be difficult and time-consuming. It is sensible to do so in a gradual way, commencing with senior managers who are more likely to be committed to demanding performance objectives. Even if they are not, it gives experience of the advantages and disadvantages of performance-related pay. It also gives pay administrators experience of pay schemes that are more complicated to operate than traditional methods.

The basis of performance-related pay systems

Simplistically, it seems only fair that people should be paid according to their contribution and a number of studies indicate that most people in business agree with this. In a classic experiment, Fossum and Fitch (1985) asked three groups of subjects – students, line managers and compensation managers – to make decisions on pay increases for hypothetical people, taking into account factors such as seniority, budget constraints and cost of living. All three groups gave far more importance to performance and contribution than other factors. Research into the attitudes of corporate boards and chief executive officers, among others, have all produced similar findings.

Theoretically, performance-related pay schemes can benefit both employers and employees. By emphasizing the importance of efficiency and effective job performance, employers can benefit from higher productivity. Higher pay can be targeted at the 'better' performers, encouraging them to stay with the company and continue to perform to a high standard. Good employees benefit from extra pay in return for extra quality of performance. According to this view, properly directed pay can reinforce appropriate behaviour, focusing effort on organizational targets and encouraging a results-based culture. However, these links must be justified and real if they are not to demoralize other members of the workforce. This is particularly important in relation to senior management. Accusations of 'fat cat' behaviour can also seriously affect stock market views of a company's organization. Widespread condemnation followed the payment of massive bonuses to individuals in the financial sector for activities described as 'socially useless' and 'gambling' that were associated with the credit crisis of 2007–2009.

PRP can be related to the performance assessment of the individual, group (team), department or company. There are several systems in common use.

Appraisal-related pay schemes

Merit pay   This is paid as part of a person's annual increase on the basis of an overall performance appraisal. The method has a long track record and is commonly regarded as an effective motivator. However, it is frequently undermined by budget restrictions, when the merit element often is set too low to motivate. It is also dependent on line managers whose training to ensure fair appraisals is often questionable (Prowse and Prowse, 2009).

There are also instances when the payment is used as a 'market supplement' to retain individuals who have skills for which there is demand but whose performance is not particularly meritorious. However, it is known that breaking the clear link between appraised performance and payment of PRP reduces the overall effectiveness of PRP as a motivator for other employees.

Individual incentives   Given as unconsolidated (one-off) payments or gifts such as holidays, golf sets or vouchers.

Collective performance schemes

Bonuses   These are paid to all staff in an organization, department or team. In common with all collective performance rewards, they are designed to reinforce corporate identity and performance.

The reward system in Japan is unusual. According to Hart and Kawasaki (1999: 4):

> Most Japanese workers receive the major part of their direct remuneration via two channels. First, and familiar to workers in other countries, they are paid in the form of regular (usually monthly) wages. Secondly, they receive bonus payments which, typically, are paid twice a year. The bonus constitutes around one-fifth to one-quarter of total cash earnings.

Bonuses paid in other countries are much smaller, so why are Japanese bonuses paid at such a level? Hart and Kawasaki offer a range of alternative explanations, including the possibility that bonuses:

> ... represent a form of efficiency wage by providing a reward for greater effort. By contrast, and at a general level, wages may reflect more systematic and structural elements of remuneration, such as seniority-based pay scales (the *Nenko* system), while bonuses are used to adjust total compensation to fluctuations in firms' economic experience. In this event, we might expect that the bonus should display more flexibility than the wage. One school of thought in this respect regards bonuses as a form of profit-sharing between the firm and its workforce. Another holds that bonuses reflect shared returns to investments in firm-specific skills and know-how.

Conrad (2010) notes a general trend towards performance-related pay in Japan, with some concerns about the exact mechanism to be used and the risk of demotivational effects.

Profit-related pay   These are schemes in which employees are allocated a payment equivalent to an agreed proportion of the organization's profits. Profit-related pay has been encouraged in the UK through tax incentives.

Option schemes   Executive share option schemes are particularly prevalent in the USA but have also become common elsewhere. They allow senior managers to benefit from the continued success of the organization through the purchase of shares at designated dates in the future at a fixed price. The more successful the company, and therefore the greater the likely increase in share value, the higher the reward to the executive. This is seen as an important incentive to motivate people who can dramatically affect the prosperity and even survival of the business.

Employee share option schemes apply to less senior staff and tend to be considerably less generous than executive schemes. Generally, a sum is allocated from company profits and used for share purchase for employees. There may also be save as you earn (SAYE) option schemes registered with the taxation authorities. These allow staff to save a proportion of their salary via the pay administration process and have it accumulated for a fixed period. This may be paid to them at the end of that time, with a bonus equivalent to the interest that could have been earned in a savings account. Alternatively, and more beneficially, the sum plus bonus can be used to purchase shares at the price prevailing at the start of the scheme. Preferential tax arrangements have been made for shares held in trust for a fixed period.

FLAVOUR OF THE (LAST) MONTH?

Kanter (1989: 233) observes that whenever any US organization comes up with a 'new' pay scheme a merit element is involved. PRP has also been a prominent feature of the attempt to commercialize practices in the public services, intended as a key factor in encouraging businesslike behaviour amongst managers.

In the UK, the earliest use of PRP in the British civil service dates back to an experiment in 1985 affecting a range of senior grades (principal to under-secretary). The scheme involved payment of a minimum £500 unconsolidated bonus paid as a one-off lump sum to no more than a fifth of eligible staff. The exercise drew a range of comments but it was decided to extend the scheme to most other grades including non-management staff. Ironically, the Review Body on Top Salaries that covered judges, permanent secretaries, senior military officers and diplomats, felt that PRP was unsuitable for politically sensitive posts.

Performance-related pay was introduced for the 800 UK National Health Service general managers in 1986 based on annual objectives, individual performance reviews and financial rewards where the achievement of objectives could be clearly demonstrated (Murliss, 1987). For general managers, the process relied on an appraisal procedure called the 'individual performance review' (IPR). The system had the following characteristics:

→ The method was objectives-based, stated wherever possible in quantifiable terms.

→ Appraisals were conducted on the 'parent–grandparent' system. Unit general managers would be assessed by the district general manager, with the chair of the regional health authority acting as 'grandparent'.

→ Managers were rated on one of five bands. 'Grandparents' had final responsibility and were required to ensure that no more than 20 per cent received the highest rating level and 40 per cent the next highest.

→ An individual at the highest level 'consistently exceeds short-term levels of performance and makes excellent progress towards long-term goals' justifying a salary increase of three–four per cent a year, up to a maximum of 20 per cent over five years.

→ At the lowest level, an individual 'meets few short-term objectives and makes little or no progress towards long-term goals' receiving no increase at all.

Kauhanen and Piekkola (2006) analyzed how features of performance-related pay schemes affect their perceived motivational effects using a Finnish survey for white-collar employees from 1999. They found that the following features are important for a successful PRP scheme:

1 Employees have to feel they are able to affect the outcomes.

2 The organizational level of performance measurement should be close to the employee – individual and team level performance measurement increase the probability that the scheme is perceived to be motivating.

3 Employees should be familiar with the performance measures.

4 The level of payments should be high enough and rewards frequent enough – levels below the median do not generate positive effects.

5 Employees should participate in the design of the PRP scheme.

Long and Shields (2005) studied the incidence of 13 forms of performance pay in 315 Canadian and Australian firms. Overall, firms in both countries showed similar incidences of most forms of performance pay, with employee profit sharing the notable exception. Firm size and unionization were among the most important predictors of individual and organizational performance pay, but neither factor predicted group performance pay. High involvement firms in both Canada and Australia used more organizational performance pay than other firms, but not more group or individual performance pay. Marsden (2010) concludes that improvement on some performance in the British Civil Service was not due to the motivational effect of PRP, but the linking of personal objectives to organizational goals. Conversely, using a meta-analysis of experimental studies, Weibel *et al.* (2010) consider that motivation is a key element in the public service use of PRP.

CRITICISMS OF PRP

There is a widespread opinion among senior managers that PRP must be a good thing – but the evidence for its effectiveness is not overwhelming. Indeed, the search for a positive relationship between PRP and good performance has been described as being like 'looking for the Holy Grail' (Fletcher and Williams, 1992). As one variable in a complex situation, it is not surprising that a connection is difficult to prove. A number of major issues can be considered.

Fairness

The concept of 'fairness' is problematic and open to interpretation, with some people seeing pay as a measure of justice (Milcovich, Newman and Milcovich, 2001: 2). What pay differentials do people consider to be fair? This may vary from country to country. Osberg and Smeeding (2006) compared attitudes in the USA with other countries towards what individuals in specific occupations 'do earn' and what they 'should earn'. Americans showed less awareness of the extent of inequality at the top of income distribution; more polarized attitudes; similar preferences for 'levelling down' at the top of the earnings distribution; but also less concern for reducing differentials at the bottom.

Some employers have gone to elaborate lengths in an attempt to make their system appear fair. This may involve sampling the work of lower-level workers, listening in on phone calls, examining files, or checking through a proportion of completed work. For example, the Bank of America has been cited as spending over a million dollars a year and employing 20 people to monitor 3500 credit card workers for their merit scheme. Not surprisingly, such attempts at 'fairness' have not been entirely popular among employees. The system seems to be distinctly Orwellian: 'Big Brother is watching you'.

Managerial judgement

The process is dependent on skilled line managers. As we have observed, for various reasons managers feel under pressure to rate their staff as above average. As Kanter (1989) says, 'far from freeing the energies of employees to seek ways to improve their performance, subjectively based merit pay systems throw them back on the merit of their bosses.' Typically such systems are cynically regarded by employees and attacked by unions as being open to abuse and favouritism. They can also result in a rash of high marks by supervisors who feel exposed to the wrath of their employees. Relationships between managers and employees are often uncomfortable, and this process tends to charge that relationship with even more emotion. But line or middle managers are often obliged to implement performance-related systems that they personally do not believe in (Harris, 2000).

Value of reward

Many senior managers seem more concerned with managing the pay bill than motivating staff, so that PRP is often budget-led, not performance-led. A frequent complaint is that the merit element is too small as a percentage of the whole – commonly from three to ten per cent. This is not enough to be a motivator for improved performance. The solution is obvious at one level: increase the merit element to a significantly motivating level such as 15–25 per cent. But this only serves to highlight the difficulty in making a judgement on who gets an increase and being seen to be fair about it (Isaac, 2001). Most employers have not felt confident enough about the process to go beyond a token percentage level.

A demotivator

There may be evidence that people who are rewarded well by PRP are duly motivated, but they are usually a minority in an organization and the effect is outweighed by the demotivation of the majority (Marsden, French and Kobi, 2000). McCausland, Pouliakas and Theodossiou (2005) found that while the predicted job satisfaction of workers receiving PRP is lower on average compared with those on other pay schemes, it has a positive effect on the mean job satisfaction of very highly paid workers. They suggest that lower-paid employees may perceive PRP to be controlling, whereas higher-paid workers derive a utility benefit from what they view as supportive reward schemes. Green and Heywood (2008) on the other hand, conclude that PRP has largely positive effects on worker satisfaction.

PRP and unions

PRP increases the likelihood of flexibility and management power. Not surprisingly, PRP has attracted hostility from many unions as collective bargaining is side-stepped. Hanley and Nguyen (2005) investigated the impact of performance-related pay at the lower end of the remuneration spectrum in Australia. Their study was based on interviews with union officials and analysis of performance appraisal and performance-related pay clauses in union enterprise bargaining agreements. These clauses ranged from minimal stipulation of existence to detailed processes and principles of design and implementation. Specific clauses in white-collar agreements suggest that they are not totally opposed. However, in blue-collar agreements the lack of such clauses is indicative of their propensity to restrict pay increases to a job classification structure. Clauses that aimed to ensure a performance-oriented culture seemed to be viewed as mere sentiment. Overall, only one union supported the notion of performance-related pay.

Conflict with the team philosophy

The obsession with individually based, performance pay conflicts with HRM's emphasis on teams where careful thought has to be given to the design of PRP systems, especially when there is an agency perspective (Mitlacher and Paul, 2009). Employee dissatisfaction can result from merit payments being too low to provide any incentive and further criticisms of the operation of the system such as:

→ Upward movement of targets: employees finding themselves on a treadmill that is continually being speeded up.

→ Employees being assessed by managers who do not know them.

→ Performance pay for junior employees being restricted by 'budgetary constraints' when this limitation does not seem to apply to senior executives.

→ Objectives being imposed rather than negotiated.

→ Subjective criteria leading to disagreements on the quality of performance, leading to a perception of unfairness.

→ Individual targets not being compatible with team performance.

Kellough and Nigro (2002) investigated GeorgiaGain, a compensation system developed for the state of Georgia (USA). Performance-related pay was the centrepiece of the initiative that was intended to include a state-of-the-art performance management system, providing performance measurement and evaluation procedures trusted by supervisors and subordinates. But Kellough and Nigro's survey of state employees found them highly critical of the reform and complaining that it had not produced the intended outcomes in most areas. The reduction of the inflation rate to low single figures has further reduced the perceived effectiveness of incentives. Merit payments of two–three per cent are not seen as much reward for exceptional performance. Indeed such payments may be viewed as insulting. Performance systems established in a high inflation period have proven to be a financial embarrassment to some companies. British Telecom scrapped a system for junior and middle managers on the grounds that managers were being overpaid in comparison with equivalents in other firms. The use of incentives seems to have declined in British manufacturing firms as managers have gained greater control over pay schemes (Arrowsmith and Marginson, 2010).

Performance and diversity

Fang and Heywood (2006) used the Workplace and Employee Survey to examine the association between payment method and ethnic wage differentials in Canada. Non-Europeans receive lower earnings than Europeans when paid by time rates. However, non-Europeans receive virtually identical earnings to their European counterparts when paid by output. They suggested that tying earnings to productivity made it more difficult for employers to discriminate. Similarly, Heywood and O'Halloran (2005) found no racial wage differential among male workers receiving output-based pay but a significant differential among those paid time rates. The racial wage differential among those receiving bonus pay, usually based on supervisory evaluation, tended to be larger than for those not receiving such bonuses.

EXECUTIVE PAY

Nowhere has the issue of performance-related pay been more controversial than in the compensation arrangements for senior executives. Bender (2004) found that many companies adopted performance-related pay despite believing that the money did not motivate executives. Instead, the reasons were due to 'best practice' in human resource management. The pay structures were designed to attract and retain executives with the potential of large earnings, focus their efforts in the direction agreed by the board and to demonstrate fairness. Variable pay was seen as a symbol of the director's success, both within and outside the organization. Bender's study suggests that companies may use performance-related pay because their competitors do, and because that legitimizes them in the eyes of the establishment.

Bebchuk and Fried (2005) studied executive pay practices in the USA and the corporate governance processes that produce them. They suggest that managerial power and influence have come to play a major role in shaping executive pay, and in ways that end up imposing significant costs on investors and the economy. Their main concerns are the distortion of incentives caused by compensation practices that fail to link pay to performance, limit executives' freedom to sell their shares, or restrict benefits paid to departing executives. They call for greater transparency, improvements in pay practices, and improvements in board accountability to shareholders.

Gordon (2005) acknowledges the strengths of Bebchuk and Fried's case for managerial power in setting executive pay but expresses three major reservations:

1   Concern about apparent lack of pay for performance does not provide sufficient explanation of the controversy over CEO pay and largely ignores popular disquiet about pay levels.

2   Many of the compensation practices identified as indicative of managerial power may have broader explanations. For example, the vast majority of employee stock options are awarded to people well below executive rank.

3   The best way of improving corporate governance may be not a wholesale expansion of shareholder power, but rather measures to increase the independence of the compensation committee.

Guy (2005) investigated the relationship between earnings differentials and CEO pay in 190 British companies between 1970 and 1990. The study concluded that top executive pay prior to 1984 was a stable function of both firm size and earnings differentials lower on the administrative ladder. The use of share options from 1984 onwards represents a change in the mode of top executive compensation and a de-linking of the pay of top executives and that of lower management. Similarly, Erturk *et al.* (2005) found that CEO pay in the UK and USA in the 1980s and 1990s increased at rates that resulted in ever widening gaps between executive and average pay. These increases, they argue, have significantly outrun any sustained increase in value attributable to management effort.

Girma, Thompson and Wright (2006) examined the impact of mergers and acquisitions on the remuneration of CEOs in the UK from 1981 to 1996. They found that CEO pay was not strongly related to company performance but, as in Guy's (2005) study, increased with firm size. CEOs involved in 'wealth-reducing' acquisitions received significantly lower remuneration than those whose deals met with market approval, suggesting that shareholder-principals had some success in penalizing managers for unwarranted empire-building mergers.

HRM IN REALITY   WHY CEO PAY KEEPS GOING UP

Regardless of economic conditions, there is one constant in the workplace: CEO salaries keep going UP. A study published in 2010 by Thomas A. DiPrete, Greg Eirich and Matthew Pittinsky puts much of the blame on the practice of compensation benchmarking.

Standard practice in American corporations, benchmarking is a process used by compensation committees to compare peer groups of executives at similar organizations in order to establish a 'fair' market salary for their CEOs. However, it seems that each year a few CEOs 'leapfrog' their peers by getting large increases in compensation that have little to do with the financial performance of their organizations. Their unjustified raises are used by other firms in subsequent benchmarks. Gradually, the study concludes, executive pay is ratcheted up for everyone through a 'contagion effect'. According to DiPrete:

> We show that rising CEO pay is not simply a function of what individual companies do, but is influenced by the behaviour of leapfroggers at other firms.

Using procedures laid out in reward management handbooks the researchers reconstructed likely peer groups for CEOs listed in Standard and Poor's annual compensation surveys. Then they looked for evidence of leapfrogging in those likely peer groups over time. They found that leapfrogging could explain around half the overall increase in CEO pay from 1992 to 2006.

Previously, the debate on the causes of ever-increasing CEO pay had mainly fallen into two groups:

→ CEOs were overpaid because of failures in corporate governance at individual organizations

→ CEOs were paid what they deserved on the basis of profits they delivered to shareholders in a 'superstar' job market.

The researchers say that their findings broaden the debate as unjustified increases for a few CEOs can lead to 'legitimate' salary increases for others. They write that 'the linkages among firms produced by the benchmarking process guarantee that firm-level governance failure becomes a factor in the environment of other firms.'

After the Enron and WorldCom scandals in the early 2000s, the Securities and Exchange Commission changed its rules to require corporations to disclose benchmarking information. The research team state that they are 'now using the new data mandated by the SEC to better understand how the network structure of peer groups affects executive pay setting in American corporations.'

DiPrete added:

> Whether the SEC regulatory change reduces the ratcheting effect of leapfrogging on CEO pay – creating more transparency about who is in the peer group and at what level the company is benchmarking – is an important question for future research.

Powerful CEOs pay employees more

Research on perceptions of fairness in executive pay and how CEO over- or underpayment cascades down to lower organizational levels was published in the September/October 2006 issue of *Organization Science*. The study looked at data from over 120 firms over a five-year period. Authors James Wade, professor at Rutgers University, Charles O'Reilly, professor at Stanford's Graduate School of Business, and Timothy Pollock at Pennsylvania State University's Smeal College of Business, used techniques of operations research (OR) in their analysis.

Key findings include:

→ **CEO overpayment has higher costs than previously realized**. It has been argued that even if a CEO is overpaid, a large company can easily absorb the cost. However, the study found that CEO pay has direct consequences for compensation at lower employee levels. The effects of CEO overpayment cascade down to subordinates at diminishing degrees. For example, where one CEO was overpaid by 64 per cent, individuals at Level Two (chief operating officer, chief finance officer, etc.) were overpaid by 26 per cent, while individuals at Level Five (division general managers) were overpaid by 12 per cent.

The cumulative effect of this systemic overpayment impacts on overall organizational performance and shareholder value.

Charles O'Reilly commented:

Given the large sums paid to some senior executives, the total cost for overpayment could be a big number – and, in some cases, significantly affect shareholder returns.

➜ **CEO pay impacts subordinate turnover**. The study found that CEOs serve as a key reference point for employees in determining whether their own pay is fair. If the CEO is overpaid, subordinates are more likely to leave. The turnover effect becomes more pronounced the farther away you get from CEO level. Even if an employee is overpaid relative to the market, they will have a greater propensity to leave if their CEO is overpaid by a larger percentage than they are.

James Wade said:

CEO compensation impacts employee retention more than we realized. Our research found that CEO overpayment is related to turnover, which can have important long-term consequences. It is quite possible that those most likely to leave because of perceived unfairness are precisely those employees coming up in the organization that would eventually rise to the top management team level.

➜ **CEO underpayment also cascades**. The study found that CEO underpayment tends to get cascaded through an organization, with multiplying effects. If the CEO is underpaid more than you are,

you are less likely to leave, but if the CEO is underpaid less than you are, you are more likely to leave. As James Wade put it, 'underpaying a CEO could reduce turnover if subordinates are underpaid less than the CEO is underpaid.'

➜ **Notions of fairness are powerful**. The study found that CEOs tend to be concerned with the perception of fairness. If the CEO is paid generously, they will typically use their influence to pay others generously as well. And, if they are seen as being underpaid, that will also have an effect.

Timothy Pollock commented:

Our research shows evidence that CEOs are concerned with fairness, and that they are likelier to share rewards than they are to share burdens. But this can be expensive and has the potential to hurt a firm's bench strength if the rewards aren't fully shared.

➜ **Powerful CEOs pay employees more**. CEOs who also serve as chairman of the board tend to pay their employees more. This effect is more pronounced at higher levels, but diminishes at lower levels. The effect disappeared at Level 5 (division general managers), but was strong at Levels two–four (the top management team through the junior vice president ranks).

What do you consider to be a fair level of pay for a CEO compared to the lowest paid employee?

Source: Reprinted with permission from HRM Guide USA (http://www.hrmguide.com).

However, Stathopoulos, Espenlaub and Walker (2005) analyzed level and composition of the pay of the top executives of a sample of UK public listed companies and found that remuneration reflected organizational performance. Executives of firms that performed badly experienced cuts in salaries, bonuses and equity-based compensation. The study also revealed increased participation and value in the equity-based schemes provided to CEOs and other executives of poorly performing firms in the longer term. CEOs of poorly performing firms were significantly more likely to be dismissed but emoluments were not directly affected during the year of departure. In the same vein, Merhebi *et al.* (2006) reversed earlier Australian studies that found no link between CEO pay and corporate performance. The study by Merhebi *et al.* suggests that Australian experience is consistent with that of firms from the USA, UK and Canada. In general, however, CEO pay seems to have mushroomed at a considerable rate, particularly in the USA. Venkatasubramanian (2009) calculated that the top Fortune 500 CEOs pay had gone up from a ratio of 40–1 (compared to their lowest paid employee) in the 1970s to 334–1 in recent years.

Perkins and Hendry (2005) highlighted the important role of non-executive directors in determining executive pay. They studied the nuances of executive pay decision-making, including remuneration committee members' reactions to corporate governance reforms. Such initiatives place non-executive directors in the role of intermediaries, explicitly assigned to resolve the conflict of interest inherent in boardroom remuneration systems, while simultaneously expected to play a team role as board members responsible for the overall strategy and operation of the company.

SUMMARY

Pay is a key element in the management of people. The importance of pay begins with pay administration that deals accurately and swiftly with payroll-related matters. Much of the information used by pay administrators is shared with the human resource function. Pay evaluation systems also impinge on human resource territory. Free market organizations are particularly concerned with performance-related pay as a motivating factor. However, this trend appears to be ideological rather than rational since practical PRP schemes that deliver the results intended are extremely difficult to construct. Current evidence shows that performance pay is likely to demotivate some people more than it motivates others.

FURTHER READING

1 *Armstrong's Handbook of Reward Management Practice: Improving Performance Through Reward*, 3rd edn (Kogan Page, 2010) by Michael Armstrong covers the ground thoroughly.

2 *Strategic Reward: Implementing More Effective Reward Management* by Michael Armstrong and Duncan Brown (Kogan Page, 2009) and

3 *Reward Management*, 2nd edn (CIPD, 2011) by Stephen Perkins and Geoffrey White (Kogan Page, 2005) also cover this topic area well.

REVIEW QUESTIONS

1 What is pay for? What effect does the minimum wage have on employer and employee attitudes to rates of pay?

2 What functions should a payroll department fulfil? Is it appropriate to merge the HR function with a payroll department?

3 What are the implications of paying different salaries for the same job?

4 Does job evaluation have a function in a modern pay system?

5 A fair day's work for a fair day's pay'. How can a company's pay system be designed to meet this criterion?

6 Outline the arguments for and against the use of performance-related pay.

7 Should executive directors be paid on a different basis from other employees?

8 What advantages do flexible benefits offer for individual employees and their employers?

9 How large does a merit payment or bonus have to be in order to provide an incentive for effective performance?

10 What are the practical consequences of using employee stock options as a motivator?

CASE STUDY FOR DISCUSSION AND ANALYSIS

Fairness

Scenario 1

A photocopying shop has one employee who has worked in the shop for six months and earns US$9 per hour. Business continues to be satisfactory, but a factory in the area has closed and unemployment has increased. Other small firms have now hired reliable workers working at US$7 an hour to perform jobs similar to those done by the photocopy shop employee. The owner of the shop reduces the employee's wage to US$7.

Is it fair to cut the worker's wage from US$9 to US$7 an hour? Compare your decision with the second scenario.

Scenario 2

A house painter employs two assistants and pays them US$9 per hour. The painter decides to change his business and go into lawn-mowing, where the going wage is lower. He tells the current workers that he will keep them on if they want to work, but will only pay them US$7 per hour.

Is this employer being fair?

CHAPTER 11
Flexibility, work–life balance and wellness

LEARNING OBJECTIVES

The purpose of this chapter is to:

→ **Debate the concept of flexible working.**

→ **Evaluate the feasibility of a work–life balance.**

→ **Discuss the role of HR practitioners in work–life balance and workplace health.**

→ **Investigate the personal, organizational and HR implications of stress.**

FLEXIBILITY

We have already observed that one of the most pronounced trends in recent years has been the replacement of full-time, long-term jobs with other types of positions. These include part-timers, 'temps', consultants, franchisees and so on. Business strategies have focused increasingly on flexible working in order to reduce employee costs of products and services (see Key concept 11.1).

KEY CONCEPT 11.1   FLEXIBILITY

The concept covers a combination of practices that enable organizations to react quickly and cheaply to environmental changes. In essence, flexibility is demanded from the workforce in terms of pay, contractual rights, hours and conditions, and working practices. This extends to the employment market, requiring jobseekers to show a willingness to move location, change occupation and accept radically different terms of employment.

Flexibility has become a much-quoted term. Neo-liberal commentators argue that, at the environmental level, competitiveness comes from the reduction of perceived 'rigidities' in the employment market. Rigidities in the job market have been pinpointed as causes of industrial decline and flexibility has become an unquestioned 'good'. Rigidity includes lack of mobility, refusal to accept new conditions, unorthodox working hours and so on. By scrapping minimum pay rates, removing legislation which limits employers' rights to hire and fire, and generally deregulating the job market, they believe that businesses will achieve the maximum degree of competitiveness (Zemanek, 2010).

Simplistically, it can be argued that the terms have an implicit political agenda: rigidity equates with worker protection and therefore left-wing, socialist attitudes; flexibility matches with 'hard' HRM, exploitation of workers and hence a right-wing, capitalist approach. In practice, flexible working can take a variety of forms that are differentially attractive to employees depending on their personal circumstances (Nadler *et al.*, 2010). For example, in an Irish study Russell *et al.* (2009) found that part-time work and flexitime tended to reduce work pressure and the conflict between work and non-work life, working from home seemed to increase levels of work pressure and work–life conflict. Blake-Beard *et al.* (2010) argue that, in order to maintain a socially sustainable workforce, organizations should make flexibility a norm, gaining an understanding of workers' lives outside the organization and allowing access to flexible working arrangements across the dimensions of gender, race, and class.

We can classify the common forms of flexibility as:

Numerical flexibility. Matching employee numbers to fluctuating work levels. This is difficult to achieve with 'regular' workers on full-time, long-term contracts.

Functional flexibility. Abolishing demarcation rules and skill barriers so that workers can take on a variety of jobs.

Pay flexibility. Offering different rates of pay for the same work – depending on geographical location and skills availability.

A further requirement is '**flexible specialization**'. Consumer demand increasingly reflects individual tastes. Purchasers want an ever-wider choice of goods, making it difficult, if not impossible, for mass production techniques to satisfy the market. The Fordist assembly-line is

HRM IN REALITY GIVE US A 6.00AM START

Many British workers would welcome the introduction of a 6.00am start, if they could go home earlier in exchange, according to research by business communications firm Your Communications.

The survey of over 2000 employees carried out in 2005 found that a majority believed they work most efficiently between 6.00am and 3.00pm.

A mere one in 20 said they were most productive between 3.00pm and 6.00pm and almost half the respondents said they could do their job as effectively from home.

Your Communications argued that this could spell the death of the traditional 9 to 5 working day. In particular, allowing employees to work flexibly from home at times best-suited to them meant that businesses could dramatically boost their productivity.

The report also concluded that employers should consider the 'obvious benefits' that flexible working schemes bring, including: strengthening staff loyalty, and improving employees' work–life balance.

'Most workers believe they work more effectively at different times of the day,' said Paul Lawton, from Your Communications. 'Flexible work arrangements, which allow them to work from home, at their clients' offices, or for that matter at airport lounges, may help them to work more productively and vary their working hours.'

What is your ideal pattern of working hours?

Source: Reprinted with permission from HRM Guide UK (http://www.hrmguide.co.uk).

---

outmoded – even if it does offer cars in colours other than black. Producers must switch equipment and employees from one product to another in a flexible but economic way. Staff must have versatile skills. Proponents of flexible specialization hold that mass production, the dominant industrial force of the 20th century, is obsolete, along with Taylorism and Fordism. Organizations in developed countries will only survive by employing a multi-skilled, highly flexible core workforce able to turn their hands to a wide variety of tasks.

Atkinson's (1984) **'flexible firm'** model combines flexibility with Japanese concepts of **'core'** and **'peripheral' workforces** (see Figure 11.1). Core workers are employed on standard contracts. Peripheral workers are employed by subcontractors, or on short-term contracts. However, Atkinson's model does without mutual obligations essential to the Japanese system: core workers provide functional flexibility – but without lifelong employment; peripheral workers and subcontractors are not rewarded with close, long-term relationships.

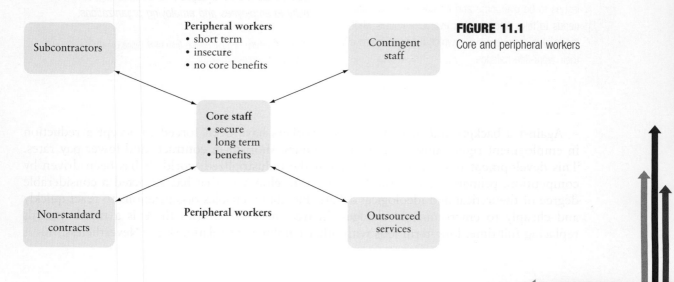

FIGURE 11.1
Core and peripheral workers

HRM IN REALITY   FLEXIBLE WORKING MAY HAMPER CAREERS

A 2006 study by business communications provider Inter-Tel questioned over 100 office-based workers about attitudes to flexible working. This identified positive reasons for applying to work flexibly but significant doubts about the likely response of employers. Significant findings included:

→ Ninety per cent of respondents agreed that all employees should have the same right to request more flexible work patterns, irrespective of domestic circumstances.

→ Thirty per cent felt their organization did not respond equitably to such requests and 54 per cent were unsure about this issue.

→ Sixty per cent believed requesting greater flexibility could have a negative impact on the careers of people without children.

→ Eighty-two per cent considered flexible working a privilege; only 18 per cent felt it should be a right.

→ Forty per cent felt their employer would not trust them to work from home.

Duncan Miller of Inter-Tel EMEA said:

> The trend for home working continues to grow. Data from the UK Office of National Statistics confirms that there are now more than two million people working from home and a further eight million opting to spend at least part of their working week outside the office. Clearly, there are still issues to be overcome and an education process needs to take place so that everyone knows what their rights are and ways in which they can improve their work–life balance.

Over two-thirds of respondents identified 'a better quality of life' as the most important reason for applying to work flexibly. Other factors centred on more time for family (22 per cent), non-work activities such as courses (six per cent), and travel (three per cent).

Duncan Miller concluded:

> We are now at a stage of technological development where people can work as effectively from their home or on the move, as they can at a desk in their company's office. Of course, flexible or home working is not feasible or suitable for all organizations, but employers should be looking at ways to address the work–life balance of their staff and be very clear on their policy in this area. A happier, healthier workforce can lead to greater productivity in the long term and increase staff retention.

New rights to flexibility may be leading to a reversal of the trend seen over the last decade. A 2001 Industrial Society (now the Work Foundation) survey of 516 human resource specialists found that 91 per cent of respondents' organizations used some form of flexible working. This compared with 84 per cent in 1998. Seventy-five per cent of respondents said that flexible working made good business sense for the organization, with almost two-thirds (63 per cent) saying that it built trust, loyalty and commitment.

Summarize the advantages and disadvantages of flexibility to employees and employing organizations.

Source: Reprinted with permission from HRM Guide UK (http://www.hrmguide.co.uk).

Against a background of globalization, workers have been forced to accept a reduction in employment rights, unsociable working hours, short-term contracts and lower pay rates. This development has occurred throughout the industrialized world. It has been driven by competition, primarily from Asia. It is also a development that has attracted a considerable degree of theoretical and ideological debate. Flexibility enables organizations to react quickly and cheaply to environmental changes. In free market countries there is a trend towards replacing full-time, long-term jobs with other employment relationships. Nevertheless, this is still a minority situation. For example, 70 per cent of workers in the UK have been employed by the same organization for over 20 years.

The idea of flexibility has definitely taken root but its theoretical basis has weaknesses. On the one hand, it is consistent with the concept of the 'virtual organization', forming and re-forming to meet particular demands. Conversely, it is doubtful that we are really moving to a 'world of quasi-bespoke production concerned with gratifying fleeting market whims' (Hyman, 1988). Rather, niche marketing is concerned with defined 'varieties' of mass produced products. Consumers are not purchasing unique cars made to their specific requirements, but red 2.3 litre high-specification models, or white 1.0 litre basic models from a controlled choice – built in factories that Henry Ford would find recognizable. The availability of such varieties has more to do with computer-controlled robots, switchable from one program to another, than with a flexible, multi-skilled workforce.

While much of the discussion on flexibility has focused on manufacturing, other industries have made long use of flexible arrangements. Thiel (2009) modelled the complex flexible schedules used in the French fresh food industry which required rapid staffing decisions on the number of employees, their hours and the source of labour: permanent, temporary, contract and subcontracted.

HRM IN REALITY   CORRECTING MYTHS ABOUT TEMPORARY WORK

A 2010 report from Canadian staffing firm Accountemps corrects common misconceptions about temporary work and its role in the current job market. Myths include:

1 Temporary assignments are mainly clerical or lower skilled – in fact the fastest growth is in professional and technical occupations, as the advantages of flexibility become increasingly apparent. Companies now hire temporary staff for positions at all levels from accounting clerk to chief financial officer.

2 Temporary work can't be included on a resume – in fact all temporary assignments should be included. The report recommends listing the staffing firm as the employer and describing the duties undertaken on various placements.

3 Temporary work will interfere with a search for permanent employment – in fact experience of temporary work can actually enhance the chance of securing full-time employment. Many organizations view interim engagements as an effective way of assessing potential employees and go on to hire on a permanent basis. Temporary workers have an opportunity to expand their skills and experience while earning an income.

4 Temporary work doesn't pay well – in fact temporary and contract positions typically pay the same as salaried ones; individuals with the most sought-after skills can often command a premium.

5 Jobseekers will have to pay to work with a staffing firm – professional staffing firms never charge jobseekers for their services; all fees are met by client companies.

Kathryn Bolt, president of Accountemps' Canadian operations said:

> As companies determine their staffing levels in response to increased business activity, many are turning to temporary employees at all levels. Temporary work has resulted in full-time employment offers for many jobseekers and is a valuable career option for professionals to consider.

What are the disadvantages experienced by temporary workers?

Source: Reprinted with permission from HRM Guide Canada (http://www.hrmguide.net/canada/).

Further problems arise in practice. Where are the necessary skilled people supposed to come from? A true transition to total flexibility requires a system for training non-permanent workers. Most employers are not equipped to provide this. Companies in countries such as Australia and the UK have been heavily criticized for under-investing in training their permanent employees. Ironically, the same countries have a weak record of providing such training on a national basis as well. In a Canadian study, Fang (2009) found that organizations relied extensively on flexible hours and extra overtime as short-term solutions to meet skill shortages.

Employees have their own views on flexibility. Hall and Atkinson (2006) investigated employee perceptions of flexibility utilized or available to them in an NHS Trust. They found that informal rather than formal flexibility was more widely used and valued, generating an increased sense of employee responsibility. Staff needed to be proactive to access formal flexibility but some did not see it as relevant to themselves. The significance of gender in the flexibility debate has been understated as the issue of family-friendly working arrangements is particularly significant to women (Atkinson and Hall, 2009). Hornung *et al.* (2009) investigated informal ('idiosyncratic') flexible working arrangements made between individual telecommuting workers and supervisors in German public administration and discovered that such deals were typically initiated by employees and were justified in terms of performance, motivation and work–life benefits.

Anderson and Kelliher (2009) argue that flexible working arrangements impact on employee engagement through a positive relationship with organizational commitment, job satisfaction and employee discretionary behaviour. Arguably, flexibility can provide a win–win solution to family and business needs, benefiting both (Thomson, 2008).

HRM IN REALITY BLURRING THE BOUNDARIES OF WORK AND HOME

Employees with flexible schedules tend to experience greater blurring of boundaries between work and other parts of their lives, especially family-related roles, according to research from the University of Toronto published in the *Journal of Family Issues* in 2010. Sociology professor Scott Schieman and PhD student Marisa Young drew on data from a national survey of more than 1200 North American workers to measure the extent of schedule control and its impact on work–family processes.

Scott Schieman explained:

Most people probably would identify schedule control as a good thing – an indicator of flexibility that helps them balance their work and home lives.

We wondered about the potential stress of schedule control for the work–family interface. What happens if schedule control blurs the boundaries between these key social roles?

Participants were asked: 'Who usually decides when you start and finish work each day at your main job? Is it someone else, or can you decide within certain limits, or are you entirely free to decide when you start and finish work?'

The study found that those with more flexibility are also more likely to work at home, attempting simultaneous work–family multitasking. Those reporting more blurring of work–family boundaries also tend to experience more conflict between roles and a consequent increase in stress. Researchers point to substantial evidence linking work–family conflict to poorer physical and mental health outcomes.

The study assessed work–family conflict by responses to questions such as:

→ 'How often have you not had enough time for your family or other important people in your life because of your job?'

→ 'How often have you not had the energy to do things with your family or other important people in your life because of your job?'

→ 'How often has your job kept you from concentrating on important things in your family and personal life?'

However, the researchers also identified benefits to flexible working.

Scott Schieman said:

People who had partial or full schedule control were able to engage in work–family multitasking activities with fewer negative consequences in terms of conflict between their work and family roles. Overall, our findings contribute to an ongoing – and complicated – debate about the costs and benefits of different forms of flexibility for workers.

Why might flexible working arrangements reduce absenteeism?

Source: Reprinted with permission from HRM Guide Canada (http://www.hrmguide.net/canada/).

WORK–LIFE BALANCE

On a common sense level it is widely accepted that well-being is enhanced by a balance between all aspects of daily life. Work is a critical area of everyday occupation but it is just one of a number of associated domains, including family life, leisure, education, and self-care that also have goal-directed activities (Anaby *et al.*, 2010).

A baseline study ('Work–life Balance 2000') conducted jointly by the Institute for Employment Research, University of Warwick and IFF Research concludes that there is a widespread demand from employees for the right to balance work and home life. It also reveals that businesses prefer to offer stress counselling for the personal consequences of long working hours (49 per cent) rather than provide assistance for childcare (nine per cent).

One in nine of full-time employees (including men with children) work more than 60 hours every week. Two-thirds of male employees believe that part-time working would damage their career prospects. At the same time there is a clear demand for greater flexibility – especially from fathers. In general, men seem to have a greater enthusiasm for working from home than do women. Virtually all the respondents to both surveys – employees and employers alike – agreed with the concept of work–life balance. But one in eight of employees still worked Saturdays and Sundays and around 20 per cent of employees worked for 24-hour/seven-day-week businesses.

Other conclusions of the study were:

→ Eighty per cent of workplaces had employees who worked more than their standard hours with 39 per cent doing so without extra pay.

→ Just 20 per cent of employers were fully aware of increased maternity leave rights and 24 per cent fully aware of new paternal leave rights.

→ Twenty-five per cent of entitled female employees took less than 18 weeks maternity leave.

→ Fifty-five per cent of employers consider it acceptable to allow staff to move from full-time to part-time work in some cases.

HRM IN REALITY LONG HOURS BAD FOR THE HEART

Research led by University College, London and published in the *European Heart Journal* found that working overtime is bad for the heart. The study forms part of the long-term follow-up of more than 10 000 London office-based civil servants (the Whitehall II study). Researchers compared people working a normal seven-hour day with those working a minimum of three hours extra. They found that this level of overtime is associated with a 60 per cent increased risk of heart-related problems (including death due to heart disease, non-fatal heart attacks and angina).

Dr Marianna Virtanen, epidemiologist at the Finnish Institute of Occupational Health said:

> The association between long hours and coronary heart disease was independent of a range of risk factors that we measured at the start of the study, such as smoking, being overweight, or having high cholesterol.
>
> Our findings suggest a link between working long hours and increased CHD [coronary heart disease] risk, but more research is needed before we can be confident that overtime work would cause CHD. In addition, we need more research on other health outcomes, such as depression and type 2 diabetes.

The Whitehall II study recruited 10 308 volunteers aged 35–55 from 20 civil service departments in 1985. The third phase (1991–1994) introduced a question on working hours. Based on an average of 11.2 years follow-up, the current research analyzes results from 4262 men and 1752 women aged between 39 and 61, up to the most recent period for which clinical data are available (2002–2004). Researchers caution that while the cohort includes several occupational grades it inevitably has no blue-collar or private sector workers.

Researchers identified 369 cases of fatal CHD, non-fatal heart attacks (myocardial infarctions) or angina. After adjusting for socio-demographic characteristics (such as age, sex, marital status and occupational grade) and 21 risk factors they found that working three to four hours overtime (but not one to two hours) was associated with a 60 per cent higher rate of CHD compared with no overtime.

Considering possible explanations, results indicate that working overtime is associated with type A behaviour pattern (a tendency towards aggressive, competitive, tense, time-conscious and hostile behaviour), psychological distress (depression and anxiety) and poor sleep patterns. In addition, researchers highlight undiagnosed high blood pressure associated with work-related stress; and 'sickness presenteeism' (employees who habitually work overtime also tend to work when ill, may ignore symptoms and not seek medical advice). Researchers also suggest that people working overtime, but in jobs where they have more freedom over work-related decisions, may have a lower risk of CHD. However, the current findings were independent of all of these factors.

Marianna Virtanen explained:

> We did not measure whether subsequent changes in these factors during the follow-up period altered the association. One plausible explanation for the increased risk could be that adverse lifestyle or risk factor changes are more common among those who work excessive hours compared with those working normal hours. Another possibility is that the chronic experience of stress (often associated with working long hours) adversely affects metabolic processes. It is important that these hypotheses should be examined in detail in the future.

Lead author Mika Kivimäki, professor of social epidemiology, concluded:

> At the moment there is no research on whether reduction in overtime work reduces CHD risk. Further research on this topic is therefore needed. Our own future research will include analyzing data over periods of time to examine whether working long hours predicts changes in life style, mental health and traditional risk factors, such as blood pressure, blood glucose and cholesterol. We hope that this research will increase understanding of the mechanisms underlying the association

between long working hours and coronary heart disease. We will also examine whether overtime work increases the risk of depression, as recent research suggests that depression increases the risk of coronary heart disease.

An accompanying editorial is provided by Gordon McInnes, professor of clinical pharmacology at the Western Infirmary, University of Glasgow. While echoing researchers' caution about the specific characteristics of the study's subjects, he nevertheless concludes that the findings may have far-reaching implications for cardiovascular risk assessment.

Gordon McInnes said:

These data from a large occupational cohort reinforce the notion that work stress attributable to overtime is associated, apparently independently, with an increased risk of coronary heart disease. A trend for risk to be related to hours of overtime worked supports this conclusion. If the effect is truly causal, the importance is much greater than commonly recognized. Overtime-induced work stress might contribute to a substantial proportion of cardiovascular disease. Physicians should be aware of the risks of overtime and take seriously symptoms such as chest pain, monitor and treat recognized cardiovascular risk factors, particularly blood pressure, and advise an appropriate lifestyle modification.

Quoting British philosopher Bertrand Russell, Gordon McInnes concluded:

'If I were a medical man, I should prescribe a holiday to any patient who considers work important'.

Reprinted with permission from HRM Guide UK (http://www.hrmguide.co.uk).

→ Twenty-four per cent of employees now work flexitime with 12 per cent working only during school terms.

→ Fifty-six per cent of women preferred flexible working after a pregnancy – for example, part-time or home-based – to having a longer maternity leave period.

A report from The Work Foundation, commissioned by UNISON, the public service union, concludes that public sector employers may 'talk the talk' on work–life balance, but in practice have limited commitment to changing standard working patterns (Visser and Williams, 2007). The survey found that three-quarters of public sector employers have initiatives and policies in place addressing work–life balance issues for at least some staff. This is considerably higher than average and includes flexible working, job sharing, home working, term-time contracts, career breaks, childcare provision, and time off to care for sick children.

However, only half of respondents felt they had real choice about their working arrangements and only just over half were aware of available work–life options. Some 53 per cent said their workplace offered flexitime; 52 per cent job sharing; 19 per cent working from home; and 32 per cent term-time working. These figures were much lower than the stated availability in all workplaces.

A third of respondents believed their employers were not committed to helping them achieve work–life balance. Some reported their managers tried to restrict uptake of flexible working by failing to communicate available options, or by dissuading people from requesting them.

The survey identified examples of the difficulties of working flexibly. For example, one respondent said that there was an unwritten policy that employees who worked 12 hour shifts were eligible for career progression, while those who did 8 hour shifts to fit around family commitments were not.

A common complaint was being made to feel like a troublemaker if the possibility of work–life balance arrangements was raised with employers. One respondent said their manager had told them 'I don't do part-time'. In several organizations, flexibility was only available to selected staff.

Respondents also reported that available work–life balance options were often inappropriate. For example, nearly three-quarters of respondents (71 per cent) expressed a strong preference for time off to care for adult dependents but fewer than half of workplaces offer this option. By contrast, 80 per cent of employers offer job sharing, but only 37 per cent of respondents say this is of use to them.

Other key survey findings include:

→   One in four said that work was too demanding.

→   A total of 30 per cent said their career had been damaged by caring responsibilities.

→   Two-thirds (66 per cent) said their job was stressful compared with 34 per cent who said home life was stressful.

→   A total of 68 per cent called for greater flexibility in working arrangements.

→   Some 66 per cent said extending work–life balance options to workers without children would be worthwhile.

The researchers suggest that respondents may be struggling to see the benefit of work–life balance policies but remain committed both to the principle and to their jobs. Some 70 per cent said they are satisfied with their job and share the values of the organization they are working for. A total of 77 per cent said they have a high degree of control over how they

HRM IN REALITY   TELECOMMUTING BETTER THAN OFFICE WORKING

Research from Brigham Young University published in the *Journal of Family Psychology* in 2010 found that telecommuters experience a better work–life balance than office-based employees even when working significantly longer hours. The study analyzed data from 24 436 IBM employees in 75 countries to identify the number of hours that had to be worked before 25 per cent reported interference with personal and family life.

Office workers with relatively inflexible schedules reached this point when their hours exceeded 38 hours per week. Those who had the possibility of telecommuting were able to achieve 57 hours per week with their time typically divided between office and home, depending on the nature of the task being undertaken. Both male and female workers appreciated the advantages of flexible working arrangements.

Lead author E. Jeffrey Hill, a professor in the school of family life, noted: 'Telecommuting is really only beneficial for reducing work–life conflict when it is accompanied by flextime.'

Formerly one of IBM's first telecommuters starting in 1990, Jeffrey Hill commented: 'Managers were initially sceptical about the wisdom of working at home and said things like, "If we can't see them, how can we know they are working?".'

The study found that more than 80 per cent of IBM managers currently agree that productivity increases when flexible working arrangements are made available. In the current economic situation, financial constraints are encouraging more widespread introduction of such schemes.

Jeffrey Hill commented: 'A down economy may actually give impetus to flexibility because most options save money or are cost-neutral. Flexible work options are associated with higher job satisfaction, boosting morale when it may be suffering in a down economy.'

Younger workers keener on web commuting
A telecommuting study from 2008, *Web Commuting & the American Workforce* commissioned by Citrix Online,

a division of Citrix Systems, Inc. has found younger workers are particularly keen on flexible working. The study showed that employees aged 18–34 are twice as likely to prefer flexible working conditions than older employees. In fact, 70% of survey respondents agreed that working remotely would be a welcome opportunity.

Termed 'web commuters' in the study, a growing number of employees performed at least some of their work away from their office, at non-standard hours, using web-based technology. The study, conducted by *the polling company, inc.* and sponsored by Citrix Online, which claims to provide easy-to-use, secure and affordable web-based services for remote computer access and online collaboration, found that:

→ Twenty-three per cent of US employees regularly worked offsite using web technology and 62% of those who do not would like to do so.

→ Employees aged 18–34 were most likely to look forward to controlling their own schedules, while respondents aged 35–44-year-olds indicated that they would value more time with family.

→ In general, the younger the worker, the more likely they were to see the value of online tools and services that allowed them to work

remotely, reflecting their greater familiarity with the Internet.

Kellyanne Conway, CEO and president of *the polling company, inc.* said: 'As baby boomers retire, employers will be forced to compete for younger workers, for whom technology is a native tongue. Offering the ability to web commute is an easy way to provide a valued benefit to this age group.'

'Anyone of any age can benefit from new, low-cost technologies that are as easy to use and as indispensable as email and cell phones,' commented Bernardo de Albergaria, vice president and general manager, global marketing and eCommerce for Citrix Online. 'Younger workers expect freedom and flexibility, and online remote access and collaboration services enable people to work on their own terms. When employers provide these tools for connecting employees with their PCs, customers, prospects and co-workers across town or halfway around the world, everyone benefits.'

Why should organizations involve themselves with non-work issues?

Source: Reprinted with permission from HRM Guide USA (http://www.hrmguide.com).

work. Some 99 per cent agreed that people work best when they can balance work and other aspects of their lives.

WORKPLACE HEALTH

According to Naidoo and Wills (2000: 270):

The relationship between work and health may appear substantial but it is viewed in different ways by different groups of people. One of the defining characteristics of the workplace setting is that it brings together a variety of groups who have different agendas with regard to work and health. The key parties are workers or employees and their trade unions or staff associations, employers and managers, occupational health staff, health and safety officers, environmental health officers and specialist health promoters.

The Chartered Institute of Personnel and Development's 2010 report on sickness absenteeism in the UK shows that absence in the National Health Service (NHS) averages 11 days per employee per year. This is significantly higher than the public sector average of 9.7 days, which, in turn is much higher than the average absence levels in the private sector of 6.4 days and 8.3 days in the non-profit sector.

HRM IN REALITY   ABSENCE MANAGEMENT IN IRELAND

A 2009 article in the *Irish Times* highlighted a campaign to control excessive absenteeism by the Health Service Executive (HSE). Under the Health Act, 2004, the HSE has assumed responsibility for Health and Personal Social Services for everyone living in the Republic of Ireland. It replaced ten regional health boards and a variety of other organisations and is now Ireland's largest employer with over 130 000 employees.

The HSE's 2009 Service Plan featured increases in service provisions and reductions in costs, including savings in staffing areas such as:

→ work practice reform (redeployment of staff, more flexible working arrangements)

→ sick leave

→ absenteeism

→ overtime

→ use of agency workers

→ allowances, and

→ a three per cent reduction in management/administration staff through planned redundancies.

According to the *Irish Times*, HSE has been auditing absenteeism levels for several months. Unpublished figures from October indicate an average level of five per cent lost hours due to absenteeism in the main teaching hospitals. However, the level in some hospital sections is much higher: for example, running at 12 per cent among general support staff at the Midwest Regional Hospital in Limerick.

The newspaper cites the intention of HSE's national HR director to eliminate 'double-digit absenteeism or inappropriately high sickness levels where they occur'.

Monitoring absenteeism

A survey by Mercer Human Resource Consulting in 2006 found that almost two-thirds (65 per cent) of Irish businesses made no attempt to calculate the annual cost of absenteeism to their companies. Moreover, the survey of top Irish businesses found that most had no idea about the impact of employee absences on their direct or indirect costs.

According to Kevin Kinsella, a consultant at Mercer Human Resource Consulting:

> Our experience in this area and indeed our research demonstrates that reporting and measurement of absence plays a very effective role in reducing absence levels. However, many companies take a casual and sporadic approach to absence management and fail to actively manage a major cost driver.

The survey also found that:

→ Twenty-six per cent of those surveyed estimated the cost of absenteeism to be more than 500 000 euros a year

→ Minor illnesses were the most frequently cited causes for absence, amounting to 33.2 per cent of days lost

→ Almost 20 per cent of absences were due to musculoskeletal illnesses and back pain

→ Ninety per cent of surveyed organizations said that 'recording' of absence was their number one tool in combating absence levels

→ Twenty per cent of surveyed organizations reported absence levels in excess of six per cent per annum

→ Sixty-five per cent did not calculate the cost of absence to their business

→ Forty-five per cent of managers whose responsibilities included dealing with employee absence had not received relevant training

→ Forty-one per cent of managers with responsibilities in this area had no formal targets.

The Mercer Human Resource Consulting survey shows that senior managers are highly aware that 'absence management' is an issue for their business, but very few companies are taking an appropriate, strategic approach to reducing absenteeism in their businesses. Kevin Kinsella said:

> There will always be short-term absence in organizations. Mercer's experience and research

suggests that there is no one 'magic cure' to manage sickness absence. The introduction of a range of simple measures such as absence reporting, early interventions on health issues, the provision of health insurance and the provision of support and training for line managers, can however, dramatically reduce absenteeism levels.

The Mercer view is that the cost of employee sick days can have an impact on overall competitiveness so it is important that organizations review and manage their absence procedures. Mercer believes that effective reporting and measurement can drive behavioral change particularly when supported by senior management.

Why are absence levels high in health services?

Source: Reprinted with permission from HRM Guide UK *(http://www.hrmguide.co.uk).*

The report shows that monitoring of absence is increasing but half of employers do not measure the cost of absence. It identifies the most effective techniques as:

→ Return-to-work interviews.

→ Trigger mechanisms to review attendance.

→ Disciplinary measures for unacceptable absence.

Ironically, public sector employers are much less likely to use disciplinary measures than private sector or non-profit employers, and have the most generous sick pay arrangements.

Health and safety are workplace issues with considerable organizational and legal implications for HR and other managers. Naidoo and Wills (2000) identify a number of benefits to organizations from the promotion of health in the workplace as (a) 'hard' benefits, such as improvements in productivity as a result of reduced sickness, absence and staff turnover; and (b) 'soft' benefits, including enhanced corporate image.

Organizations may introduce specialist occupational health staff tasked with the following (Naidoo and Wills, *ibid.*):

→ Surveillance of the work environment, such as monitoring the effects of new technology.

→ Introducing initiatives and providing advice on the control of hazards.

→ Surveillance of employee health including assessing fitness to work and analyzing sickness/absence reports.

→ Srganizing first aid and emergency responses.

→ Involvement with adaptation of work and working environment to the worker.

Changes away from large, labour-intensive manufacturing organizations towards more fragmented, technology-based industries have dramatically altered the nature of occupational health over the last few decades – in developed countries, at least. Boyd (2001) argues that health and safety (as a topic) occupies a somewhat rhetorical role in HRM literature. Boyd looked at HRM and the management of health and safety in the airline industry and found that airlines have adopted a short-term cost-cutting approach to both in response to increasingly competitive trading conditions. The focus has been on reducing operating costs, achieving immediate productivity gains and prioritizing profit over employee health and safety.

HRM IN REALITY HEALTH AND SAFETY NOT OVERREGULATED

Recent research from the University of Liverpool and Liverpool John Moores University in 2010 found that safety in the workplace has been adversely affected by policy changes relating to health and safety over the last ten years, with reduced levels of enforcement by the Health and Safety Executive (HSE). These findings challenge the perception that health and safety is overregulated.

The report entitled *Regulatory Surrender: death, injury and the non-enforcement of law* found that inspections of business premises fell by 69 per cent and investigations of health and safety-related incidents by 68 per cent. The study also identified a 48 per cent reduction in prosecutions of organizations for breaching HSE regulations.

Dr David Whyte, reader in sociology at the University of Liverpool, said:

The idea that health and safety has 'gone mad' does not seem to hold true. The collapse in inspection, investigation and enforcement has dramatically reduced the chances of businesses being detected and prosecuted for committing safety offences. Most serious injuries now are not even investigated. For example, only a third of

amputations are now investigated by the Health and Safety Executive.

Researchers explain that the new UK government elected in May 2010 announced a wide-ranging review of health and safety regulations in response to claims that industry had been 'saturated' by legislation passed by the outgoing administration. The Liverpool study concluded that the HSE's inspection and enforcement powers had been reduced, resulting in increased numbers of employees at risk of suffering work-related accidents or injuries.

Professor Steve Tombs, of Liverpool John Moores University, commented:

HSE's senior management have effectively surrendered to the Government's lighter touch regulatory agenda. Not only is the agency now more vulnerable to further 'reviews' of regulation, but workers too are increasingly vulnerable – as managements are far less likely to respond to workers' demands to comply with the law in the absence of a credible enforcement threat.

Source: Reprinted with permission from HRM Guide UK (http://www.hrmguide.co.uk/).

HRM IN REALITY HR CHANGES CAN INCREASE STRESS

Research funded by the Economic and Social Research Council as part of its Future of Work programme has found that teamworking and other contemporary employment practices can put as much strain on a woman's family relationships as working an extra 120 hours a year.

The study by Patrick McGovern, Stephen Hill, Colin Mills and Michael White entitled *Market, Class, and Employment* found significant changes in British job prospects and conditions over the period 1984–2004.

Despite competitive market pressures employers have maintained long-term career relationships with their employees. However, introduction of practices such as team-based forms of work organization, individual performance-related pay, and an emphasis on development of individual potential has demanded greater effort and higher performance.

Researchers found that while these human resource management practices are thought to improve staff morale and to form an essential element in successful business performance, the resulting stress has an adverse impact on employees' family relationships. Women are generally more affected than men and are less likely to get support from male partners also in pressurized jobs. Both are more likely to experience anxiety about childcare.

Researchers highlight ICT surveillance as a significant new source of strain at work. They found that 52 per cent of all employees (20 per cent of workplaces) have their work monitored by computerized systems. This has led to a sharp increase in work-related stress reflected in feelings of exhaustion and anxiety. The study found an overall 7.5 per cent increase among employees subject to ICT surveillance compared with those in similar jobs supervised in more traditional ways. Administrative and white-collar staff in settings such as call centres reported a 10 per cent increase.

Michael White commented: 'Computers and IT systems are bringing surveillance to most workplaces. Now for the first time we can see how this development is damaging employees' well-being.'

Researchers found that recent US employment practices have not been replicated in Britain. It might have been assumed that highly competitive market conditions would result in both private and public sector employers resorting to hire and fire practices, temporary jobs and a decline in training and career planning. While British employers continue to use redundancy to adjust employee numbers, in general they remain committed to retention and long-term development.

The study found that the proportion in permanent employment remains above 90 per cent and increased during the 1990s. Fixed-term or casual employment grew in the 1980s but declined in the subsequent decade. Researchers argue that increased use of communication techniques, employee participation, team organization, training and development, and performance rewards are indicative of efforts to maintain a long-term workforce.

Researchers suggest that the decline in trade union recognition and membership could increase the chances of unfair treatment but found that this has been mitigated in part by a growth in alternative forms of employee engagement such as meetings with management and consultation. The study found that by 2000 about one third of employees were participating in individual pay bargaining. Researchers note that this is more likely to occur in non-unionized workplaces and is leading to increasing inequality. Managers and professionals are more likely to negotiate personal pay deals; women are less likely to bargain over pay when recruited or to be represented by a union. Thus the ability of women to challenge the gender pay gap is doubly limited.

The research concluded that class differences in job rewards have increased since the early 1990s. Pay inequality increased between 1992 and 2000, reflecting substantial increases in average earnings for senior managers and significant though lower gains for other managers. Pay for individuals in semi-routine and routine occupations either saw no real increase or declined.

Other benefits such as occupational pensions, sickness pay and paid holidays also showed a marked class difference in favour of higher managerial and professional groups which tended to increase over time. There was a similar gap in job desirability, reflecting both pay and other factors such as flexibility and autonomy. Researchers conclude that inequality in pay and benefits will probably continue to grow. Managers and professionals are more able than other groups to benefit from increasing opportunities for personal pay bargaining and performance deals.

Patrick McGovern commented:

> The major story about work in Britain is not that it has become more precarious or fragmented, rather it has become more demanding while the returns have become more unequal. The major winners in the so-called new economy are professional and managerial employees who have actually moved further ahead of the rest of the labour force.

Why might HR practices increase stress?

Source: Reprinted with permission from HRM Guide UK (http://www.hrmguide.co.uk/).

HRM IN REALITY

HEALTH EFFECTS OF WORK-RELATED STRESS AND SHIFT WORK

Research from the University of Michigan Medical School published in 2010 in the *American Journal of Gastroenterology* found that nurses working shift patterns, especially those rotating between day and night, had a significantly higher risk of developing irritable bowel syndrome (IBS) and abdominal pain than those permanently on daytime rotas.

Lead author Sandra Hoogerwerf, assistant professor of internal medicine said: 'We know that people participating in shift work often complain of gastrointestinal symptoms such as abdominal pain, constipation and diarrhea. These are the same symptoms as IBS.'

The researchers explain that IBS is the most common functional bowel disorder. It is not amenable to diagnostic testing but is identified by clinical symptoms such as recurrent episodes of abdominal pain or cramping associated with altered bowel habits.

The study recruited 399 nurses working three shift patterns: 214 on permanent day duty; 110 on permanent nights and 75 rotating between the two. More than 85 per cent were women. Researchers identified a higher prevalence of IBS and abdominal pain in participants working shifts, particularly those rotating between day and night. This finding was independent of reported sleep disturbances.

Sandra Hoogerwerf explained:

> 'We know the colon has its own biological clock and that's what increases the likelihood of having a bowel movement in the first six hours of the day. Shift work can cause chronic disruption of that biological rhythm, resulting in that clock to constantly be thrown off and needing to adjust, creating symptoms of diarrhea, bloating, constipation and abdominal pain and discomfort.'

The researchers suggest that patients with IBS should be alerted to the possible impact of their work schedule on their condition.

Stress and coronary heart disease

Research from Université Laval's Faculty of Medicine published in the *Journal of the American Medical Asso-*

ciation in 2007 has demonstrated that chronic job strain after a first heart attack may double the risk of suffering a second one.

The researchers explain that previous studies had confirmed a relationship between work-related stress and a first coronary heart disease (CHD) event, but the few studies conducted on the association with recurrent CHD were limited in scope and inconsistent in their findings.

Researchers led by Chantal Brisson followed a group of 972 people aged 35 to 59 who had suffered a heart attack. They were interviewed at six weeks, two and six years after returning to work concerning their health, lifestyle, socio-demographic status, and degree of work stress. A job was defined as stressful 'if it combined high psychological demands (heavy workload, intense intellectual activity, and important time constraints) and little control over decision-making (lack of autonomy, creativity, and opportunities to use or develop skills).'

The study found that 124 participants suffered a second heart attack and 82 experienced unstable angina. People reporting high levels of work stress at six weeks and two years were twice as likely to suffer another CHD event. Researchers found that the risk remained the same after allowing for variables such as severity of the first heart attack, other health conditions, family history, lifestyle, socio-demographic status, personality, and other work-environment factors. They also found that job strain did not increase the probability of experiencing a second CHD event during the first two years.

Chantal Brisson commented: 'It makes sense on a biomedical level, since the pathological process at the source of the CHD requires some time before it can manifest itself.'

The researchers conclude that these findings should alert employers to the need to protect people from potentially harmful situations when they return to work after a heart attack.

Chantal Brisson said:

> Employers and occupational health service professionals must find ways to modify the psychological demands of a job or the level of

control over decision-making for people returning to work after a heart attack. It can be done, and encouraging autonomy, creativity, and the development of professional abilities in the workplace is not incompatible with a company's productivity.

Source: Reprinted with permission from HRM Guide USA (http://www.hrmguide.com).

Stressors include a long list of factors. Too much or too little work may both be stressful. De-layering, downsizing, rightsizing: changes in organization and job structure are rife in modern industry and are perceived as stressful by those who are made to change.

Where job numbers are slashed, the remaining workforce may be pressurized and also be concerned about the future of their own jobs. The 2:3:2 formula – half the people doing three times the work for twice the money – brings its own pressures.

The UK Health and Safety Executive (HSE) has published research showing that occupational groups reporting highest levels of work-related stress were teaching, nursing, management, professionals, other education and welfare (including social workers), road transport and security (including police and prison officers). In each of these groups at least one in five reported high stress (two in five among teachers). Full-time workers were more likely to report high stress than part-time employees.

High levels of stress were reported most frequently by people in managerial and technical occupations, those educated to degree level and those earning more than £20 000. Non-white employees reported comparatively higher levels of stress than white workers but it is pointed out that the numbers involved were small. Little difference was reported in stress levels between male and female workers.

Alker and McHugh (2000) looked at the rationale used for introducing employee assistance or advisory programmes (EAPs) in UK organizations. They found that support was more likely to be given for organizational change than for more humanistic reasons. They offer the explanation that this is consistent with managers' work roles.

 SUMMARY

This chapter has focused on the relationship between forms of flexible working, the consequences on work–life balance and employee health and well-being in the workplace. Competitive pressure has placed extra burdens on employees, especially those with career aspirations. These burdens can cause health problems, particularly those that are stress-related. HR practitioners have at least a moral responsibility to deal with such matters and encourage the setting up of supportive mechanisms such as employee assistance programmes.

 FURTHER READING

1 *Flexible Working* by John Stredwick and Steve Ellis, 2nd edn (CIPD, 2005) covers the subject from policy to practice.

2 *How to Reduce Workplace Conflict and Stress: How Leaders and Their Employees Can Protect Their Sanity and Productivity from Tension and Turf Wars* by Anna

KEY CONCEPT 12.2 UNITARISM VERSUS PLURALISM

The unitarist view is implicit in American models of HRM. It holds that the interests of employees and the firm should be the same. Pluralism, on the other hand, recognizes that every organization is composed of different interests that are not balanced. Pluralists accept that conflict is natural and are concerned with the means by which it can be managed.

Unions attempted to counter negative perceptions by introducing ethical training in order to stress their legitimacy, morality and organizational effectiveness (Cohen, 2008).

Geare *et al.* (2006) suggest that HRM theorists appear to believe that unitarism is the norm in employment relationships. At the same time, theorists see HRM as the means to achieving unitarism through the introduction of high commitment management systems in the workplace. But they point out that a number of authors have questioned these assumptions. Van Ruysseveldt *et al.* (1995: 2) contend that '... no modern society has ever accepted a purely individualistic determination of the employment relationship.'

The study by Geare *et al.* attempted to identify current employment values and beliefs of workers and management and examined the extent to which these influence, or are influenced by, the adoption of high commitment practices in the workplace. Curiously, they found that managers considered employment relationships in general to be pluralist, but their own organizations to be unitarist.

'Self-reliance' became the prevailing ethos. Everything outside one's own control was treated as a potential enemy to be dominated. This applied as much to trade unions as it did to competitors. Elsewhere in the democratic world, such an extreme position was unusual. Nevertheless, it cannot be assumed that there is a common agenda between employers and the employed that can be 'managed'. There is an inevitable, if latent, tension between the two (Blyton and Turnbull, 1994: 4).

Historically, unions attempted to replace individual bargaining with collective bargaining (see Key concept 12.3) in order to increase employees' power and counter employers' attempts to create competition between workers. This required solidarity between union members. Union goals were to obtain standardized wages and optimal conditions. Employers tended to prefer dealing with employees on an individual basis.

KEY CONCEPT 12.3 COLLECTIVE BARGAINING

Collective bargaining takes place between employers and trade unions when employees are members of trade unions that undertake to negotiate on their behalf in matters such as pay, working conditions, other benefits, and work allocation; and employers recognize trade unions and their officials as legitimate bargaining agents.

Braverman (1974) regarded the weakness of workers in the employment relationship as an inevitable consequence of the management role, concluding that managers were responsible to the market as well as to shareholders and employees. Businesses would not survive without increasing levels of productivity and efficiency provided by the creativity, imagination and problem-solving abilities of the workforce. However, these same qualities could be used to resist managers' aspirations for change.

Employees had their own objectives that frequently differed from management goals. Under the 19th century craft-based system of production, individual employees held a considerable degree of power through their possession of knowledge. Managers frequently had no idea what workers were doing. Scientific management and Fordism offered the prospect of de-skilling jobs and removing knowledge, and hence bargaining power, from the workforce. Braverman's original analysis has been criticized for oversimplification; most workers were unskilled or semi-skilled. Fordism led to a relative standardization of the employment relationship throughout the developed world until around 1980, with the following characteristics (Van Ruysseveldt et al., 1995: 2):

→ Permanent, full-time jobs.

→ Wage increases on the basis of experience and training.

→ Extra payments for inconvenient or anti-social arrangements.

→ Regular working hours and a clearly defined working week.

→ Paid holidays.

→ The right to collective representation and some consultation on changes to working practices.

Trade unions conducted negotiations with employers within this framework. This form of employee relations was associated with vertical and horizontal division of labour, hierarchical management and close supervision. However, this pattern of working life has disintegrated under the pressures of competition from newly-developing countries and the introduction of flexibility. In consequence, the 'traditional' role of trade unions has been undermined.

Union activity traditionally focused on people within the internal employment market. Under newer working practices, the core workforce can be reduced to insignificant numbers and many companies have made a practice of actively discouraging unionization. The use of short-term or part-time contracts has increased. Variable working hours have become a valuable source of flexibility. Extended opening hours have allowed employers to increase profits by maximizing use of equipment and accommodation. The extent of these changes leads Van Ruysseveldt et al. (1995: 7) to conclude that pre-1980s analytical and theoretical frameworks for studying employee relations are outdated.

There are significant differences in union density (proportion of the workforce who are trade union members) between Canada and the USA, and also between and within industry sectors. The prevailing explanation for this difference (see Johnson, 2002) is that mandatory voting has discouraged unionization in the USA whereas card-checking (counting the number of existing union members) has encouraged unionization in Canada. There was a marked increase in the proportion of Canadian provinces covered by mandatory voting between 1993 (18 per cent) and 2000 (62 per cent).

In 2008 union density in Canada was 30.4 per cent (Statistics Canada Labour Force Survey). According to the US Bureau of Labor Statistics, union density was 12.3 per cent in 2009, representing a 10 per cent fall in membership. Part of an ongoing trend, this also reflects the impact of recession on manufacturing and construction. More than 37 per cent of US government workers were union members in 2009. For the first time, there were more union members in the public sector than the private sector, even though the private sector has five times more jobs.

Union density in Australia fell from 50.2 per cent in 1970 to 22 per cent of full-time and 15 per cent of part-time workers in 2009. After long-standing decline, membership has risen in the last two years for which figures are available.

In New Zealand union density fell from 55.2 per cent in 1970 to 17.9 per cent in 2009. Of 159 registered unions, 44.6 per cent have less than 100 members; women make up 59.9 per cent of union members (Household Labour Force Survey).

In 2008 union density in Canada was 30.4 per cent (Statistics Canada *Labour Force Survey*).

According to the US Bureau of Labor Statistics, union density was 12.3 per cent in 2009, representing a 10 per cent fall in membership.

ORGANIZATIONS AND EMPLOYEE RELATIONS

Earlier in this chapter we observed that traditional industrial relations assumed a formal structure in which management and staff negotiated pay levels and working conditions such as hours of work, grade demarcation, holiday and sick leave entitlement. In some organizations the same structure was used for grievance and disciplinary matters, agreeing levels of performance, attendance requirements – such as shift hours – and work procedures. Within this mechanism, staff were represented by one or more trade unions or staff associations.

In recent years large organizations in free market countries have attempted to emphasize individual rather than collective bargaining through mechanisms such as:

→ Introduction of personal contracts that, for example, allow employers to offer pay increases to those employees, sometimes at the expense of union members.

→ Organizational change methods such as team briefings, that allow managers to disseminate information throughout the organization in meetings (usually monthly), simultaneously collecting ideas and criticisms to be channeled upwards.

→ Quality circles that emphasize direct dialogue between staff and management to improve procedures.

It is not surprising that unions have often resisted the introduction of change methods of this nature because they depend on staff and management talking directly to each other, thereby removing a main source of union power – the filter or gatekeeper of information and innovation. In such situations, collective bargaining has often been restricted to primary issues of pay, holidays and discipline, removing unions from negotiation about procedures.

Individualized systems stress commitment from employees, yet the trend towards downsizing and restructuring imposes a 'fear of commitment' among managers and employees alike (Rousseau, 1995: xii). HR policies that emphasize the individual contribute to this fear since they remove any collective employee defence against the employer. 'Divide and rule.' Hendry (1995: 57) acknowledges a 'more sophisticated pluralist technique which sees the unitary organization as "bad" because the denial of individual and group interests actually makes for a less effective organization.' In other words, there is a valid criticism that the integrating activities of HRM can rub out the healthy diversity that is essential for future development: 'Such paradoxes, discrepancies, and ambiguities highlight the fact that organizational life is beset by paradoxes, and that (mercifully) managers and organizations cannot get a handle completely on human behaviour.'

Peters (1987) distinguishes two contradictory philosophies operating in modern business organizations:

Minimize human resources. Workers are pure costs. New methods and equipment are now available globally. Businesses in the developed world can: cut employee costs to match those of poorer countries; or switch to industries that are not labour intensive. This involves actual and threatened redundancies, transferring operations to lower-wage countries and automation.

Increase the value of the people element. Employees are assets. This approach emphasizes flexibility and creativity and aims to eliminate unnecessary routine by: the intelligent use of technology; and retraining workers for more complex or varied tasks. According to Peters it should be tied to profit-linked bonuses to ensure commitment.

The first approach leads to industrial conflict. Managers must make cuts and be aggressive towards staff. Workers defend their position and oppose change. The second approach is collaborative. It seeks partnership between workers and employers for mutual benefit. Peters argues that both approaches deliver short-term profits but only the second can maintain competitiveness in the long term.

Other management writers advocate a new form of employee relationship based on cooperation, for example the Major Projects Agreement (MPA) implemented in the construction of London Heathrow Airport's Terminal 5 (Deakin and Koukiadaki, 2009). Kanter (1989: 127) argues that the adversarial model is unsuitable for contemporary business conditions. 'Teaming up' is the route to growth and survival. Corporations need to seek strategic alliances – cooperative arrangements to achieve business goals. Such alliances should be made with unions as well as other businesses. Kanter defines these as 'stakeholder alliances' or 'complementary' coalitions. Stuart and Lucio (2002) found that while some unions were extremely enthusiastic, most companies did not reciprocate. Oxenbridge and Brown (2002) found a dichotomy between production sector firms that nurtured collective bargaining through informal partnership relationships, and service sector businesses that contained collective bargaining tightly through formalized partnership agreements. Haynes and Allen (2001), meanwhile, found equally distinct polarization among unions – some saw partnership as a potentially effective strategy for restoring union influence, others viewed the concept as fatally flawed. For the union representatives and line managers who are engaged in trying to make a social partnership work, the process is one of both accommodation and antagonism (Rittau and Dundon, 2010).

Participation is also a matter of delegation – involving everyone downwards within the organization as well as stakeholder partners. It requires a change in behaviour from managers who have previously exercised power in a clear-cut, overtly decisive fashion. A consensus style requires patience; willingness to discuss ideas at an early stage; and ability to listen. Not all managers can make the transition. Partnerships require managers with team leadership skills.

EMPLOYEE RELATIONS STRATEGIES

Strategic management styles towards employee relations have been classified to demonstrate a variety of approaches, ranging from authoritarian and anti-unionist to more sophisticated and inclusive strategies (see Table 12.1). In the same way, employees may adopt various styles in response. Trade unions also have varying interpretations of their role, reflecting the cultural, historical and legislative background in which they operate.

TABLE 12.1
Strategic management styles towards employee relations

Basic	Purcell and Sissons (1983)	Gunnigle *et al.* (1994)
1 **Authoritarian.** Typical small company style. Boss rules absolutely – staff have simple 'take it or leave it' choice. Works if employees accept situation – e.g. where there is little or no opportunity to change jobs. Seen in some large organizations.	1 **Traditional.** Fire-fighting – managers pay little attention to employee relations until trouble arises. Low pay levels. Hostile to unions. Prevails in authoritarian small businesses but seen in larger companies when workers have little choice in their employment.	1 **Anti-union.** Little or no consideration of employee relations. No collective arrangements such as union representation. Low concern for employee needs. Aggressive opposition to collective bargaining and union recognition.
2 **Individual.** Negotiation between management and individuals. Possible for staff teams to discuss common interests jointly. Non-authoritarian. Emphasis on commitment to company goals. Managers reasonable and approachable. No collective body representing staff.	2 **Paternalist.** More benevolent, humanistic style; close parallels with HRM approach. Employers consider unions unnecessary because conditions are so generous. Employee relations concentrate on getting employees to identify with the objectives of the business.	2 **Paternalist.** Concern for employee needs but rejects union recognition and collective bargaining. Little sophistication in human resource policies.
3 **Collective.** Dominant method in Western world from 1945 until approx. 1980. Since then, social and free market economies have taken different paths. Social market economies, e.g. Germany, have industry or company-wide trade unions (or staff associations) negotiating with management on behalf of the staff. Free market economies continue to make extensive use of this approach but management literature and HRM emphasize individual bargaining. Many companies utilize both strategies.	3 **Consultative.** Ideal form of employee relations in some eyes. Emphasis is on informal rather than formal systems of bargaining with continuous dialogue. Unions are fully recognized. 4 **Constitutional.** Similar to consultative approach but emphasis on formal regulatory agreements to control the relationship between powerful parties on either side. Found in social market economies and strongly encouraged by European Union social policy. 5 **Opportunistic.** Responsibility for employee relations left to individual divisions/subsidiaries, leaving no common approach and an emphasis on unit profitability.	3 **Sophisticated paternalist.** Emphasizes welfare and well-being of individual staff. Sophisticated HR policies for resourcing, development, reward and communication. Rejects unions and collective bargaining. Equates to 'traditional HRM' – values employees because this is seen to benefit organization. 4 **Sophisticated unionized.** Recognizes trade unions but carefully prescribed union role (e.g. single union agreement). Mixed collective and individual arrangements, incorporating HR policies. Neo-pluralist model with HRM-type policies designed to foster consensualism and employee commitment. 5 **Traditional unionized.** Pluralist approach typified by adversarial industrial relations. Collective bargaining but multiple unions complicate matters.

In many developed countries, dependence on company rules and regulations that clarified what was expected of both employees and employers has been overtaken by the trend towards flexibility and empowerment of staff. This has resulted in 'fuzzier' boundaries between required behaviour and that which is regarded as inappropriate. Employees – particularly managers – have been given greater discretion on decision-making in free market economies. This has been encouraged by 'neo-liberal' governments throughout the world. Within the European Union, however, there has been a countervailing emphasis on formal rules because of the predominance of social market economies. Typically, most large organizations continue to have formal rules on:

1 *Timekeeping*
   — Normally expected times of attendance, often with monitoring ('clocking-in').
   — Sanctions for lateness.

2 *Absence*
   — An approval mechanism for absence.
   — Authorization for taking annual leave.
   — A reporting procedure when people are absent from the workplace.
   — The need for medical self-certification or a doctor's certificate.

3 *Health and safety*
   — Requirements for appearance or cleanliness, e.g. protective clothing, wearing jewellery.
   — Special hazards such as chemicals and dangerous machinery.
   — Prohibition of smoking, alcohol or drugs.

4 *Gross misconduct*
   — Offences regarded as being serious enough to lead to dismissal without notice.
   — Theft, fraud, deliberate falsification of records.
   — Fighting, assault on another person.
   — Deliberate damage to company property.
   — Serious incapability through alcohol or being under the influence of illegal drugs.
   — Serious negligence that causes unacceptable loss, damage or injury.
   — Serious acts of insubordination.
   — Unauthorized entry to computer records.

5 *Use of company facilities*
   — Use of telephone for private calls.
   — Admission to company premises outside working hours.
   — Use of company equipment, e.g. computers, photocopiers, for personal reasons.
   — Abuse of emails and the Internet.

6 *Discrimination*
   — Overt discrimination but also sexual harassment and racial abuse.

The enforcement of such rules is a sensitive issue, requiring some kind of formal or informal disciplinary system. Butterfield *et al.* (2005) see disciplinary punishment as an inevitable element of a manager's job. Reviewing literature on the subject, they conclude that although managers typically regard punishment as being justified by deterrence or 'just desserts' (commensurate with the level of offence), the latter is the normal motive for any disciplinary sanction. Impression management plays a significant role: managers are concerned about their reputations to be fair but effective disciplinarians. Actions that are perceived to be unfair will elicit bad reactions from employees, ranging from sullen lack of cooperation to outright hostility or subversion. Butterfield *et al.* argue that there are specific elements of discipline that are important such as: the timeliness of the punishment; the perceived justice of the punishment; the use of constructive criticism; and keeping the punishment private.

Discipline is not only negative, in the sense of being punitive or preventative, it also makes a positive contribution to organizational performance. An effective organization cannot survive if its members behave in an anarchic way. Order within an organization depends on an appropriate mixture of each of these forms of discipline. Within the context of HRM, however, the emphasis has moved away from managerial discipline towards self and, especially, team discipline. Nevertheless, most organizations continue to have institutionalized disciplinary procedures, largely determined by management. Internet use at work is an interesting and growing disciplinary problem at work.

Dismissal is the ultimate expression of such procedures and also one of the most unpleasant aspects of human resource management. It may arise because of disciplinary issues such as persistent absenteeism, failure of an employee to perform adequately despite support and training, or as a strategic requirement arising from a change in direction by the organization. Most managers regard the 'exiting' process with distaste – often it is more stressful for the sacking manager than the victims. Dismissal inevitably follows some form of conflict.

HRM IN REALITY INTERNET USE AT WORK

Research by MyJobGroup.co.uk, the operator of the UK's largest network of regional jobsites, found that more than half of British workers access social media websites while at work. Based on a survey of 1000 employees, the study found that of those acknowledging use of sites such as Facebook, Twitter and Myspace, one-third report spending more than 30 minutes a day and nearly six per cent more than an hour.

The report suggests that the cost to the UK economy could be as much as £14 billion in lost productivity, with SMEs likely to be most adversely affected.

The study found that many respondents were in denial about the negative impact on efficiency. Only 14 per cent admitted to being less productive as a result and 10 per cent claimed social media had made them more productive. There was widespread resistance to banning use of social media during working hours, with over two-thirds of respondents (68 per cent) supporting some form of access.

Lee Fayer, managing director of MyJobGroup.co.uk commented:

Our results clearly show that UK workers are spending increased time whilst at work on social media networks, which, left unchecked, could have negative repercussions on the productivity of many companies across the country.

Whilst we're certainly not kill-joys, people spending over an hour per day in work time on the likes of Facebook and Twitter are seriously hampering companies' efforts to boost productivity, which is more important than ever given the fragile state of our economy.

Companies would do well to monitor use of social networking sites during work hours and ensure that their employees are not abusing their freedom of access to these sites.

Has internet misuse become the greatest discipline problem in modern organizations?

Source: Reprinted with permission from HRM Guide UK (http://www.hrmguide.co.uk/).

HRM IN REALITY CAREER EXITS

According to the 2006 survey on employee exits by career publisher Vault.com, 61 per cent of respondents have exited a job on bad terms with their employer.

Based on 706 responses from American employees in a variety of industries, the survey found the main reasons for leaving were disagreements with management (73 per cent), disagreements with co-workers (12 per cent), or to start employment with a new company immediately (14 per cent).

One respondent commented, 'Owners of the company were liars, cheaters, and didn't treat their employees well'. Another said, 'My manager wanted me to do something that violated FDA regulations, and then he got HR to begin disciplinary steps because I was disobedient'.

Almost half (47 per cent) did not give notice in person, but instead called or emailed their manager. One respondent explained, 'After having it out with my boss's boss, I called my boss and told him I quit. The

funny thing was, at the same time I was in his voice-mail, his boss paged him and told him to fire me.'

Types of bad exits included:

→ screaming matches (42 per cent)

→ negative mass emails (24 per cent)

→ negative speeches at company meetings (18 per cent)

→ vandalized or stolen company property (12 per cent)

→ physical scuffles (four per cent).

About half of respondents (52 per cent) witnessed or took part in a domino effect in which one person's exit caused others to leave the company soon afterwards.

Source: HRM Guide USA *(http://www.hrmguide.com).*

CONFLICT

Where does conflict come from? Conflict has both positive and negative aspects as we can see in Table 12.2. A number of basic psychological causes are apparent, regardless of the overt justification for a dispute (McKenna, 1994: 418):

Frustration and aggression. Disagreement often reflects frustration – feelings of being ignored, of being pressurized or of blocked promotion. Any point of difference, no matter how irrelevant, may spark a reaction to frustration. This may appear in the form of verbal aggression, seemingly out of proportion to the importance of the supposed dispute. Clearly, the dispute masks problems that are attributable to poor communication, lack of empowerment and mistrust.

Different objectives. The rhetoric of HRM states that organizations should aim for shared goals between management and staff. However, in practice, managers and employees have different priorities. Managers may focus on efficiency and cost-effectiveness, whereas employees want higher pay and longer holidays. Unless there are mechanisms, such as team briefings or quality circles, by which mutual understanding of these goals can be improved, differences are likely to be brought to a head at some stage.

Different values. These could be political – a difference in belief about the purpose of business for example – or a disagreement about the manager's right to manage. Many

TABLE 12.2
Consequences of conflict

Positive	Negative
Clearing the air. Allowing people to air their grievances can sometimes lead to an improved atmosphere after the disagreement has finished. This serves to bring 'hidden agendas' out into the open.	**Wasting time and energy**. A simple decision can be quick to implement, but negotiation can take an inordinate amount of time. Often participants forget original purpose of negotiation and get caught up with fighting a war.
Understanding each other's position. When both sides of an agenda are brought out into the open, people must think through their own case in order to express it clearly; and grasp the other point of view in order to challenge it.	**Stress**. Conflicts can become quite personal, abusive and threatening. The postures taken by the two sides can lead to further stress. Mental exhaustion may come from prolonged debate.
Modification of goal. One side may realize how unpopular or impractical the consequences of their argument may be.	**Worsening the situation**. Conflict may highlight problems, dislikes and grievances better left unstated. Tension may escalate debate into action: strikes, lock-outs, work-to-rule, threatened or implied redundancies. Consequences may be unpleasantness with worse morale and industrial relations after negotiations than before.

managers believe that they have the authority to issue instructions without being challenged by their staff. On the other hand, some employees consider that managers have this right only if they are prepared to explain their decisions, account for the consequences of their actions, and are prepared to accept questions and criticisms.

Jealousy. Individual employees can be sensitive to other members of staff being paid more than them, or getting extra perks. The conflict arises from jealousy or loss of status.

Culture. The tradition of 'us and them' (employees versus management) continues to exist in many organizations, particularly those using an authoritarian style of people management. New staff and management are quickly encouraged to accept the 'normality' of this perspective. In other cases, a change in the management approach disturbs the prevailing employee relations culture.

Conflict is an inevitable feature of negotiating and bargaining. Trained negotiators are taught to deal with conflict, expecting both negative and positive aspects to appear during the process. This will be easier to understand when we consider specific models of negotiation later in this chapter.

Issues of conflict and discipline may not be resolved at local level. Many countries have mechanisms by which disputes may be taken to an outside body, usually in the form of industrial tribunals or arbitration bodies.

TRIBUNALS AND ARBITRATION SYSTEMS

To what extent can differences between employers and workers be resolved through **arbitration** or legal tribunals? It is the view in many countries that an impartial, legally based process has a significant role to play in a number of circumstances. Industrial tribunals take many forms, some making legally binding judgements, others not setting a precedent in law. Even in the latter case, however, they have a long-term effect since they establish a set of values and influence the behaviour of others. If there is a judgement on a case of significant racial discrimination, for example, the resulting publicity may lead to a moderation of racist behaviour as people fear the possibility of similar action against themselves.

Chelliah and D'Netto (2006) analyzed 342 decisions in 17 industries by arbitrators in the Australian Industrial Relations Commission to assess whether employees benefited from arbitration. They found that 50.6 per cent of arbitration decisions were in favour of employees but only 10.8 per cent of complainants were reinstated. They suggest that employers need to look at ways of creating a more harmonious workplace. Employees do not benefit much from arbitration and reaching a settlement through mediation may be a better option.

In the UK, the **Advisory, Conciliation, and Arbitration Service (Acas)** plays a similar role to that formerly conducted by the Australian Industrial Relations Commission in relation to collective disputes. It provides services including:

Binding arbitration. Acas can appoint an arbitrator provided that the two parties agree to accept the arbitrator's decision.

Voluntary conciliation. Acas provides a calm environment and help on defining the important issues. Acas conciliation staff act as facilitators and do not make judgements or attempt to impose solutions.

Mediation. Intermediate between arbitration and conciliation. Acas mediators make advisory recommendations that are aimed at preventing disputes from degenerating into industrial action. These recommendations are not binding on the parties involved.

Acas also plays a major role in promoting agreed settlements in disputes taken to industrial tribunals.

HRM IN REALITY ACAS 2009/2010

In 2009/2010 the Advisory, Conciliation, and Arbitration Service (Acas) dealt with 905 requests for collective conciliation of which 44 per cent involved pay and 14 per cent trade union recognition. The majority (94 per cent) were at least partially resolved.

Some 87 421 individual employment tribunal cases were referred for conciliation; almost all (97 per cent) were successfully resolved. This represents an overall increase of 13 per cent over the previous 12 months.

Nearly 10 000 cases were referred to the pre-claim service introduced in April 2009 that offers prompt conciliation designed to prevent disputes escalating. Results show that tribunal cases have been avoided in about 70 per cent of cases. Acas estimates that simply completing the necessary paperwork for an employment tribunal costs the average employer £2000.

The Acas helpline received over one million calls over the period; redundancy, dismissals, discipline and grievance were the most common issues raised. The service is receiving an increasing number of calls about company survival, addressing subjects such as short-time working schemes.

In April 2010 the Acas Model Workplace went online. This interactive assessment tool offers employers ten modules covering different areas of employment relations including performance management and employee representation. Aimed primarily at organizations with 100–300 employees, the Model Workplace is intended to: help employers assess the effectiveness of people management in their organization; give practical guidance on good employee relations; and connect employers to useful resources.

Ed Sweeney, chair of Acas said:

As the country begins to emerge from its longest and deepest recession for more than 60 years businesses have been looking for support and guidance. Acas has helped thousands of businesses over the past year. We have provided advice in the employment relations field, from short practical courses on issues such as improving

attendance and managing change, through to in-depth tailored support. Concern about employment issues and, in particular, redundancies, has remained high.

John Taylor, chief executive officer of Acas commented:

This has been a very tough year for British business and we have seen demand for our services, especially around dealing with redundancy, increase greatly. As well as continuing to provide conciliation in individual and collective disputes, we have also looked at our other services and the value for money we provide and have identified new ways of improving the British workplace through effective employee relations.

Source: Reprinted with permission from HRM Guide UK (http://www.hrmguide.co.uk).

THE NEGOTIATING PROCESS

Negotiation is an ancient art. It is important in fields as diverse as diplomacy, buying and selling, arranging relationships (marriages, business partnerships), as well as employee relations. Negotiation is a form of decision-making where two or more parties approach a problem or situation wanting to achieve their own objectives – which may or may not turn out to be the same. In the employee relations arena, negotiation usually takes place within the collective bargaining environment.

Participants enter the process with widely different views: some, typically on the employee side, will view it as being fundamental to industrial democracy, fairness and good business conduct; others see it as a barrier to efficiency, a view more prevalent on the management side. The latter view sees negotiation as compromise and second-best to winning: possibly worse than giving in! As can be seen from Table 12.3, the process also has its own jargon.

Negotiation is not simply a matter of 'splitting the difference' so that neither side achieves what it wants. It can produce an outcome that meets both sets of goals. In negotiating, both sides must have some goals in common and some that conflict. For example, employers and employees will all want the business to survive and expand. However, employers might resist high pay rises to keep costs down, whereas the staff will want increases to boost employee morale. Usually, bargaining takes place because neither side has the power or the authority to force a decision on the other and preserve a harmonious working atmosphere.

Therefore, both sides will open negotiations knowing that they will have to move from the opening position and that there will have to be sacrifices on one item to achieve advantages on another. Even in those ideal circumstances, such as the traditional German model, where deliberate confrontation is not acceptable, there will be an element of conflict between the two sides.

There is also an implicit assumption that the two parties have the same amount of power in the bargaining situation. This is almost certainly not the case and the degree of power will change during the process of negotiation; the location of greatest power may well

Statement	Translation
We explored all options	Everybody talked a lot
A great deal of additional work will be necessary	Nobody understood it
The results were inconclusive	Nothing happened
While no agreement was reached, definite progress was made	Nobody budged an inch
It is hoped that this report will stimulate interest in the problem	Let somebody else do it next time

TABLE 12.3

Communication in collective bargaining

Source: Adapted from *Toctanic* (undated, circa 1989), unofficial staff publication, British Telecom International.

switch backwards and forwards between the two sides as they achieve positions of advantage. Whatever the actual degree of power, advantages will come from both sides preserving the appearance or illusion of power. There is value, therefore, in playing a game of bluff.

Many texts imply that the methods of bargaining can only be learned through experience and may well suggest that negotiation, like most interpersonal skills, is instinctive rather than learned. Perhaps, the basic requirement is a combination of a competitive, assertive style with a devious and resilient personality. In fact, study of the bargaining process indicates regular patterns and processes that people tend to go through. Gates (2006) provides an overview of skills needed for successful negotiations and seeks to identify the benefits of training key staff in negotiations skills. The study finds that only five per cent of the UK's training budget is spent on negotiations skills development. However, it makes a significant difference to the performance of all staff, both in internal and external negotiations.

Studies of industrial negotiations have indicated that many disputes worsen because of the following factors:

→ Lack of clarity of aims or goals by one or both sides.

→ Poor understanding of the detailed situation.

→ The apparent dispute is not the real problem.

MODELS OF BARGAINING

There are several models of the bargaining process, the clearest of which identifies four main stages (Lyons, 1988: 110):

1 *Initial positioning.* Both parties set out their positions and requirements in an emphatic, firm way aimed at giving the impression that there is no possibility of budging from those positions. The situation can appear hopeless at this stage.

2 *Testing.* The next stage is a less formal probing of the other side's demands, testing out which are really unmovable and which might bend in the right circumstances.

3 *Concession.* Some tentative proposals and concessions are exchanged on which detailed negotiations can take place.

4   *Settlement.* Finally, agreement is reached and the package of new terms is settled and actioned. Lyons argues that successful negotiation requires specific skills, examined in the following subsections.

Analysis

This may be defined as the ability to analyze a situation not only in terms of one's own position and goals but also those of the other side. There should be a long-term perspective – rarely is it clear that one should begin to consider the consequences of the whole process at this basic stage. The analysis must include a decision on which elements can be agreed on an 'I win/you win' basis, as opposed to those which are 'I win/you lose'. It is not worthwhile winning one of the latter if the advantage is trivial in comparison with the longer-term bad feelings that may arise as a consequence.

This phase is frequently glossed over but in fact is possibly the most important. It is the stage at which one should work out what the highest and lowest gains you and your opponent are likely to accept. Additionally, there must be a clear understanding of what the other side really want as opposed to what you think they might want.

Effective argument

This has to be carefully balanced between being forceful and being reasonable. The whole point of negotiation is to convince the other side of the merits of your argument as against their own. It is a change process. It is important to avoid cheap point-scoring and abuse in order to preserve mutual respect and avoid distraction from irrelevant side issues.

Signals of cooperation

The skill of sensing and giving signals of cooperation and possible compromise. Kanter (1989: 156) found that the participants in successful 'business partnerships' were 'very adept at "reading" signals that indicated whether partner representatives can be trusted'. On the 'tit-for-tat' principle, maximum opportunity comes from rewarding cooperation or compromise with a compromise of your own. On the other hand, one does not reward the opposition for sticking to an unmovable position: every offer one makes has to be conditional on cooperation in return. It may be necessary to keep communication going in order for this process to happen. In the case of a complete deadlock, it may even be necessary to have 'talks about talks'. All offers and threats must have credibility, remembering that it is not real power that matters but the appearance of it.

Attention to detail

Lastly, the final conclusion of negotiations requires the ability to attend to detail, making sure that all aspects are taken care of and there is no way for the other side to avoid its agreed obligations.

➡ SUMMARY

'Employee relations' broadens the study of industrial relations to include wider aspects of the employment relationship, including unionized and non-unionized workplaces, personal contracts and socio-emotional, rather than contractual, arrangements. This is an area with diverse ideological underpinnings and political ramifications. Governments have taken an active part in determining its conduct, sometimes disallowing any form of employee voice and framing legislation to encourage individual or collective arrangements. In Europe, harmonization is leading to the establishment of works councils across the EU, giving a new role for collective representation. Australia and New Zealand have seen some of the most significant changes in employee relations legislation in recent years. Negotiation, bargaining and mediation are some of the most significant employee relations activities in which human resource specialists are involved.

FURTHER READING

1 *Reassessing the Employment Relationship* edited by Paul Blyton, Edmond Heery and Peter Turnbull (Palgrave Macmillan, 2010) places employee relations in a wide HR context.

2 *Employment Relations* by Ed Rose (FT–Prentice Hall, 3rd edition, 2008) and

3 *Contemporary Employment Relations: A Critical Introduction* by Steve Williams and Derek Adams-Smith (OUP Oxford, 2nd edition, 2009) provide good overviews of the field.

4 *International and Comparative Industrial Relations* edited by Greg Bamber, Russell Lansbury and Nick Wailes (Sage Publications, 5th edition, 2010) compares different countries.

5 *Managing Conflict in the Workplace: How to Develop Trust and Understanding and Manage Disagreements* by Shay and Margaret McConnon (How to Books, 4th edition, 2010) takes a win–win approach to workplace conflict.

6 *The Essential Guide to Mediation and Conflict Resolution* by Norah Doherty and Marcelas Guyler (Kogan Page, 2008) is a comprehensive guide.

7 *The Mind and Heart of the Negotiator* by Leigh L. Thomson (Prentice Hall, 4th edition, 2008) looks at the skills of negotiation and bargaining.

REVIEW QUESTIONS

1 What are the key differences between unitarist and pluralist views of employee relations?

2 What is meant by the employment relationship? To what extent is it reasonable to say that employee relations should encompass all employment relationships?

3 Do trade unions have a role to play in the modern workplace? Discuss the view that employee relations is an outmoded concept that has no place in organizations managed according to the principles of HRM.

4 What are the principal factors responsible for the changes in union power over the last few decades?

5 How central is the German system of employee relations to the European Union's 'social partnership' model?

6 Are works councils a handicap or a benefit to business efficiency?

7 Is it wise for governments to suppress independent trade unions?

8 What should trade unions do to be 'new realists' in employee relations?

9 What are the key skills of negotiation?

10 Should all disputes be resolved by arbitration?

11 Review the positive and negative aspects of conflict in the workplace. Is conflict healthy?

CASE STUDIES FOR DISCUSSION AND ANALYSIS

Middleton Council/Euro Vehicles

1 Middleton Council covers a large urban area bordered by open country. Most of its 300 staff work in the main office complex, Delta House, located in the old town centre. A new shopping mall has opened immediately between the council offices and the old market, transforming a derelict area into a fashionable district. The staff are delighted since they now work in a pleasant and prestigious locality with a massive choice of shops and eating places nearby.

The council has been re-elected after promising a considerable improvement in services. However, all available funds have been devoted to maintaining things as they are. After much debate it has been decided that costs could be cut dramatically by renting out Delta House to a commercial firm and transferring the staff to much cheaper accommodation at the edge of town. The savings could be used to pay for new services promised in the election.

The staff are unionized and have a reputation for resisting changes, no matter how small.

How would you advise the council to proceed?

2 Euro Vehicles manufactures vans and other light commercial vehicles. Because of severe competition and a declining market, the workforce has been reduced from 11 300 to 2800 in the last three years and the remaining employees are fearful of further redundancies. There are three unions in the two remaining plants, representing clerical, engineering and supervisory staff. Partly as a result of the recent cuts they are all suspicious of management intentions. Management is authoritarian, based on a rigid departmental structure and values technical competence and seniority over anything else. Most of the managers have been promoted from the engineering and production side of the company and are in their 40s and 50s.

The company's production is largely devoted to basic van models built to a 15-year-old design and sold to large utility companies at a very keen price. Marketing is almost non-existent and the Research and Development department was closed as a cost-cutting measure three years ago. The company is currently owned by a large conglomerate that left the management alone until recently but with strict, detailed financial controls. Consequently, the company has been consistently profitable but with a shrinking level of production and increasingly outdated manufacturing equipment. The conglomerate has decided that this 'hands-off' approach is no longer satisfactory. They are prepared to make a major investment but only if they can be convinced that this will be effectively managed.

You have been brought in as a consultant to look at the current organization and to recommend changes that would improve the situation.

How would you go about this?

What are the implications for employee relations?

CONCLUSION

We began this volume with an analysis of the concept of HRM. We found that interpretations of human resource management range from formal models to comparatively loose portrayals of the territory with which HRM should be concerned. There is general agreement on its underlying philosophy, linking people management to business objectives in a strategic, integrated and coherent way. Beyond that, however, commentators and practitioners interpret HRM in different ways, depending on personal agendas and vested interests. As a result HRM ranges from 'soft', humanistic attempts to win over staff and achieve heart-felt commitment, to 'hard'-nosed extraction of maximum effort at minimum cost.

Senior executives do not have a consistent view of HRM – any more than they have a shared understanding of management. Many do not perceive any distinction between general management and managing people. Even less do they wish to be involved with fine academic distinctions between different models of HRM. The actual 'doing' of HRM is passed to middle managers who are responsible for its implementation and can be held (conveniently) accountable for any failures. People policies and practices must be integrated and coherent for HRM to be effective but this division of labour leads to a significant weakness: it offers scope for a dislocation between strategic intentions and the conduct of people management at ground level.

Regardless of the rationale or the nature of its practice, HRM has become a common label for various forms and functions of people management. In English-speaking countries, the term has replaced 'personnel management' in many contexts. Following a South African study by Wood and Els (2000) we can identify four distinct patterns of practice:

1 A simple change in nomenclature of relevant personnel sections where, in a number of cases, staff were not seen as managers but instead were viewed as a distinct, relatively junior category of employee.

2 A broadened personnel function encompassing clearly delineated areas such as training and development.

3 HRM practitioners play an important strategic role as facilitators in the adoption of progressive industrial relations policies, rather than developing a vision for managing human resources across the organization.

4 True strategic HRM.

The adoption of human resource management has been driven by a range of stakeholders with different interests and expectations. It has been interpreted differently around the world but globalization has encouraged an increasing convergence. In the past, new management concepts have generally come from North America. However, the worldwide economy is changing. China, India and Brazil appear destined to be major influences at the beginning of the 21st century and they are not dominated by US-style free market ideas. HR specialists are no longer able to focus solely on their own local employment markets as global competition and outsourcing become dominant factors in the allocation of human resources.

What is clear is that the central tenet of 'soft' HRM – the belief that HRM regards employees as valuable assets and not just costs – is rarely translated into action. The practices associated with HRM are often introduced for reasons of expediency rather than any serious belief in its principles. Indeed, it is arguable that the practice of HRM is rife with hypocrisy and rhetoric. Many organizations in free market countries feel that competitive forces make it impossible to commit themselves to their employees. People management in these firms is firmly focused on cost-cutting. A conflict arises from the inherent contradiction between typical HRM themes such as encouraging long-term employee engagement and short-term cost-effectiveness.

This leads to the question of whether HRM is no more than a matter of fine words. Employees quickly learn to mistrust official rhetoric and instead practise the art of 'sense-making': looking for cues that indicate the route for success or, at least, survival. Informal messages are transmitted through the choice of people who are rewarded and those whose skills are developed. For example, large-scale redundancies – determined at short notice by senior managers – have followed soothing statements about the importance of human resources to an organization's future.

Is there any evidence that the implementation of HRM has a significant effect on national or organizational economic performance? After all, this is the justification implicit in HRM models for valuing the human resource above all others. Progress has been made in conceptualizing the problem and measuring results. Improvements in HR metrics have resulted in clear evidence for the effectiveness of HRM initiatives, especially when they are delivered in strategic 'bundles'. Fashionable concepts such as 'knowledge management', 'human capital management' and 'talent management' overlap with many features of human resource management and are often delivered as part of the same package of management initiatives. The evidence appears to support the view that 'calculative' practices, such as short-term contracts, lack of employer commitment to job security, low levels of training and unsophisticated human resource practices have been negatively correlated with corporate performance. In contrast, positive correlations have been found between good corporate performance and high-engagement organizations, especially when HR initiatives are introduced as a comprehensive, coherent package, or 'bundle' of practices.

GLOSSARY

Advisory, Conciliation, and Arbitration Service (Acas)
Founded in 1975, this is a UK public body with the ambition to 'improve organizations and working life through better employment relations'. It is run by a council with representatives from business, unions, and the independent sector and has approximately 800 staff in England, Scotland and Wales. There are 11 main regional centres plus a head office in London. ACAS defines its services as follows: *Conciliating:* the act of reconciling or bringing together the parties in a dispute with the aim of moving forward to a settlement acceptable to all sides. *Arbitrating:* an independent arbitrator or arbiter (in Scotland) deciding the outcome of a dispute. The decision may well be binding in law. *Mediating:* acting as an intermediary in talking to both sides. The aim is for the parties to resolve the problem between themselves but the mediator will make suggestions along the way.

Ageism Discrimination on the grounds of age is prevalent but often unrecognized. Legislation against ageism is becoming common in developed countries.

Application forms (blanks) Usually sent out to jobseekers who respond to some kind of job advertising. The form or blank is a template for the presentation of personal information that should be relevant to the job applied for. This ensures that all candidates provide the desired range of information in the same order of presentation to facilitate comparison and preparation of a short-list for further selection procedures.

Appraisals Appraisals rate individuals on quasi-objective criteria or standards deemed to be relevant to performance. Traditional appraisals rated individuals on a list of qualities, primarily work-related attitudes and personality traits. *See also* 'Performance assessment'.

Arbitration Arbitration is a long-standing alternative to court-based litigation. For example, the first institute for arbitration in Denmark was set up in Copenhagen in 1894. The process has a number of variant forms but, in essence, nominated third-parties (arbitrators) can make decisions which are binding on the parties to a dispute. Arbitration procedures can range between the informal and more rule-based systems and are similar to court procedures. Generally, arbitration is seen as providing such benefits as confidentiality, flexibility, speed and relative cheapness.

Assessment centre A concept and not necessarily a place. Normally used for selection or employee development, participants are given a variety of exercises, tests, role plays, interviews, etc. over a period of days. Several rates contribute to the assessment.

Attitudes Attitudes are dispositions held by people – towards or against – people, things and ideas. They have individual components based on factors such as personality and understanding, and social elements derived from shared experiences and cultural history. Attitudes are complex systems of belief, evaluation, emotion and behaviour.

Australian Council of Trade Unions (ACTU) Formed in 1927, the Australian Council of Trade Unions is the peak council and national centre representing the unionized Australian workforce. The ACTU holds a Congress every three years that sets out a clear set of policies and objectives for unions. The core activity of unions remains the improvement and representation of workers through workplace and industry activity and collective bargaining. The ACTU also has policies on a range of other issues which affect workers, their families and their communities.

Australian Industrial Relations Commission (AIRC) The AIRC was a national tribunal dealing with employment issues including dispute settlement and unfair dismissal. Replaced by Fair Work Australia in 2010.

Behavioural consistency Maintaining a set of desired behaviours consistently in the workplace. Desired behaviours may be agreed ways of behaving towards customers, team behaviour, etc.

Benchmarking Direct comparisons of different measures between an organization and 'best practice' competitors in the same business sector. This indicates the gap in performance, costs, morale, etc., between that organization and industry best practice.

Best Fit Matching human resource management and strategy as closely as possible to organizational requirements.

Best practice Strategies, activities or techniques that are viewed as being highly effective. Note that what is best practice in one context may not work in another.

Biodata Roberts (1997, p.: 10) describes biodata as a 'set of questions framed around "coincidences" in the lives of good performers.' People who are good at a particular job are likely to be more similar to each other than to individuals selected at random from the general population. Such similarities extend beyond work-related factors into hobbies, sports and social activities.

Change strategy An organizational or HR strategy aimed at implementing planned change.

Charisma Weber regarded charisma as one of three sources of authority (the other two being 'rational', and 'traditional'), portraying it as a magical and hypnotic force based on direct personal contact. In modern life charisma is often fake – a product of carefully orchestrated mass communications.

Cloning Cloning, or 'elective homogeneity' is the tendency for selectors to pick people like themselves, thereby reducing the breadth of skills and personalities in an organization. Simply matching the set of characteristics possessed by previous successful post holders, it is a safe, conservative way to fill jobs. As a low risk, but backward-looking approach, it is unlikely to meet the future needs of the organization.

Co-determination Cooperation between employees and management in policymaking.

Collective bargaining Collective bargaining takes place between employers and trade unions when: employees are members of trade unions which undertake to negotiate on their behalf in matters such as pay, working conditions, other benefits, and work allocation; and employers recognize trade unions and their officials as legitimate bargaining agents.

Collectivism The opposite of individualism – a preference for being part of a group. In employment relations, a process of combining into unions or staff associations for the purpose of negotiation with management.

Collectivization As individuals, most employees have a limited amount of power in comparison to their employers. But employees can pool the power they have. Through collectivization, workers are able to band together to protect their mutual interests. From the late 19th century onwards, trade unions have fought to improve pay and conditions for their members

Commitment Commitment is defined as the degree of identification and involvement which individuals have with their organization's mission, values and goals. This translates into: their desire to stay with the organization; belief in its objectives and values; and the strength of employee effort in the pursuit of business objectives.

Competence Organizations must have the capability to meet changing needs. In current parlance this is often expressed in terms of competences – skills, knowledge and abilities. These are qualities possessed by the people who work for those organizations. Competences can be brought into businesses through the recruitment of skilled individuals. They can also be developed within existing people by investing in training, education and experiential programmes.

Confucian dynamism Acceptance of the legitimacy of hierarchy and valuing of perseverance and thrift, without undue emphasis on tradition and social obligations that could impede business initiative.

Congruence One of the '4 Cs' of the Harvard model. An organization should be regarded as a system whose elements and activities have to fit together.

Contingency 'It depends'. Adapting theory to reality.

Core In resourcing terms, core staff are crucial to the organization and the last to be outsourced.

Cost-effectiveness Expressed in terms of profitability, cost-effectiveness has been used extensively as the justification for large-scale job cuts. But as a reflection of the value of its human assets, an organization has a duty to use its people wisely. In itself, there is nothing wrong with an attention to cost – provided that it does not become the one and only management criterion.

Counselling interview In the context of performance and employee development, an interview in which strengths and weaknesses and development actions are discussed. Typically, it follows a performance assessment.

Cover letters Introductory letters that accompany CVs or Resumes.

Critical incidents technique A set of procedures for systematically identifying behaviours which contribute to success or failure of individuals or organizations in specific situations.

Culture An all-pervasive system of beliefs and behaviours transmitted socially. Specifically it consists of the set of values – abstract ideals – and norms or rules held by a society, together with its material expressions. *See also* 'Corporate culture'.

Demographic trends Long-term changes in a country's population density, age profile, etc.

Development *see Human Resource Development (HRD)*

Direct *see Direct Discrimination*

Disability Discrimination Acts Legislation enabled to deter discrimination against people on the grounds of disability.

Downsizing Term used to describe sacking, dismissing or otherwise making redundant a substantial proportion of an organization's workforce.

Economically active Includes the employed – those in paid work – and the unemployed – those who are looking for paid work but are unable to find it.

Economic turbulence Cyclical and non-cyclical changes in the economy that cause periods of high or low demand for goods, services and employees.

Employee analysis Modern computer packages offer extensive possibilities for modelling the total profile of an organization's human resources. Employees can be classified in a variety of ways, such as function, department or grade.

Employee relations Employee relations is an alternative label for 'industrial relations'. It is not confined to unionized collective bargaining but encompasses all employment relationships. It goes beyond the negotiation of pay and benefits to include the conduct of the power relationship between employee and employer.

Employee resourcing Resourcing is the process by which people are identified and allocated to perform necessary work. Resourcing has two strategic imperatives: first, minimizing employee costs and maximizing employee value to the organization; secondly, obtaining the correct behavioural mix of attitude and commitment in the workforce

Employee turnover Measurable incidence of people joining and leaving the organization.

Employment market The employment market comprises all those people who are available for work. Neo-classical economics views this potential workforce as forming a labour market. The market is affected by national or regional supply and demand for appropriately skilled employees. It is constrained by demographic factors such as the number of young people leaving schools and universities and by cultural variables such as expectations for mothers to stay at home looking after children.

Employment relationship A formal and informal relationship between the employing organization and an employee. The informal element is sometimes referred to as the psychological contract – an undocumented understanding about the nature of employment within the organization. Regarded by neo-classical economists as an exchange of labour for pay, The employment relationship is also a power relationship in which the employer has the formal authority to direct effort towards specific goals, whereas the employee can – informally – frustrate the achievements of those objectives.

Equal access A situation where disadvantaged groups are not barred from entry into organizations but may be confined to lower levels of work.

Equal chance A situation where everyone has the same right, for example, to apply for a vacancy or be considered for promotion.

Equal opportunity policy A written statement of commitment to fair, non-discriminatory human resource management.

Equal share Access is free to any position within an organization and all groups are represented at all levels. May require a quota systems or 'Affirmative action' to achieve this situation.

Equality Act (UK) Act of 2010 that replaces older legislation such as the Race Relations Act 1976 and the Disability Discrimination Act 1995.

Flexibility The concept covers a combination of practices which enable organizations to react quickly and cheaply to environmental changes. In essence, flexibility is demanded from the workforce in terms of pay, contractual rights, hours and conditions, and working practices. This extends to the employment market, requiring jobseekers to show a willingness to move location, change occupation and accept radically different terms of employment. *See also* 'Numerical flexibility', 'Functional flexibility', 'Flexible firm', 'Flexible pay', 'Flexible specialization'.

Flexible firm Atkinson's model combining flexibility with Japanese concepts of 'core' and 'peripheral' workforces.

Flexible specialization Allocation of time and labour according to consumer demand. Staff receive extra training and resources to widen their specialist skills.

Gender All human societies divide themselves into two social categories called 'female' and 'male' (this does not exclude other categories). Each category is defined on the basis of varying cultural assumptions about the attributes, beliefs and behaviours expected from males and females. The gender of any individual depends on a complex combination of genetic, body, social, psychological and social elements, none of which is free from possible ambiguity or anomaly. Traditionally, sexual differences have been used to justify male-dominated societies in which women have been given inferior and secondary roles in their working lives.

Graphology Handwriting analysis to identify features of personality – popular as a selection technique in continental Europe.

Harvard model The Harvard Business School generated one of the most influential models of HRM. The Harvard view provides a strategic map of HRM territory which guides all managers in their relations with employees. Beer *et al.* (1984) who devised this approach recognized an element of mutuality in all businesses – that employees are significant stakeholders in an organization.

Headhunting Recruitment method aimed at identifying star performers.

Human capital Economic growth creates employment, but economic growth partly depends on skilled human resources – a country's human capital. The concept encompasses investment in the skills of the labour force, including education and vocational training to develop specific skills.

Human resource development (HRD) A strategic approach to investing in human capital. It draws on other human resource processes, including resourcing and performance assessment to identify actual and potential talent. HRD provides a framework for self-development, training programmes and career progression to meet an organization's future skill requirements.

Human resource flow Movement of people through an organization commencing with recruitment.

Human resource management A philosophy of people management based on the belief that human resources are uniquely important to sustained business success. An organization gains competitive advantage by using its people effectively, drawing on their expertise and ingenuity to meet clearly defined objectives. HRM is aimed at recruiting capable, flexible and committed people, managing and rewarding their performance and developing key competencies. *See also* 'Hard HRM', 'Soft HRM'.

Human resource planning (HRP) A process which anticipates and maps out the consequences of business strategy on an organization's human resource requirements. This is reflected in planning of skill and competence needs as well as total headcounts.

Human resource strategy Overall plan for staffing, developing and rewarding employees and outsourced human resources tied to business objectives.

Image The apparent totality of knowledge and abilities as outwardly presented by an individual or group. Can be false. See also 'Impression management'.

Impression management A deliberate process in which a personal image is learned or acquired through training. *See also* 'Image'.

Indirect The opposite of direct or obvious.

Individualism Opposite of collectivism. Preference to work individually rather than as part of a group.

Induction Initial orientation and training of a new recruit.

Industrial democracy Egalitarian notion of worker involvement in decisionmaking.

In-group Favoured and usually long-standing members of a society, department or organization.

Institutionalized racism An indirect and largely invisible process which can be compared with cloning and the glass ceiling. It is a term encompassing the often unintentional barriers and selection/promotion procedures which serve to disadvantage members of ethnic minority groups.

Japanization A term that first came into vogue in the mid-1980s. It is used as a label for the attempts of Western firms to make practical use of 'Japanese' ideas and practices and as a description of the presence and impact of Japanese subsidiaries overseas.

Job analysis The process of job analysis is that of gathering and analysing job-related information. This includes details about tasks to be performed as part of a job and the personal qualities required to do so. Job analysis can provide information for a variety of purposes including: determining training needs, development criteria, appropriate pay and productivity improvements. For resourcing purposes, job analysis can generate job and personnel specifications.

Job description List of essential tasks involved in a particular job.

Labour market The setting in which people who can provide labour meet those who need labour. Labour markets can be: internal, within an organization, or external, outside the organization. Labour market is a somewhat old-fashioned term which implies physical labour as opposed to the time, knowledge and intellectual effort required in many modern jobs. 'Job market' or 'employment market' are more meaningful in today's context. *See* 'Employment market'.

Learning A process of acquiring skills and knowledge.

Manpower planning (obsolete) 'A strategy for the acquisition, utilization, improvement and retention of an enterprise's human resources' (anonymous government publication cited in Pratt and Bennett (1989, p.: 101). *See also* 'Human resource planning'.

Mentoring Individual–individual support in an organization providing guidance on career development, learning and performance.

Michigan Significant in HRM for the matching model developed by its business school.

Minimum wage Lowest allowable level of pay within a state or country.

Occupational segregation Disproportionate representation of particular groups in specific sectors, job-types or levels of responsibility. Horizontal segregation places men and women, for example, in different jobs, such as chambermaids (women) and porters (men). Vertical segregation places one group in better-paid positions than another group, so that men are better represented at managerial levels while women are concentrated in lower, administrative jobs.

Option scheme Right to buy shares in an employing organization, often at a favourable price.

Organization The means by which human and other resources are deployed so that work gets done.

Organizational development (OD) Methodology of change characterized by an ongoing series of relatively small improvements.

Organizational goals The logical starting point for human resource management lies in an organization's goals – the reasons for its existence. Most modern businesses express these goals in the form of a mission statement. The allocation and control of human resources serves to assist or constrain the achievement of these objectives.

Particularism A form of discrimination favouring particular groups and individuals over others. It derives from a reliance on personal relationships such as ethnic origin, religion or tribal community. It contrasts with universalism in which personal relationships are ignored and emphasis is on other criteria such as qualifications, expertise and ability to do the job.

Performance A critical element in HRM, the management of which can lead to enhanced competitiveness.

Performance assessment One of the many people management techniques which 'classify and order individuals hierarchically' (Townley, 1994, p.33). Modern assessment is often focused on competences. *See also* 'Appraisals'.

Performance management 'A strategic and integrated approach to increasing the effectiveness of organizations by improving the performance of the people who work in them and by developing the capabilities of teams and individual contributors.' (Armstrong and Baron, 1998)

Performance-related pay (PRP) Pay based on merit as assessed by a performance management process.

Peripheral workforces Secondary or less crucial workers as opposed to core employees.

Personality Generally expressed in terms of types or traits, the latter form the basis of most personality tests used for resourcing and the documentation employed for many performance appraisal systems. An alternative approach is to regard personality as an artefact of a particular set of circumstances. In other words, apparent personality depends on the meaning individuals give to a particular situation.

Personnel specification 'The demands of the job translated into human terms' (Arnold, Robertson and Cooper, 1991, p.: 95). Personnel specifications list 'essential' criteria which must be satisfied, and other criteria which rule out certain people from being able to do the job.

Person perception The perception and evaluation of other people using cues such as facial expression, posture, gesture, tone of voice, etc.

Pluralism The acceptance of several alternative approaches, interests or goals within the same organization or society. A view which recognizes that every organization is composed of different interests which are not balanced. Pluralists accept that conflict is natural and are concerned with the means by which it can be managed.

Positive action Measures to prevent discrimination by insisting, for example, on non-discriminatory recruitment procedures, training programmes and pay rates. This does not include any preferential treatment for disadvantaged groups.

Power distance The perceived status differences between people with high and low degrees of power.

Psychometric model The dominant approach to selection in British and US textbooks. In its traditional form, it grounds the 'best-person' model in psychological theory and testing. It embodies the use of refined techniques to achieve the best 'match' between job characteristics identified by formal job analysis and individual characteristics measured by psychological tests, structured interviews and other assessment methods.

Race discrimination Unfavourable treatment on the grounds of race or ethnic origin.

Reorganization A move from one form of organization to another. For example, a business may change from a divisional to a network structure.

Restructuring Breaking up and recombining organizational structures in order to reduce costs, eliminate duplication and achieve greater efficiency.

Reward management Management of pay, benefits and other forms of compensation.

Rewards Pay, incentives, bonuses and other means of compensating individuals for the effort and time they devote to work.

Selection A key element of employee resourcing in which successful applicants are evaluated and chosen by means of interviews and tests.

Sexual harassment Definitions vary considerably but most are agreed that it is sexual attention which is unwanted, repeated, and affects an employee's work performance or expectations from her/his job. However, it is possible for one incident to be sufficiently severe to be regarded as harassment. It differs from sexual banter or flirting since it is one-way; it does not have the involvement and acceptance of both parties. In the USA, the Equal Employment Opportunity Commission has extended the definition of sexual harassment to include a range of actions which lead to a 'hostile work environment'. This definition includes unwelcome touching, joking, teasing, innuendos, slurs, and the display of sexually explicit materials.

Social market A term coined by Alfred Müller-Armack, Secretary of State at the Economics Ministry in Bonn, Federal Republic of Germany between 1958 and 1963. He defined the social market as an economic system that combined market freedom with social equilibrium. In this kind of economic system the government plays a regulating role and creates the framework for market processes, going beyond securing competition to ensure social equity.

Soft planning Human resource planning based on factors other than numbers of employees.

Stakeholders Recognizably separate groups or institutions with a special interest in an organization. These include shareholders, employees, managers, customers, suppliers, lenders and government. Each group has its own priorities and demands and fits into the power structure controlling the organization.

Strategic HRM Directing people, processes and HR systems to achieve strategic objectives so that individual goals are tied to the business needs of the whole organization.

Substance The body of competences, knowledge and experience required to fulfil a particular function.

Synergy Making the new whole worth more than its old parts, sometimes described as $2 + 2 = 5$. Synergies involve economies from integrating activities, horizontally or vertically; but also unrealized potential for new ideas, products or processes by melding expertise from the different sources into centres of excellence.

Talent management A strategic and integrated approach to developing a skilled and competent workforce, involving targeted recruitment, development and retention.

Targeting Quotas for the employment of particular groups have been enforced in the USA. In Europe quota systems have been applied to the disabled and, in a few countries, other groups such as ex-servicemen but enforcement was not usually strict. *See also* 'Affirmative action'.

Tokenism The employment or promotion of isolated individuals to represent their gender or colour. For example, a 12-member board of directors with one token woman and one token ethnic minority person.

Turnover *See* 'Employee turnover'.

Uncertainty avoidance How people deal with conflict, particularly aggression and the expression of feelings. High uncertainty avoidance favours precise rules, teachers who are always right and superiors who should be obeyed without question. Low uncertainty avoidance favours flexibility, discussion and delegation of decisionmaking.

Unitarism A managerialist stance which assumes that everyone in an organization is a member of a team with a common purpose. The unitarist view is implicit in American models of HRM. It embodies a central concern of HRM, that an organization's people, whether managers or lower-level employees, should share the same objectives and work together harmoniously. From this perspective, conflicting objectives are seen as negative and dysfunctional.

World view A set of values and beliefs held by members of a particular culture. This is meaningful to its members but alien to others.

Abrahart, A. and Verme, P. (2001) 'Labor market policies: theoretical background', in I.D. Ortitz (ed.) *Social Protection in Asia and the Pacific*, Asian Development Bank.

Adams, K. (1991) 'Externalisation vs specialisation: what is happening to personnel?', *Human Resource Management Journal* 1(4): 40–54.

Adobor, H. and Daneshfar, A. (2006) 'Management simulations: determining their effectiveness', *The Journal of Management Development* 25(2): 151–68.

Aguinis, H., Michaelis, S.E. and Jones, N.M. (2005) 'Demand for certified human resources professionals in internetbased job announcements', *International Journal of Selection and Assessment* 13(2): 160–71.

Alker, L. and McHugh, D. (2000) 'Human resource maintenance? Organisational rationales for the introduction of employee assistance programmes', *Journal of Managerial Psychology* 15(4): 303–23.

Allan, C., Brosnan, P. and Walsh, P. (1999) 'Human resource strategies, workplace reform and industrial restructuring in Australia and New Zealand', *International Journal of Human Resource Management* 10(5): 828–41.

Alonderiene, R. (2010) 'Enhancing informal learning to improve job satisfaction: Perspective of SMEs managers in Lithuania', *Baltic Journal of Management* 5(2): 257–87.

Al–Raisi, A., Amin, S. and Tahir, S. (2010) 'Determinants of performance management system in UAE public sector', *International Journal of Trade and Global Markets* 3(3) (26 August): 267–79.

American Management Association (2000) *Auditing Your Human Resources Department*, AMACOM.

Anaby, D. Jarus, T., Backman, C. and Zumbo, B. (2010) 'The Role of Occupational Characteristics and Occupational Imbalance in Explaining Well–being', *Applied Research in Quality of Life* 5(2) (June): 81–104.

Anderson, D. and Kelliher, C. (2009) 'Flexible working and engagement: the importance of choice', *Strategic HR Review* 8(2): 13–18.

Anderson, N., Salgado, J. F, and Hülsheger, U.R. (2010) 'Applicant Reactions in Selection: Comprehensive meta–analysis into reaction generalization versus situational specificity', *International Journal of Selection and Assessment* 18(3) (September): 291–304.

Anderson, N. and Witvliet, C. (2008) 'Fairness Reactions to Personnel Selection Methods: An international comparison between the Netherlands, the United States, France, Spain, Portugal, and Singapore', *International Journal of Selection and Assessment* 16(1) (March): 1–13.

Andrisani, P. and Nestel, G. (1976) 'Internal-external control as contributor to and outcome of work experience', *Journal of Applied Psychology* 61: 156–65.

Antila, E. (2006) 'The role of HR managers in international mergers and acquisitions: a multiple case study', *International Journal of Human Resource Management* 17(6): 999–1020.

Arasli, H. and Tumer, M. (2010) 'Nepotism, Favoritism and Cronyism: a study of their effects on job stress and job satisfaction in the banking industry of North Cyprus', Social *Behavior and Personality: an international journal* 36(9): 1237–1250.

Ardichvili, A. and Kuchinke, K.P. (2009) 'International Perspectives on the Meaning of Work and Working: Current Research and Theory', *Advances in Developing Human Resources*, 11, (2): 155–67.

Argyle, M. (1991) *Cooperation: The Basis of Sociability*, Routledge.

Armstrong, M. (1987) 'Human resource management: a case of the emperor's new clothes?', *Personnel Management* (August): 31–4.

Armstrong, M. (1992) *Human Resource Management: Strategy and Action*, Kogan Page.

Armstrong, M. (1994) *The Reality of Strategic HRM*, paper presented at the Strategic Direction of Human Resource Management Conference, Nottingham Trent University, 14–15 December.

Armstrong, M. and Baron, A. (1998) *Performance Management: The New Realities*, Chartered Institute of Personnel and Development (CIPD).

Arnold, J., Robertson, I.T. and Cooper, C.L. (1991) *Work Psychology*, Pitman.

Arrowsmith, J. and Marginson, P. (2010) 'The decline of incentive pay in British manufacturing', *Industrial Relations Journal* 41(4): 289–311.

Atkinson, C. and Hall, Laura (2009) 'The Role of Gender in Varying Forms of Flexible Working', *Gender, Work and Organization* 16(6): 650–666.

Atkinson, J. (1984) 'Manpower strategies for flexible organizations', *Personnel Management* (August): 28–31.

Ausburn, L. (2004) 'Course design elements most valued by adult learners in blended online education environments: an American perspective', *Educational Media International* 41(4): 327–37.

Autor, D.H. and Houseman, S.N. (2010) 'Do Temporary–Help Jobs Improve Labor Market Outcomes for Low–Skilled Workers? Evidence from "Work First"', *American Economic Journal: Applied Economics* 2(3): 96–128.

Awad, G.H., Cokley, K. and Ravitch, J. (2005) 'Attitudes toward affirmative action: a comparison of color-blind versus modern racist attitudes', *Journal of Applied Social Psychology* 35(7): 1384–99.

Bach, S. (2005) *Managing Human Resources: Personnel Management in Transition*, Wiley–Blackwell.

Bacha, E. (2010) 'The relationships among organizational performance, environmental uncertainty, and employees' perceptions of CEO charisma', *The Journal of Management Development* 29(1): 28–37.

Balsam, S., Gifford, R. and Kim, S. (2007) 'The effect of stock option grants on voluntary employee turnover', *Review of Accounting and Finance* 6(1): 5–14.

Ban, C. (2010) 'Reforming the staffing process in the European Union institutions: moving the sacred cow out of the road', *International Review of Administrative Sciences*, Mar 2010; 76: 5 24.

Bangerter, A., König, C.J., Blatti, S. and Salvisberg, A. (2009) 'How Widespread is Graphology in Personnel Selection Practice? A case study of a job market myth', *International Journal of Selection and Assessment* 17(2): 219–230(12).

Barclay, J.M. (2001) 'Improving selection interviews with structure: organisations' use of "behavioural" interviews', *Personnel Review* 30(1): 81–101.

Barry, M. and May, R. (2004) 'New employee representation: legal developments and New Zealand unions', *Employee Relations* 26(2): 203–23.

Bassett-Jones, N. (2005) 'The paradox of diversity management, creativity and innovation', *Creativity and Innovation Management* 14(2): 169–75.

Bates, R. (2002) 'Liking and similarity as predictors of multisource ratings', *Personnel Review* 31(5): 540–52.

Beachler, D.W. (2009) 'Victory and the Promise of Reform: Labor and the 2008 Election', *Working USA* 12(2): 265–77.

Beal, B. (2004) 'Psychological search for Hilton hotel managers', *Human Resource Management International Digest* 12(1): 30.

Beaumont, P.B. (1992) 'The US human resource management literature: a review', in G. Salaman (ed.) *Human Resource Strategies*, Sage.

Bebchuk, L.A. and Fried, J.M. (2005) 'Pay without performance: overview of the issues', *Journal of Applied Corporate Finance* 17(4): 8–23.

Beer, M., Spector, B.A., Lawrence, P.R., Mills, Q. and Walton, R.E. (1984) *Managing Human Assets*, Harvard Business Press.

Bender, R. (2004) 'Why do companies use performance-related pay for their executive directors?', *Corporate Governance* 12(4): 521–33.

Bendl, R. and Schmidt, A. (2010) 'From "Glass Ceilings" to "Firewalls" Different Metaphors for Describing Discrimination', *Gender, Work and Organization* 17(5): 612–34.

Bennis, W. (1990) 'Managing the dream: leadership in the 21st century', *Training: The Magazine of Human Resource Development* 27(5): 44–6.

Ben-Tovim, G., Gabriel, J., Law, I. and Stredder, K. (1992) 'A political analysis of local struggles for racial equality', in P. Braham, A. Rattansi and R. Skellington (eds) *Racism and Antiracism*, Sage.

Bercusson, B. (2002) 'The European social model comes to Britain', *Industrial Law Journal* 31(3): 209–44.

Bertua, C., Anderson, N. and Salgado, J.F. (2005) 'The predictive validity of cognitive ability tests: a UK metaanalysis', *Journal of Occupational and Organizational Psychology* 78(3): 387–409.

Bevan, S. and Thompson, M. (1992) *Merit Pay, Performance Appraisals and Attitudes to Women's Work*, IMS Publications.

Biggs, D. (2006) 'The decline of the temporary worker: a regional perspective', *Local Economy* 21(3): 249–63.

Birdi, K., Clegg, C., Patterson, M., Robinson, A., Stride, C.B., Wall, T.D., and Wood, S.J. (2008) 'The Impact of Human Resource and Operational Management Practices on Company Productivity: A Longitudinal Study', *Personnel Psychology*, 61: 467–501.

Blackman, M.C. (2002a) 'The employment interview via the telephone: are we sacrificing accurate personality judgments for cost efficiency?', *Journal of Research in Personality* 36(3): 208–23.

Blackman, M.C. (2002b) 'Personality judgment and the utility of the unstructured employment interview', *Basic and Applied Social Psychology* 24(3): 241–50.

Blake–Beard, S., O'Neill, R., Ingols, C., Shapiro, M. (2010) 'Social sustainability, flexible work arrangements, and diverse women', *Gender in Management: An International Journal* 25(5): 408–25.

Blanksby, M. and Iles, P. (1990) 'Recent developments in assessment centre theory, practice and operation', *Personnel Review* 19(6): 33–42.

Blanton, H., George, G. and Crocker, J. (2001) 'Contexts of system justification and system evaluation: exploring the social comparison strategies of the (not yet) contented female worker', *Group Processes and Intergroup Relations* 4(2): 126–37.

Blickle, G., Schneider, P.B., Meurs, J.A. and Perrewé, P.L. (2010) 'Antecedents and Consequences of Perceived Barriers to Obtaining Mentoring: A Longitudinal Investigation', *Journal of Applied Social Psychology* 40(8): 1897–920.

Blinkhorn, S. and Johnson, C. (1990) 'The insignificance of personality testing', *Nature* 348(6303): 671–2.

Blyton, P. and Turnbull, P. (1992) *Reassessing Human Resource Management*, Sage.

Blyton, P. and Turnbull, P. (1994) *The Dynamics of Employee Relations*, Macmillan.

Bourne, A. and Haddon, D. (2010) 'An evidence–based approach to developing HR strategy: transformation in Royal Mail', *Strategic HR Review* 9(1): 10–16.

Boxall, P. (1996) 'The strategic HRM debate and the resource based view of the firm', *Human Resource Management Journal* 6(3): 59–75.

Boxall, P. and Macky, K. (2009) 'Research and theory on high–performance work systems: progressing the high–involvement stream', *Human Resource Management Journal* 19(1): 3–23.

Boxall, P. and Purcell, J. (2003) *Strategy and Human Resource Management*, Palgrave Macmillan.

Boyatzis, R.E. (1982) *The Competent Manager*, John Wiley & Sons.

Boyd, C. (2001) 'HRM in the airline industry: strategies and outcomes', *Personnel Review* 30(4): 438–53

Braham, P., Rattansi, A. and Skellington, R. (eds) (1992) *Racism and Antiracism*, Sage.

Branine, M. (2008) 'Graduate recruitment and selection in the UK: A study of the recent changes in methods and expectations', *Career Development International* 13(6): 497–513.

Braverman, H. (1974) *Labor and Monopoly Capital: The Degradation of Work in the Twentieth Century*, Monthly Review Press.

Bray, M. and Underhill, E. (2009) 'Industry differences in the neoliberal transformation of Australian industrial relations', *Industrial Relations Journal* 40(5): 372–92.

Breakwell, G.M. (1990) *Interviewing*, BPS/Routledge.

Bret, B.J., Matthews, M.C., Hartley, D.L., and Whitaker, D.H. (2009) 'Using Biodata to Predict Turnover, Organizational Commitment, and Job Performance in Healthcare', *International Journal of Selection and Assessment* 17(2): 189–202.

Brewster, C. (2002) *Transfer of HRM Practices around the World*, paper presented at Human Resource Management across Countries: the Cultural Dimension Conference, Athens University of Economics and Business, 17 October 2002.

Brewster, C., Croucher, R., Wood, G. and Brookes, M. (2007) 'Collective and individual voice: convergence in Europe?' (2007) *International Journal of Human Resource Management* 18(7): 1246–62.

Brewster, C. and Tyson, S. (eds) (1991) *International Comparisons in Human Resource Management*, Pitman.

Briggs, C. (2001) 'Australian exceptionalism: the role of trade unions in the emergence of enterprise bargaining', *The Journal of Industrial Relations* 43(1): 27–43.

Brown, M. and Heywood, J.S. (2005) 'Performance appraisal systems: determinants and change', *British Journal of Industrial Relations* 43(4): 659–79.

Brown, M., Hyatt, D. and Benson, J. (2010) 'Consequences of the performance appraisal experience', *Personnel Review* 39(3): 375–96.

Brown, M., Metz, I., Cregan,C. and Kulik, C.T. (2009) 'Irreconcilable differences? Strategic human resource management and employee well-being', *Asia Pacific Journal of Human Resources*, Dec 2009; 47: 270–294.

Brown, S. and Seidner, C. (1998) *Evaluating Corporate Training: Models and Issues*, Kluwer Academic Publishers

Brown, W. (1994) *Bargaining for Full Employment*, Employment Policy Institute.

Bruine de Eruin, W. (2005) 'Save the last dance for me: unwanted serial position effects on jury evaluations', *Acta Psychologica* 118: 245–60.

Bryman, A. (1992) *Charisma and Leadership in Organizations*, Sage.

Brynin, M. (2006) 'Gender, technology and jobs', *The British Journal of Sociology* 57(3): 437–53.

Buono, A.F. (1991) 'Managing strategic alliances: organizational and human resource considerations', *Business and the Contemporary World* 3(4): 92–101.

Busolt, U. and Kugele, K. (2009) 'The gender innovation and research productivity gap in Europe', *International Journal of Innovation and Sustainable Development* 4, (2–3): 109–122.

Butterfield, K.D., Treviño, L.K., Wade, K.J. and Ball, G.A. (2005) 'Organizational punishment from the manager's perspective: an exploratory study', *Journal of Managerial Issues* 17(3): 363–82.

Byham, W. (1984) 'Assessing employees without resorting to a "centre"', *Personnel Management* (October): 55.

Byrne, B. (2009) 'Not just class: towards an understanding of the whiteness of middle–class schooling choice', *Ethnic and Racial Studies* 32(3): 424–441.

Cakar, F. and Bititci, U.S. (2001) *Human Resource Management as a Strategic Input to Manufacturing*, paper presented at the International Working Conference on Strategic Manufacturing, 26–29 August, 2001, Aalborg, Denmark.

Callaghan, G. and Thompson, P. (2002) '"We recruit attitude": the selection and shaping of routine call centre labour', *Journal of Management Studies* 39(2): 233–54.

Campbell, J.P., Dunnette, M., Lawler, E. and Weick, K. (1970) *Managerial Behavior, Performance and Effectiveness*, McGraw-Hill.

Carter, J.L and Hill, G.J E. (2007) 'Critiquing environmental management in indigenous Australia: two case studies', *Area* 39(1): 43–54.

Cascio, W.F. (1998) *Applied Psychology in Human Resource Management*, Prentice-Hall.

Chakkarath, P. (2010) 'Stereotypes in social psychology: The "West–East" differentiation as a reflection of western traditions of thought', *Psychological Studies* 55(1): 18–25.

Chapman, D. and Webster, J. (2006) 'Toward an integrated model of applicant reactions and job choice', *International Journal of Human Resource Management* 17(6): 1032–57.

Chatterjee, S. (2007) 'Why is synergy so difficult in mergers of related businesses? *Strategy and Leadership* 35(2): 46–52.

Chelliah, J. and D'Netto, B. (2006) 'Unfair dismissals in Australia: does arbitration help employees?', *Employee Relations* 28(5): 483–95.

Chung, T.Z. (1991) 'Culture: a key to management communication between the Asian-Pacific area and Europe', *European Management Journal* 9(4): 419–24.

Chung, Y.B., Coleman, M. and Gfroerer, A. (2003) 'Career coaching: practice, training, professional, and ethical issues', *The Career Development Quarterly* 52(2): 141.

CIPD (2000) *Recruitment Survey Report 14*, June, Chartered Institute of Personnel and Development.

CIPD (2006) *Recruitment, Retention and Turnover, Annual Report*, Chartered Institute of Personnel and Development.

Clarke, A.C. (1973) *Profiles of the Future: An Inquiry into the Limits of the Possible*, HarperCollins.

Clarke, L. (2006a) 'Sexual relationships and sexual conduct in the workplace', *Legal Studies* 26(3): 347–68.

Clarke, L. (2006b) 'Valuing labour', *Building Research and Information* 34(3): 246–56.

Claydon, T. (2001) 'Human resource management and the labour market', in I. Beardwell and L. Holden, *Human Resource Management: A Contemporary Approach*, Pearson.

Clemente, M.N. and Greenspan, D.S. (1999) *Empowering Human Resources in the Merger and Acquisition Process: Guidance for HR Professionals in the Key Areas of M&A Planning and Integration*, Clemente, Greenspan and Co.

Coetzer, A. (2006) 'Managers as learning facilitators in small manufacturing firms', *Journal of Small Business and Enterprise Development* 13(3): 351–62.Cohen, M. (2008) 'Union Ethics Training: Building the Legitimacy and Effectiveness of Organized Labor', *WorkingUSA* 11(3): 363–82.

Collis, B., Bianco, M., Margaryan, A. and Waring, B. (2005) 'Putting blended learning to work: a case study from a multinational oil company', *Education, Communication and Information* 5(3): 233–50.

Combs, J., Liu, Y., Hall, A. and Ketchen, D. (2006) 'How much do high–performance work practices matter? A meta–analysis of their effects on organizational performance' *Personnel Psychology*, 59: 501–28.

Conboy, H., Brine, A. and Clarke, J. (2010) 'Emerging technologies as change agent within and across organisational cultures', Source: *International Journal of Web Based Communities* 6(3): 269–83.

Conrad, H. (2010) 'From Seniority to Performance Principle: The Evolution of Pay Practices in Japanese Firms since the 1990s', *Social Science Japan Journal* 2010; 13: 115–35.

Cooper, R. and Ellem, B. (2008) 'The Neoliberal State, Trade Unions and Collective Bargaining in Australia', *British Journal of Industrial Relations* 46 (3): 532–54.

Corbridge, M. and Pilbeam, S. (1998) *Employment Resourcing*, Financial Times/Pitman Publishing.

Cowey, A. (2005) 'Finance training can be fun and effective', *Industrial and Commercial Training* 37 (7): 355–60.

Cox, J. and Tapsell, J. (1991) *The Writing on the Wall: Graphology and Its Validity in Personality Assessments*, paper presented at the British Psychological Society Conference, Cardiff.

Cox, T. Jr., O'Neill, P.H. and Quinn, R.E. (2001) *Creating the Multicultural Organization: A Strategy for Capturing the Power of Diversity*, John Wiley & Sons.

Cressey, P. (1993) 'Employee participation', in M. Gold (ed.) *The Social Dimension: Employment Policy in the European Community*, Macmillan.

Crittan, P. (1993) *Investing in People: Towards Corporate Capability*, Butterworth-Heinemann.

Damaske, S. (2009) 'Brown Suits Need Not Apply: The Intersection of Race, Gender, and Class in Institutional Network Building', *Sociological Forum* 24(2): 402–24.

Davison, H.K. and Burke, M.J. (2000) 'Sex discrimination in simulated employment contexts: a meta-analytic investigation', *Journal of Vocational Behavior* 56(2): 225–48.

Day, D.V. and Schleicher, D.J. (2006) 'Self-monitoring at work: a motive-based perspective', *Journal of Personality* 74(3): 685–714.

Dayan, K., Fox, S., and Kasten, R. (2008) 'The Preliminary Employment Interview as a Predictor of Assessment Center Outcomes', *International Journal of Selection and Assessment* 16(2): 102–111.

Deakin, S. and Koukiadaki, A. (2009) 'Governance Processes, Labour Management Partnership and Employee Voice in the Construction of Heathrow Terminal 5', *Industrial Law Journal* 38(4): 365–89.

Dechawatanapaisal, D. and Siengthai, S. (2006) 'The impact of cognitive dissonance on learning work behavior', *The Journal of Workplace Learning* 18(1): 42–54.

Deckop, J.R. (ed) (2006) *Human Resource Management Ethics*, Information Age Publishing.

De Graft-Johnson, A., Manley, S. and Greed, C. (2005) 'Diversity or the lack of it in the architectural profession', *Construction Management and Economics* 23(10): 1035–43.

de Meijer, L.A.L., Born, M., van Zielst, J., and van der Molen, H.T. (2007) 'Analyzing Judgments of Ethnically Diverse Applicants During Personnel Selection: A study at the Dutch police', *International Journal of Selection and Assessment* 15(2): 139–52.

DeNisi, A.S. and Pritchard, R.D. (2006) 'Performance appraisal, performance management and improving individual performance: a motivational framework', *Management and Organization Review* 2(2): 253–77.

Dick, P. and Nadin, S. (2006) 'Reproducing gender inequalities? A critique of realist assumptions underpinning personnel selection research and practice', *Journal of Occupational and Organizational Psychology* 79(3): 481–98.

Dickinson, J. (2006) 'Employees' preferences for the bases of pay differentials', *Employee Relations* 28(2): 164–83.

Dierendonck, D. van, Haynes, C., Borrill, C. and Stride, C. (2007) 'Effects of upward feedback on leadership behaviour toward subordinates', *The Journal of Management Development* 26(3): 228–38.

Dipboye, R.L. (2007) 'Eight outrageous statements about HR science', *Human Resource Management Review* 17: 96–106.

Dipboye, R.L., Gaugler, B.B., Hayes, T.L. and Parker, D. (2001) 'The validity of unstructured panel interviews: more than meets the eye?', *Journal of Business and Psychology* 16(1): 35–49.

DiPrete, T.A., Eirich, G. and Pittinsky, M. (2010) "Compensation Benchmarking, Leapfrogs, and the Surge in Executive Pay." *American Journal of Sociology* (May).

Dominelli, L. (1992) 'An uncaring profession: an examination of racism in social work', in P. Braham, A. Rattansi and R. Skellington (eds) *Racism and Antiracism*, Sage.

Downey, L.A., Papageorgiou, V. and Stough, C. (2006) 'Examining the relationship between leadership, emotional intelligence and intuition in senior female managers', *Leadership and Organizational Development Journal* 27(4): 250–64.

Drenth, P.J.D. and Algera, J. (1987) 'Personnel Selection', in P.B. Warr (ed.) *Psychology at Work*, Penguin.

Driscoll, M. (2002) *Web-Based Training: Designing e-Learning Experiences*, Jossey-Bass/Pfeiffer.

Druker, J. and Stanworth, C. (2004) 'Mutual expectations: a study of the threeway relationship between employment agencies, their client organisations and white-collar agency temps', *Industrial Relations Journal* 35(1): 58–75.

Drydakis, N. and Vlassis, M. (2010) 'Ethnic Discrimination in the Greek Labour Market: occupational access, insurance coverage and age offers', *The Manchester School* 78(3): 201–18.

Dulewicz, V. (1991) 'Improving assessment centres', *Personnel Management* (June): 50–5.

Dunning, D., Heath, C. and Suls, J.M. (2004) 'Flawed self-assessment: implications for health, education and the workplace', *Psychological Science and the Public Interest* 5(3): 69–106.

Ebbinghaus B. (2003) 'Ever larger unions: organisational restructuring and its impact on union confederations', *Industrial Relations Journal* 34(5): 446–60.

Eder, R. and Harris, M. (1999) 'Employment interview research: historical update and introduction', in R. Eder and M. Harris (eds) *The Employment Interview Handbook*, Sage Publications.

Eiser, J.R. (1994) *Attitudes, Chaos and the Connectivist Mind*, Blackwell.

Ehnert, I. (2009) *Sustainable Human resource Management: a Conceptual and Exploratory Analysis From a Paradox Perspective*, Physica-Verlag.

Eleftheriou, A. and Robertson, I. (1999) 'A Survey of Management Selection Practices in Greece', *International Journal of Selection and Assessment* 7(4): 203–208.

Elkjaer, B. (2001) 'The learning organization: an undelivered promise', *Management Learning* 32(4): 437–52.

El-Kot, G. and Leat, M. (2008) 'A survey of recruitment and selection practices in Egypt', *Education, Business and Society: Contemporary Middle Eastern Issues* 1(3): 200–12.

Ellin, A. (2004) 'What your handwriting says about your career', *New York Times* (late edition (East Coast) New York, N.Y.), 18 July: 10.1.

Ellinger, A.D., Ellinger, A.E., Yang, B. and Howton, S.W. (2002) 'The relationship between the learning organization concept and firms' financial performance: an empirical assessment', *Human Resource Development Quarterly* 13(1): 5–21.

English, G. (1991) 'Tuning up for performance management', *Training and Development Journal* (April): 56–60.

Entrekin, L. and Chung, Y.W. (2001) 'Attitudes towards different sources of executive appraisal: a comparison of Hong Kong Chinese and American managers in Hong Kong', *International Journal of Human Resource Management* 12(6): 965–87.

Erturk, I., Froud, J., Johal, S. and Williams, K. (2005) 'Pay for corporate performance or pay as social division? Rethinking the problem of top management pay in giant corporations', *Competition and Change* 9(1): 49–74.

Fairris, D. and Askenazy, P. (2010) 'Works Councils and Firm Productivity in France', *Journal of Labor Research* 31(3): 209–29.

Fang, A. (2009) 'Workplace responses to vacancies and skill shortages in Canada', *International Journal of Manpower* 30(4): 326–48.

Ficery, K., Herd, T., and Pursche, W. (2007) 'Where has all the synergy gone? The M&A puzzle', *Journal of Business Strategy* 28(5): 29–35.

Flanders, A. (1970) *Management and Unions*, Faber & Faber.

Flesher, J. (2009) 'The Meaning of Working: A Perspective From Practice', *Advances in Developing Human Resources* 11(2): 253–60.

Fletcher, C. (2001) 'Performance appraisal and management: the developing research agenda', *Journal of Occupational and Organizational Psychology* 74(4): 473–87.

Fletcher, C. and Williams, R. (1992) 'The route to performance management', *Personnel Management* (October): 42–7.

Fontanin, M. (2010) 'E-learning contribution to the building of a multi-generational workplace learning community in an academic library: observations drawn from practice', *Library Hi Tech News incorporating Online and CD Notes* 27(2): 15–19.

Forbes, R. (1996) 'Performance management', *HR Monthly*, November 1996, Australian Human Resource Institute.

Ford, T.E. (2000) 'Effects of sexist humor on tolerance of sexist events', *Personality and Social Psychology Bulletin* 26(9): 1094–107.

Fortin, N.M. (2005) 'Gender role attitudes and the labour-market outcomes of women across OECD countries', *Oxford Review of Economic Policy* 21(3): 416–38.

Flynn, M. (2010) 'Mandatory retirement in the police service: the case of the London MPS', *Policing: An International Journal of Police Strategies and Management* 33(2): 376–391.

Fofack, H. (2009) 'Determinants Of Globalization And Growth Prospects For Sub-Saharan African Countries', *Research Working papers*, World Bank, November: 1–34.

Forstenlechner, I. and Al–Waqfi, M.A. (2010) 'A job interview for Mo, but none for Mohammed: Religious discrimination against immigrants in Austria and Germany', *Personnel Review* 39(6): 767–84.

Fossum, J. and Fitch, M. (1985) 'The effects of individual and contextual attributes on the sizes of recommended salary increases', *Personnel Psychology* 38(autumn): 587–602.

Foster, C. and Harris, L. (2005) 'Easy to say, difficult to do: diversity management in retail', *Human Resource Management Journal* 15(3): 4–17.

Fowler, A. (1987) 'When chief executives discover HRM', *Personnel Management* (January): 3.

Frazer, R.A. and Wiersma, J.J. (2001) 'Prejudice versus discrimination in the employment interview: we may hire equally, but our memories harbour prejudice', *Human Relations* 54(2): 173–91.

Freidank, C–C, Velte, P. and Weber, S. (2010) 'The changing German corporate governance system normative implications and empirical evidence', *International Journal of Corporate Governance* 2(1): 42–57.

French, W.L. and Bell, C.H. (1990) *Organization Development: Behavioral Science Interventions for Organization Improvement*, 4th edn, Prentice-Hall.

Frijters, P., Shields, M.A. and Price, S.W. (2005) 'Job search methods and their success: a comparison of immigrants and natives in the UK', *The Economic Journal* 115(507): F359–F376.

Fuller, A., Beck, V. and Unwin, L. (2005) 'The gendered nature of apprenticeship: employers' and young people's perspectives', *Education + Training* 47(4–5): 298–311.

Furnham, A. (1990) *The Protestant Work Ethic: The Psychology of Work-related Beliefs and Behaviours*, Routledge.

Furnham, A. (1992) *Personality at Work*, Routledge.

Furnham, A. (2008) 'HR Professionals' Beliefs About, and Knowledge of, Assessment Techniques and Psychometric Tests', *International Journal of Selection and Assessment* 16(3): 300–305.

Gall, G. (2007) 'Turning full circle? Changing industrial relations in the magazine industry in Britain', *Personnel Review* 36(1): 91–108.

Gates, S. (2006) 'Time to take negotiation seriously', *Industrial and Commercial Training* 38(5): 238–41.

Gates, S., and Langevin, P. (2010) 'Human capital measures, strategy, and performance: HR managers' perceptions', *Accounting, Auditing & Accountability Journal* 23(1): 111–132.

Gazioglu, S. and Tansel, A. (2006) 'Job satisfaction in Britain: individual and job related factors', *Applied Economics* 38(10): 1163–71.

Geare, A., Edgar, F. and McAndrew, I. (2006) 'Employment relationships: ideology and HRM practice', *International Journal of Human Resource Management* 17(7): 1190–208.

Geerlings, W.S.J. and van Veen, K. (2006) 'The future qualities of workforces: a simulation study of the long-term consequences of minor selection decisions', *International Journal of Human Resource Management* 17(7): 1254–66.

Giangreco, A., Sebastiano, A. and Peccei, R. (2009) 'Trainees' reactions to training: an analysis of the factors affecting overall satisfaction with training', *International Journal of Human Resource Management* 20(1): 96–111.

Gibb, S. (2002) *Learning and Development: Processes, Practices and Perspectives at Work*, Palgrave/Macmillan.

Giddens, A. (1989) *Sociology*, Polity Press.

Giles, E. and Williams, R. (1991) 'Can the personnel department survive quality management?', *Personnel Management* (April).

Gilley, J.W. and Gilley, A.M. (2002) *Strategically Integrated HRD*, Perseus Books Group.

Girma, S., Thompson, S. and Wright, P.W. (2006) 'The impact of merger activity on executive pay in the United Kingdom', *Economica* 73(290): 321–39.

Glover, J. (1988) *I: The Philosophy and Psychology of Personal Identity*, Penguin.

Godard, J. (2010) "What Is Best for Workers? The Implications of Workplace and Human Resource Management Practices Revisited" *Industrial Relations* 49(3): 466–88.

Good, K. and Taylor, I. (2008) 'Botswana: A Minimalist Democracy', *Democratization* 15(4): 750–65.

Gordon, J.N. (2005) 'A remedy for the executive pay problem: the case for "compensation discussion and analysis"', *Journal of Applied Corporate Finance* 17(4): 24–35.

Gospel, H. and Sako, M. (2010) 'The unbundling of corporate functions: the evolution of shared services and outsourcing in human resource management', *Ind. Corp. Change*, Mar 2010; 10.1093/icc/dtq002.

Goss, D. (1994) *Principles of Human Resource Management*, Routledge.

Graham, H.T. and Bennett, R. (1992) *Human Resources Management*, 7th edn, M&E Handbook Series, Pitman.

Graham, M. (2005) 'How to maximize your investment in IT training', *Human Resource Management International Digest* 13(2): 3–4.

Green, C. and Heywood, J.S. (2008) 'Does Performance Pay Increase Job Satisfaction?', *Economica* 75(300): 710–28.

Gregg, P. and Wadsworth, J. (2010) *The UK Labour Market and the 2008 2009 Recession*, June 2010, Paper No. CEPOP25: CEP Occasional Papers, London School of Economics.

Gubman, E. (2004) 'HR strategy and planning: from birth to business results', *HR. Human Resource Planning* 27(1): 13–24.

Guest, D. (1987) 'Human resource management and industrial relations', *Journal of Management Studies* 24(5): 503–21.

Guest, D. (1989) 'Personnel and HRM: can you tell the difference?', *Personnel Management* (January): 48–51.

Guest, D. (1992) 'Right enough to be dangerously wrong: an analysis of the In Search of Excellence phenomenon', in G. Salaman (ed.) *Human Resource Strategies*, Sage.

Guest, D.E. (1997) 'Human resource management and performance: a review and research agenda', *International Journal of Human Resource Management* 8(3): 263–76.

Gunz, H. (1990) 'The dual meaning of managerial careers: organizational and individual levels of analysis', *Journal of Management Studies* 26(May): 3.

Guthrie, J.; Flood, P., Liu, W., and MacCurtain, S. (2009) 'High performance work systems in Ireland: human resource and organizational outcomes', *International Journal of Human Resource Management* 20(1): 112–25.

Guy, F. (2005) 'Earnings distribution, corporate governance and CEO pay', *International Review of Applied Economics* 19(1): 51–65.

Haire, M. (1959) 'Psychological problems relevant to business and industry', *Psychological Bulletin* 56: 169–94.

Hakim, C. (2006) 'Women, careers, and work-life preferences', *British Journal of Guidance and Counselling* 34(3): 279–94.

Hall, L. and Atkinson, C. (2006) 'Improving working lives: flexible working and the role of employee control', *Employee Relations* 28(4): 374–86.

Hall, R. (2006) 'Temporary agency work and HRM in Australia: "cooperation, specialisation and satisfaction for the good of all?"', *Personnel Review* 35(2): 158–74.

Hallier, J. (2009) 'Rhetoric but whose reality? The influence of employability messages on employee mobility tactics and work group identification', *International Journal of Human Resource Management* 20(4): 846–68.

Hamblin, A.C. (1974) *Evaluation and Control of Training*, McGraw-Hill.

Hamilton, E.A., Gordon, J.R. and Whelan-Berry, K.S. (2006) 'Understanding the work-life conflict of never-married women without children', *Women in Management Review* 21(5): 393–415.

Hammonds, K.H. (2005) 'Why we hate HR', *Fast Company* 97(August): 40.

Handy, C. (1989) *The Age of Unreason*, Business Books.

Hanley, G. and Nguyen, L. (2005) 'Right on the money: what do Australian unions think of performance-related pay?', *Employee Relations* 27(2): 141–59.

Hanson, P. (2001) *The M&A Transition Guide: A 10-Step Roadmap for Workforce Integration*, John Wiley & Sons.

Harbridge, R. and Walsh, P. (2002) 'Globalisation and labour market deregulation in Australia and New Zealand: different approaches, similar outcomes', *Employee Relations* 24(4): 423–36.

Harper, B. (2000) 'Beauty, stature and the labour market: a British cohort study', *Oxford Bulletin of Economics and Statistics* 62(1): 771–800.

Harper, B. and Haq, M. (2001) 'Ambition, discrimination, and occupational attainment: a study of a British cohort', *Oxford Economic Papers* 53(4): 695–720.

Harris, L. (2000) 'Rewarding employee performance: line managers' values, beliefs and perspectives', *International Journal of Human Resource Management* 12(7): 1182–92.

Hart, R.A. and Kawasaki, S. (1999) *Work and Pay in Japan*, Cambridge University Press.

Hatcher, T. (2006) 'An Examination of the Potential of Human Resource Development (HRD) to Improve Organizational Ethics' in *Human Resource Management Ethics*, ed. John R. Deckop, IAP.

Hausknecht, J.P. (2010) 'Candidate Persistence and Personality Test Practice Effects: Implications for Staffing System Management', *Personnel Psychology* 63(2, Summer): 299–24.

Haynes, P. and Allen, M. (2001) 'Partnership as union strategy: a preliminary evaluation', *Employee Relations* 23(2): 164–93.

Hebl, M.R. and Skorinko, J.L. (2005) 'Acknowledging one's physical disability in the interview: does "when" make a difference?', *Journal of Applied Social Psychology* 35(12): 2477–92.

Heery, E. and Salmon, J. (2000) 'The insecurity thesis', in E. Heery and J. Salmon *The Insecure Workforce*, Routledge.

Heilbroner, R.L. (1953) *The Worldly Philosophers: The Lives, Times and Ideas of the Great Economic Thinkers*, Simon and Schuster.

Helman, C.G. (1990) *Culture, Health and Illness*, 2nd edn, Butterworth-Heinemann.

Hempel, P.S. (2001) 'Differences between Chinese and Western managerial views of performance', *Personnel Review* 30(2): 203–26.

Hendry, C. (1995) *Human Resource Management: A Strategic Approach to Employment*, Butterworth-Heinemann.

Hermelin, E., Lievens, F., and Robertson, I.T. (2007) 'The Validity of Assessment Centres for the Prediction of Supervisory Performance Ratings: A meta–analysis', International Journal of Selection and Assessment 15(4): 405–11.

Herpen, M., Praag, M. and Cools, K. (2005) 'The effects of performance measurement and compensation on motivation: an empirical study', *De Economist* 153(3): 303–29.

Herriot, P. and Fletcher, C. (1990) 'Candidate-friendly selection for the 1990s', *Personnel Management* (February): 32–5.

Heywood, J.S. and O'Halloran, P.L. (2005) 'Racial earnings differentials and performance pay', *Journal of Human Resources* 40(2): 435–52.

Highhouse, S. (2010) 'Stubborn Reliance on Intuition and Subjectivity in Employee Selection', *Industrial and Organizational Psychology* 1(3): 333–42.

Hills, P. (2009) 'Costs down, talent up', *Strategic HR Review* 8(4): 29–33.

Hinton, P.R. (1993) *The Psychology of Interpersonal Perception*, Routledge.

Hitzeman, S.E. (1997) *The Strategic Positioning of Today's Benefit Department*, IAHRM.

Hofstede, G. (1980) *Culture's Consequences: International Differences in Work-related Values*, Sage.

Hofstede, G. (1994) *Cultures and Organizations*, HarperCollins (amended paperback edition of the 1991 McGraw-Hill publication).

Hofstede, G. and Bond, M.H. (1988) 'The Confucius connection: from cultural roots to economic growth', *Organizational Dynamics* 16(4): 4–21.

Hogenesch, K. (2004) 'A new science for finding the right employee?', *NZ Business* 18(2): 10.

Hollenbeck, G.P. (2009) 'Executive Selection – What's Right … and What's Wrong', *Industrial and Organizational Psychology* 2(2): 130–43.

Holmes, T.H. and Rahe, R.H. (1967) 'The social readjustment rating scale', *Journal of Psychosomatic Research* 11: 213–8.

Hornung, S., Rousseau, D.M. and Glaser, J. (2009) 'Why supervisors make idiosyncratic deals: antecedents and outcomes of i–deals from a managerial perspective', *Journal of Managerial Psychology* 24(8): 738–64.

Horwitz, F.M., Bravington, D. and Silvis, U. (2006) 'The promise of virtual teams: identifying key factors in effectiveness and failure', *Journal of European Industrial Training* 30(6): 472–94.

Horwitz, F.M., Browning, V., Jain, H. and Steenkamp, A.J. (2002) 'Human resource practices and discrimination in South Africa: overcoming the apartheid legacy', *International Journal of Human Resource Management* 13(7): 1105–18.

Hossain, M.A. and Tisdell, C.A. (2005) 'Closing the gender gap in Bangladesh: inequality in education, employment and earnings', *International Journal of Social Economics* 32(5): 439–53.

Howitt, D. and Owusu-Bempah, J. (1990) 'Racism in a British journal', *Psychologist* (September): 396–9.

Hoxie, R.F. (1923) *Trade Unionism in the United States*, 2nd edn, Appleton-Century Crofts; reproduced in W.E.J. McCarthy (ed.) (1972) *Trade Unions*, Penguin.

Hui, C.H. (1990) 'Work attitudes, leadership styles, and managerial behaviours in different cultures', in R.W. Brislin (ed.) *Applied Cross-Cultural Psychology*, Sage.

Husband, C. (1991) *Race, Conflictual Politics and Anti-racist Social Work: Lessons from the Past for Action in the 90s*, Northern Curriculum Development Project Setting the Context for Change, Central Council for Education and Training in Social Work, Leeds.

Huysman, M. (2000) 'An organizational learning approach to the learning organization', *European Journal of Work and Organizational Psychology* 9(2): 133–45.

Huzzard, T. (2001) 'Discourse for normalizing what? – The learning organization and the workplace trade union response', *Economic and Industrial Democracy* 22(3): 407–31.

Hyman, R. (1988) 'Flexible specialization: miracle or myth?', in R. Hyman and W. Streek (eds) *New Technology and Industrial Relations*, Blackwell.

Iles, P. (2001) 'Employee resourcing', in J. Storey (ed.) *Human Resource Management: A Critical Text*, 2nd edn, Thomson Learning.

Iles, P. and Salaman, G. (1995) 'Recruitment, selection and assessment', in J. Storey (ed.) *Human Resource Management: A Critical Text*, Routledge.

International Labour Organization (2000) *Decent Work and Poverty Reduction in the Global Economy*, paper submitted by the International Labour Office to the Second Session of the Preparatory Committee for the Special Session of the General Assembly on the Implementation of the Outcome of the World Summit for Social Development and Further Initiatives, April 2000.

Isaac, J.E. (2001) 'Performance related pay: the importance of fairness', *The Journal of Industrial Relations* 43(2): 111–23.

Jamroq, J.J. and Overhot, M.H. (2004) 'Building a strategic HR function: continuing the evolution', *HR. Human Resource Planning* 7(1): 51–63.

Jenkins, A. (2001) *Companies' Use of Psychometric Testing and the Changing Demand for Skills: A Review of the Literature*, Centre for the Economics of Education, London School of Economics and Political Science.

Johnson, G. and Scholes, K. (1984) *Exploring Corporate Strategy*, Prentice-Hall.

Johnson, S. (2002) 'Card check or mandatory representation vote? How the type of union recognition procedure affects union certification success', *Economic Journal* (April):344–61.Judge, T.A. (2009) 'Core Self–Evaluations and Work Success', Source: *Current Directions in Psychological Science* 18(1): 58–62.

Kagaari, J.R.K., Munene, J.C. and Ntayi, J.M. (2010) 'Performance management practices, information and communication technology (ICT) adoption and managed performance', *Quality Assurance in Education* 18(2): 106–125.

Kalra, V.S., Abel, P. and Esmail, A. (2009) 'Developing leadership interventions for Black and minority ethnic staff: A case study of the National Health Service (NHS) in the UK', *Journal of Health, Organisation and Management* 23(1): 103–118.

Kanter, R.M. (1989) *When Giants Learn to Dance*, Simon and Schuster.

Kauhanen, A. and Piekkola, H. (2006) 'What makes performance-related pay schemes work? Finnish evidence', *Journal of Management and Governance* 10(2): 149–77.

Kavanagh, M.H. and Ashkanasy, N.M. (2006) 'Acceptance of change during a merger', *British Journal of Management* 17(1): S81–S103.

Kearns, P. (2003) *HR Strategy: Business Focused Individually Centred*, Butterworth-Heinemann.

Keenoy, T. (1990) 'HRM: a case of the wolf in sheep's clothing', *Personnel Review* 19(2): 3–9.

Keenoy, T. and Anthony, P.D. (1992) 'HRM: metaphor, meaning and morality', in P. Blyton and P. Turnbull (eds) *Reassessing Human Resource Management*, Sage.

Kellaway, L. (2001) 'INSIDE TRACK: A prelude to platitudes: handing out staff guidelines to good and bad "behaviours" is surely a sign that an organisation is in deep trouble', *Financial Times* (December): 17.

Kellough, J.E. and Nigro, L.G. (2002) 'Pay for performance in Georgia state government: employee perspectives on GeorgiaGain after 5 years', *Review of Public Personnel Administration* 22(2): 146–66.

Kessler, I. (1995) 'Reward systems', in J. Storey (ed.) *Human Resource Management: A Critical Text*, Routledge.

Kessler, I. (2001) 'Reward system choices', in J. Storey (ed.) *Human Resource Management: A Critical Text*, 2nd edn, Thomson Learning.

Kettley, P. (1996) *Personal Feedback: Cases in Point*, IES Report 326, Institute of Employment Studies.

Khilji, S.E. and Wang, X. (2006) '"Intended" and "implemented" HRM: the missing linchpin in strategic human resource management research', *International Journal of Human Resource Management* 17(7): 1171–89.

Kidder, J. (2006) '"It's the job that I love": bike messengers and edgework', *Sociological Forum* 21(1): 31–54.Kilburn, B. and Cates, T. (2010) 'Leader behavior: gatekeeper to voluntary upward feedback', *Management Research Review* 33(9): 900–910.

Kirkpatrick, D. (1994) *Evaluating Training Programs: The Four Levels*, Berrett-Koehler Publishers, Inc.

Kirkwood, A. (2009) 'E-learning: you don't always get what you hope for', *Technology, Pedagogy and Education* 18(2): 107–121.

Kirkwood, J. (2009) 'To grow or not? Growing small service firms', *Journal of Small Business and Enterprise Development* 16(3): 485–503.

Kline, B. (1993) *The Handbook of Psychological Testing*, Routledge.

Kochan, T. and Dyer, L. (2001) 'HRM: an American view', in J. Storey (ed.) *Human Resource Management: A Critical Text*, 2nd edn, Thomson Learning.

König, C.J., Melchers, K.G., Kleinmann, M., Richter, G.M., and Klehe, U. (2007) 'Candidates' Ability to Identify Criteria in Nontransparent Selection Procedures: Evidence from an assessment center and a structured interview', International *Journal of Selection and Assessment* 15(3): 283–92.

Koritsas, S., Coles, J. and Boyle, M. (2010) 'Workplace Violence towards Social Workers: The Australian Experience', *British Journal of Social Work* 40(1): 257–71.

Krajewski, H.T., Goffin, R.D., McCarthy, J.M., Rothstein, M.G. and Johnston, N. (2006) 'Comparing the validity of structured interviews for managerial-level employees: should we look to the past or focus on the future?', *Journal of Occupational and Organizational Psychology* 79(3): 411–32.

Kramer, L.A. and Lambert, S. (2001) 'Sex-linked bias in chances of being promoted to supervisor', *Sociological Perspectives* 44(1): 111–27.

Kraus, V. and Yonay, Y.P. (2000) 'The effect of occupational sex composition on the gender gap in workplace authority', *Social Science Research* 29(4): 583–605.

Krause, D.E., Kersting, M., Heggestad, E.D., Thornton, and George C. (2006) 'Incremental Validity of Assessment Center Ratings Over Cognitive Ability Tests: A Study at the Executive Management Level *International Journal of Selection and Assessment* 14(4): 360–371.

Krings, F. and Olivares, J. (2007) 'At the doorstep to employment: Discrimination against immigrants as a function of applicant ethnicity, job type, and raters' prejudice', *International Journal of Psychology* 42(6): 406–417.

Kuchinke, K.P. (2009) 'Changing Meanings of Work in Germany, Korea, and the United States in Historical Perspectives', *Advances in Developing Human Resources* 11(2): 168–88.

Kuhn, T.S. (1962) *The Structure of Scientific Revolutions*, University of Chicago Press.

Kumra, S. and Vinnicombe, S. (2010) 'Impressing for Success: A Gendered Analysis of a Key Social Capital Accumulation Strategy', *Gender, Work and Organization* 17(5): 521–46.

Kutcher, E.J. and Bragger, J.D. (2004) 'Selection interviews of overweight job applicants: can structure reduce the bias?', *Journal of Applied Social Psychology* 34(10): 1993–2022.

Lane, H.W., Distefano, J.J. and Maznevski, M.L. (1997) *International Management Behavior*, Blackwell.

Langtry, R. and Langtry, B. (1991) 'Why managers keep an eye on their image', *The Independent Business News*, 3 November.

Lappalainen, P. (2001) *The Challenges Posed by the EU Anti-Discrimination Directives*, paper presented at the Sixth International Metropolis Conference, Workshop on Anti-discrimination legislation, 27 November, 2001, Rotterdam, the Netherlands.

Lautenschlager, G.J. (1994) 'Accuracy and faking of background data', in G.A. Stokes, M.D. Mumford and W.A. Owens (eds) *Biodata Handbook*, Consulting Psychologists Press.

Lawrence, P. (1993) 'Human resource management in Germany', in S. Tyson, P. Lawrence, P., Poirson, L. Manzolini and C.F. Vincente (eds) *Human Resource Management in Europe: Strategic Issues and Cases*, Kogan Page.

Lee, H.W. (2006) 'International human resource management can be achieved through cultural studies and relevant training', *The Business Review* 5(2): 95–100.

Lee, S. (2004) 'Seniority as an employment norm: the case of layoffs and promotion in the US employment relationship', *Socio-Economic Review* 2(1): 65–86.Lee, H.W. (2006) 'International human resource management can be achieved through cultural studies and relevant training', *The Business Review* 5(2): 95–100.

Legge, K. (1989) 'Human resource management: a critical analysis', in J. Storey (ed.) *New Perspectives in Human Resource Management*, Routledge.

Legge, K. (1995) *Human Resource Management: Rhetorics and Realities*, Macmillan Business.

Legge, K. (2001) 'Silver bullet or spent round? Assessing the meaning of the high commitment management/performance relationship', in J. Storey (ed.) *Human Resource Management: A Critical Text*, 2nd edn, Thomson Learning.

Legge, K. (2004) *Human Resource Management: Rhetorics and Realities*, Palgrave Macmillan.

Leibfried, S. and Pierson, P. (2000) 'Social policy: left to courts and markets?', in H. Wallace and W. Wallace (eds) *Policy-Making in the European Union*, Oxford University Press.

Levashina, J., Morgeson, F.P., and Campion, M.A. (2009) 'They Don't Do It Often, But They Do It Well: Exploring the relationship between applicant mental abilities and faking', *International Journal of Selection and Assessment* 17(3): 271–81.

Lewis, C. (1985) *Employee Selection*, Hutchinson.

Lewis, P. (1991) 'Eight steps to the successful appointment of a training consultant', *Journal of European Industrial Training* 15(6): 25–9.

Li, A. and Bagger, J. (2006) 'Using the BIDR to distinguish the effects of impression management and self-deception on the criterion validity of personality measures: a meta-analysis', *International Journal of Selection and Assessment* 14(2): 131–41.

Li, J., Brake, G., Champion, A., Fuller, A., Gabel, S. and Hatcher–Busch, L. (2009) 'Workplace learning: the roles of knowledge accessibility and management', *The Journal of Workplace Learning* 21(4): 347–64.

Lievens, F., Highhouse, S. and De Corte, W. (2005) 'The importance of traits and abilities in supervisors' hirability decisions as a function of method of assessment', *Journal of Occupational and Organizational Psychology* 78(3): 453–70.

Lindbeck, A. and Snower, D. (1988) *The Insider-Outsider Theory of Unemployment and Employment*, MIT Press.

Long, R.J. and Shields, J.L. (2005) 'Performance pay in Canadian and Australian firms: a comparative study', *International Journal of Human Resource Management* 16(10): 1783–811.

Lyons, P. (1988) 'Social interaction', in A.G. Cowling, M.J.K. Stanworth, R.D. Bennett, J. Curran and P. Lyons (eds) *Behavioural Sciences for Managers*, 2nd edn, Edward Arnold.

Mackay, J. (1992) 'Tying the knot: the human side of acquisitions', *Human Resources* (autumn): 10–14.

Macky, K. and Boxall, P. (2007) 'The relationship between "high–performance work practices" and employee attitudes: an investigation of additive and interaction effects', *International Journal of Human Resource Management* 18(4): 537–67.

Mahoney–Phillips, J. and Adams, A. (2010) 'Getting the measure of HR', *Strategic HR Review* 9(1): 5–9.

Maltby, A. and Mackie, S. (2009) 'Virtual learning environments help or hindrance for the "disengaged" student?' *ALT-J* 17(1): 49–62.

Margerison, C. (1991) *Making Management Development Work*, McGraw-Hill.

Marginson, P., Edwards, P.K., Armstrong, P. and Purcell, J. (1993) Executive Summary of Findings. *Second Company Level Industrial Relations Survey*, Industrial Relations Research Unit (mimeo).

Marsden, D. (2010) 'The Paradox of Performance–Related Pay Systems' in *Paradoxes of Modernization* (June): 185–203.

Marsden, D., French, S. and Kobi, K. (2000) *Why Does Performance Pay Demotivate? Financial Incentives Versus. Performance Appraisal*, Centre for Economic Performance, London School of Economics and Political Science.

Marti, M., Bobier, D. and Baron, R.S. (2000) 'Right before our eyes: the failure to recognize non-prototypical forms of prejudice', *Group Processes and Intergroup Relations* 3(4): 403–18.

Martin, J.P. and Stancanelli, E. (2002) 'Tackling some myths about temporary jobs', *OECD Observer*, 26 June.

Mason, P.L. (2000) 'Understanding recent empirical evidence on race and labor market outcomes in the USA', *Review of Social Economy* 58(3): 319–38.

Massingham, P. and Diment, K. (2009) 'Organizational commitment, knowledge management interventions, and learning organization capacity', *The Learning Organization: An International Journal* 16(2): 122–142.

Mathis, R.L. and Jackson, J.H. (2007) *Human Resource Management*, South–Western.

Mattoo, A., Subramanian, A. (2009) 'Criss–Crossing Globalization', *Research Working papers*, World Bank, (November): 1–36.

Mauboussin, M.J. (2010) 'Surge in the Urge to Merge: M&A Trends and Analysis', *Journal of Applied Corporate Finance* 22(2): 83–93.

Matlay, H. (2002) 'Industrial relations in the SME sector of the British economy: an empirical perspective', *Journal of Small Business and Enterprise Development* 9(3): 307–18.

Maurer, R. (1996) *Beyond the Wall of Resistance: Unconventional Strategies That Build Support for Change*, Bard Press.

McCausland, W.D., Pouliakas, K. and Theodossiou, I. (2005) 'Some are punished and some are rewarded: a study of the impact of performance pay on job satisfaction', *International Journal of Manpower* 26(7–8): 636–59.

McClintock, E.A. (2010) 'When Does Race Matter? Race, Sex, and Dating at an Elite University', *Journal of Marriage and Family* 72(1): 45–72.

McCormick, E.J. and Ilgen, D. (1987) *Industrial and Organizational Psychology*, 8th edn, Unwin Hyman.

McDonald, S. (2010) 'Right place, right time: serendipity and informal job matching', *Socio– Economic Review* 8(2): 307–31.

McDowall, A. and Saunders, M.N.K. (2010) 'UK managers' conceptions of employee training and development ', *Journal of European Industrial Training* 34(7): 609–30.

McDermott, E., Mangan, J. and O'Connor, M. (2006) 'Graduate development programmes and satisfaction levels', *Journal of European Industrial Training* 30(6): 456–71.

McIlwee, T. and Roberts, I. (1991) *Human Resource Management*, Elm Publications.

McKinnon, R. (2010) 'An ageing workforce and strategic human resource management: Staffing challenges for social security administrations', *International Social Security Review* 63(3–4): 91–113.

McLaughlin, V. and Mott, C. (2010) 'Leadership brand equity: HR leaders' role in driving economic value', *Strategic HR Review* 9(4): 13–19.

McKenna, E. (1994) *Business Psychology and Organizational Behaviour*, Lawrence Erlbaum Associates.

Melchers, K.G., Kleinmann, M., and Prinz, M.A. (2010) 'Do Assessors Have Too Much on their Plates? The Effects of Simultaneously Rating Multiple Assessment Center Candidates on Rating Quality', *International Journal of Selection and Assessment* 18(3): 329–41.

Melé, D. (2005) 'Exploring the principle of subsidiarity in organisational forms', *Journal of Business Ethics* 60(3): 293–305.

Merhebi, R., Pattenden, K., Swan, P.L. and Zhou, X. (2006) 'Australian chief executive officer remuneration: pay and performance', *Accounting and Finance* 46(3): 481–97.

Meriac, J., Woehr, D. and Banister, C. (2010) 'Generational Differences in Work Ethic: An Examination of Measurement Equivalence Across Three Cohorts', *Journal of Business and Psychology* 25(2): 315–24.

Metcalf, D., Hansen, K. and Charlwood, A. (2001) 'Unions and the sword of justice: unions and pay systems, pay inequality, pay discrimination and low pay', *National Institute Economic Review* 176(1): 61–75.

Milcovich, G.T., Newman, J.M. and Milcovich, C. (2001) *Compensation*, 7th edn, McGraw-Hill.

Miles, R.E. and Snow, C.C. (1984) 'Designing strategic human resource systems', *Organizational Dynamics* (summer): 36–52.

Miller, A.F., Jnr and Hanson, M. (1991) 'The smile on the face of the leadership tiger', *Personnel Management* (October): 54–7.

Miller, P. (1989) 'Managing corporate identity in the diversified business', *Personnel Management* (March): 36–9.

Mills, A.J. and Murgatroyd, S.J. (1991) *Organizational Rules: A Framework for Understanding Organizational Action*, Open University.

Ming Chia, Y. (2005) 'Job offers of multi-national accounting firms: the effects of emotional intelligence, extra-curricular activities, and academic performance', *Accounting Education* 14(1): 75–93.

Mintzberg, H. (1994) *The Rise and Fall of Strategic Planning*, Prentice-Hall.

Mitki, Y., Herstein, R. and Jaffe, E.D. (2007) 'Learning mechanisms for designing corporate identity in the banking industry' *The International Journal of Bank Marketing* 25(7): 452–68.

Mitlacher, L.W. and Paul, C. (2009) 'Performance– based pay systems for teams: explaining the design of performance–based pay systems for teams from an expanded agency theory perspective', *International Journal of Business Performance Management* 11(3): 171–86.

Mobius, M.M. and Rosenblat, T.S. (2006) 'Why beauty matters', *The American Economic Review* 96(1): 222–35.

Molander, C. and Winterton, J. (1994) *Managing Human Resources*, Routledge.

Moore, S. (2006) 'The relationship between legislation and industrial practice: a study of the outcome of trade union recognition', *Employee Relations* 28(4): 363–73.

Morgan, A., Cannan, K. and Cullinane, J. (2005) '360° feedback: a critical enquiry', *Personnel Review* 34(6): 663–80.

Morgan, G. (1986) *Images of Organization*, Sage.

Morris, D., Bakan, I. and Wood, G. (2006) 'Employee financial participation: evidence from a major UK retailer', *Employee Relations* 28(4): 326–41.

Moscoso, S. (2000) 'Selection interview: a review of validity evidence, adverse impact and applicant reactions', *International Journal of Selection and Assessment* 8(4): 237–47.

Moscoso, S. and Salgado, J.F. (2004) 'Fairness reactions to personnel selection techniques in Spain and Portugal', *International Journal of Selection and Assessment* 12(1–2): 187–96.

Mosel, J.N. and Goheen, H.W. (1958) 'The validity of the employment recommendation questionnaire in personnel selection', *Personnel Psychology* 2: 487–90.

Mount, M., Ilies, R. and Johnson, E. (2006) 'Relationship of personality traits and counterproductive work behaviors: the mediating effects of job satisfaction', *Personnel Psychology* 59(3): 591–622.

Moy, J.W. (2006) 'Are employers assessing the right traits in hiring? Evidence from Hong Kong companies', *International Journal of Human Resource Management* 17(4): 734–54.

Moye, M.J. and Henkin, A.B. (2006) 'Exploring associations between employee empowerment and interpersonal trust in managers', *The Journal of Management Development* 25(2): 101–17.

Moynahan, B. (1993) 'Creating harassment-free work zones', *Training and Development* (May): 67–70.

Moynihan, D.P. and Pandey, S.K. (2010) 'The Big Question for Performance Management: Why Do Managers Use Performance Information?', *Journal of Public Administration Research and Theory* 20(4): 849–866.

Mulin, C. and Reen, H. (2010) 'Arkadin develops employee talent through e-learning', *Strategic HR Review* 9(5): 11–16.

Murji, K. (2006) 'Using racial stereotypes in anti-racist campaigns', *Ethnic and Racial Studies* 29(2): 260–80.

Murliss, H. (1987) 'Performance-related pay in the public sector', *Public Money* (March): 29–33.

Murphy, K.R. and Cleveland, J.N. (1995) *Understanding Performance Appraisal: Social, Organizational and Goal-based Perspectives*, Sage.

Nadler, J.T., Cundiff, Nicole, L., Lowery, M.R. and Jackson, S. (2010) 'Perceptions of organizational attractiveness: The differential relationships of various work schedule flexibility programs', *Management Research Review* 33(9): 865–76.

Nadler, L. and Nadler, Z. (1989) *Developing Human Resources*, Jossey-Bass.

Naidoo, J. and Wills, J. (2000) *Health Promotion: Foundations for Practice*, 2nd edn, Balliere Tindall/RCN.

Needle, D. (1994) *Business in Context: An Introduction to Business and its Environment*, 2nd edn, Chapman and Hall.

Noblet, A., Teo, S.T.T., McWilliams, J. and Rodwell, J. (2005) 'Which work characteristics predict employee outcomes for the public-sector employee? An examination of generic and occupation-specific characteristics', *International Journal of Human Resource Management* 16(8): 1415–30.

Nolan, C., Conway, E., Farrell, T. and Monks, K. (2010) 'Competency needs in Irish hotels: employer and graduate perspectives', *Journal of European Industrial Training* 34(5): 432–54.

Nolan, K.P. and Harold, C.M. (2010) 'Fit with what? The influence of multiple self–concept images on organizational attraction', *Journal of Occupational and Organizational Psychology* 83(3): 645–62.

Nowack, K.M. (1991) 'A true training needs analysis', *Training and Development Journal* (April): 69–73.

Nowicki, M.D. and Rosse, J.G. (2002) 'Managers' views of how to hire: building bridges between science and practice', *Journal of Business and Psychology* 17(2): 157–70.

Nurse, L. (2005) 'Performance appraisal, employee development and organizational justice: exploring the linkages', *International Journal of Human Resource Management* 16(7): 1176–94.

Osberg, L. and Smeeding, T. (2006) '"Fair" inequality? Attitudes toward pay differentials: the United States in comparative perspective', *American Sociological Review* 71(3): 450–73.

Ohemeng, F. (2010) 'The dangers of internationalization and "one–size–fits–all" in public sector management: Lessons from performance management policies in Ontario and Ghana', *International Journal of Public Sector Management* 23(5): 456–78.

Oxenbridge, S. and Brown, W. (2002) 'The two faces of partnership?: an assessment of partnership and co-operative employer/trade union relationships', *Employee Relations* 24(3): 262–76.

Paik, Y., Vance, C.M. and Stage, H.D. (2000) 'A test of assumed cluster homogeneity for performance appraisal management in four Southeast Asian countries', *International Journal of Human Resource Management* 11(4): 736–50.

Panari, C., Guglielmi, D., Simbula, S. and Depolo, M. (2010) 'Can an opportunity to learn at work reduce stress?: A revisitation of the job demand–control model', *The Journal of Workplace Learning* 22(3): 166–79.

Pantazis, C. (2002) 'Maximizing e-learning to train the 21st century workforce', *Public Personnel Management* 31(1): 21–7.

Papalexandris, N. (1991) 'A comparative study of human resource management in selected Greek and foreign-owned subsidiaries in Greece', in C. Brewster and S. Tyson (eds) *International Comparisons in Human Resource Management*, Pitman.

Parding, K. and Abrahamsson, L. (2010) 'Learning gaps in a learning organization: professionals' values versus management values', *The Journal of Workplace Learning* 22(5): 292–305.

Pedler, M., Boydell, T.H. and Burgoyne, J.G. (1989) 'Towards the learning company', *Management Education and Development* 2(3): 19–41.

Peeters, H. and Lievens, F. (2006) 'Verbal and nonverbal impression management tactics in behavior description and situational interviews', *International Journal of Selection and Assessment* 14(3): 206–22.

Pennell, K. (2010) 'The role of flexible job descriptions in succession management', *Library Management* 31(4–5): 279–90.

Peppas, S.C. (2006) 'Diversity in the workplace: Hispanic perceptions of the hiring decision', *Employee Relations* 28(2): 119–29.

Perkins, S.J. and Hendry, C. (2005) 'Ordering top pay: interpreting the signals', *Journal of Management Studies* 42(7): 1443–68.

Perryer, C., Jordan, C., Firns, I. and Travaglione, A. (2010) 'Predicting turnover intentions: The interactive effects of organizational commitment and perceived organizational support', *Management Research Review* 33(9): 911–923.

Peters, T.J. (1987) *Thriving on Chaos*, Alfred A. Knopf.

Peters, T.J. and Waterman, R.H. (1982) *In Search of Excellence*, Harper and Row.

Pettijohn, L.S., Parker, R.S., Pettijohn, C.E. and Kent, O.L. (2001) 'Performance appraisals usage, criteria and observation', *The Journal of Management Development* 20(9): 754–71.

Pfeffer, J. (1998) *The Human Equation: Building Profits by Putting People First*, Harvard Business School Press.

Pheng, L.S. and Yuquan, S. (2002) 'An exploratory study of Hofstede's cross-cultural dimensions in construction projects', *Management Decision* 40(1): 7–16.

Philp, T. (1990) *Appraising Performance for Results*, McGraw-Hill.

Phillimore, J. (2000) 'The limits of supply-side social democracy: Australian labor, 1983–95', *Politics and Society* 28(4): 557–87.

Pollitt, D. (2005) 'HR transformation lowers costs and boosts efficiency at AstraZeneca: site and functionally based service makes way for "one team" approach', *Human Resource Management International Digest* 13(6): 6–11.

Poole, M. (1990) 'Editorial: human resource management in an international perspective', *The International Journal of Human Resource Management* 1(1): 1–16.

Porter, M. (1990) *The Competitive Advantage of Nations*, Free Press.

PPRU (1999) *Report for The Office of The Data Protection Registrar (UK)*, Personnel Policy Research Unit.

Preble, J. F. (2010) 'Toward a Framework for Achieving a Sustainable Globalization' *Business and Society Review* 115(3): 329–366.

Price, A.J. (1997) *Human Resource Management in a Business Context*, Thomson Learning.

Price, A.J. (2000) *Principles of Human Resource Management: An Action-Learning Approach*, Blackwell.

Price, A.J. (2005a) 'Learning and development methods, interventions and practices', in J. Swart, C. Mann, S. Brown and A.J. Price (eds) *Human Resource Development: Strategy and Tactics*, Butterworth-Heinemann.

Price, A.J. (2005b) 'The e-learning revolution', in J. Swart, C. Mann, S. Brown and A.J. Price (eds) *Human Resource Development: Strategy and Tactics*, Butterworth-Heinemann.

Proost, K., Schreurs, B., DeWitte, K., and Derous, E. (2010) 'Ingratiation and Self–Promotion in the Selection Interview: The Effects of Using Single Tactics or a Combination of Tactics on Interviewer Judgments', *Journal of Applied Social Psychology* 40(9): 2155–69.

Prowse, P. and Prowse, J. (2009) 'The dilemma of performance appraisal', *Measuring Business Excellence* 13(4): 69–77.

Purcell, J. (1989) 'The impact of corporate strategy on human resource management', in J. Storey (ed.) *New Perspectives on Human Resource Management*, Routledge.

Purcell, J. (2001) 'The meaning of strategy in human resource management', in J. Storey (ed.) *Human Resource Management: A Critical Text*, 2nd edn, Thomson Learning.

Purcell, K. (2002) *Employers in the New Graduate Labour Market: Recruiting from a Wider Spectrum of Graduates*, Employment Studies Research Unit, University of the West of England.

Raia, A.P. (1974) *Managing by Objectives*, Scott, Foresman.

Rainbird, H. and Maguire, M. (1993) 'When corporate need supersedes employee development', *Personnel Management* (February): 34–7.

Ramamoorthy, N., Gupta, A., Sardessai, R.M. and Flood, P.C. (2005) 'Individualism/collectivism and attitudes towards human resource systems: a comparative study of American, Irish and Indian MBA students', *International Journal of Human Resource Management* 16(5): 852–69.

Ranzijn, R., Carson, E., Winefield, A.H. and Price, D. (2006) 'On the scrap-heap at 45: the human impact of mature-aged unemployment', *Journal of Occupational and Organizational Psychology* 79(3): 467–79.

Rasmussen, E. and Lind, J. (2003) 'Productive employment relationships: European experiences', *New Zealand Journal of Industrial Relations* 28(2): 158–69.

Razack, S., Faremo, S., Drolet, F., Snell, L., Wiseman, J., Pickering, J. (2009) 'Multiple mini–interviews versus traditional interviews: stakeholder acceptability comparison', *Medical Education* 43(10): 993–1000.

Revans, R.W. (1972) 'Action learning – a management development programme', *Personnel Review* (autumn).

Rhinesmith, S.H. (1996) *A Manager's Guide to Globalization – Six Skills for Success in a Changing World*, 2nd edn, Irwin.

Rice, A.K., Hull, J.M. and Trist, E.L. (1950) 'The representation of labour turnover as a social process', *Journal of Human Relations* 3.

Rittau, Y. and Dundon, A. (2010) 'The roles and functions of shop stewards in workplace partnership: Evidence from the Republic of Ireland', *Employee Relations* 32(1): 10–27.

Rizov, M. and Croucher, R. (2009) 'Human resource management and performance in European firms', *Cambridge Journal of Economics* 33(2): 253–72.

Roberts, G. (1997) *Recruitment and Selection: A Competency Approach*, Chartered Institute of Personnel and Development.

Robinson, D. and Hayday, S. (2009) *The Engaging Manager*, IES Report 470, November, Institute of Employment Studies.

Rodger, A. (1952) *The Seven Point Plan*, National Institute for Industrial Psychology.

Rosania, R.J. (2000) *The Credible Trainer*, American Society for Training and Development

Rosenbloom, J.S. (2001) *The Handbook of Employee Benefits*, 5th edn, McGraw-Hill.

Ross, R. and Schneider, R. (1992) *From Equality to Diversity: A Business Case for Equal Opportunities*, Pitman.

Roth, P.L., Bobko, P. and Mcfarland, L.A. (2005) 'A meta-analysis of work sample test validity: updating and integrating some classic literature', *Personnel Psychology* 58(4): 1009–37.

Rothwell, W.J., Prescott, R.K. and Taylor, M.W. (1998) *The Strategic Human Resource Leader: How to Prepare Your Organization for the Six Key Trends Shaping the Future*, Davies-Black Publications.

Rousseau, D.M. (1995) *Psychological Contracts in Organizations: Understanding Written and Unwritten Agreements*, Sage.

Rowden, R.W. (2001) 'Exploring methods to evaluate the return from training', *American Business Review* 19(1): 6–12.

Rowden, R.W., Jnr and Conine, C.T. (2005) 'The impact of workplace learning on job satisfaction in small US commercial banks', *The Journal of Workplace Learning* 17(4): 215–30.

Rumpel, S. and Medcof, J.W. (2006) 'Total rewards: good fit for tech workers', *Research-Technology Management* 49(5): 27–35.

Russell, C., Mattson, J., Devlin, S. and Atwater, D. (1990) 'Predictive validity of biodata items generated from retrospective life experience essays', *Journal of Applied Psychology* 75: 569–80.

Russell, H., O'Connell, P.J. and McGinnity, F. (2009) 'The Impact of Flexible Working Arrangements on Work–life Conflict and Work Pressure in Ireland', *Gender, Work and Organization* 16(1): 73–97.

Rynes, S.L., Brown, K.G., and Colbert, A.E. (2002) 'Seven common misconceptions about human resource practices: Research findings versus practitioner beliefs,' *Academy of Management Executive* 16(3).

Rynes, S.L., Gerhart, B. and Minette, K.A. (2004) 'The importance of pay in employee motivation: discrepancies between what people say and what they do', *Human Resource Management* 43(4): 381–94.

Sambrook, S. (2001) 'HRD as an emergent and negotiated evolution: an ethnographic case study in the British National Health Service', *Human Resource Development Quarterly* 12(2): 169–93.

Sartori, R. (2010) 'Face validity in personality tests: psychometric instruments and projective techniques in comparison', *Quality and Quantity* 44(4): 749–759.

Sayal, A. (1990) 'Black women and mental health', *Psychologist* (January): 24–7.

Schinkel, S., van Dierendonck, D. and Anderson, N. (2004) 'The impact of selection encounters on applicants: an experimental study into feedback effects after a negative selection decision', *International Journal of Selection and Assessment* 12(1–2): 197–205.

Schleicher, D.J., Venkatamarani, V., Morgeson, F.P. and Campion, M.A. (2006) 'So you didn't get the job … now what do you think? Examining opportunity-to-perform fairness perceptions', *Personnel Psychology* 59(3): 559–90.

Schuler, R.S. (1990) *Personnel and Human Resource Management*, 4th edn, West Publishing,

Schuler, R.S., Jackson, S.E. and Storey, J. (2001) 'HRM and its link with strategic management', in J. Storey (ed.) *Human Resource Management: A Critical Text*, 2nd edn, Thomson Learning.

Sealy, R., Vinnicombe, S. and Doldor, E. (2009) *The Female FTSE Board Report 2009*, Cranfield School of Management.

Seijts, G.H. and Kyei–Poku, I. (2010) 'The Role of Situational Interviews in Fostering Positive Reactions to Selection Decisions', *Applied Psychology An International Review* 59(3): 431–53.

Sen, A. (2002) 'How to judge globalism', *The American Prospect* 13(1): 1–14.

Senge, P.M. (1990) *The Fifth Discipline: The Art & Practice of The Learning Organization*, Currency Doubleday.

Servage, L. (2005) 'Strategizing for workplace e-learning: some critical considerations', *The Journal of Workplace Learning* 17(5–6): 304–17.

Sheehan, C. (2009) 'Outsourcing HRM activities in Australian organisations', *Asia Pacific Journal of Human Resources*, Aug; 47: 236–53.

Shen, J. and Darby, R. (2006) 'Training and management development in Chinese multinational enterprises', *Employee Relations* 28(4): 342–62.

Shih, H.-A., Chiang, Y.-H. and Kim, I.-S. (2005) 'Expatriate performance management from MNEs of different national origins', *International Journal of Manpower* 26(2): 157–76.

Shiner, M. (2010) 'Post–Lawrence Policing in England and Wales: Guilt, Innocence and the Defence of Organizational Ego', *British Journal of Criminology* 50(5): 935–53.

Shiner, M. and Modood, T. (2002) 'Help or hindrance? Higher education and the route to ethnic equality', *British Journal of Sociology of Education* 23(2): 209–32.

Sivanandan, A. (1991) *Black Struggles Against Racism*, Northern Curriculum Development Project Setting the Context for Change: Anti-Racist Social Work Education, Central Council for Education and Training in Social Work, Leeds.

Sleator, R.D. (2010) 'The evolution of eLearning Background, blends and blackboard', *Science Progress* 93(3): 319–34.

Sloman, M. (1994) 'Coming in from the cold: a new role for trainers', *Personnel Management* (January): 24–7.

Smith, M. (1991) 'Selection in organizations', in M. Smith (ed.) *Analysing Organizational Behaviour*, Macmillan.

Smith, M., Gregg, M. and Andrews, R. (1989) *Selection and Assessment: A New Appraisal*, Pitman.

Smith, M. and Robertson, I.T. (1993) *The Theory and Practice of Systematic Personnel Selection*, 2nd edn, Macmillan.

Snell, A.F., Sydell, E.J. and Lueke, S.B. (1999) 'Towards a theory of applicant faking: integrating studies of deception', *Human Resources Management Review* 9: 219–42.

Snyder, M. (1974) 'The self-monitoring of expressive behaviour', *Journal of Personality and Social Psychology* 30: 526–37.

Song, J.H. and Kim, H.M. (2009) 'The integrative structure of employee commitment: The influential relations of individuals' characteristic in a supportive learning culture', *Leadership and Organization Development Journal* 30(3): 240–55.

Stathopoulos, K., Espenlaub, S. and Walker, M. (2005) 'The compensation of UK executive directors: lots of carrots but are there any sticks?', *Competition and Change* 9(1): 89–105.

Steensma, H. and Groeneveld, K. (2010) 'Evaluating a training using the "four levels model"', *The Journal of Workplace Learning* 22(5): 319–31

Sternberg, R.J. (1994) 'Thinking styles: theory and assessment at the interface between intelligence and personality', in R.J. Sternberg and P. Zuzgis (eds) *Personality and Intelligence*, Cambridge University Press.

Stevens, J. and Walsh, T. (1991) 'Training and competitiveness', in J. Stevens and R. Mackay (eds) *Training and Competitiveness*, NEDO, Kogan Page.

Stewart, L.D. and Perlow, R. (2001) 'Applicant race, job status, and racial attitude as predictors of employment discrimination', *Journal of Business and Psychology* 16(2): 259–75.

Stone-Romero, E.F., Stone, D.L. and Hyatt, D. (2003) 'Personnel selection procedures and invasion of privacy', *Journal of Social Issues* 59(2): 343–68.

Storey, J. (1994) 'How new-style management is taking hold', *Personnel Management* (January): 32–5.

Storey, J. (ed.) (1995) *Human Resource Management: A Critical Text*, Routledge.

Storey, J. (ed.) (1989) *New Perspectives on Human Resource Management*, Routledge.

Storey, J. (ed.) (2001) *Human Resource Management: A Critical Text*, 2nd edn, Thomson Learning.

Strebler, M.T., Robinson, D. and Bevan, S. (2001) *Performance Review: Balancing Objectives and Content*, IES Report 370, Institute of Employment Studies.

Stuart, M. and Lucio, M.M. (2002) 'Social partnership and the mutual gains organization: remaking involvement and trust at the British workplace', *Economic and Industrial Democracy* 23(2): 177–200.

Subeliani, D. and Tsogas, G. (2005) 'Managing diversity in the Netherlands: a case study of Rabobank', *International Journal of Human Resource Management* 16(5): 831–51.

Sulcic, V. (2010) 'The key factors for acquired knowledge through e–learning', *International Journal of Innovation and Learning* 7(3): 290–302.

Tamkin, P., Cowling, M. and Hunt, W. (2008) *People and the Bottom Line*, Report Number 448, Institute for Employment Studies.

Tamkin, P., Yarnall, J. and Kerrin, M. (2002) *Kirkpatrick and Beyond: A Review of Models of Training Evaluation*, IES Report 392, Institute for Employment Studies.

Tampakoudis, I.A. (2010) 'Visiting the paradox of the upward trends of mergers and acquisitions in the USA in times of poor financial performance', *International Journal of Trade and Global Markets* 3(4): 341–58.

Tan, H.H. and Chee, D. (2005) 'Understanding interpersonal trust in a Confucian-influenced society', *International Journal of Cross Cultural Management* 5(2): 197–212.

Tannock, S. (2008) 'The problem of education–based discrimination', *British Journal of Sociology of Education* 29(5): 439–49.

Taylor, S. (2006) 'Communicating across cultures', *The British Journal of Administrative Management* (June/July): 12–13.

Tennenbaum, B. (2005) 'Hire the write way', *Pest Control* 73(8): 112.

Thiel, D. (2009) 'Dynamic modelling of labour assignment flexibility in the French fresh food industry', *Journal of the Operational Research Society* 60(5): 652–62.

Thomson, P. (2008) 'The business benefits of flexible working', *Strategic HR Review* 7(2): 17–22.

Thomson, R. and Mabey, C. (1994) *Developing Human Resources*, Butterworth-Heinemann.

Thomas, S.L. and Vaught, S. (2001) 'The write stuff: what the evidence says about using handwriting analysis in hiring', *S.A.M. Advanced Management Journal* Autumn(66): 4.

Thornton, W. and Thornton, S. H. (2009) 'India in Search of Itself: The Crisis and Opportunity of Indo–Globalization', *New Political Science* 31(2): 183–200.

Tichy, N.M., Fombrun, C.J. and Devanna, M.A. (1982) 'Strategic human resource management', *Sloan Management Review* 23(2): 47–61.

Tight, M. (2000) 'Critical perspectives on management learning: a view from adult/continuing/lifelong education', *Management Learning* 31(1): 103–19.

Toner, G.A. (2009) 'New ways of thinking about old crimes: Prosecuting corruption and organized criminal groups engaged in labor–management racketeering', *Journal of Financial Crime* 16(1): 41–59.

Tootell, B., Blackler, M., Toulson, P., and Dewe, P. (2009) 'Metrics: HRM's Holy Grail? A New Zealand case study', *Human Resource Management Journal* 19(4): 375–392.

Torrington, D. and Hall, L. (1991) *Personnel Management: A New Approach*, 2nd edn, Prentice-Hall.

Torrington, D. and Hall, L. (1995) *Personnel Management: HRM in Action*, 3rd edn, Prentice-Hall.

Townley, B. (1989) 'Selection and appraisal: reconstituting "social relations?"', in J. Storey (ed.) *New Perspectives on Human Resource Management*, Routledge.

Townley, B. (1994) *Reframing Human Resource Management*, Sage.

Triandis, H.C. (1990) 'Theoretical concepts that are applicable to the analysis of ethnocentrism', in R.W. Brislin (ed.) *Applied Cross-Cultural Psychology*, Sage.

Triandis, H.C. (1995) 'A theoretical framework for the study of diversity', in M.M. Chemers, S. Oskamp and M.A. Costanzo (eds) *Diversity in Organizations: New Perspectives for a Changing Workplace*, Sage.

Trompenaars, F. and Hampden-Turner, C. (1997) *Riding the Waves of Culture*, 2nd edn, McGraw-Hill.

Truss, C. (1999) 'Soft and hard HRM', in L. Gratton (ed.) *Strategic Human Resource Management: Corporate Rhetoric and Human Reality*, Oxford University Press.

Truxillo, D.M., Bauer, T.N., Campion, M.A. and Paronto, M.E. (2006) 'A field study of the role of big five personality in applicant perceptions of selection fairness, self, and the hiring organization', *International Journal of Selection and Assessment* 14 (3): 269–77.

Truxillo, D.M., Bodner, T.E, Bertolino, M., Bauer, T.N., and Yonce, C.A. (2009) 'Effects of Explanations on Applicant Reactions: A meta–analytic review', *International Journal of Selection and Assessment* 17(4): 346–61.

Turnasella, T. (1999) 'The salary trap', *Compensation and Benefits Review* 31(6): 2–3.

Twenge, J.M., Campbell, S.M., Hoffman, B.J. and Lance, C.E. (2010) Generational 'Differences in Work Values: Leisure and Extrinsic Values Increasing, Social and Intrinsic Values Decreasing', *Journal of Management*, Sep, 36: 1117–1142.

Tyson, S. (1989) 'The management of the personnel function', *Journal of Management Studies* 24 (September): 523–32.

Tyson, S. (1995) *Human Resource Strategy*, Pitman.

Tyson, S. (2006) *Essentials of Human Resource Management*, Butterworth–Heinemann.

Tziner, A., Joanis, C. and Murphy, K.R. (2000) 'A comparison of three methods of performance appraisal with regard to goal properties, goal perception, and ratee satisfaction', *Group and Organization Management* 25(2): 175–90.

Ulrich, D. (1997) *Human Resource Champions: The Next Agenda for Adding Value and Delivering Results*, Harvard Business School Press.

Van Ark, B. (2006) 'Europe's Productivity Gap: Catching Up or Getting Stuck?', June, *Conference Board Economic Working Paper–EPWP #06–02*.

Vandenberghe, C. (1999) 'Organizational culture, person-culture fit, and turnover: a replication in the health care industry', *Journal of Organizational Behavior* 20: 175–84.

Van Iddekinge, C.H., Sager, C.E., Burnfield, J.L. and Heffner, T.S. (2006) 'The variability of criterion-related validity estimates among interviewers and interview panels', *International Journal of Selection and Assessment* 14(3): 193–205.

Van Ruysseveldt, J., Huiskamp, R. and van Hoof, J. (1995) *Comparative Industrial and Employment Relations*, Sage.

Venkatasubramanian, V. (2009) 'What is Fair Pay for Executives? An Information Theoretic Analysis of Wage Distributions', *Entropy*, 11(4): 766–81.

Viitala, R. (2005) 'Perceived development needs of managers compared to an integrated management competency model', *The Journal of Workplace Learning* 17(7): 436–51.

Visser, F. and Williams, L. (2007) *Work–life balance in the public sector: rhetoric vs. reality*, Work Foundation.

Visser, J. (2006) 'Union membership statistics in 24 countries', *Monthly Labor Review* (January): 38–49.

Vranken, M. (1999) 'The role of specialist labour courts in an environment of substantive labour law deregulation: a New Zealand case study', *International Journal of Comparative Labour Law and Industrial Relations* 15(3): 303–28.

Wadsworth, J. (2010) *Immigration and the UK Labour Market: The Evidence from Economic Research*, April, Paper No. CEPEA006: CEP Election Analysis, London School of Economics.

Waddill, D.D. (2006) 'Action e-learning: an exploratory case study of action learning applied online', *Human Resource Development International* 9(2): 157–71.

Waight, C.L and Stewart, B.L. (2005) 'Valuing the adult learner in e-learning: part one – a conceptual model for corporate settings', *The Journal of Workplace Learning* 17(5–6): 337–45.

Waldman, D.A. and Atwater, L.E. (2001) 'Attitudinal and behavioral outcomes of an upward feedback process', *Group and Organization Management* 26(2): 189–205.

Walker, H.J., Feild, H.S.,Giles, W.F.and Bernerth, J.B.(2008) 'The interactive effects of job advertisement characteristics and applicant experience on reactions to recruitment messages', *Journal of Occupational and Organizational Psychology* 81(4): 619–38.

Walton, J. (1999) *Strategic Human Resource Development*, Financial Times/Prentice Hall.

Wang, J., Hutchins, H.M. and Garavan, T.N. (2009) 'Exploring the Strategic Role of Human Resource Development in Organizational Crisis Management', *Human Resource Development Review*, March, 8: 22–53.

Warr, P. (1987) *Psychology at Work*, 2nd edn, Penguin.

Watkins, L.M. and Johnston, L. (2000) 'Screening job applicants: the impact of physical attractiveness and application quality', *International Journal of Selection and Assessment* 8(2): 76–84.

Watson, T. (2003) *Towards a Grown-Up and Critical Academic HRM and the Need to Grow Out of Infantile 'Hard And Soft HRM', 'Rhetoric and Reality' and Functionalist Habits to Engage Critically with the Adult World of Employment Management*, paper presented at Critical Management Studies 2003, Lancaster University, 7–9 July.

Webber, G. and Williams, C. (2008) 'Mothers in "Good" and "Bad" Part–time Jobs: Different Problems, Same Results', *Gender Society*, December, 22: 752–77.

Weber, M. (1947) *Max Weber: The Theory of Social and Economic Organization*, translated by A.M. Henderson and Talcott Parsons, The Free Press.

Webster, E.C. (1964) *Decision Making in the Employment Interview*, Industrial Relations Centre, McGill University, Montreal.

Weibel, A., Rost, K. and Osterloh, M. (2010) 'Pay for Performance in the Public Sector Benefits and (Hidden) Costs', *Journal of Public Administration Research and Theory* 20(2): 387–412.

Weisner, W.H. and Cronshaw, S.F. (1988) 'A meta-analytic investigation of the impact of interview format and degree of structure on the validity of the employment interview', *Journal of Occupational Psychology* 61: 275–90.

Weiss, D.S. (1999) *High Performance HR: Leveraging Human Resources for Competitive Advantage*, John Wiley & Sons Ltd.

Weiss, M. (2002) 'Modernizing the German works council system: a recent amendment', *International Journal of Comparative Labour Law and Industrial Relations* 18(3): 251–64.

Whitehill, A.M. (1991) *Japanese Management: Tradition and Transition*, Routledge.

Wilson, F. (2005) 'Caught between difference and similarity: the case of women academics', *Women in Management Review* 20(4): 234–48.

Wolf, A. and Jenkins, A. (2006) 'Explaining greater test use for selection: the role of HR professionals in a world of expanding regulation', *Human Resource Management Journal* 16(2): 193–213.

Wolf, M.G. (1999) 'Compensation: an overview', in L.A. Berger and D.R. Berger (eds) *The Compensation Handbook*, 4th edn, McGraw-Hill.

Wolter, S., Mühlemann, S. and Schweri, J. (2006) 'Why some firms train apprentices and many others do not', *German Economic Review* 7(3): 249–64.

Wood, R. and Baron, H. (1992) 'Psychological testing free from prejudice', *Personnel Management* (December): 34–7.

Woodhams, C. and Lupton, B. (2006) 'Gender-based equal opportunities policy and practice in small firms: the impact of HR professionals', *Human Resource Management Journal* 16(1): 74–97.

Wright, M. and Storey, J. (1994) 'Recruitment', in I. Beardwell and L. Holden (eds) *Human Resource Management*, Pitman.

Wright, P.M., and McMahan, G.C. (1992). 'Theoretical Perspectives for Strategic Human Resource Management', *Journal of Management*, 18, 295–320.

WTO (2006) *Trade Picks up in Mid-2005, but 2006 Picture is Uncertain*, Press Release, 11 April, World Trade Organization.

Wyatt, M.R.R., Pathak, S.B. and Zibarras, L.D. (2010) 'Advancing selection in an SME: Is best practice methodology applicable?', *International Small Business Journal*, June; 28: 258–73.

Yalcinalp, S. and Gulbahar, Y. (2010) 'Ontology and taxonomy design and development for personalised web–based learning systems', *British Journal of Educational Technology* 41 (6, November): 883–96.

Yang, I. (2005) 'Group leadership in Korea', *The Business Review* 4(2): 73–9.

Zemanek, H. (2010) 'Competitiveness Within the Euro Area: The problem that still needs to be solved', *Economic Affairs* 30(3, October): 42–7.

Zickar, M.J., Gibby, R.E. and Robie, C. (2004) 'Uncovering faking samples in applicant, incumbent and experimental data sets: an application of mixed-model item response theory', *Organizational Research Methods* 7(2): 168.

INDEX